Homelands

Anthem Studies in Population Displacement
and Political Space

Homelands

War, Population and Statehood in Eastern Europe
and Russia, 1918–1924

NICK BARON AND PETER GATRELL

Anthem Press

This edition first published by Anthem Press 2004
Anthem Press is an imprint of
Wimbledon Publishing Company
75–76 Blackfriars Road
London SE1 8HA

This selection © Wimbledon Publishing Company 2004
Individual articles © individual contributors

The moral right of the authors to be identified as the
authors of this work has been asserted

All rights reserved.
No part of this publication may be reproduced,
stored in a retrieval system, or transmitted, in any form
or by any means, without the prior permission in writing of
Wimbledon Publishing Company, or as expressly permitted
by law, or under terms agreed with the appropriate
reprographics rights organization.

British Library Cataloguing in Publication Data
Data available

Library of Congress in Publication Data
A catalogue record has been applied for

ISBN 1 84331 120 8 (hbk)
ISBN 1 84331 121 6 (pbk)

1 3 5 7 9 10 8 6 4 2

Designed by Abe Aboody
Typeset by Alliance Interactive Technology, Pondicherry, India
Printed in India

CONTENTS

List of Maps — vii
List of Tables — viii
Acknowledgements — x
Contributors — xi

Introduction — 1
Nick Baron and Peter Gatrell

1 War, Population Displacement and State Formation in the Russian Borderlands, 1914–1924 — 10
  Peter Gatrell

2 Latvian Refugees and the Latvian Nation State during and after World War One — 35
  Aija Priedite

3 In Search of National Support: Belarusian Refugees in World War One and the People's Republic of Belarus — 53
  Valentina Utgof

4 In Search of a Native Realm: The Return of World War One Refugees to Lithuania, 1918–1924 — 74
  Tomas Balkelis

5 Population Displacement and Citizenship in Poland, 1918–24 — 98
  Konrad Zielinski

6 The Repatriation of Polish Citizens from Soviet Ukraine to Poland in 1921–2 — 119
  Kateryna Stadnik

7 'Sybiraki': Siberian and Manchurian Returnees in Independent Poland — 138
  Łucja Kapralska

8 Refugees in the Urals Region, 1917–1925 — 156
  Gennadii Kornilov

9 Armenia: the 'Nationalization', Internationalization and
   Representation of the Refugee Crisis   179
   Peter Gatrell and Jo Laycock

   Conclusions: On Living in a 'New Country'   201
   Peter Gatrell and Nick Baron

   Notes   209
   Index   261

LIST OF MAPS

Map 1: Eastern Europe and the Soviet Union (1923 borders)   xiv
Map 2: Western Borderlands of the Former Russian Empire   xvi
Map 3: America and the Near East, 1914–1923   xvii

LIST OF TABLES

Chapter 3: IN SEARCH OF NATIONAL SUPPORT: BELARUSIAN REFUGEES IN THE FIRST WORLD WAR AND THE PEOPLE'S REPUBLIC OF BELARUS
1. Ethnic background of refugees registered and re-evacuated by the Belarusian Administration in 1921 — 70

Chapter 4: IN SEARCH OF A NATIVE REALM: THE RETURN OF FIRST WORLD WAR REFUGEES TO LITHUANIA, 1918–1924
1. Population displaced from Lithuania to Russia during World War One — 97
2. Return of refugees to Lithuania after World War One — 97

Chapter 6: THE REPATRIATION OF POLISH CITIZENS FROM SOVIET UKRAINE TO POLAND IN 1921–2
1. Estimated number of Poles on the territory of Soviet Ukraine expressing a wish to leave for Poland (as of 18 April 1921) — 126
2. Number of Poles registered for re-evacuation in the uezds of Donetsk province (as of 28 June 1921) — 127
3. Number of Poles resident in and re-evacuated from Donetsk province, between summer 1921 and spring 1922 — 135

Chapter 8: REFUGEES IN THE URALS REGION, 1917–1925
1. Distribution of refugees in Russia (*Tsentroplenbezh* data, 1 December 1919) — 161
2. 'First wave' refugees on the territory of Ekaterinburg province in 1920 — 165
3. Refugees within Ekaterinburg province, April 1921 — 166
4. Refugee transports (data from 1 January to 1 September 1921) — 166
5. Refugees passing through Ekaterinburg train station, 1 April–1 October 1922 — 167
6. Refugee traffic through Ekaterinburg train station, September 1921 — 170
7 The scale of famine in Ekaterinburg province, 1921 — 171

8. The scale of operations of Urals' 'Bandit Groups' 173
9. Food rations, established by *Tsentroplenbezh* decree,
   1 January 1920 176

ACKNOWLEDGEMENTS

We would like to thank, first and foremost, the UK Arts and Humanities Research Board, for funding the five-year collaborative project in the Department of History of the University of Manchester ('Population Displacement, State-Building and Social Identity in the Lands of the Former Russian Empire, 1917–1930', reference B/RG/AN993/APN9265) of which this volume is one outcome. More information on the project can be found at the website: *http://www.art.man.ac.uk/history/ahrbproj/details.htm.*

We also acknowledge those members of the Project team who are not represented in this volume: Professor Pavel Polian, Dr Aldis Purs, Dr Irina Silina and Iurii Bassilov. Their support and contributions to our discussions have been invaluable. Several colleagues, including Professor Boris Kolonitskii and Dr Hilary Pilkington, gave us helpful advice at an early stage of the Project by enabling us to make contact with scholars in central and eastern Europe.

We hope that the numerous archivists and librarians who have assisted all the contributors to this book will accept a general expression of our gratitude. We would also like to thank Tom Penn, commissioning editor at Anthem Press, for his enthusiastic support for this volume and the new series in which it appears, and Freda Diggle of the School of History and Classics in Manchester University, for the administrative back-up she has provided in such a friendly and capable manner.

We dedicate this book to Professor RW Davies, erstwhile director of the Centre for Russian and East European Studies, University of Birmingham, and a firm advocate of the kind of collaborative endeavour of which this volume is an example. Bob Davies has encouraged both editors of this book in ways too numerous to mention.

VALENTINA UTGOF is a graduate of Brest State University, Belarus, and the European University in St. Petersburg. Her recent publications include 'Reevakuatsiia belorusskikh bezhentsev pervoi mirovoi voiny, nachal'nyi etap, struktury, formy, organizatsiia' ['The re-evacuation of Belarusian refugees of World War One: first stage, structures, forms, organization'], in MM Krom, ed., *Istochnik, istorik, istoriia* [*Source, Historian, History*], European University Press, St Petersburg, 2002. She is currently working on nationality questions in Belarus during the interwar period.

KONRAD ZIELINSKI is a lecturer at the Maria Curie-Sklodowska University in Lublin, where he teaches modern Jewish history and culture. His recent publications include *Zydzi Lubelszczyzny 1914–1918* [*Jews in Lublin Province, 1914–1918*], Lublin, Lubelskie Towarzystwo Naukowe, 1999, and a co-authored monograph with Nina Zielinska about a famous Lublin rabbinical school in the 1930s *Jeszywas Chachmej Lublin (Uczelnia Mędrców Lublina)*, Lublin, Wydawnictwo UMCS, 2003. He has also co-edited (with Monika Adamczyk-Garbowska) the volume *Ortodoksja–Emancypacja–Asymilacja. Studia z dziejów ludności żydowskiej na ziemiach polskich w okresie rozbiorów* [*Orthodoxy–Emancipation–Assimilation. Studies on Polish Jewry during the partition of Poland*], Lublin, Wydawnictwo UMCS, 2003. His current research investigates the history of Polish populations in early Soviet Russia and their attitudes towards the War of 1920, and Polish–Jewish relationships during and after World War One.

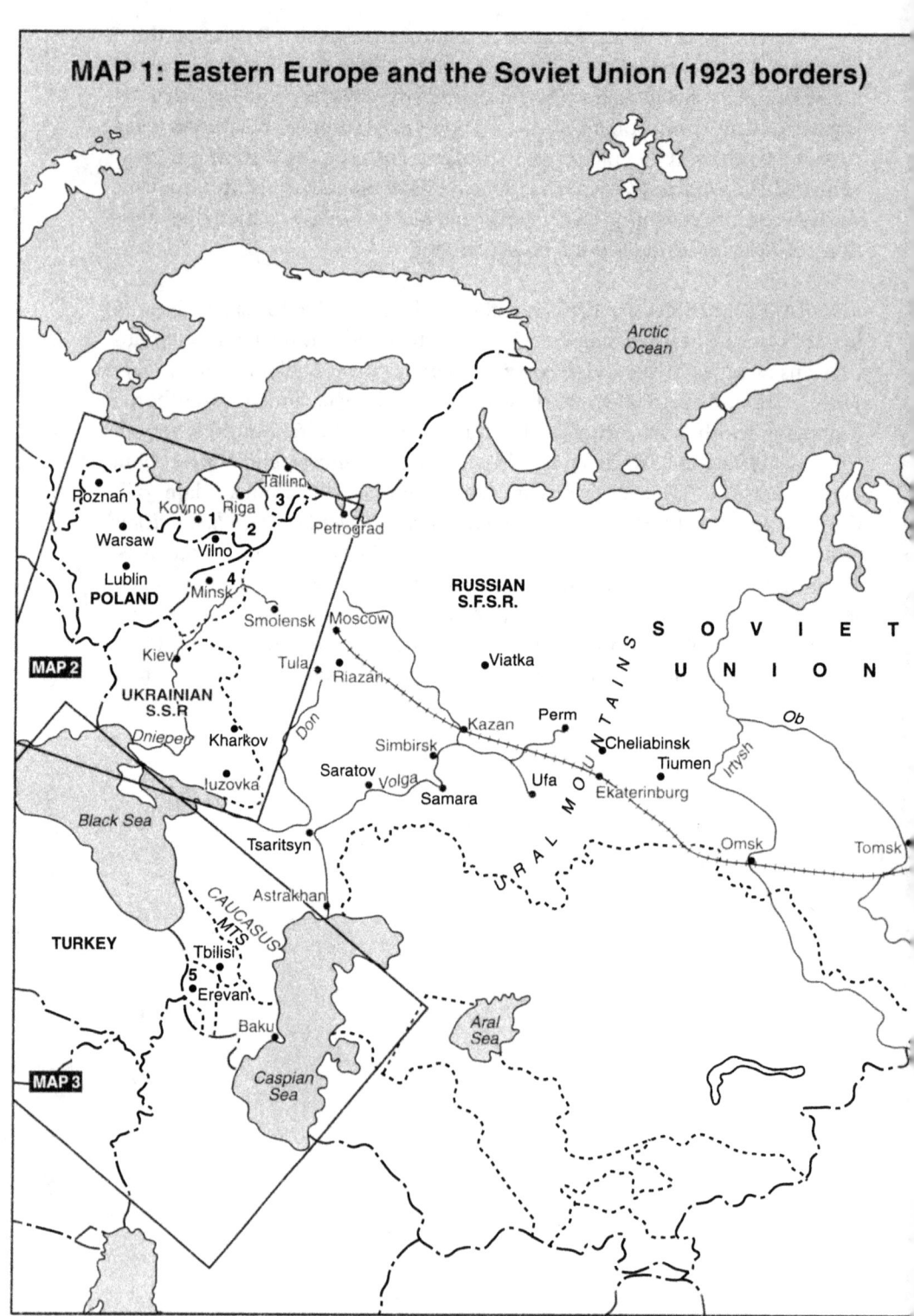

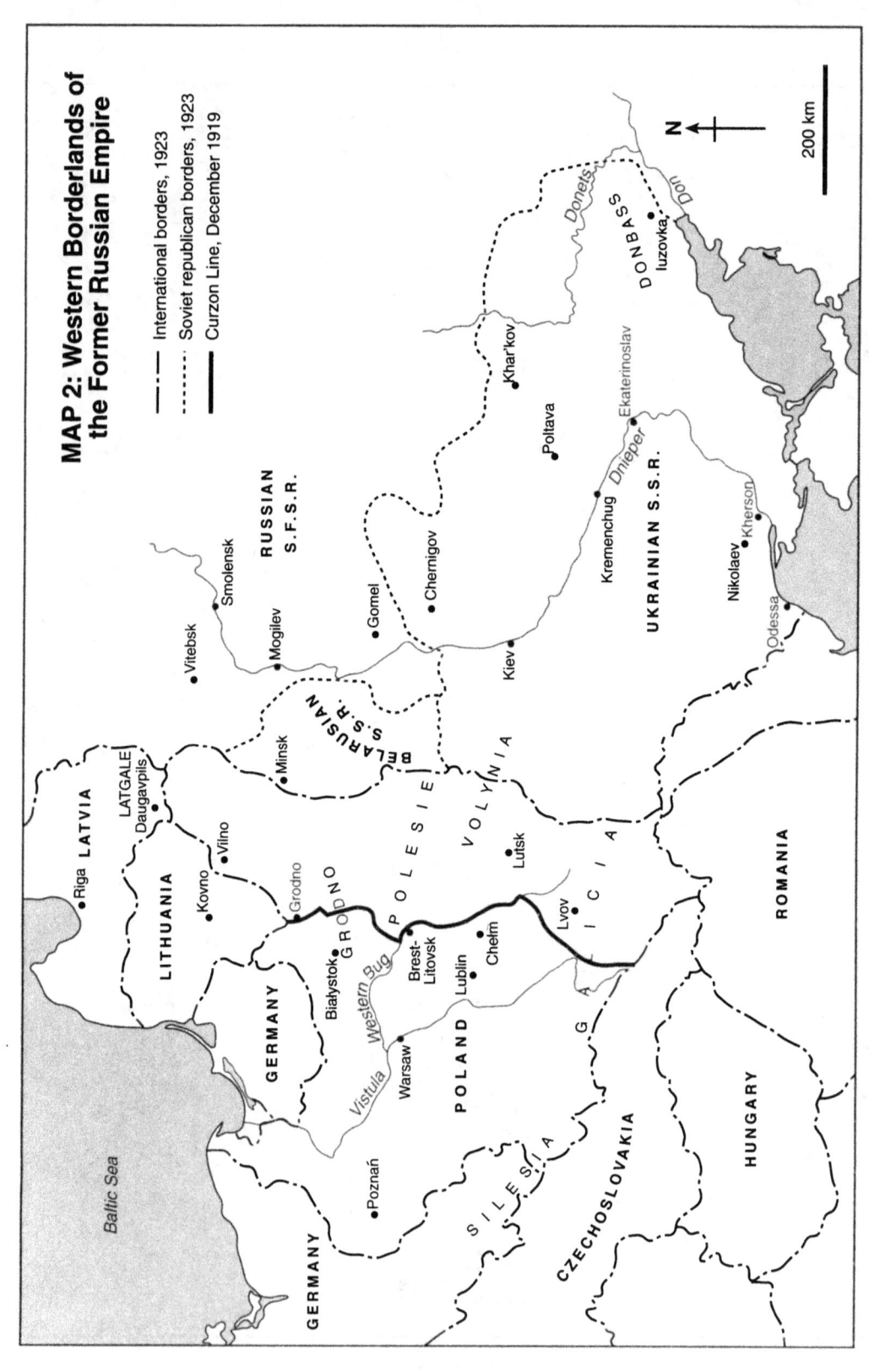

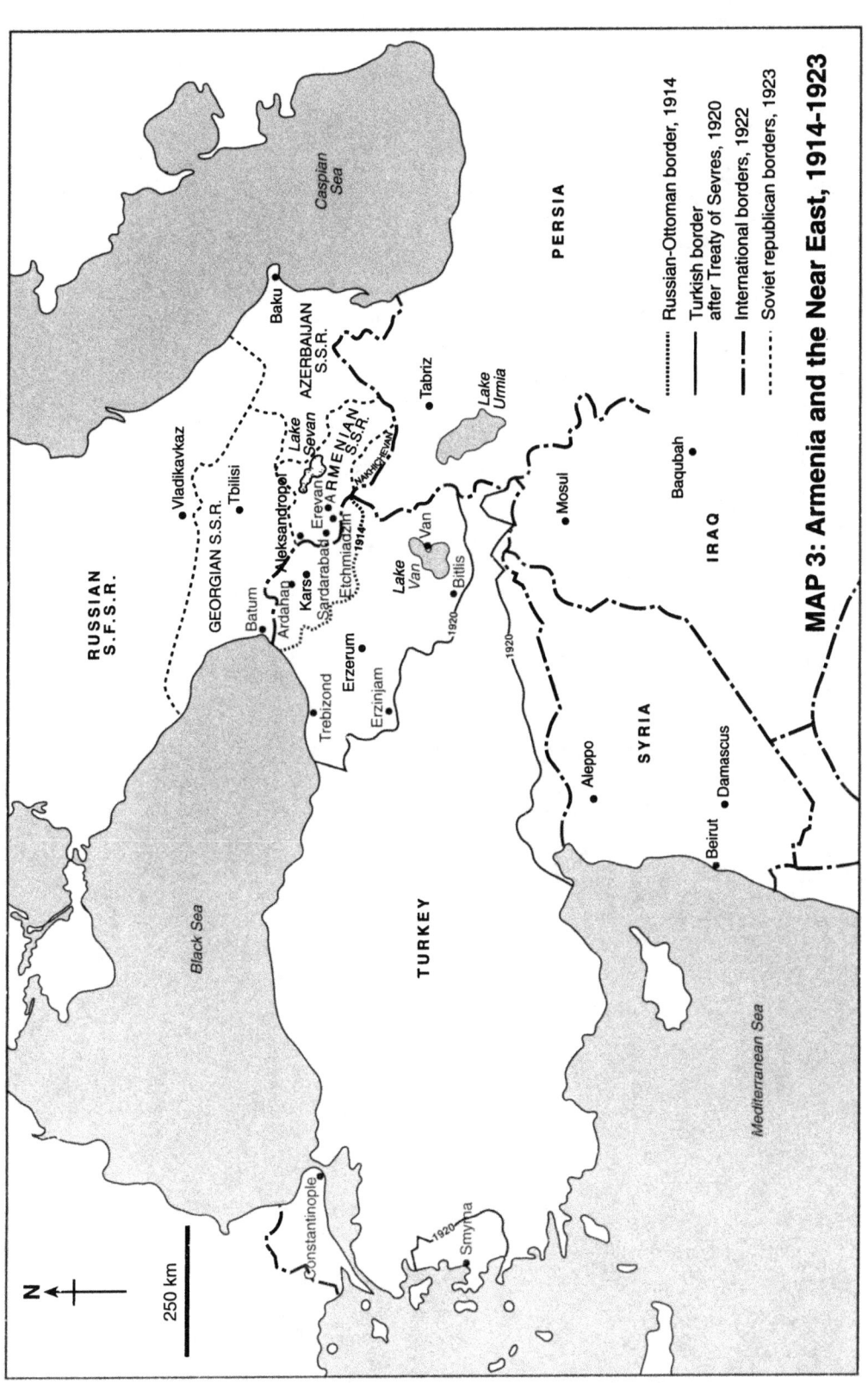

CONTRIBUTORS

TOMAS BALKELIS is a doctoral student in history at the University of Toronto, Canada. He is currently completing his thesis 'In Search of a Native Realm: The Making of the Lithuanian Intelligentsia, 1883–1914' and has recently completed 'Nation Building and World War One Refugees in Lithuania', forthcoming in *Journal of Baltic Studies*. His interests include nationalism, collective memory, ethnicity and forced migrations in East Central Europe.

NICK BARON is a lecturer at the University of Nottingham, UK, where he works on Russian and East European history and historical geography. From 1999–2003, he was research fellow in history at the University of Manchester, UK. His publications include the monograph *Soviet Karelia: Planning, politics and Terror in Stalin's Russia, 1920–1939*, London, RoutledgeCurzon, 2004, several edited volumes and numerous journal articles. He is currently working on child displacement in twentieth-century eastern Europe and on Soviet cartography and spatial cultures in the interwar period.

PETER GATRELL is professor of economic history at the University of Manchester, where he was Head of the School of History and Classics between 1997 and 2002. His most recent book *A Whole Empire Walking: Refugees in Russia during World War I*, Bloomington, Indiana University Press, 1999, won the Wayne Vucinich Prize of the American Association for the Advancement of Slavic Studies and the Alec Nove Prize of the British Association for Slavonic and East European Studies. He will shortly be publishing a monograph on Russia's economy and society during World War One.

ŁUCJA KAPRALSKA is a lecturer in sociology in the Department of Applied Social Science of the University of Science and Technology in Kraków, Poland. Her historical research explores questions of ethnicity and social identity in Polish society from 1914–1939, and she also studies social problems of contemporary Poland. Her most recent publication is *Pluralizm kulturowy i etniczny a odrębność regionalna Kresów południowo–wschodnich w latach*

1918–1939 [*Cultural and Ethnic Pluralism in the South–Eastern Borderland Region of Poland, 1918–1939*], Kraków, Wydawnictwo NOMOS, 2000. Her current research focuses on returnees from Russia in interwar Poland.

GENNADII KORNILOV is a professor, doctor of history and senior researcher at the Institute of History and Archeology of the Urals Branch of the Russian Academy of Sciences, Ekaterinburg. He is a specialist in Russian historical demography, agrarian history and the study of historical sources, and has participated in numerous international projects. His latest publications include the two-volume work (co-edited with VV Maslakov) *Prodovol'stvennaia bezopasnost' Urala v XX veke. Documenty i materialy* [*Food security in the Urals in the twentieth century. Documents and Materials*], Russian Academy of Sciences, Ekaterinburg, 2000, and the monograph *Istoriki Urala XVIII–XX veka* [*Historians of the Urals in the 18th to 20th centuries*], Russian Academy of Sciences, Ekaterinburg, 2003.

JO LAYCOCK is a PhD student at the University of Manchester, where she is writing a dissertation entitled 'Armenia in the British and French imagination, 1880–1930'. She has recently returned from a research visit to Erevan.

AIJA PRIEDITE is an associate professor at the University of Latvia, where she teaches the history of philosophy in Latvia and Latvian cultural history. Her recent publications include the co-edited work (with Ainārs Dimants and Dace Lüse) *Eiropas idejas Latvijā. Populāra Latvijas rakstnieku un domātāju Eiropas antoloģija. Sast* [*European ideas in Latvia. Anthology of writings by popular Latvian writers and thinkers on Europe*], Rīga, Pētergailis, 2003, and 'The Establishment of a Discourse about National Identity in Latvia in the late 19th and early 20th Centuries', in *Humanities and Social Sciences. Latvia*, Vol. 4 (25), 1999. Since 2000 she has directed the Latvian Council of Science project 'National Identity Discourse in the History of Ideas in Latvia'.

KATE STADNIK is currently enrolled on the PhD programme at the Centre for Social Studies of the Central European University in Warsaw. Previously she received a Candidate of Sciences degree in history. She is also working as an historian and social researcher in a number of interdisciplinary projects focusing on ethnicity, migration and youth studies. Her recent publications include 'Inter-Ethnic Coexistence in Ukraine: the Case of the Donetsk region' in Ch. Lord & O Strietska-Ilina (eds) *Parallel Cultures: majority/minority relations in the countries of the former Eastern Bloc* (Ashgate, 2001).

Introduction

NICK BARON AND PETER GATRELL

The present volume explores the complex interactions between population displacement and territorial, political and social organization in the modern world. It focuses on a particular time and place, namely the aftermath of World War One in the former Russian empire, placing population movements at the heart of debates about the process of imperial collapse and state-building. Here we take the opportunity to articulate our theoretical standpoint and justify our choice of historical case studies.

Our starting point is the recognition that states tend to privilege place of being above space of movement.[1] We maintain that the state's need to mobilize resources, for example to maintain its internal and external security, predisposes it to register, record and, as appropriate, freeze the passage of the uprooted and itinerant.[2] For state officials, immobility and rootedness are the desired norm. The state may encourage or promote migration, for developmental or other reasons, but its officials seek to ensure that this is an orderly process. Such predispositions tend to be strongly reinforced by observing refugee itineracy, which (whether considered with compassion or hostility) appears to confirm the normative and, moreover, essentialized nature of ideas of 'roots', 'home' or 'homeland'.[3] The evidence comes in the form of the actions of policymakers, politicians and officials active in immigration control or refugee welfare, who seek to isolate, encamp, quarantine, examine, classify and at times expel newcomers and strangers. We maintain further that these assumptions are shared by members of the professional intelligentsia and that they have become part of the 'common sense' of public opinion. Historians are not immune from these ways of seeing. In analogous manner, they strive to relocate the migrant or refugee in historical place and time, by assigning them identities qualified by place of origin, sojourn or destination, by time of departure, arrival or return, or by imputed motivation. It is thereby easy to overlook the stubbornly undocumented or unclassifiable dimensions of migrant agency, and to dismiss the fluid, cross-cutting and often contradictory nature of the itinerant's social and self-identification.

This 'itinerant' perspective, which we counterpose to the traditional 'sedentary' way of seeing, seems a particularly appropriate means of elucidating the period after World War One. This era was characterized by extreme flux, in the form of massive population displacements, shifting territorial borders and cultural boundaries, and new political and social formations in the process of self-definition and delimitation.[4] To be sure, for many populations the experience of flux did not represent an aberration or departure from a sedentary and unchanging normality. From the west of Ireland to east of the Pale of Settlement, Europeans had been 'on the move' under various forms of incentive or coercion for many generations.[5] What was new in eastern Europe after 1918 was the sudden reconfiguration of power and territory. This process 'dis-placed' not only those who migrated, but also those who remained rooted in the region but found that the larger political unit to which they belonged had changed, and with it their locus in social time and space.[6]

Why have these questions of history become newly urgent? To a large extent the widespread fascination with post-1918 developments derives from the collapse of the USSR and the 'Soviet bloc', and from violent conflicts in the Balkans and Caucasus during the 1990s. As is well known, most of these recent wars have been the result of state-building projects which mobilized essentialist ideas of ethnicity and national territory and produced major displacements of population, both within state borders and beyond. At the time of writing (summer 2003), involuntary population displacement continues to take place. What is more, the break up of the Soviet Union itself has led to immense uncertainty and upheaval, not least because so many Russians lived 'beyond Russia', in emerging states such as Kazakhstan, Latvia, and Ukraine. What would become of these 'displaced' persons? Where do they belong? Whose responsibility are they? These are pressing questions in post-Communist Europe. The relationship between population and political space remains problematic.[7]

The magnitude of population displacement in the contemporary world also gives rise to a plethora of initiatives designed to 'manage' the 'refugee crisis'. Nation states now debate as a matter of urgency the need to monitor the flow of refugees. International organizations intervene to formulate programmes of one kind or another, for example, to relieve distress in countries of origin, but they have great difficulty in affecting the drift of policy in potential recipient countries.[8]

Many of these current dilemmas and tragedies, as well as national and international responses to them, have their antecedents (in some cases, their origins) in the aftermath of World War One, when the new states of eastern Europe first sought to define themselves in terms of territory, population and citizenship. Established states are concerned to settle, regulate and order their constituent populations, in the belief that this will ensure internal security, social cohesion, fiscal efficiency and an equitable allocation of limited welfare resources. They are also concerned to inculcate in their populations a sense of a collective 'home', as a focus of affective identification. The exigencies of new state-building in the post-imperial territories of eastern Europe lent added urgency to the strivings of political leaders and government officials to 'fix' their populations and define their new 'homelands'. As we shall see from the research presented in this volume, all the new states which arose on the territory of the former tsarist empire (including Soviet Russia) attached great importance to the discourse of itinerancy versus sedentarism. Problems of population movement and settlement preoccupied their government institutions, including the military, as well as non-governmental organizations. They loomed large on the agenda of postwar governments and were never far from the forefront of discussions at meetings of new transnational institutions, notably the League of Nations.[9] They also figure widely in postwar novels and other forms of artistic expression, becoming part of the cultural landscape of the 1920s.[10]

The authors have kept these formulations and perspectives in mind as they elucidate aspects of population and statehood at a crucial juncture in modern European history when, in the words of Tomas Masaryk, the entire continent took on the aspect of a 'laboratory atop a mass graveyard.'[11] Our contention is that populations – their sheer number, their categorization, their multiple representation, in short their 'problematization' – formed a crucial part of the period's experimental and combustible politics of state-building, which laid the foundations of contemporary eastern Europe.

This volume is conceived as an interlinked set of essays, authored by scholars from various disciplines, on the themes of population displacement, state-building and social identity in eastern Europe. The geographic focus is the territories that until 1917 comprised the Russian empire whose wartime history was the subject of a recent book by one of the editors of this volume.[12] Following World War One, the empire of the Romanovs fragmented. The states that emerged from the wreckage of the former empire were Poland, Latvia, Lithuania and Estonia. In 1923 the Soviet Union constituted itself as a federation of republics, including Belarus, Ukraine, Armenia, Georgia and Azerbaijan, all of them polities that had enjoyed a brief moment as independent states. The temporal coverage of this volume extends roughly from Soviet Russia's decision to sue for peace with the Central Powers in December 1917 to the formation of the Soviet Union at the very beginning of 1924. The process of repatriation, however, persisted in some countries until 1925 and beyond.

This focus draws our attention to two major processes. Firstly, to state-formation, a topic of widespread diplomatic and public interest during the 1920s and again during the 1990s when the USSR collapsed, giving rise to sovereign states that disavowed the political and economic principles upon which the Soviet state had originally been founded and which since 1945 had been adopted throughout what came to be called the Soviet bloc.[13] The new eastern European states of the post-1918 era confronted myriad problems. Amongst the most pressing were the need to delimit their territories and defend their borders, to assemble state bureaucracies, to secure resources for the conduct of government business, to rebuild shattered economies, and of course to establish the basis for international commercial, financial and diplomatic relations. New states, in short, had to be pieced together by social, political, economic and cultural means.[14]

Secondly, most of the eastern European successor states after 1918 chose to constitute themselves as nation-states, on the grounds that the prolonged European war had validated the nationalist claims that each 'nation' should have its 'own' titular state. Soviet Russia, later the USSR, was ostensibly the exception to this, defining its statehood in social rather than in national terms (as the 'dictatorship of the proletariat'), but even there ethnic and national categories played a major role in shaping the new state's territorial system, political structure and social relations. In the newly independent nation-states, political leaders and state officials spoke of loyalty in terms of a population's historical 'rootedness' in a defined place, and it was those roots that governed membership of the nation-state and the entitlements that derived from citizenship. By the same token, other defined population 'elements' were excluded from this imagined community.[15] Affective affiliations to place were recast and mobilized as legal, political or scientific discourses, defining the identities both of a supposedly 'native' population and of those to be excluded from the 'nation'.[16] Such discourses assigned social values to individuals and groups as citizen (rather than as alien), as a member of the majority (rather than a minority), as a repatriate (rather than as a refugee), and as a 'healthy cell' of the body politic (rather than as a 'bacillus' of social contagion).[17] Naturally, space and its markers (for example, borders and landscapes) are significant determinants in structuring these schema of difference, since most forms of nationalism aspire to occupy a space designated as the 'homeland', and the nation-state defines itself as the instrument for protecting the integrity of the territory and the welfare of its core population. In effect, those who do not belong in this bounded national space are figuratively, and sometimes physically, 'dis-placed'.[18]

As the contributors to this book show, processes of state-construction and nation-building during and immediately after World War One entailed both territorial reconfiguration and a confrontation with the scattering of populations. Indeed, questions of space were inseparable from questions of population. We have chosen to concentrate on several specific case studies, for three main reasons. First, the numerically most important population movements involved Russia, Lithuania, Poland, Ukraine, Armenia and (to a lesser extent) Latvia and Belarus. Second, population movements in these countries involved significant 'unmixing' of peoples and therefore generate particularly illuminating material.[19] Third, these states were the focus of greatest international preoccupation, expressed in terms of direct foreign intervention, in Wilsonian attempts to implement the experiment of 'self-determination', and in international measures to confront pan-European epidemics and the presence of large numbers of Russian and Armenian refugees.

The leaders of these new states, many of whom had been primed and shaped by the painful experience of World War One, encouraged a new style of politics. Both in Soviet Russia and in the new nation-states, leaders made similar assumptions about displaced populations, staking a claim to the loyalty of favoured groups, defining their entitlements and responsibilities, and questioning in turn the affiliation of minority groups that found themselves within the orbit of the state. They were joined in this project by a professional intelligentsia – doctors, lawyers, social workers, teachers, statisticians – that practised disciplinary techniques upon the refugee population. (We use this term to convey both the knowledge derived from a discipline-based professional training, and the effects that the application of that knowledge were expected to have.) In many ways, the war had enabled these caseworkers (which is what they were) to secure their status and to gain credibility.

Displaced populations had their own aspirations, of course; the interplay between their hopes and fears, on the one hand, and the cultural-political ambitions of the state, on the other, constitute an important field of study, and we aim to shed light on these issues.[20] In keeping with the approach adopted in the editors' earlier work, we seek in this volume to do more than catalogue the demographics of displacement and chronicle undeniable human hardship.[21] Instead, we aim to explore the multiple interrelations between population displacement, state-construction and the constitution of social identities. While acknowledging the physical and mental trauma of forced migration, and the objectification of displaced populations in post-imperial policies and discourses, we have encouraged the contributors to this volume, where possible, to consider also the ways in which refugees and returnees played an active part in negotiating the organizational and cultural preconditions of state-formation and, at times, in subverting state attempts to impose transparency and order.[22] Although the practice of population displacement is an expression of overt state power, we should not assume that the state had it all its own way. This is another way of saying that the discourse of helplessness – so prevalent in the representation (and the archival documentation) of forced population displacement – must be carefully deconstructed.[23]

This discourse persists to this day. To be sure, it can go hand in hand with the crystallization of a humanitarian impulse, giving credence to institutional claims to intervene and to professional attempts to relieve suffering. More often, in the hands of some politicians it underpins immigration controls. Even in benign hands, the prevalent depiction of destitution, illness and incapacity comes at a price. All too easily we are confronted by an undifferentiated image of a 'victimized' population, lacking in agency. Any individual self-assertiveness often generates feelings of mistrust amongst government officials and settled populations. Passivity and knowing one's (new) place, rather than activism on the part of the displaced, are the forms of behaviour that call forth sympathy and assistance.[24]

There are important lessons here for all those who study forced migration, wherever it occurs and however unpleasant its manifestations.[25] Underlying humanitarian intervention is a recurrent sense of a 'people without history' (Eric Wolf's phrase), whose prior social networks, cultural achievements and political practices have been obliterated in the emphasis upon abjection. In Liisa Malkki's words 'understanding displacement as a human tragedy and looking no further can mean that one gains no insight at all into the lived meanings that displacement and exile can have for specific people'.[26] In this 'age of extremes' it is important to acknowledge the capacity for human resourcefulness on the part of the displaced, and their readiness to assert a sense of self-worth, frequently against all the odds.

We hope that these remarks will help readers of this book to understand why the topics of population displacement, state-building and social identity should be matters of vital concern not only to contemporary political scientists, demographers, policymakers, journalists and others, but also to historians. The collapse of empires and the emergence of new states in eastern Europe, the displacement of populations, and uncertainty about social identities in unravelling polities are all issues on which historians have something to contribute to public debate.

Peter Gatrell's opening chapter provides an introduction to the origins and broad implications of population displacement in imperial Russia during World War One. It outlines the basic domestic and international changes that affected the entire region between the end of the war in eastern Europe and the stabilization of post-imperial European frontiers and regimes by 1924. It thus serves to introduce the main themes that recur throughout this volume. The context having been established, subsequent chapters take up the story with a series of detailed case studies.

In chapter 2, Aija Priedite, a philosopher and historian of nationalism, considers the contribution of Latvian refugees and refugee organizations in Russia during World War One to the emergence of the idea of a Latvian nation-state, and traces the relationship between the troubled and prolonged process of postwar refugee repatriation and the incipient state's struggle to assert its independence and forge its new identity. Valentina Utgof in chapter 3 also explores the impact of World War One on the development of national consciousness and the role of refugee welfare agencies in creating preconditions for national statehood, in this case in relation to the rapidly abortive efforts to establish an independent Belarusian people's republic in the period 1917–20. Next, Tomas Balkelis' contribution focuses on the return of wartime refugees to a new Lithuanian 'homeland' between 1918 and 1924, and the new state's efforts to 'domesticate' them as national citizens against a background of new armed conflict and fresh displacements within and across its borders.

Chapters 5 and 6 investigate population movements across the new, and still unstable, Polish–Ukrainian state border in the early postwar years. First, Konrad Zielinski offers an insight into how independent Poland strove to control the influx of returning refugees across this border, legislating to define its community of national citizens in such a way as to preclude the return of many former residents of its territory, notably Jews and Ukrainians, and engaging in further discriminatory practices of immigration control and registration. The sociologist Kateryna Stadnik next focuses on newly sovietized Ukraine on the other side of the border in 1921–2, where the authorities were just as concerned to regulate population transfers into and out of their territory, organizing contingents of refugees intended for repatriation to Poland according to their own categorizations and closely monitoring them for their political attitudes.

While most of these chapters give due attention to the 'itinerant' voices of the refugees themselves, their own categories of identification, their objectives and ambitions, and the sources and effects of their decision-making, Łucja

Kapralska's contribution in chapter 7 focuses primarily on refugee agency and identity as distinct from (indeed, often in conflict with) state ideologies and practices. Having outlined the history of Polish deportees, wartime refugees and prisoners of war in Siberia and the Far East, and traced their arduous return to a newly independent 'homeland', she describes how many of these repatriates struggled to integrate into the life of the new Polish state, and reflects on ways in which they sought throughout the interwar period to sustain the particular collective spirit they identified with their shared experience of Siberian exile.

A majority of these 'Siberian' Poles returned home in 1920–2 through the Urals region of the new Russian Socialist Federal Soviet Republic (from the beginning of 1924, the USSR), which is the focus of chapter 8 by the demographic historian Gennadii Kornilov. He details three waves of refugee movements through the Urals between 1915 and 1925: firstly, wartime refugees and, later, returnees; secondly, forced migrants of the Russian Civil War; and thirdly, refugees from the central and southern Russian famine. His chapter concentrates on establishing the numbers of these refugees, describing their conditions and analysing the Soviet authorities' efforts to organize their registration and welfare.

The final case study, by Peter Gatrell and Jo Laycock, moves to the southern periphery of the former Russian empire to consider the relationship between Armenian population movements and state-building projects in the early postwar years. The authors pay particular attention to the consequences of the Armenian 'genocide' and subsequent foreign humanitarian interventions for the emergence and short-lived success of the Armenian national movement, and to the strongly gendered representations of 'the' Armenian refugee in contemporary nationalist and international discourse.

Although all contributing authors have offered conclusions to their own papers, the editors attempt a summing-up of the book's main themes in a short final chapter, in which they also indicate some possible directions for future research. So pertinent are these issues, and so little explored is the surviving evidence, that this book does not claim to offer conclusive answers. We hope nevertheless that this volume provides a good guide to the questions to ask and the approaches to adopt.

NOTE ON TERMINOLOGY

Strictly speaking, contemporary international law confined the term 'refugee' to Russian and Armenian refugees who no longer enjoyed the protection of, respectively, the Soviet and Turkish governments, and who had 'not acquired another nationality.' The refugee could not demand the protection of the host state: 'above all, he has no claim as of right to continued residence, and he is liable to expulsion if his presence for any reason is no longer desired.' New states, such as Poland, distinguished between 'repatriates' (who were ethnically Polish) and 'refugees', applying that term to all 'foreigners'. Sir John Simpson deployed the term 'fugitives' to characterize those who fled the borderlands in 1915 for the relative safety of the Russian interior, but who returned after 1918: 'they were not stateless, homeless wanderers.'[27] Another definition was provided by the Refugee Department of the American Joint Distribution Committee: 'by repatriate is meant that class of non-combatants, before the war resident in what is now Poland, Lithuania or Latvia, who, because of military operations in their territories during the World War and afterwards, fled, or were compulsorily evacuated, from their homes into the interior of Russia, and who, at the termination of hostilities, desired and were permitted by the Governments concerned to return to their homes.'[28] Where legal distinctions were important, we have endeavoured to use the appropriate term, although this has not always been possible, for example where contemporary usage is unclear.

1
War, Population Displacement and State Formation in the Russian Borderlands, 1914–24

PETER GATRELL

The Russian revolution, the collapse of the Russian empire, and the ensuing Civil War (1917–21) had profound consequences for the displacement of population. In 1917, as a result of the world war, the number of displaced persons (defined as men in uniform, foreign prisoners of war, and refugees) in Russia exceeded 17.5 million, equivalent to more than 12 per cent of the total population. The revolution generated fresh population displacement, adding to Russia's woes. In towns and cities, the severe economic collapse in 1917–18 compelled tens of thousands of Russian workers to leave for the villages in search of means of subsistence, thereby reversing a generation of sustained urban in-migration before World War One. Millions of other men and women experienced the Civil War as population displacement – as conscripts in the Red and White armies, or as members of various irregular military units, including the numerous peasant armies that fought Reds and Whites with equal determination. Fresh population displacement also resulted from the German military occupation of the western borderlands of the former Russian empire that came to an end only in November 1918. The prolonged dislocation caused by the Russian Civil War, battles between Polish, Lithuanian, and Ukrainian troops, the Soviet – Polish war, and continued turmoil in the Caucasus, all contributed to further migrations. Having failed to overthrow the new regime, anti-Bolshevik elements hastened to exit Russia. Most of them left, never to return, forming a large refugee and stateless population that was eventually scattered across three continents.[1]

This chapter provides an overview of the causes and consequences of population displacement during the years 1914–24, when the old empire fragmented as a result of war and revolution. It looks at population movements during World War One, and then proceeds to examine the implications for population displacement of the collapse of the Russian empire, the conflicts unleashed by the Bolshevik revolution and the terms of the postwar peace settlement. Many of the issues it raises are taken up by other contributors to this volume.

WORLD WAR ONE: HUMANITY UPROOTED

The war that broke out in 1914 was widely expected to be of short duration. Huge European armies were thought likely to engage in military manoeuvres, without great consequence for civilian populations. This vision quickly evaporated. The armies of the belligerents had a seemingly inexhaustible capacity to absorb fresh manpower, transporting troops – often across great distances – in order to confront the enemy. For hundreds of thousands of these men, the war resulted in captivity and thus further displacement. Unexpectedly, civilians also experienced war as displacement. Civilian populations scattered as they sought to escape either punitive action or subjugation by enemy forces. Belgian civilians sought refuge in Holland or Britain; Serbian refugees made their way to Albania and Greece; Polish and Lithuanian refugees fled to the Russian interior. Belligerent states also contributed to population displacement by deporting entire groups that were deemed capable of aiding the enemy: the deportation of Armenian civilians by Ottoman Turkish troops was the most egregious example of state-sponsored migration. World War One turned into a prolonged conflict in which civilian suffering in Belgium, Serbia, Armenia, Lithuania, Poland and elsewhere registered alongside the trauma of the Somme and Gallipoli.[2]

Nowhere was this unexpected drama of civilian population displacement more evident than in the Russian empire. The rapid German advance into Poland in 1914 prompted nervous tsarist officials to abandon their posts; civilians, fearful of enemy brutality, joined them in the journey eastwards. The simultaneous Russian occupation of Austrian-ruled Galicia was accompanied by the expulsion or flight of civilians opposed to the campaign of Russification. In 1915, the continued German onslaught in Russia's north-western territories, combined with Austria's reconquest of Galicia, created further waves of refugees. They had been forced to leave their homes, either by the threat of enemy violence or at the behest of the Russian high command. According to a decree issued in 1915, 'refugees (*bezhentsy*) are those persons who have abandoned localities threatened or already occupied by the enemy, or who have been evacuated by order of the military or civil authority from the zone of military operations.'³ Domestic military considerations, and not just enemy violence, created the conditions for displacement.⁴

The attempt to identify the refugee population for administrative and legal purposes betrayed uncertainties about the origins of displacement – was it caused by the Tsar's troops who targeted particular groups, or by enemy troops who behaved in an uncivilized fashion, provoking civilians to lose a sense of self-control? According to one explanation, 'as soon as our troops withdraw, the entire population becomes confused and runs away.'⁵ Sometimes people fled lest they lose contact with relatives on Russian territory, including fathers and sons who were currently serving in the tsarist army. This did not necessarily imply a move to distant locations; during the initial phase of retreat refugees would often stay close by Russian troops, in the hope or expectation that the army would quickly recapture land from the enemy, allowing them to go home. Many peasants, however, despaired of continuing to farm when their horses and livestock had been badly depleted by requisitioning. They expressed a wish to seek a better life 'in the depths of Russia.'⁶ Other motives also came to the surface. Sometimes civilians were warned that 'voluntary' departure was the only alternative to almost certain conscription by the enemy. Civilians were also prompted to leave their homes by the fear of being terrorized by enemy troops. Nor were these fears misplaced: 'rumours are rife that the Germans have behaved abominably towards the local population.'⁷

Yet displacement was by no means solely dictated by a fearful civilian response to punitive action by the enemy. Russian army regulations permitted the military authorities to assume absolute control over all affairs in the theatre of operations. This jealously guarded licence provided one of the main impulses behind population displacement. Within the extensive theatre of operations the Russian high command was accused of pursuing a scorched earth policy, and of driving civilians from their homes. General Nikolai Ianushkevich, Chief of Staff to the supreme commander of Russian forces, ordered the destruction of crops in Galicia and elsewhere; livestock, farm equipment and church bells were removed to the safety of the rear. Reports reached army headquarters that entire villages had been destroyed. The army sometimes removed civilians indiscriminately from districts close to the front. In the words of one group of refugees, 'We didn't want to move, we were chased away ... we were forced to burn our homes and crops, we weren't allowed to take our cattle with us, we weren't even allowed to return to our homes to get some money'.⁸ Ianushkevich singled out Jews for special treatment, encouraging what the Minister of the Interior termed 'a pogrom mood' in the army.⁹ But the crude and desperate measures employed by the Russian army were not applied exclusively to the Jewish population of the Russian empire. Gypsies were deported from the vicinity of the front in July and August 1915. German subjects of the Tsar were, like Jews, Poles and Ukrainians (the largest group in the province of Volynia), an object of military distrust. The German settlers' protestations of loyalty to Russia, manifested over several generations, did not spare them either deportation or the expropriation of their lands in 1915 and 1916.[10] So widespread were the army's tactics that a leading tsarist official believed that 'refugees' constituted a minority of the displaced population, compared to the hundreds of thousands of those who had been forcibly displaced.[11]

Population displacement also characterized the conduct of war on the southern borderlands of the empire. Turkey entered the war on the side of the central powers in November 1914. Six months later, Russian troops crossed the border. Held up by a Turkish counter-offensive, Russian commanders ordered troops to withdraw. In chaotic circumstances, some of the local Armenian population managed to flee to the relative safety of the Caucasus; others were left behind in the hasty Russian retreat. Turkish radicals blamed Armenians for the defeats already suffered by the Ottoman army in the winter of 1914 and early 1915, and charged them with having instigated uprisings against Turkish rule. Those Armenians who remained on Ottoman-controlled territory suffered a terrible fate. Emergency legislation provided for the deportation of communities suspected of espionage or treason. Hundreds of thousands of Ottoman Armenians were disarmed, arrested and deported, being forced to endure long and humiliating marches to the south from which many never recovered. Many were simply butchered. A minority of victims managed to escape to safety, either to Syria or to Russian-controlled Transcaucasus. A quarter of a million Armenians managed to flee across the Russian border during August 1915. Perhaps as many as one-fifth of them died en route. By the beginning of 1916 105,000 ex-Ottoman Armenians sought refuge in Erevan, whose population in 1914 barely reached 30,000.[12]

This wartime displacement of Russia's civilian population was, in all likelihood, unprecedented in its intensity. In the words of Eugene Kulischer, 'in two short years the movement of refugees and evacuees was as considerable as it had been during the migration to Siberia over a 25-year period' from 1885.[13] Reliable estimates suggest that refugees numbered at least 3.3 million at the end of 1915. One careful calculation, taking account of under-registration, put the total number at just over six million by the beginning of 1917.[14] As a result, refugees probably accounted for something like five per cent of the total population.

One of the striking features of Russia's wartime history was the extent of voluntary as well as governmental intervention.[15] Municipal authorities, diocesan committees, private charitable activity, and the semi-official Tatiana committees (taking their name from Tsar Nicholas's second daughter) established schools, orphanages and other facilities for refugees. The main Tatiana Committee devoted resources to tracing family members who had become separated. Peasant communities and rural co-operatives harnessed their established mechanisms of self-help to the task of assisting the newcomers. Nor were these efforts confined to Russian activists. The British (and, later, the American) Society of Friends established hospitals, orphanages and workshops in Samara, as well as shelters in Moscow for refugees in transit.[16] Granted, there were turf wars and confusion over lines of responsibility. Population displacement generated further political rivalry and intrigue. Nevertheless, the war brought about an impressive relief effort.

Humanitarian initiatives provided additional evidence of a newly emerging professional ethos in late imperial Russia, giving social workers, doctors, psychiatrists, lawyers and others extensive practice in observing, counting, examining and managing the Tsar's subjects. This body of expert opinion helped to crystallize a popular image of the sick, desperate and sometimes depraved refugee, whose 'essence' enabled professionals to constitute in turn a sense of their own purpose and identity. We can trace this process through the medium of specialist journals, but it was also evident in newspaper articles of a purely factual kind, dramatic tales of refugee journeys, and the calculated use of photographs and other images. Refugees themselves found it difficult to challenge that categorization, because the humanitarian efforts were couched in pervasive terms of degradation and disease. As we shall see, similar devices were at work in postwar eastern Europe.[17]

Crucially, because resources were thinly stretched, the tsarist state devolved some of the responsibility for refugee relief on to newly formed 'national committees' (Latvian, Armenian, Polish, Jewish and Lithuanian – but rarely Russian, Ukrainian, Belarusian, still less German).[18] These committees mobilized 'national' opinion at home and abroad. This aspect of refugeedom inspired among an emerging patriotic elite a sense of national calamity which itself gave rise to a vision of national solidarity. Deliberate action was needed, in the words of the Latvian activist Janis Goldmanis, to ensure that Latvians avoid 'the lot of the Jews, to be scattered across the entire globe.' Polish activists spoke of 'preserving the refugee on behalf of the motherland'. Goldmanis was not alone in articulating a vision of a reclaimed homeland, whose farms should in due course be repopulated by 'people who think and act in a Latvian manner'.[19] The leader of the Lithuanian Welfare Committee, Martynas Yčas, a lawyer and former Duma deputy, boasted in his memoirs that his organization had 'prepared the people for future action and created the foundations for a future cultural and political edifice. It unearthed the buried name of Lithuania and forced even non-Lithuanians to recognise that we ourselves were masters of our country.' Members of the Committee proclaimed the need to ensure that Lithuanian refugees retained a sense of what it meant to be 'Lithuanian', meaning that they needed to stay together.[20] These elites had both cause and opportunity to engage in a new politics, designed to instruct the refugee population in their rights and responsibilities. Refugeedom gave the elites direct access to a nascent national community. Refugee relief instructed the displaced farmer or labourer about what it meant to be Armenian, Polish, Jewish or Latvian. Several contributors to the present volume take up this theme, confirming that population displacement during World War One helped to breed and to legitimize national politics upon which they could capitalize during the early years of independence.[21] Even where, as in the case of Ukrainian and Belarusian refugees, the tsarist state frustrated attempts by a patriotic elite to create dedicated national organizations, the very act of denial fostered both a sense of disappointment and a readiness to confront official discrimination.[22]

In sum, the wartime displacement of population in the Russian empire transformed political space and debate. The conduct of politics assumed a nationalist aspect, as leading members of the non-Russian intelligentsia seized the new opportunities that were created by refugeedom. The old regime battled to cope with the social and economic consequences of refugee population movements, but found itself exposed to public obloquy. Local authorities expressed alarm about the 'flood' of refugees that threatened to 'overwhelm' provincial towns and cities. Professional experts and volunteer relief workers discovered a sense of purpose and identity in fresh forms of humanitarian intervention. Refugees did not 'cause' the Russian revolution, but they exposed political power struggles and transformed the terms of public debate about 'space', borders, and territory.[23]

The Provisional Government inherited an unstable polity, in which Russia's dispossessed social groups clamoured for freedom and justice. Alongside radical workers, peasants, sailors and soldiers, ethnic minority leaders proclaimed the need for greater autonomy within a Russian federation. Many members of the government were sympathetic to this demand, but insisted that any resolution of nationalist claims would have to await the successful conclusion of the war effort. The most that the government would commit itself to was the acceptance of self-rule for Poland, whose independence had in any event been granted in principle by Germany in November 1916, as a means of courting popular support for the German war effort against imperial Russia. To be sure, while Poland (like Lithuania) remained under German occupation the issue of independence was purely notional. But the Provisional Government's stance opened the door for members of the non-Russian intelligentsia to demand greater political rights. Estonia established a national council on 30 March 1917, and the Finnish parliament (Diet) actually declared independence on 23 June, provoking a bitter rift with the Provisional Government. Another important moment was the 'First Universal', issued by the Ukrainian Rada (council) on 10 June for a separate legislative assembly in Kiev, and the establishment of a 'General Secretariat', amounting in practice to a separate political authority. This initiative was not and should not be taken as a definite indication of a groundswell of popular support for independence on the part of Russia's national minority populations. Yet where underlying social and economic grievances coincided with the nationalist agenda, popular 'ethnic mobilization' proceeded apace. In Ukraine, for example, the peasantry increasingly associated freedom with the dispossession of Russian and Polish landlords, and the redistribution of land to Ukrainians. But the route from ethnic mobilization to the adoption of independence as a political strategy was by no means straightforward. The realization of national independence hinged above all on external patronage and on the Bolsheviks' readiness to support national self-determination. Once those conditions were met, imperial unity ended.[24]

REVOLUTION, PEACEMAKING, AND THE ONSET OF CIVIL WAR IN RUSSIA

The Bolshevik revolution of October 1917 had profound consequences for Russia's external relations and for the internal configuration of its territory. In the first place, the revolution led directly to Russia's withdrawal from the war, in accordance with the Bolshevik slogan 'peace without annexations'. The Bolsheviks fully expected that revolution in Russia would be replicated elsewhere in Europe, and that proletarian solidarity would produce a lasting peace. In the meantime, the Bolsheviks entered into negotiations with Germany in November 1917, concluding an armistice in early December. In the second place, the revolution brought about the fragmentation of the old imperial polity, as the Bolshevik doctrine of self-determination implied. These developments were closely related.[25] In January 1918 Germany recognized Ukrainian independence (the Germans had already invited a Ukrainian delegation to the negotiations at Brest-Litovsk). Within two months Lithuania and Latvia received similar recognition, although (as in Poland) this remained something of a fiction, given the continued presence of German occupation forces. Belarusian nationalists declared independence on 25 March 1918, although their claim to statehood was disputed by Lithuania, the latter enjoying German backing. Russia's new rulers had already accepted the independence of Finland in December 1917, but they drew a distinction between their recognition of Finnish independence and the independence granted to 'puppet' states by imperialist powers.[26]

Far from bringing peace and stability, however, the Bolsheviks' stance exposed Russia's borderlands to continued German and Turkish encroachment, partly because German patience with Trotsky's negotiating stance ('neither war nor peace') ran out, and partly because the collapse of the Russian army meant that no military force stood in their way. German troops advanced on Dvinsk and entered Ukrainian territory, while consolidating their position in Belarus and the Baltic region. Turkish troops continued to advance into Armenia, leading to the recapture of Erzinjan and Erzerum in February 1918; the fortress of Kars fell into Turkish hands two months later. Finally, after weeks of tortuous negotiations (as well as bitter wrangling among the Bolshevik leadership), Soviet Russia signed the Treaty of Brest-Litovsk on 3 March 1918, accepting the harsh terms dictated by 'the Hohenzollerns and the Habsburgs'. Under this treaty, the Bolsheviks renounced all the tsarist empire's western regions. Turkey added to Russia's humiliation by demanding the cession of the border provinces of Kars, Ardahan and Batum, which had been in Russian hands since 1878.[27]

This process had immediate implications for population displacement. Some refugees, filled with enthusiasm for the Bolshevik triumph, made plans to return to the land they had left, in the hope or expectation that they could contribute to a radical reconstruction of their homeland.[28] Others, on the contrary, wished to escape political persecution and the worsening economic crisis on Russian territory. To be sure, plans to return were difficult to implement, for a variety of reasons: the eruption of fresh military conflict (see below); the devastation of the means of communication; the loss or destruction of personal documentation, and so forth. All the same, between May and November 1918, around 400,000 refugees of various nationalities left Soviet Russia for territory that was still under German occupation. More cautious elements adopted a wait-and-see policy. Others threw in their lot with the Bolsheviks, at least for the time being, from their temporary bases in Russian or Ukrainian cities such as Viatka, Perm, Rostov and Kiev, rejecting the 'national' committees in favour of class-based organizations.[29]

The disintegration of the Russian empire was followed by another shock, namely the collapse of the German war effort at the end of 1918. By conceding defeat in its long struggle for supremacy in Europe, Germany renounced its occupation of Poland and Lithuania, as well as Ukraine, where it had sponsored a virulently anti-Bolshevik regime. New opportunities opened up in eastern Europe. In the Caucasus, the capitulation of Turkey prompted British and French troops to occupy much of the region and enabled Armenian troop units to occupy eastern Anatolia. The imminent peace negotiations seemed likely to complete the transformation of Europe, by legitimizing the creation of new nation-states, as advocated in Woodrow Wilson's 'Fourteen Points'.[30] The great powers and their invited guests gathered at Versailles in January 1919 to formulate a European peace settlement that would, among other things, determine international boundaries.[31] Sceptics, such as the novelist Joseph Conrad, bemoaned the rupture in traditional diplomacy and warned against the threat posed by Bolshevism: fixing borders seemed to him 'like people laying out a tennis court on a ground that is already moving under their feet'.[32] Whatever Conrad's misgivings, the peace treaty that was signed in July 1919 prescribed most of Europe's frontiers, with the conspicuous exception of Poland's borders with its eastern neighbours, where the proposed 'Curzon line' aroused the ire of Polish statesmen.[33]

Peacemaking in Paris did not mean the end of armed conflict in eastern Europe. The political future of these new states remained desperately uncertain. From a nationalist point of view, they had achieved freedom by escaping German, Austrian and Russian oppression alike; and, in the Caucasus, Armenian leaders looked to the Allies to keep Turkey in check. At stake now was the territorial integrity, political viability and social stability of newly formed polities. They shared borders with the new Soviet state, and deep-rooted social and economic problems led radical elements to entertain hopes of indigenous revolution. Like the bourgeois governments in western Europe, the leaders of the 'successor states' were deeply suspicious of Soviet intentions towards eastern Europe, not least since the Bolsheviks had already shown themselves adept at conducting propaganda among Czech, Hungarian, Serb, Romanian and German prisoners of war. Populations were not just liable to be displaced; they found themselves the targets of a carefully orchestrated campaign for hearts and minds.[34]

With serious repercussions for population displacement, conflicts erupted on the borderlands of empire, in Ukraine, Belarus, the Baltic states, in Poland and in the Caucasus. Already, in the winter of 1918, the German withdrawal from the Baltic region allowed Soviet troops and Bolshevik commissars to attempt to influence the political future of the region. They met with a strong rebuff in Estonia. Lithuania, having succeeded in appropriating military equipment left behind by the retreating German army, drove the Red Army from Vilno (in Lithuanian, Vilnius), and established a bourgeois state.[35] In Latvia, by contrast, the infant national government was confronted by the militant pro-Bolshevik Latvian Rifle Regiment. A bitter Civil War developed, with considerable loss of life. The complicating factor here was the continued presence of the German Freikorps, military freebooters under the control of General von der Goltz, who planned to restore the power of the Baltic German nobility. As late as October 1919, German irregulars were still trying to dominate Latvia.[36]

In Poland, a new republic came into being in November 1918, led by Józef Piłsudski, who was wedded to the restoration of Poland's 'historic' (pre-1772) borders. The new Polish government laid claim to Vilno and found itself in direct confrontation with Lithuania, whose government mounted a counter-claim. The dramatic Polish occupation of Vilno in 1920 remained a source of anger in Lithuania throughout the interwar period.[37] In similar vein, Poland vied with Ukraine for control of Galicia, a dispute that had led to a Polish invasion and armed conflict during the first half of 1919; a final settlement (in Poland's favour) was only reached in March 1923. Meanwhile, the realization of Piłsudski's nationalist vision was bound to have serious implications for those non-Polish minorities who were to be abruptly incorporated into the new state.[38]

Poland also secured control of the western part of Belarus in February 1919, a measure that seemed at first to many of its inhabitants preferable to rule by Moscow – or indeed by Germany, whose forces remained there until November 1918. However, the Belarusians' attitude rapidly changed as a result of the iron grip of Polish administration, which promoted the Polonization of economic, cultural and religious life. A serious health crisis complicated matters still further. As in Galicia, there were widespread reports of pogroms against the Jewish population.[39] Polish rule was challenged by an alliance between Russia and Lithuania, but this alliance proved short-lived. When Poland and the Soviet state signed a peace treaty at Riga in March 1921, they agreed to the partition of Belarus. The persistent Polish repression led to the impoverishment of the Belarusian population, around 100,000 of whom emigrated, some of them to Latvia. By contrast, the Sovietization of eastern Belarus led to a 'nativization' (*korenizatsiia*) programme that promoted the influx of a well-disposed professional and cultural intelligentsia from the Baltic states and from Polish-occupied western Belarus.[40]

Having agreed to form an independent Transcaucasian Federation with Georgia in April 1918, Armenia and Azerbaijan almost immediately came to blows over the assertion of rival claims to territory. Georgia's declaration of independence on 26 May brought a speedy end to the Federation. Meanwhile Georgia and Armenia only narrowly averted war in December 1918, thanks to British mediation, a reminder that the rival European powers all had commercial, economic and political ambitions in the Caucasus. As in the Baltic, this federation came to naught, because it made more sense for each of these fledgling states to come to a separate understanding with their more powerful neighbours, Turkey and Russia.[41]

Following victory in the armed conflict with Armenia in the autumn of 1920, Turkey once more re-established its control over large parts of Anatolia. In December Armenia was obliged to renounce the claims to north-eastern Anatolia that had been granted by the Treaty of Sèvres four months earlier on 10 August 1920.[42] The Red Army took control of Erevan that same month. Soviet Armenia was born, but in accordance with the agreement between Russia and Turkey (signed in Moscow in March 1921), and subsequently confirmed by the Treaty of Kars (signed in October 1921 by Turkey, Armenia, Georgia and Azerbaijan) its territory was severely reduced in comparison to the claims that Armenia had staked hitherto. Although the USA sent material aid to Armenia, no direct military assistance was forthcoming. (President Woodrow Wilson had seriously contemplated the creation of an American mandate over Armenia, but nothing came of this proposal.[43]) The Treaty of Lausanne (24 July 1923) confirmed Turkey's territorial demands and put paid to the vision of a 'Greater Armenia'.[44]

The Bolshevik revolution and the collapse of the old Russian empire had a significance that went far beyond Russia's borders. These events injected fierce new energies into the complex interplay of radical, liberal and reactionary tendencies in postwar Europe.[45] The Entente powers feared that world revolution emanating from Soviet Russia would destroy not only the fiercely won European status quo, but also the global imperial order which they had just expended so much energy to maintain. Throughout Europe and North America, politicians and diplomats developed the idea of a 'cordon sanitaire', to protect the population from the Bolshevik 'infection' and the 'flood of barbarism', lest it grip the minds of poor peasants and workers and encourage them to think of following in the footsteps of Russia's dispossessed.[46] In the febrile political atmosphere created by events in Russia during 1917, bourgeois fears of expropriation were no less real than proletarian hopes of a better world. For these reasons, counter-revolutionary wars were launched on Latvian, Lithuanian, Polish and Caucasian territory, as well as across European and Asiatic Russia. As well as by direct military intervention, the international powers sought through diplomatic, political and economic interference to dictate the territorial and social form of the new polities emerging from the wreckage of the tsarist empire. To be sure, ideology and class interests were not the sole motors of the European diplomacy of containment. France, for instance, supported the ambitious territorial claims of the new Polish government vis-à-vis Lithuania, as a means of creating a client state and forestalling a revival in Germany's political and military fortunes. The French Prime Minister Georges Clemenceau hoped for a strong Russian state for the same reason, provided of course it was non-Bolshevik. Other politicians claimed that Europe had a duty to intervene, in order to prevent the spread of 'barbarism ... to the vast regions of Northern and Central Asia'.[47]

This intervention was closely bound up with the onset of Civil War in Russia itself. The struggle for supremacy in Russia after October 1917 took the form of prolonged and bloody encounters between the newly formed Red Army and the Bolsheviks' White opponents. Since the Whites were committed to maintaining the integrity of the old empire, it was clear that the outcome of the Civil War would ultimately decide the fate of national self-determination. Complicating the picture further was a parallel conflict launched in 1920 by peasant armies which resisted Bolshevik and White forces alike to secure food, fodder and manpower for their campaigns.[48]

We can illustrate some of the consequences of war by considering the White movement in Siberia. The first phase of the struggle for supremacy over Siberia was marked by the uprising in May and June 1918 of Czech prisoners of war, who sought to take part in the war against Germany in order to achieve Czech independence. Taking up arms against the Soviet regime, whose troops stood in their way, they joined forces with the Bolsheviks' SR opponents. By the end of the year, Admiral Kolchak had imposed his own authoritarian rule on these anti-Bolshevik forces in Siberia. Prosperous citizens sought to escape from Bolshevik supremacy in central European Russia by taking refuge in the major Siberian cities controlled by the Whites, notably Cheliabinsk and Omsk. Many refugees, having sold their valuables, found themselves in desperate straits. As the White movement finally collapsed, in November 1919, these 'refugees' fled further eastwards to Krasnoiarsk, Irkutsk, and thence to Vladivostok, in the company of Kolchak's bedraggled army. One eye-witness depicted them as 'men moving like living dead through the taiga.'[49]

On the southern front, too, military confrontation gave rise to forced population movements. Here the White Volunteer armies under Denikin had enjoyed conspicuous success during 1918, only to be driven from the north Caucasus and the Don region by Soviet troops in the spring of 1919. Cossack troops, who endured a tempestuous relationship with Denikin, were now exposed to Bolshevik wrath. The Bolsheviks engaged in wholesale removal of Cossacks from the Don Territory, with the intention of replacing them with a more reliable 'healthy element'.[50] Further west, in Ukraine, the frequent changes of regime prompted continuous movements of population. Thus when Kiev came under the control of the fiercely anti-Bolshevik Hetman Skoropadskii in March 1918, White Russian refugees from Soviet-controlled territory quickly entered the city in order to take shelter from Bolshevik terror. Many of them found work in Ukrainian government agencies. But this proved a short-lived refuge: Skoropadskii was driven out, along with his German masters, in

December. Further bewildering changes of regime prompted similar movements of population.[51]

These internal hostilities and external conflicts were given added momentum by the war that broke out between Soviet Russia and Poland in 1920. The Polish – Soviet war interrupted the hesitant attempts to repatriate those refugees who had been displaced during World War One.[52] Polish troops quickly captured territory in Belarus and Ukraine, Piłsudski having reached an understanding with the Ukrainian nationalist leader Semen Petliura, according to which Ukraine would forfeit its western borderlands (Eastern Galicia), in exchange for Poland's help in driving the Bolsheviks from the rest of Ukraine. In May 1920 the Poles took Kiev and drove out the Soviet regime. But the Polish occupation lasted barely a month, and Soviet troops chased the Poles back to the edge of Warsaw. Much remains to be done to trace the population movements that occurred as a result of the Soviet – Polish War. During the Polish occupation of Belarus and Eastern Galicia, contemporaries observed that the roads in and out of towns such as Minsk were crowded with refugees and 'speculators'.[53] Conversely, the Soviet counter-offensive prompted an exodus of propertied Poles from towns such as Bialystok in the eastern territories, 'bringing with them [to central Poland] pestilence and disease in epidemic form', while the subsequent collapse of Belarus's short-lived attempt at independence also impelled Belarusian refugees to flee to Poland.[54] The war finally came to an end with the Treaty of Riga in March 1921. Poland, more than any other state (with the exception of Armenia), was faced with an enormous problem of refugee relief.[55] Its officials exacerbated the situation by ordering displaced persons who settled close to the frontier with Soviet Russia to leave the region; some of these were deported to Russia.[56]

Many civilians who fled the western borderlands in 1915 had found refuge in villages in the central regions of Russia, as well as further east.[57] Here the local peasant population had initially offered them shelter and food, in return for which refugees worked as craftsmen or performed other services. However, as living conditions in the countryside deteriorated, relations between refugees and host communities turned sour. As 'outsiders', refugees were normally excluded from the redistribution of land that took place in 1918; in any case, few of them had the equipment or draft animals to work the land on their own account. During the late summer of 1919, an eye-witness in Tambov – himself displaced – watched as desperate refugees combed the floor of the village barn for scraps of rye. Their only hope was to make the journey back to their former homes in the west, a hope that the chaotic condition of Russian transport frequently rendered futile.[58]

When famine struck the provinces of the middle Volga in 1921, thousands of refugees who still remained on Soviet territory, including many who had been supported by Quaker relief measures, now embarked on the difficult journey in search of food. For some this meant venturing long distances to regions in the east of Russia. For others it meant travelling towards westwards. The Soviet railway system struggled to cope with the numbers involved. Contemporaries bemoaned the fact that the 'stream' of refugees was accompanied by a renewed typhus epidemic.[59] A Quaker relief worker operating close to the Polish – Soviet border spoke for many when he described the conditions in which refugees found themselves:

> Ten or fifteen peasants live in a dug-out; there is no ventilation, there is very little firewood, they all huddle together at night to keep warm. One of the ten or fifteen gets typhus, and then they all get typhus ... There is nothing to do but to wait for one of two things – recovery, or non-recovery, in these horrible infected dug-outs.[60]

The same source estimated that half a million refugees left Russia, 'quietly and without confusion', to return to Poland between 1918 and July 1921. In the following six months an additional half million had left in a 'rush', leaving one million more 'waiting to return to their homes.' The American writer Anna Louise Strong confirmed this bleak assessment of the refugee crisis, to which she added some comments of her own on the ethnic composition and affiliation of the displaced population: 'By far the largest part of these returning refugees are not Polish by nationality, although they now owe allegiance to the Polish government ... They are White Ruthenians and Ruthenians whose language is Russian.'[61] Her brief remarks draw attention to the fact that resettlement and relief efforts were closely bound up with nationality politics, as well as with economics and public health. We turn to these issues in the following section.

THE FRAMEWORK OF RESETTLEMENT AND RELIEF

Once a peace treaty had been signed between Russia and Germany, many refugees began to explore the possibility of returning to the lands that they had been forced to quit in 1915 and 1916. In the immediate weeks following Brest-Litovsk, the Soviet government entrusted the administration of re-evacuation to the national organizations that had sprung up during the war, thereby validating the national project that had become attached to refugeedom. Provincial agencies, such as the Grodno central committee of united voluntary organizations, actively sought to establish the size and local of the Belarusian refugee population. Much of their work was subsequently taken over by a new

Soviet authority.⁶² At the end of April 1918 the Soviet Central Administration for Prisoners of War and Refugees (abbreviated as *Tsentroplenbezh*) came into being; by this time, however, local and regional soviets had begun to claim a more prominent role in determining the future of refugees, with the aim of supplanting purely 'national' bodies. *Tsentroplenbezh* launched a fresh registration of refugees on Soviet territory.⁶³ National organizations continued to apply themselves to the task of refugee relief and to engage in cultural and educational projects to promote 'national consciousness' among the 'inert masses'. Only in June 1918 did Soviet regional authorities undertake to curtail the activities of private organizations in the sphere of refugee relief.⁶⁴

It would be idle to pretend that refugees necessarily obeyed bureaucratic injunctions, whether issued by national committees or Soviet agencies. Official documents giving an entitlement to return were issued in accordance with strict criteria.⁶⁵ Yet refugees were perfectly capable of embarking on their own quest to return home, without going through official channels. Just as tsarist officials had complained in 1915 about the 'spontaneous' 'flood' of refugees eastwards from the front, now their Bolshevik counterparts (as well as non-governmental organizations) complained about the 'unplanned' return movement that threatened to unleash a public health catastrophe across Soviet space. Rumours flourished after Brest-Litovsk that Belarusian farmers would forfeit their land unless they claimed title to it within a matter of weeks. But those who attempted to travel home found that the German army stood in their way.⁶⁶

As indicated earlier, the discourse of the 'Bolshevik threat' was also closely bound up with population displacement. Nowhere were the ethnic dimensions of political affiliation more acute than in Poland, which had acquired territory in Eastern Galicia, Volynia and Polesie, whose impoverished and mixed population of Ukrainians, Belarusians, Jews and Russians resented rule from Warsaw. It was not difficult for Polish politicians to depict them variously as revanchist, Bolshevik or 'alien', and to develop programmes of resettlement designed to increase the Polish presence on these lands.⁶⁷

Prevalent too was a state-centric view that returnees were potential subversives and, at the very least, a burden on scarce resources. They had to be screened lest they import a 'virulent Bolshevik fever'.⁶⁸ Nor was this harsh appraisal entirely a figment of bourgeois imagination: the Commissariat for Polish Affairs in Moscow hoped to send home Polish refugees as 'conscious workers of the revolution'.⁶⁹ One outcome of this stance was a much more rigorous attitude towards border controls, the counterpart to a programme for protecting newly defined national space from epidemic hazards associated with displaced persons. The historical record testifies to official anxiety concerning the 'spontaneous' return journeys made by refugees, who evaded stringent controls over movement.[70] Another outcome was the impulse to isolate and, where possible, to expel 'dangerous' categories of population. In each instance Polish and Ukrainian Jews in particular tended to lose out, as Konrad Zielinski and Kate Stadnik demonstrate in their contributions to this volume. Such tactics cast a lengthy shadow over interwar politics in the successor states.

This reminds us that states also drew upon new (or recast) representations of difference also in formulating health, welfare and education policies. New rulers sought to protect the health of the nation by quarantining and isolating displaced groups that threatened to 'contaminate' the 'core' citizenry. Paul Weindling has carefully traced this process in eastern Europe. He shows, among other things, that the demonization of Jewish minorities as inherently 'unclean' reached a new pitch in 1915 and 1916, while the war promoted the emergence of extensive statist and technocratic programmes for the elimination of infectious disease. These projects for national hygiene were given a further impetus by the post-1917 movements of refugees and prisoners of war, and the associated anxieties about the spread of typhus across borders, which could only be checked if rigorous efforts were made to stem the tide of displaced persons.[71] In a nicely ironic juxtaposition, the Polish Minister of Health appointed a 'typhus czar'.[72] International efforts made by the Red Cross, by the American Joint Distribution Committee and by the American–Polish Relief Expedition demonstrated that concern for the health of displaced persons was not confined to the new national governments of eastern Europe and the USSR. In the midst of the typhus epidemic in 1919, Hoover dramatically pronounced that 'the pestilence had begun to move westward like a prairie fire', along with the desperate refugee population.[73] An American captain enthused that 'with such inducements as hot water, soap, clean towels and above all new underwear, *we can wash Poland*.'[74]

Population politics also implied a fresh conceptualization of 'land'. Economic and political aspects of land reform in central and eastern Europe have received a good deal of attention. Less well researched are the cultural meanings that attached to land in the aftermath of war and political upheaval.[75] Land – fought over, pockmarked by shell, infested by weeds, and littered with unexploded bombs, barbed wire and other detritus – assumed a particular significance. References to land conjured up images of despoliation and memories of displacement. 'While ploughing, I see that not only are ditches ripped open by shrapnel, but that within the land there are lots of splinters that will threaten bare footed people for a long time', wrote the Latvian refugee Alfreds Goba in a diary entry for October 1918.[76] Relief workers painted a graphic picture of refugees who sheltered in dugouts that had been abandoned by

German soldiers, permitting the new occupants to live like 'modern cavemen'.[77] Protracted warfare had 'de-natured' vast swathes of land, turning fertile land into desert. Certain landscapes were essentialized by an emerging scientific discourse of ecology that frequently assumed a nationalist tone. Some patriotic leaders invested it with a newly acquired 'national' significance: that is, the soil became a 'sacred' space that had not only been despoiled by the enemy but also 'fertilized' (as Piłsudksi put it) by the blood of its menfolk.[78] More prosaically, in 1924 the Latvian 'Joint Committee for the Economic and Cultural Integration of the Border Zone' considered using the land vacated by non-Latvian refugees to settle ethnic Latvian farmers near the border. Land reform was to compensate ethnic minorities, if necessary, with land in western Latvian districts where they would be outnumbered by and, ideally, assimilated into the local Latvian majority populations.[79] For Jewish leaders, too, land acquired a new significance, as a means of establishing new settlements in Ukraine and Crimea. As farmers, Jews would be able to avoid being exposed to the hardship and violence that Jewish tradesmen and their families had encountered in the townships of Russia and Ukraine. In Joseph Rosen's words, 'we must not overlook the eugenic value of the colonisation project. No other people is so greatly in need of the revitalising effect of an agricultural element, as is the Jewish people.' In this formulation the land-population nexus represented economic opportunity, eugenic improvement and self-protection – a wager on the most sturdy and strong 'human material'.[80]

The romanticized discourse of blood-soaked land reached its apogee among pro-Armenian writers, for whom the nation's future was closely linked to the efforts of the population to 'restore' the land to its former condition. Its supporters in western Europe emphasized the long and 'troubled' history of Christian Armenia at the hands of Turkish oppressors, culminating in the genocide of 1915. However, the return of some Armenian refugees to their homes in 1916 following a Russian advance exposed them to renewed attack when Russian troops finally withdrew. Those who survived crossed to Persia at the beginning of 1918. This protracted upheaval provided a rich vein of stories about Turkish (and Kurdish) atrocities, but would in due course generate schemes for the 'renewal' of the Armenian peasantry.[81]

No survey of postwar population displacement in the former Russian empire would be complete without mentioning the emigration from Russia of the Bolsheviks' political opponents, although it is not part of our purpose to trace their circumstances in exile. Civilians and military personnel escaped Soviet Russia in large numbers between the end of 1917 and 1922. Their numbers have been put at around 2 million, although recent research proposes a lower figure. They exited from the north-west provinces to Estonia (following the defeat of

Yudenich's army in November 1919), from Vladivostok in the Far East (in the aftermath of Admiral Kolchak's humiliation in November 1920), and from the south (in the wake of the defeats suffered by the White generals Denikin and Wrangel in 1920). Not all of these emigrants were ethnic Russians; they included Baltic German landowners, Greek merchants and Karelian peasants. But the majority were Russian.[82] Many exiles believed that they were leaving Russia only for a short while, until such time as the Bolshevik regime was overthrown. Thus they settled in what were deemed 'temporary' refugee camps in Turkey (particularly in Constantinople), Bulgaria, Yugoslavia and Greece (Lemnos). Those who had sufficient funds – members of the Russian aristocracy or ex-businessmen – made their way to Poland, Czechoslovakia and to western Europe, leaving impoverished officers and other ex-servicemen behind. Having evacuated the remnants of his Cossack army from Crimea, in 1921 Wrangel succeeded in persuading the Yugoslav government to allow them to settle in Yugoslavia. In the longer term, 'colonies' of largely Russian nationalist exiles were formed in cities such as Constantinople, Harbin, and (later on) Paris, Prague, Warsaw and Berlin. By 1922, twenty per cent of the total Russian refugee population had settled in Poland and around seventeen per cent in the Far East.[83] The Russian émigrés aroused in some observers a sense of fear about the political consequences of psychological distress: 'there is nothing they can do but loaf and starve. It is no wonder if they have lost, or are losing, all hope, and all morale, all sense of being members of and co-operators in a reasonable world. *Of such stuff are Bolsheviks made.*'[84]

Soviet aspirations and practice from an early stage thus convinced thousands of people that they did not have a secure future in Russia. Hence the 'wave' of applicants for emigration who arrived at the Polish, Latvian or Lithuanian frontiers, and whose claims were processed by bewildered, overstretched and often prejudiced officials.[85] In 1922 the Soviet state withdrew diplomatic recognition and protection from the Russian exiles who were scattered across Europe and the Far East. This had profound consequences for hundreds of thousands of people who, as an official of the League of Nations put it, 'cannot travel, marry, be born, or die without creating legal problems to which there is no solution.'[86]

The large-scale Russian and Armenian emigration draws our attention to the role of international agencies in addressing population displacement. The architects of the new European order did not take direct account of wartime and postwar population movements, but other bodies could not fail to deal with the consequences of war and diplomatic action.[87] In the grand project of social and economic reconstruction, the military delegation and the humanitarian mission frequently went hand in hand, explicitly so in the case of Herbert

Hoover's Polish Typhus Relief Expedition, which was staffed by members of the US army. The American Red Cross established a presence in Poland in March 1919. The US-based Young Men's Christian Association sent a team to eastern Europe, as did the Save the Children Fund. The American Jewish Joint Distribution Committee (JDC) became heavily involved in refugee and anti-typhus work from 1919 onwards. The JDC established offices throughout the region. By 1921–2 its Refugee Department had responsibility for 200,000 refugees in Poland, the Baltic States and Romania.[88] The League of Nations maintained a small epidemic commission in Warsaw.[89] This activity was replicated in Armenia, Anatolia, Cilicia, Syria and elsewhere, where British and American missionaries, Near East Relief, the League of Nations and other agencies were all involved in the welfare of Armenian refugees.[90] Finally, the British Society of Friends (Quakers) was active in Russia since the early days of the war, its field workers being joined in 1918 by American Friends.[91]

The displacement of population supported a stronger doctrine of bureaucratic and expert intervention at an international level. As the French delegate to the Inter-Governmental Conference on the Refugee Question put it in 1926:

> Extensive experience in the matter of placing refugees [has] shown that better results could be obtained if a professional selection of the refugees were effected before their departure.[92]

The suggestion here was that refugees would be counted, inspected, 'sorted' in situ, to determine their suitability for resettlement. Quaker relief workers similarly spent much time creating a bureaucratic record of refugees:

> Information concerning each child and refugee family was carefully entered, relationships traced and noted, and responsibilities allotted when the moment to move arrived. Even questions of land-ownership for parentless children were recorded, so that a claim could be made on their behalf when they got home.[93]

Similarly, the staff of the American JDC insisted on the need for 'case individualisation' that 'made it possible to follow the progress of each applicant personally', thereby helping to avoid what it termed 'moral degeneration'.[94]

A more general point was also being conveyed. By invoking 'professionalism' it was implied that refugees would submit to the power of technocracy, both for their own good and for the sake of the 'settled' population. Thus, eastern European ministers of health agreed on a rigorous programme to combat the typhus epidemic. Only after a period of quarantine might the refugees be discharged with the all-important 'certificate of delousation'. In some Polish towns, American soldiers who belonged to the American Polish Typhus Relief Expedition awarded prizes for the cleanest houses and people. In more active mode they also:

> spent the entire day prowling around the town and dropping irregularly and unexpectedly at some house which, if then dirty, was required to be instantly cleaned, the men staying until the work had been done then writing the name of the inhabitants in a little book.

In short, typhus borne by refugees became a powerful metaphor for refugeedom. It also served to draw attention to post-imperial state-building and the triumph of patriotic leadership. In Herbert Hoover's words, 'Rats, lice, famine, pestilence – yet they [Poles] were determined to build a new nation.'[95]

TOWARDS A REFUGEE-CENTRED PERSPECTIVE: NARRATING AND NEGOTIATING DISPLACEMENT

Thus far we have largely evaded a key question: how did refugee populations experience displacement? At first glance it might be expected that we can answer this question by considering the stories of displacement told by refugees themselves, but this is much more problematic than at first appears. The refugee voice emerges only rarely in the documentary record. More common are the tales told by those who encountered or acted on behalf of the refugee population.

The humanitarian narrative constitutes a particular genre, in which the relief effort serves as a record of individual self-realization. Stories of 'adventure' are couched in terms of overcoming obstacles and confronting danger. They are juxtaposed alongside the passivity of the tired and sick refugees, whose experiences were presumed to have left them incapable of telling a coherent story, let alone making informed or 'rational' judgements about the future. The sense of embarking upon an adventure that needs to be told contrasts sharply with the denial of refugees' own history and capacity for narration.[96]

The assumption that refugees needed to be acted for, rather than be allowed to act for themselves, reflected in part the age and gender composition of the refugee population. It also reflected a belief that those refugees who used their wit, whether to make ends meet or to negotiate the obstacles that were placed before them, contributed to making life difficult for relief workers and for officialdom.[97] Generally speaking, it seemed as if only intensive efforts on the part of relief workers prevented refugees from becoming entirely overwhelmed by their condition. The paradox is obvious: passivity was a precondition of the selfsame humanitarian assistance that was designed to overcome lethargy and to restore 'moral dignity'. These underlying assumptions supported the view that refugees' voices had no claim to public attention.

To be sure, we can gain occasional glimpses of refugees' declared aspirations. In May 1919 a group of Polish teachers in Riazan petitioned the Soviet administration for refugees (*Tsentroplenbezh*) to return to Poland:

> We have a natural wish to go back to our native country, where a new and brighter future awaits us in free Poland ... we are anxious to re-establish contact with our families who remained behind there, and we have a passionate desire to serve our homeland during the difficult time of its foundation.[98]

Some refugees believed that they could contribute to the revival of Russia's economic fortunes. A sympathetic eyewitness recounted the story of a nineteen-year-old Belarusian refugee, Jascha Onishchuk, who lived with his widowed mother in the village of Podgornyi, in Tambov province. Jascha's brother had joined the Red Army. He himself was impressed by the rich soil of Tambov and believed that agricultural productivity could be improved if the local peasant population adopted improved methods of cultivation, such as were practised in the western borderlands. But Jascha's hopes were soon dashed. Having joined the Bolshevik Party in order to avoid being drafted into the Red Army, the local peasants murdered him in 1920, as a representative of the 'commissarocracy'.[99]

There are also exceptions to the argument that humanitarian intervention stifled a sense of refugees' history. Mabel Elliott, the American medical director of Near East Relief allowed her articulate Armenian interpreter to speak of her experiences as a refugee. Yet Elliott was compelled to admit that 'somehow our minds could never quite meet theirs [i.e. the Armenians]; there was always something oblique there – a starting from different angles. Somehow we never got quite close to them...'[100] In November 1921 the Quaker relief worker Florence Barrow listened to the stories of some of the refugees who returned to Poland after having been forced to leave their homes in 1915.[101] Her single-minded pursuit of refugee families is touching and remarkable; Barrow tracked Polish refugees whom she had first encountered during 1916 in the Quaker settlements in the mid-Volga region. The extant stories mix despair and hope in equal measure, as in the account of the Harek family, three sisters who had been orphaned in 1915 after the family had been expelled from a village south of Brest-Litovsk. The elder sister was adopted by a school teacher in Pinsk, leaving the younger two (Domna, then aged 12, and Feokla, aged 8) to move eastwards, where they eventually settled in the Quaker home in Mogotova, Buzuluk district, Samara province. In 1920 the sisters made the long journey home:

They found that their house, happily undestroyed, had however been removed to a neighbouring village by another refugee who was occupying it. Domna found refuge in the miserably overcrowded hut of a relation, while Feokla undertook the care of a child of very undesirable parents not far off.

Two of the Friend workers found them in these sad conditions and arranged for Feokla to attend the school for spinning and weaving at Kobryn (sic). The man who had carried off their house was made to pay something towards the cost of a new one, but as this was not enough, more was given to them to build a new one, where Domna soon joined her sister. When they were again visited in 1925, they were full of hope for the future. Domna had married an industrious young man, who was setting to work to cultivate their land, and had already acquired some stock, while the girls were busy at their weaving. All trace of their sister had been lost, sad to say, and they feared they should never see her again.

Nothing survives of the sisters' unmediated attempts to recount their experiences. Others were even more unfortunate. Six surviving members of the Polcycko family returned to the village of Chojnicki:

> The good little new house of which she had told us in 1916 was now a ruin. The roof had fallen in, the stove and chimney had tumbled down, and there were neither windows nor doors, and a thick covering of snow partly covered the debris. A more hopelessly desolate looking place would hardly be imagined. They still own their land, but have neither plough nor horses...

In these interviews, something of a bond seems to have been forged between the Quaker missionary and her informants. Perhaps this reflects a shared sense of female strength and masculine incapacity; one refugee's father had gone from being 'a strong, fine-looking man' to being 'an absolute wreck'. 'In the autumn of 1915, father, mother, and four daughters had left the house, and now only the father, aged and ill, had returned, and one child.'[102] It may be stretching matters, but this served as a metaphor for Poland itself: damaged and enfeebled, but with the potential to recover itself with appropriate assistance from those with the right combination of selfless devotion, capital investment and expert knowledge.

All the same, the limitations of this project are evident. The case history underscores the helplessness of the refugee family. Florence Barrow's initiative demonstrates the scope for the Quaker volunteers to offer advice and to make their own observations on the plight of the refugee population. The refugee voice is all but submerged. When it does emerge it carries significant weight.[103]

Against this background it is intriguing to realize that some refugees were encouraged to record their experiences.[104] Occasionally refugees kept diaries in which they recorded their tortuous attempts to return to their homes. The diary of the Latvian Alfreds Goba is an excellent example.[105] Goba, who was studying in Moscow at the outbreak of World War One, fled to Baku in late 1915, where he joined the Latvian exile community and in 1917 married a young Latvian woman. In spring 1918, as navigation on the Volga opened, he wrote impatiently in his diary that 'soon we will start again on an unknown road.' His young wife was now pregnant, but Goba was preoccupied with Latvia's national birth. His diary fused dreams of Latvian independence with visions of an idealized national landscape as a place of future happiness, which he contrasted with his present exile. He wrote in March 1918: 'Only in an independent Latvian state could Latvian culture flourish. Oh, what happiness to live in an independent state.'[106] This fusion of the personal and the political was quite remarkable. In April 1918, Goba and his wife left with six other Latvians on a steamer which took them as far as Tsaritsyn on the Volga. Goba was happy to be travelling in a group, his sense of national solidarity deepened by the common experience of exile and resolution to return: 'If we are to drown, at least we will all drown together.' After three months of travelling, they reached Latvia in mid-July. Goba found the Germans in control and the country ruined. His father's house in Zemgale on the Daugava river was 'devastated, torn down and the grass is overgrown . . .' Domestic destruction was symbolic of the state of the country, in which not only the physical infrastructure but also the fabric of government and of people's allegiance had to be reconstructed from scratch:

> Everything falls apart, as if a hill was on it. There are so many things to do and think that at first a person is dumbfounded. You have to know what kind of authority is here, and in a judicial sense, what is allowed and what is forbidden. What kind of obligations, and what kind of rights. The masses complain that the Germans suppress them. How do they suppress them? What rights do I have? I have to relearn all of my surroundings and conditions.[107]

It is difficult to establish the extent to which newly emerging states capitalized on this enthusiasm by encouraging returnees to make public their experiences of the journey they made to and from distant lands. Certainly, so far as can be ascertained, there are few instances in which returnees were lionized as heroic individuals who had kept the flag of national identity flying in the Russian interior. To be sure, Anna Louise Strong recounted one tale of determination and leadership:

> A tall young Jewish farmer, standing at the door of his still unfinished stone hut in the biting November wind, told me how he organised his group: "I come from a small town near Kiev. I have no trade. For five years I served under Nicholas and five in a German prison camp. When I came home my

people, who were once rich, were ruined. The bandit bands had been seven times looting through our town. So I called a meeting in the theatre and said, It is impossible to live as we are. Brother cheats brother, and we all lie to the tax collector, yet the taxes eat us all up ... Let us take up land and live by honest work.".... [108]

As we have seen, however, it was much more common for states and officials to inscribe on the refugee population their own vision of the nation's future. Refugees were encouraged or obliged to be passive characters in the state-building narrative.

Finally, when refugees were invited to give voice to their concerns and aspirations, they might insist on the incommensurability of experience. As one Armenian refugee told Mabel Elliott, 'I can't really tell you what it was like. You must live through things like that, to understand them'.[109] For some displaced persons, refugeedom could never be fully narrated. It does not seem fanciful to suggest that this enabled them to claim a privileged standpoint of their own, and thus to turn the tables on those who observed them.

CONCLUDING REMARKS: 'WAR AFTER THE WAR'[110]

We can sum up as follows. Many civilians who had been displaced into the Russian interior during World War One fervently wished to return to their former abode in newly independent native lands. Others chose, or were forced, to remain where they were. Economic deprivation and famine (in 1921–2) imposed additional burdens on displaced and settled populations. Political uncertainty in this enormous contested space only served to multiply these dilemmas and difficulties. The refugee population was swelled by newly displaced persons, the result of German military occupation of the western borderlands of the former empire. Subsequently, the prolonged dislocation of the Russian Civil War, battles between Polish, Lithuanian and Ukrainian troops, the Soviet–Polish war, and continued turmoil in the Caucasus, prompted additional displacement, to which was added large-scale emigration by Russians, Armenians and others. Some populations stayed physically where they were, but found that borders had moved instead, effectively resulting in their political expatriation. Thus the years of war, revolution, and peacemaking between 1917 and 1921 marked renewed population displacement on a massive scale.

The leadership of the new polities – by which is meant those in command of both 'bourgeois' and 'proletarian' governments – had to decide if, when and how these citizens would be 'repatriated'. Only after lengthy negotiations did the states that emerged on the wreckage of the old Russian Empire reach binding diplomatic agreements that paved the way for organized return.[111] The process of return subjected individual refugees to great stress. It put pressure on government budgets. It imposed heavy demands on fledgling bureaucracies and relief workers, who were at times overwhelmed by the scale and character of population movement. As people returned, the new successor states of eastern Europe embarked on programmes to consolidate a sense of affiliation to the new national homeland, identifying those who 'belonged' by virtue of ethnicity or who might conceivably be 'nationalized' into membership of the new nation-state. As we have seen, this placed many Jewish refugees in a more precarious position than their non-Jewish counterparts: the contributors to this book take up this particular issue in relation to Poland and the Baltic states. This scrutiny went hand in hand with a stringent health screening of the displaced population. In the longer term, state construction was associated with programmes of social reform, fiscal stabilization and economic modernization, without which any attempt to assist chosen refugees to rebuild shattered lives would be inconceivable.[112] For their part, the Bolsheviks created an entirely new polity according to ethno-territorial principles.[113] In Soviet Russia, too, ethnicity was hugely significant, but now wedded to the principle of proletarian dictatorship. In each instance, controlling and moving populations facilitated a spatial reordering of the new state in political, economic, national or strategic terms. In Russia the propertied and military elites went into exile; those upper strata who remained behind on Soviet soil soon found themselves excluded from membership of the new state. These disabilities had their counterpart in 'bourgeois' Europe, where land settlement and other measures tended to privilege certain claims at the expense of others, and where migration was likewise promoted for developmental reasons. As a result of these multiple pressures, practices, and – certainly – opportunities, population displacement continued to characterize the politics of interwar Europe.[114]

2
Latvian Refugees and the Latvian Nation State during and after World War One

AIJA PRIEDITE

INTRODUCTION

World War One inflicted upon the Latvian people, as upon so many others, an unprecedented displacement of population. In Latvia's case this was accompanied by considerable economic destruction. However, these misfortunes also enabled national mobilization, stimulating political activity, which flourished particularly after the February Revolution of 1917. Growing disappointment with the tsarist institutions that dealt inadequately with refugee relief, indignation at the tactics of the Russian army commanders on the Riga front during the winter of 1916–17, and the collapse of parliamentary democracy in Russia – all this radicalized those Latvians who found themselves in foreign parts. At the same time, leaders of Latvian refugee organizations on Russian soil began to promote the idea of independence. They formulated programmes of institutional change at a national level and provided the ideological basis for later state-building activities.

In nationalist historiography, the formation of an independent state is considered to be the summit of each national movement, crowning a process of development that may stretch back over decades. Miroslav Hroch speaks of a first phase ('Phase A') that is characterized by a purely theoretical interest of scholars in national culture, history and folklore. The second phase ('Phase B') is a period of patriotic agitation and the beginnings of political campaigning for the national idea. The transition from phase B to phase C, the creation of a new, mass-supported national movement, is crucial for the characterization of national politics. The Latvian nation followed this course for almost seventy years, beginning in the 1850s with the Young Latvian movement, and culminating in the declaration of an independent Latvian state on 18 November 1918.

However, the development of the idea of Latvia as a state cannot be equated solely with the history of the national movement. The most important aspect of the prehistory of the Latvian nation-state was connected with the emergence of mass politics.[1]

In terms of Hroch's model, studies of Latvian nationalism have concentrated on Phases B and C.[2] Recent publications reject the applicability of Phase C, arguing that before 1918 Latvian nationalism did not grow into a political movement, and that the foundation of the nation-state did not reflect the popular will. Thus Detlef Hening believes that 'the mass movement generated by national self-awareness (setting aside the famous Latvian Riflemen's Regiment in 1915) can be observed only in the period of the "singing revolution", that is only in 1988.'[3] In his opinion, the foundation of an independent Latvia in 1918 did not rest upon popular political mobilization, because no mass demonstrations took place then comparable with those in 1988-9. Hening argues that:

> Until the October 1917 coup, no group within Latvian society expressed demands for an independent state. In many conceptions, which mostly developed from various social democratic schools of thought, emphasis was variously placed on cultural, economic or political autonomy within a reformed Russia ... Why did the views of the Latvian political elite change so suddenly in favour of founding an independent state in 1918?[4]

To be sure, the start of Phase C in the history of any national movement is hard to locate, because we have no clear criteria to determine how large its base has to be in order to call it a mass movement. Do a few thousand conscious participants meet the criteria, or must a majority of the nation subscribe to the nationalist cause?

Although any organized national movement must be led by a core of activists, it is hard to believe that the decisive factor in the establishment of the Latvian state was the will of a few liberally inclined politicians. Political pragmatism has been one of the most important elements of Latvian national thought, but as Uldis Ģērmanis points out, the objective would never have been achieved if the politically active part of Latvian society had not already embraced the ideology of political nationalism, and if the central Latvian political organizations had not directly and ceaselessly struggled for the achievement of the maximum demand of the Latvian national programme – a sovereign Latvia.[5] I would argue that they were enabled to do so in part as a consequence of the international situation – the geopolitical collapse of two empires during World War One and the revolution in Russia – which created a favourable situation for the declaration of independence in November 1918.

Within this broad context, other socio-political considerations also loomed large. Population displacement in particular was of considerable significance.

The aim of this chapter is to trace the genesis of the Latvian state in this wider context. My contention is that an analysis of the Latvian national movement during World War One must encompass three mutually connected aspects, namely national ideology, collective psychology and institutional arrangements. National ideology did not develop in isolation from the social psychological mood among a large refugee population, which amounted to something like one-third of the entire Latvian population. The realization of independence was unthinkable without an institutional framework created and accepted by the proponents of a national movement. These last two aspects are mentioned only in passing in Latvian historiography or are not mentioned at all, possibly because an extremely important role in the creation of a sovereign Latvia was played by refugees and refugee organizations, none of them actually on Latvian soil.[6]

THE DEVELOPMENT OF THE IDEA OF A LATVIAN STATE DURING WORLD WAR ONE

At the beginning of World War One, Latvians generally thought of themselves as loyal citizens of the Russian state who were ready to carry out their patriotic duty and submit to the orders of civil and military institutions.[7] Following a fresh attack by the German army on Kurzeme in July 1915, the Supreme High Command ordered the destruction of crops and the evacuation of the entire province. The retreating Russian army burned houses and farm buildings, so that nothing of material value would fall into German hands. This was followed by the evacuation of factories and their workers from Riga and Daugavpils. Deprived of the means of support, virtually all social classes and age groups became refugees.

Historians have attempted to weigh the losses and gains for the Latvian nation brought about by the war. The 'losses' column is made up of statistics about the dead, the numbers of people who fled from Latvia as refugees, and of enormous material losses. The 'gains' column usually includes the considerable activation of Latvian national aspirations, which expressed itself in the organization of national military units, the unification of Latgale with the rest of Latvia, and the strengthening of rights to autonomy and independence. The Moscow-based newspaper *Dzimtenes Atbalss* (*Echo of the Fatherland*), with a circulation of 10,000 and a much larger readership, began to propagate the idea of an independent Latvia; this gained increasing currency during 1917.[8]

Yet it would be wrong to associate the growth of Latvian political nationalism entirely with World War One. Latvian political nationalism grew out of the 1905 revolution, when the Latvian Social Democratic Association (LSDA), led by M Valters, E Rolavs, and E Skubiķis, came into its own.⁹ To be sure, the nationalist demands of the LSDA did not as yet strike a popular chord. The stance toward the national question of the leadership of the Latvian Social Democratic Party (LSDP) – at this time Latvia's largest political party – had a much greater ideological impact. Its platform included a paragraph on 'the right of self-determination for all nations living within the current borders of Russia', and 'broad political and economic autonomy for the provinces'. Neither in 1905 nor in 1917 did the Social Democratic Party actively campaign for these demands.¹⁰ All the same, the contribution of the LSDA to the history of Latvian nationalist thought and to state-building extended far beyond the narrow confines of the LSDA itself. The nationalist movement capitalized on the opportunities presented by World War One. Writers such as Jānis Akuraters and Kārlis Skalbe played an important role in fostering the idea of independence, both in their homeland and among Latvian refugees in the Russian interior.¹¹

The development of Latvian nationalist ideology during World War One may be divided into two stages. The first, until the summer of 1917, was characterized by demands for Latvia's autonomy, demands which built upon plans developed during and after the 1905 revolution. Prominent members of the LSDP adopted the programme of political nationalism. Mensheviks such as M Skujenieks and F Cielēns, as well as many members of the intelligentsia, moved away from the SDP and the Revolutionary Socialist (formerly the LSDA) parties, and created the newspapers *Līdums* and *Dzimtenes Atbalss* as fora for their nationalist views. The idea of Latvian autonomy was also supported by J Zālītis and J Goldmanis, both of them members of the State Duma. A broad discussion with members of the Latvian press and representatives of various national organizations in Latvia and Russia was convened in Goldmanis's Petrograd apartment in the autumn of 1916. At this meeting, P Zālīte presented a new plan for the autonomy of Latvia, which took as its model the constitution of Australia as a Dominion of the British Commonwealth.¹² *Dzimtenes Atbalss* published 'The basic principles of the unity of Latvia', setting out the project for political autonomy. Meanwhile the Latvian press reflected a progressive disillusionment with the policies of the Russian state. Latvians' loyalty toward Russia had brought them only substantial material and human losses. Any residual allegiance was eroded by the incompetence of the Russian army leadership on the Riga front and by the senseless sacrifices of Latvian riflemen during the 'Christmas battles' of January 1917.¹³ Developments soon after the February 1917 revolution showed that the idea of autonomy was gaining ground. The Latvian Social Democrats (LSD) changed their earlier negative attitude toward autonomy, as evidenced by its resolution on the national question at the fifth party congress on 22 July 1917. A conference on 12 August in Riga Castle showed that representatives of practically all Latvian political tendencies (including the Bolsheviks) were in favour of political autonomy for Latvia in a federal republic of Russia. The only exception was the ultra-conservative People's Party, but this was by no stretch of the imagination a significant political force.

The hopes invested in the democratic revolution of February 1917 were summed up in the slogan, 'A free Latvia in a free Russia'. It was expected that democracy in Russia would generate respect for the rights of nationalities. The declarations of loyalty by Latvians to the Russian state seemed to many of them to entitle Latvia to national rights after the war. However, the stance of the L'vov and Kerenskii governments toward non-Russian nationalities, which dragged out the implementation of the national and political demands of the nationalities, quickly led to disillusionment with Russia's parliamentary democracy and to a rapid radicalization of Latvian nationalist thought.

In this second stage the decisive role in the formulation of Latvian national demands belonged to the Latvian National Democratic Party (LNDP), which was founded in Moscow in the spring of 1917. Its core were the publicists of the newspaper *Dzimtenes Atbalss*, which at this time became the party's ideological platform. The LNDP developed its activities primarily amongst Latvian refugees and Latvian colonies in Russia. Within three weeks 1,000 new members had joined the party. *Dzimtenes Atbalss* began to propagate the idea of an independent Latvia in the summer of 1917, especially after the First All-Russian Congress of Soviets failed to give any tangible support to non-Russian nationalities. The contributions to *Dzimtenes Atbalss* showed that the slogan of the moderates, 'A free Latvia in a free Russia', had lost its appeal. Ernests Blanks captured the new doctrine in his phrase: 'Where Latvia begins, Russia ends.' As Blanks saw it, the decisive factor in killing off the idea of federation was the chauvinism of a large nation toward its smaller neighbour, threatening Latvia's cultural, political and economic autonomy. His conclusion was unequivocal: 'Federation with Russia is not our ideal, it is only a compromise. Our ideal is a sovereign Latvia.'[14] *Dzimtenes Atbalss* and *Līdums* both supported the creation of a national centre which would represent the will of the whole nation in the shape of a Latvian Provisional National Council. This heralded a new stage in the history of the Latvian national movement, the hallmark of which was practical activity aimed at creating a national provisional government. This significant expression of political will would culminate in the declaration of independence in November 1918.

THE INSTITUTIONAL FRAMEWORK OF
THE LATVIAN NATIONAL MOVEMENT

Simultaneously with the development of national political thought during World War One, the institutionalization of the Latvian national movement occurred in new locations. Newly formed refugee welfare organizations became the basis for a different kind of national politics, and their leaders would eventually form part of the political elite in independent Latvia.[15] Refugee welfare organizations initially united under a support society called 'Baltija'. Its network covered Latvia. The evacuation of the country and the rapid growth in the number of refugees led in 1915 to the formation in Petrograd of the Latvian Central Welfare Committee (LCWC). The LCWC eventually embraced about 260 local refugee organizations and agencies, some of them as far away as Siberia, Central Asia and Transcaucasia. By 1916 around 2,000 refugee relief workers were employed by the LCWC.[16]

The creation of this network needs to be set in the context of social organization after the 1905 revolution. Latvian social life and cultural activities took place within a range of societies. Šilde notes that alongside earlier choral and temperance societies there arose groups with more avowedly political aims, such as the Latvian Central Society for Agriculture, and the Latvian Farmers' Economic Society. Businesses and co-operatives also took on a new lease of life.[17] Commenting on this trend, the newspaper *Latvija* wrote in 1914 that 'the life of the societies is one of, if not the main, forms of social life, in which, in spite of reactionary punishments, our nation's self organization and determination are expressed. Societies have already become an essential part of our cultural life.'[18]

World War One and the widespread movement of Latvian refugees brought about an adjustment of the practical objectives being pursued by leaders of the Latvian national movement. Political demands for autonomy became secondary. Analysing Latvian politics in 1916, *Līdums* noted that refugee problems and support for the Latvian Riflemen had become the most important matters for both the Latvian representatives in the State Duma and for the representatives of social organizations. It would be more accurate to say that the discourse of national politics had been displaced onto issues of population migration and military organization.[19]

From its inception, the LCWC was led by Pastor Vilis Olavs. Olavs was widely known as a national ideologue, who had been the editor of the newspaper *Pēterburgas Avīzes*. In his articles on the unity of the Latvian nation, he had demanded not just the unification of the inhabitants of Latgale (the Latvians living in Vitebsk province) with those in the Baltic provinces, but had also drawn attention to the Latvian colonists in Russia, who from the 1880s onward had drifted away from their homeland to seek a better life, and who were seriously in danger of losing their national identity. Olavs put their number at around 200,000. In his view, the wave of refugees during World War One threatened to repeat this situation. Olavs assumed a moral responsibility toward the Latvian refugees, newly 'cast into foreign lands'.[20] Under his leadership the LCWC did not confine itself to technical issues relating to the material needs of refugees. The LCWC became instead an institution at the very centre of Latvian political life, representing Latvians and defending their interests.[21] Its status was confirmed by the fact that the leading parliamentarians Zālītis and Goldmanis were involved in it from its inception. Both men frequently coordinated their political activities in the Duma with the LCWC board.[22]

The next shift in Latvian political opinion took place in the autumn of 1917. In early September the German army occupied Riga and surged forward across Latvia's territory. The indifference of Russian politicians toward the Baltic became obvious. The Russian army began to collapse. The Russian Provisional Government ignored the aspirations of Russia's minorities. The death-knell for Latvian autonomy sounded in October 1917. After the Bolshevik revolution, the 'Russian orientation' forfeited credibility, and from the autumn of 1917 Latvian national politics followed two other paths. The burgeoning Latvian Provisional National Council represented the first course. This orientation pinned its hopes on an Allied victory in the world war, and the realization of the promise of national self-determination. The Democratic Bloc, founded in Riga at the end of September 1917 by politicians, who tried to develop cooperation with the German Reichstag and its left-wing parties, represented the second orientation, but its activities are not relevant to the argument advanced in the present chapter.

In May 1917 proposals were made for the creation of a broad body to represent the nation that could organize elections for a Latvian Constitutional Assembly and in the meantime handle pressing political matters, so as to prevent the loss of popular support on the issue of territorial unification. The final decision to set up the Latvian Provisional National Council (LPNC) was taken on 13 October 1917, when representatives of the biggest Latvian organizations and parties met in Petrograd. The LPNC was founded with the direct support of the LCWC, and from its inception refugee representatives played an active part at various levels of this important body. Kristaps Bachmanis and Kārlis Skalbe, who were officially representing the Latvian National Democratic Party but were also known as activists in refugee relief organizations in Moscow, were elected to the board of the LPNC. Jāzeps Rancāns, Arveds Bergs, Zigfrīds Meierovics, Pēteris Zālīte, Frīdrihs Grosvalds and Jānis Brūmels worked in the sections of the LPNC, while Jānis Čakste, Jānis Kreicbergs and Zigfrīds Meierovics were elected as foreign delegates. Following the liquidation of the LCWC in Petrograd in January 1918, its members continued to work in the foreign section of the National Council.[23] The practical work of supporting refugees became virtually impossible after the Bolshevik seizure of power, since funding was withdrawn. The LPNC dedicated itself instead to propaganda in support of an independent, democratic republic of Latvia.

Notwithstanding the destruction of the Latvian press after the October revolution and the lack of transport links with the colonies, Latvian refugees took a notable interest in the work of the LPNC. From April 1918 onwards, a periodical issued by the LPNC's foreign section kept Latvian refugees in Russia informed of political developments.[24] From May 1918 onwards Latvian refugees and colonists in Ukraine and southern Russia could read the newspaper *Atvase* [*Offspring*] published in Khar'kov, which also followed the LPNC line. Articles about the Latvian nation and its national political strivings also appeared in major Russian newspapers, such as *Utro Rossii*. Latvian refugee organizations and individual refugees gave moral and financial backing to the LPNC, demonstrating an impressive degree of cooperation in support of a common objective. Territorial sections of the LPNC were established in Moscow, Ufa, Kazan', Tbilisi, Samara, Smolensk, Orel, Pskov, Kiev, Odessa, Khar'kov, Ekaterinoslav and elsewhere. These undertook important administrative responsibilities. A good example is the Khar'kov Latvian National Council, which issued Latvian passports to Latvian citizens even before November; these documents were recognized by local authorities, and by the Latvian Ministry of the Interior, which later exchanged them for official passports. In this way, the LPNC became a kind of embryonic or proto-state.[25]

The twin centres of the Latvian national movement in Siberia and the Far East from the summer and autumn of 1918 were Vladivostok and Omsk. Both towns saw the creation of new organizations to support the local Latvian population. A congress in Irkutsk saw the establishment of the 'Latvian National Council of Siberia and the Urals'. The members of its executive included the most prominent Latvian historian, Professor Arveds Švābe, executive secretary, and Professor Pēteris Šmits, honorary president. The organization was dedicated to the defence of the rights of Latvians, and in particular to the relief of refugees, whose cultural needs were acknowledged and who were given assistance with registration and re-evacuation. The Council also established contacts with the foreign diplomatic corps.[26]

Another important organizational vehicle of the Latvian national movement was the Latvian Self-Determination Union, established in March 1918. This non-partisan union advocated the convocation of a Latvian Constitutional

Assembly, on the grounds that Latvia's political future required the support of a wide spectrum of democratically inclined Latvians. The Union published a pamphlet, founded support sections in Moscow, Tver, Rybinsk, Tula, Khar'kov, Briansk, Roslavl', Vitebsk, Kazan', Vladivostok and elsewhere, and conducted a broad information campaign among refugees by sending its propaganda teams all over Russia. More than 40,000 individuals and numerous organizations signed a protest petition organized by the Union, against German plans to annex Latvian territory.[27]

REPRESENTATIONS OF LATVIAN REFUGEES IN THE RUSSIAN INTERIOR

Refugees had in the first place to deal with the pronounced image of Latvians in the Russian state as unwelcome foreigners. Initial patriotic sentiment – that refugees were real citizens of the state who boldly turned their backs on the enemy and headed deep into Russian territory – began to fade within days of their leaving Latvian territory. The refugees were looked upon with suspicion, fear and contempt. The Russians did not understand the misfortune of the Latvians and did not take any interest in them. Even worse, there were unconcealed attempts to profit from the flood of refugees by raising prices for apartment rents, food and other essential goods. The selfsame Russian government, which had urged Latvians to leave the German-occupied territories, now turned its back on the refugees at the most difficult time of their lives. This awareness bitterly contrasted with the fact that the mobilized Latvian men were fighting for the good of the country while their wives, children and old folk were abandoned to their fates. Latvian refugees felt themselves to be war victims who had followed government orders, but were now experiencing disappointment and a lack of hospitality from the Russian people.[28]

In 1915 and early 1916 various press publications drew attention to the fact that ordinary Russian people considered the Latvians to be *nemtsy*, or Germans, because the decisive factor in determining people's identity was their religion. The inhabitants of Kurzeme and Zemgale were mostly Lutherans, a fact that was noted in their identification documents. For the Russians, Lutheranism meant a 'German' faith, a perception strengthened by the 'Germanic' surnames of the Latvians. Portrayed as Germans, Latvian refugees were often denied work and humanitarian aid, while in the larger cities they were sometimes the victims of street fights, organised attacks and pogroms. As a result of these attitudes, in August 1915 the Latvian press began publishing the slogan, 'Refugees, get yourselves proof of your nationality!'[29] Meanwhile Olavs used the Russian press to deploy a more positive self-image:

Help us! Our language is foreign to you, most Latvians are foreign to you by their faith, our surnames sounds strange to Russian ears – but we are yours. For more than 700 years we have suffered from German abuse, and thanks to us, the Baltic did not become a German land. We are your advance guard, which is now taking the first blow on its breast.[30]

Latvian refugees' religion had become a symbolic marker of their difference in the context of Russian orthodoxy and culture. An inability to satisfy their religious needs (due to the small number of Latvian pastors) served to intensify a perception that Latvians had become God's abandoned people. This self-image was in turn supported by the historical analogy drawn between Latvians and ancient Hebrew captives. In this way, a prevailing sense of collective nostalgia assumed a religious character.[31]

Negative images in Russia also included a popular view that refugees were 'parasites'. To be sure, this image applied to all nationalities, not just the Latvians. Latvian refugees were often employed in jobs, such as forestry, where they were paid less than local inhabitants. When they turned down these jobs, or expressed displeasure at the low pay, this was interpreted as a refusal to work at all. In the summer of 1916 the Tatiana Committee came up the idea of holding an exhibition which would help the inhabitants of Russia develop an understanding of the minority nations of Russia swept up in the refugee wave. It was hoped that this exhibition could be organized on the 'nationality principle' so that Russians could understand what the refugees had lost in their homelands, the difficulties faced by the refugees, and the situation in their current places of residence. Unfortunately, the exhibition was postponed until the autumn of 1917 and in the end never took place at all.[32]

Against the background of this adverse publicity and these negative public attitudes, members of the Latvian patriotic intelligentsia sought to promote a more positive self-image. Crucial in this respect were the activities of the Latvian Central Welfare Committee (LCWC), local refugee committees and other Latvian organizations, which devoted considerable attention to the educational, cultural and spiritual needs of the refugees. The very first Latvian Refugee Congress (30–31 August 1915) adopted a resolution calling for the establishment in Moscow of a Cultural Bureau to take care of refugees' cultural needs. The Moscow Latvian Society and Petrograd Welfare Society worked alongside and in cooperation with the Cultural Bureau to organize gatherings of the Latvian intelligentsia. Latvian theatre companies operated in Moscow and Petrograd. Latvian musical life also developed in these cities, with choral and symphonic concerts presented by renowned Latvian artists. Important exhibitions of sculpture were also held.[33]

There was an active cultural life among Latvian colonies in many parts of

European Russia and in Siberia, where refugees brought in fresh ideas and strengthened links with Latvia. The long-established Moscow Latvian community supported the '1917 Fund', organized by the National Democratic Party with the aim of popularizing Latvian culture and science. Attempts were also made to arrange for the dissemination of nationalist propaganda overseas.[34] The Tatiana Committee helped finance schools.[35] By the end of 1916, over 12,000 children attended these schools, although this was only a fraction of the total number of registered refugee children. The LCWC's schools gave children the opportunity to commence their studies in their native language, whereas in the unoccupied part of Latvia teaching was only allowed in the Russian language. The Education Section of the Cultural Bureau started to develop a new Latvian national schools project. Its work laid the foundations of the education system of the Republic of Latvia.[36]

The large amount of attention paid to culture and education grew out of justified concerns about the loss of national identity and potential 'assimilation' in the new places of residence. The numerous Latvian colonies already established in European Russia and Siberia from the 1880s onward were seen as examples of this negative tendency. *Dzimtenes Atbalss* made this the subject of an article in its first issue, confirming the point that vernacular culture is one of the most important elements forming what Anthony Smith has termed the ethnic model of the nation.[37]

BEYOND WORLD WAR ONE

The repatriation process fell into three stages, corresponding to events in Russia and to changes in Latvian–Russian relations. Repatriation began in the wake of the Brest-Litovsk peace treaty, when Latvia was of course still under German control. The legal basis for the return of refugees to Latvia was established later, by a series of agreements beginning with the Refugee Re-evacuation Agreement (22 June 1920) and the Latvian–Soviet Russian Peace Treaty (11 August 1920). These were followed by an 'Agreement on the Optants' (22 July 1921) and by the Convention on Refugee Repatriation from Ukraine.

The Brest-Litovsk peace treaty granted the inhabitants of the Baltic provinces the right of return to their former place of residence. Germans were the first to use this opportunity. Latvians could leave Russia provided they were in possession of certificates testifying that they were natives of Latvia. Unfortunately, the Bolsheviks had closed Latvian national organizations, including the LCWC, which left no Latvian representatives to issue certificates. Thanks to Kārlis Zariņš, a well known refugee relief official who established contacts with the German Consul-General and the Baltic German Committee, an agreement was struck whereby Latvian identity papers would be issued to the refugees by himself and his deputies, Reverend J Grīnbergs and Dr O Voit in Petrograd, and by Reverend Kārlis Irbe in Moscow.[42] Irbe, later Bishop of the Latvian Evangelic Lutheran Church, recalled that the Baltic German Committee was very suspicious about refugees, insisting that no Latvian Bolsheviks be permitted to leave for Latvia. The Baltic Germans finally agreed that refugees would be issued with proof of membership of a religious congregation in Latvia, on the grounds that no church member could possibly be a Bolshevik.[43] Many thousands of Latvian refugees received these certificates, which were accepted both by the Bolshevik government and the German authorities beyond the demarcation line.[44] The well-known Latvian politician Ādolfs Klīve was one such beneficiary:

> ... I was content with a certificate in German, issued in my real name and stating that I was a member of Vecumnieki parish, returning to my home in Bauska, Kurzeme province. These certificates were issued at the German embassy, where a special department was headed by Dr.Schiemann, who later on became a member of the Saeima [Parliament].[45]

The certificate enabled Klīve to cross the border in Valka without any difficulty. Other trains went via Toroshino (15 km from Pskov), Sebezh and Polock. In Latvia, all entrants were placed in quarantine in Inchukalns or Krustpils and received vaccination against contagious diseases.

The issue of repatriation became the responsibility of the Bolsheviks in the autumn and winter of 1918, when they finally gained control of territories occupied by the Germans. As early as March 1918, the Commissariat of Latvian National Affairs was formed as part of the Russian Commissariat of Nationalities. The CLNA started to register Latvian refugees in the summer. The first trainloads of refugees departed for Latvia in September and October. Some 400,000 refugees left between May and November 1918, although it is not known how many were ethnic Latvians, nor what proportion was re-evacuated due to the initiative of the Baltic German Committee or the CLNA.[46] When the Soviet Latvian Republic was established, the organized re-evacuation of refugees shrank. Their departure was delayed on the grounds that it would lead to an outflow of qualified workers and jeopardize successful enterprises in Russia. The rubber factory 'Kaučuks' is a perfect example. Its workforce founded a re-evacuation committee in early 1919, and repeatedly expressed a desire to return to Latvia, together with families and belongings. The CLNA had already approved this, but its decision was revoked by Aleksei Rykov (chairman of the Supreme Council of the National Economy, VSNKh) who dismissed the re-evacuation committee.[47] Latvians were also drafted to serve in the new Red

Army. Soviet officials controlled the purchase of railway tickets in order to prevent spontaneous return of refugees.[48] Hence only small numbers of Latvians were repatriated in 1919.[49] When warmer weather set in during the spring of the following year, several hundred refugees managed to cross the border illegally every day, but they had to leave their belongings behind in Russia.[50]

The most intensive return of the refugees to Latvia took place in 1920–2, following the Latvian–Russian Refugees Re-evacuation Agreement. The regulations were worked out to the smallest detail, stipulating the amount of luggage and money, jewellery, food, clothing, footwear, toiletries and so on. The Agreement also established the general principles of re-evacuation, for example, giving preference to refugees from areas with lower living standards, promoting the reunion of divided families, and making both states responsible for the transportation of refugees and their belongings. The Agreement also confirmed two ports of exit from Russia: Rozenova station on the former Ventspils-Rybinsk railway line and Zhogov on the Petrograd-Warsaw line.[51]

In Latvia itself, the Department of POWs and Refugees at the Ministry of the Interior (established in July 1919) and the Refugees and Colonies Department in the Ministry of Foreign Affairs (founded in February 1920) took charge of repatriation. In April 1920 the Latvian Refugee Re-evacuation Society (LRRS) came into being. This was a public organization with branches in Riga and six more Latvian towns. Its founding members were officials from former refugee organizations in various Russian cities, such as Moscow, Odessa, Samara, Petrograd, Khar'kov and Taganrog. The LRRS gave financial support to refugees. It opened shelters and asylums, as well as shops selling cheap goods to newcomers in Rezekne and Riga. The Society also kept in touch with refugees in Russia, Ukraine, Crimea and Caucasus, informing them of the terms of the Re-evacuation Agreement. Although it received no financial support from the financially hard-pressed Latvian government, the LRRS played a crucial part in the repatriation process.[52]

Aside from technical matters, such as quarantine and disinfecting, and the establishment of orphanages and asylums for handicapped people, Latvia's official agencies had to confront the issue of refugees' loyalty to the new state. So-called refugee 'liberation commissions' were set up in Rezekne and Riga, aimed at establishing refugees' identity, aspirations and political past. These commissions gained a lot of publicity. The Latvian press emphasized that, in order to obtain official documents such as a provisional passport, each refugee needed two referees to guarantee that he or she was not a communist agent. This condition was sometimes hard to meet.[53]

The repatriation of Latvian refugees encountered considerable difficulties in Russia. Latvian Bolsheviks on Russian territory adopted a wholly negative attitude towards 'White Latvia' and depicted the return of their compatriots to Latvia as a 'betrayal' of class consciousness.[54] Hoping to stem the outflow of qualified workers, the Bolsheviks compiled lists of returnees who had little to contribute to economic reconstruction, such as the sick, infirm or handicapped. Professional people and skilled workers, on the other hand, found it difficult to obtain permission to leave Russia.[55] Hermanis Kaupins, who became an official of the LRRS after returning to Latvia, told the newspaper *Laukstrādnieks* [*Farm-Hand*] that the Bolsheviks objected to agitation in support of a return to Latvia and hindered the activity of independent refugee organizations.[56] The very existence of the Re-evacuation Agreement was concealed; copies of the paper *Krievijas Cīņa* [*Russia's Fight*], which had published the text of the Agreement, were 'lost in the post' and failed to reach readers.[57]

Such measures nevertheless proved ineffective, and the Bolsheviks resorted to other methods. Repression of Latvian activists took place in various Russian cities. Ten LPNC members, including their leader R Glāznieks, were imprisoned in Irkutsk (Glāznieks himself was later executed). V Jākobsons, a representative of the Latvian government, was arrested in Rostov-on-Don. Lieutenant A Vilips was sentenced to death in Krasnoiarsk. V Grīnbergs was arrested and shot dead in Kuban. Zaļkalns was arrested and sentenced to three months penal servitude for being in contact with the Latvian peace delegation. These are not the only such examples. The Soviet authorities occasionally assigned Latvians jobs in distant locations, preventing them from boarding the train home.[58] When drafting the lists of repatriates, *Tsentroplenbezh* took a close interest in persons with a so-called 'exchange value', such as popular artists, scholars, professionals and politicians who were illegally seized and held hostage, in order to be exchanged for communist underground activists who had been arrested in Latvia. Seventeen people were sent to Latvia in April 1920 to be exchanged in this way, among them the philosopher Aleksandrs Dauge, professors V Mincs and K Blahers and their families, as well as several Social-Democratic politicians. The Latvian press was filled with numerous complaints about the obstacles placed in the way of repatriation by the Soviet side. It seemed that hardly any individual could leave for Latvia without waiting in Moscow for at least one or two months, often spent in railway carriages.[59]

The return of refugees was promoted by the Latvian Consulates in Petrograd and Omsk (1921–2), Harbin, Arkhangel'sk and Murmansk, and by the Vice-Consul in Tbilisi. The Refugee and Optants Commission continued to be attached to Latvia's Embassy in Moscow until 1924. In all, some 240,000 individuals returned to Latvia by 1928, and optant rights were granted to 6,500 individuals, that is, around half of those who had applied for it. About 400 hostages were exchanged. Most refugees – some 225,000 – returned to Latvia before 1924. But as many as 186,000 Latvians remained in Soviet Russia for various reasons, while around 60,000 people left Latvia for Russia.[60]

What kind of life did the returnees enjoy in independent Latvia? It is difficult to answer this question with great certainty. Their socio-economic status and class identity remain for the most part unknown. Latvian industry had been destroyed during the war. In 1922 the size of the industrial workforce stood at 32,000, one third of its prewar level. Latvian industry consisted mainly of small industrial enterprises. Disproportionately large numbers were employed as civil servants, imposing a heavy burden on the state budget. Notwithstanding calls that Latvia should not become a bureaucratic state, the number of civil servants continued to grow.[61]

Land reform, designed to reconstruct the postwar Latvian economy, changed Latvian agriculture radically. The relevant legal framework was completed by the autumn of 1920. The underlying motives were to curb the Germanization of Latvia and to grant the veterans of the War of Independence in 1919–20 a piece of land. Landless peasants – potential supporters of the Communists – would be provided with land and equipment.[62] New farms sprang up, but not all individuals who wished to become farmers in Latvia were able to do so. The Latvian government and its diplomatic representatives failed to do everything necessary to assist the return of those Latvian colonists who had left for Russia long before the outbreak of the world war. The Latvian Embassy in Moscow reported that only one quarter of these colonists could return from Russia with sufficient savings to start a new life in independent Latvia.[63]

One more indicator of the depressed economic conditions was the level of unemployment. In 1921–2 the number of registered unemployed stood at 6,000, or 0.5 per cent of the population. This figure undoubtedly underestimated the actual total of unemployed. The majority were refugees returning from Soviet Russia. The Latvian government provided 53 million roubles to local authorities to provide public works programmes, with the aim of repairing war damage and providing some work for refugees.[64]

It is important to emphasize those aspects of refugees' activities that have traditionally been regarded as the sphere of cultural activity. The first initiatives came from among the circle of Latvian Lutheran ministers who, with participation of Goldmanis and Zālītis, had already begun to work on the reform of Lutheran congregations in March 1916. The main objective was to eliminate the historic patronage rights enjoyed by the Baltic Germans and to establish a new and democratic form of church administration. These ministers drafted a new structure for the Latvian Evangelic Lutheran church, which was implemented in September 1919.[65] Another event of lasting importance was the congress of the Latvian teacher representatives in Dorpat in June 1917. This congress discussed projected legislation on schools and the reform of orthography, making the Latin script compulsory in all Latvian territory (this was necessary because of the consolidation of Latgale with the rest of the Latvian territory). A college committee, headed by professor Jēkabs Osis, also started work on a project for the new University of Latvia.[66] Finally, in May 1917, a conference of Latvian lawyers discussed the need for a new legal system.[67]

Permanent changes in Latvian historical consciousness also need to be counted as an outcome of World War One. For a country long regarded as a 'nation without history', the war enabled the creation of new quasi-mythical national heroes. Chief among these were the Latvian Rifle Regiments, formed in the second half of 1915, whose exploits laid the foundation for the a Latvian epic literature during the 1920s and 1930s. Classics of Latvian literature, as well as visual arts, the Latvian War museum and the designation of sacred territory (Tīrelpurvs and Nāves sala) helped to sustain memories of battle and of sacrifices made by the Riflemen at the famous 'Battle of Christmas Eve'. During the independence period no year passed without extensive celebration of this day. Roads leading to the Brethren Cemetery were overcrowded, and churches and meeting-halls were filled to capacity. Collective memory celebrated the Riflemen's patriotism as the culmination of Latvia's striving for freedom and national independence. About half of all participants in the war of independence were national Riflemen, and almost all army officers were former Riflemen. There is no unanimity in Latvian historiography concerning the activity of the Latvian Red Riflemen during 1917–20, and their motives in serving the Bolshevik regime. Some émigré Latvian historians portrayed them as nationalists fighting for the independence of Latvia as promised by Lenin, and such an interpretation has become popular in textbooks. The issue is too complex to unravel in the present chapter. But it is worth mentioning that, after demobilization, Trotsky placed the Latvian Riflemen on the same footing as Latvian refugees. In 1921–2 around 11,400 Latvian soldiers were thereby able to return to their homeland.[68]

CONCLUSIONS

The movement for Latvian independence drew upon prewar social and political activism, but it acquired new momentum as a result of wartime developments, in particular the displacement of Latvian civilians. Ideas of 'national freedom' that were already gaining currency before the war now found a larger and more receptive audience. The historiography has underestimated the growth of Latvian national consciousness and mobilization as a result of the war. To focus exclusively on a narrow circle of liberal politicians, writers and intelligentsia is to miss this point. On the other hand, to concentrate on quantitative indices (such as participation in mass strikes and demonstrations) is to overlook qualitative changes in national consciousness. As this chapter has shown, Latvian refugees helped create a structure of political, social and professional organizations that articulated collective aspirations and facilitated collaboration in pursuit of national goals.[69]

Demands for autonomy, and later on for outright independence, were advanced by a new generation of activists, some of whom had campaigned for greater cultural and social freedom during and after the 1905 revolution. These activists came to greater prominence during the war. The main outlets for their views were newspapers such as *Dzimtenes Atbalss* and *Lidums*. Some commentators accused the Latvian politicians of showing excessive loyalty toward Russia, of being indecisive and of lacking political maturity. This chapter supports instead the view that the development of Latvian national thought corresponded to the changing political situation and the possibilities for realizing Latvia's political demands.

The bitter experience of Latvian refugees helped to deflate the jingoistic mood of many Latvians. Newspaper comment and the memoir literature reflect the moral challenge and psychological trauma inflicted upon Latvian refugees during the war. Here it is argued that this experience helped to make Latvian refugees receptive to the idea of an independent state. The effectiveness of any national ideology is largely dependent upon the intellectual and cultural resources on which it draws. The Latvian example during World War One shows the importance of 'emotional resources' – disappointment, exhaustion, pain, humiliation and nostalgia on the one hand and, on the other, pride for a newly acquired heroic ethno-history. These feelings could help consolidate a large group of people just as successfully as could clearly defined positive ideals. The nascent Latvian state, which had to be built from ruins, had no pragmatic values that it could promise its inhabitants in advance. But it could draw upon a wellspring of wartime sacrifice.

Latvian refugees in Russia made more specific and assertive demands than Latvians who remained in Latvia. One reason is that the latter encountered opposition from the German authorities and then had to confront the Bolshevik terror. Another is that Moscow had become the main centre for the cultural and political activities of Latvian patriotic intelligentsia during the war. Numerous refugee agencies in Russia became effective organizational structures capable of demonstrating the organizing abilities of nascent national leaders and serving to promote a sense of ethnic identity. The work done by organizations such as the LCWC had a very important political meaning for the Latvian national movement.

The majority of Latvian Refugees returned to Latvia by 1924, most of them immediately following the Refugee Re-evacuation Agreement signed on 22 June 1920. However, the process of re-evacuation was uneven. Despite the political agreements signed by both sides, the Soviet authorities in Russia placed a number of obstacles in the way of Latvian returnees. One of the main reasons was the Soviet desire to stem the outflow of skilled Latvian workers and technical specialists, in order to minimize economic decline in Russia.

One of the results of the war was a permanent change in Latvian historical consciousness, brought about by the actions of the Latvian Riflemen. Latvian collective memory during the 1920s and 1930s celebrated their patriotism and sacrifice as the culmination of Latvia's search for freedom and national independence. Such feelings of pride in a glorious past served to strengthen national identity during the early years of Latvia's independence. But another element in this interwar discourse concerned Latvia's refugees. World War One is fixed in Latvian historical memory as an emotionally charged period of 'the refugee times'. Although relatively brief, this was a dynamic period in the history of the country, characterized by rapid changes in social relations, a loss of loyalty to the Russian state and the creation of a new national identity. The social history of the Latvian refugees is still in its infancy. This chapter is a contribution to this emerging historiography.

3
In Search of National Support: Belarusian Refugees in World War One and the People's Republic of Belarus

VALENTINA UTGOF*

INTRODUCTION

During the turbulent years of World War One, the territory of Belarus was exposed to population displacement on a huge scale, as a consequence of the German advance and subsequent occupation of the western borderlands of the Russian empire. The war inflicted great suffering on the civilian population. Some estimates suggestion that 1.4 million civilians – Poles, Jews, Lithuanians, Russians and others, as well as Belarusians – were displaced from Vilno, Grodno, Minsk, Vitebsk and Mogilev provinces.[1] Other estimates are higher still.[2] In all likelihood, more than 20 per cent of the population of this region had to leave their homes and seek refuge further east. Their departure was accompanied by the evacuation of fixed assets, including schools and other facilities.[3] Meanwhile the German army of occupation established the notorious *Land Ober Ost* on territory inhabited by Lithuanians, Poles, Jews and, of course, Belarusians, who were especially numerous in the so-called 'Military Administration Belastok-Grodno'.[4]

At the same time the war created an opportunity to instil a sense of national consciousness among the displaced Belarusian population. Members of the patriotic elite were actively involved in shaping the social and political life of the country, whether or not they remained on the territory of Belarus. The emerging Belarusian intelligentsia, admittedly small in number, threw itself energetically into relief work among refugees. Many eminent intellectuals took a keen interest in this kind of work. Their expectations and the results they achieved form an important element of this chapter.

As other contributions to this book demonstrate, the Russian revolution and European peace settlement significantly affected the relocation of the displaced population. The German occupation of Belarus, having been extended under the peace treaty at Brest-Litovsk, lasted until the end of 1918. Throughout the war German intervention had important implications not only for population displacement but also for the political future of Belarus itself. As World War One came to an end and German troops withdrew, the new politics of Belarusian nationalism created unprecedented opportunities for state-formation. But the circumstances were complicated still further, first by a resurgent Poland that threatened to undermine Belarusian claims of independence and territorial integrity, and second by the forces of Bolshevism that portrayed themselves as representatives of the interests of the Belarusian working class and peasantry.[5] The period following the German withdrawal provided no respite for the population of Belarus, much of whose territory was a battleground between Poland and Soviet Russia. Only with the Treaty of Riga (18 March 1921) did a degree of stability return to Belarus, at the price of its dismemberment. The western provinces of Grodno and Vilno, as well as part of Minsk, were appropriated by Poland. Minsk, Mogilev and part of Vitebsk province formed the Belarusian Soviet Socialist Republic that came into existence in January 1919. Further additions to the territory of the BSSR followed in 1924 and 1926.[6]

In the event, some of those displaced during World War One and who returned to their homes opted to remain on Soviet Belarusian territory. Others decided to settle in Poland where they sought to maintain Belarusian culture in what they hoped would be a temporary exile. The difficulties they encountered have been reasonably well covered in the literature.[7]

This chapter outlines the activities of the Belarusian organizations that were established during World War One in order to assist the large refugee population. It examines the implications for Belarusian politics of attempts to define the role of these relief organizations against the background of an emerging Belarusian statehood, in particular the People's Republic of Belarus, which came into being in March 1918. Chronologically it concentrates on issues raised by Belarusian population displacement in the period preceding and immediately following the October revolution.

WAR AND THE ORIGINS OF REFUGEE RELIEF IN BELARUS

The first Belarusian organizations to provide assistance to refugees came into being during the spring of 1915.[8] At the end of April, activists in Vilno established the Belarusian Society for Assisting the Victims of War (BSAVW).[9] The new Society was dominated by the veteran socialists Anton Luckiewicz, Vaclaw Ivanowski and Vaclav Lastowski, all of whom had played a prominent part in public life before the war, notably as part of the circle that established the Belarusian Socialist Hramada and the progressive newspaper *Nasha Niva* [*Our Field*], which was described as 'the river into which all Belarusian literary creation flowed'.[10] The war encouraged them in their declared aspiration 'to move further out into the region, into the most remote corners of the region', and by implication to establish contact with the population of rural Belarus.[11] To some extent they succeeded in this aim. By August 1915 the BSAVW had already opened branches in Grodno, Vilno and Vitebsk provinces. Additional branches were planned for settlements in Minsk and Mogilev, as well as in other parts of Grodno province.[12] However the BSAVW could not expand its activities in the region by simply opening new branches here and there, as its executive committee acknowledged.[13]

A lack of resources hindered the laudable efforts of the BSAVW to provide assistance to refugees. With a modest monthly membership fee of just three rubles, subscriptions failed to cover expenditure. Donations and proceeds from concerts and lectures organized by the Society were insufficient to facilitate any extension of its activities.[14] The Society attempted to obtain the support of the Main Committee of the All-Russian Union of Towns, one of Russia's 'public organizations' (*obshchestvennye organizatsii*), citing the refusal of the governor of Vilno to include the BSAVW in the list of organizations entitled to receive grants from the semi-official Tatiana Committee.[15] Although the Union did eventually accede to this request, its grant of 500 rubles made little real difference to the scale of operations of the Society. The BSAVW was told to apply in future to the plenipotentiary of the All-Russian Union of Towns at the North-Western Front, NV Dmitriev, on the grounds that he was responsible for the region in which the BSAVW operated.[16] Much depended on the Tatiana Committee, which gradually improved the level of support, authorizing grants totalling 78,000 rubles in the seven months between April and November 1916.[17] The Lithuanian Committee also furnished the BASVW with some funds. The Society was thus able to open student dormitories.[18]

In July 1915 the refugee registration office in Vilno reported that the combined refugee population of Vilno province and city stood at 71,525. This figure did not remain stable. After the German occupation of Vilno at the beginning of September 1915, most Belarusian national activists were forced to flee, although the BSAVW continued its activities in their absence. Throughout the summer months the number of refugees continued to grow and, as the military situation deteriorated, welfare centres for refugees had to be relocated. A branch of the BSAVW had already been formed in Minsk in July. Its executive committee included prominent leaders of the Belarus national movement, such as Sha Jadvigin,[19] Vladislav Golubok,[20] Vsevolod Fal'skii[21] and Zos'ka

Veras.[22] The executive committee was chaired by Viktor Chausov, an attorney by profession.[23] The section established an orphanage and a night shelter for refugees, as well as soup kitchens. These endeavours echoed the work of other newly established national committees in Russia.[24]

The BSAWV attempted to build up a working relationship with other agencies that arranged relief programmes for Belarusian refugees. Chausov participated in the meetings of organizations further afield.[25] Early in 1916 he established close contact with the Petrograd-based Belarusian Society for Assisting the Victims of War, among whose leaders were AP Eremich, Cz A Rodzievicz, and Bronislav Epimakh-Shipillo. Epimakh-Shipillo had already come to prominence more than a decade earlier, as a teacher in the Catholic seminary in St Petersburg and as the founder, along with Eduard Budz'ko, of the Belarusian Christian Democratic Party.[26] The goals of the Petrograd Society were defined as 'providing assistance to the population suffering from war-related damage', by organizing soup kitchens, shelters and canteens for refugees, supplying them with warm clothes and fuel, providing medical aid for sick and wounded refugees, and issuing refugees leaving Petrograd with a one-off grant to cover their expenses on food, education and seed, to assist them in re-establishing their households.[27] The Petrograd Society confined itself to the relief of Belarusian refugees in the capital. By contrast, the Vilno and Minsk societies sought to expand their activities to all western provinces. These differences would become more serious as time wore on.

EDUCATIONAL AND CULTURAL WORK

One of the most remarkable features of the wartime population displacement was the opportunity it gave for national activists to engage in proselytizing work among refugees. Educational and cultural work took priority. In November 1916 the Belarusian Society in Petrograd, led by Vaclav Ivanowski, planned to open a primary school for Belarusian refugees.[28] Even on occupied territory some concessions were extracted from the German administration. In Vilno, for example, Anton Luckiewicz received permission to open a Belarusian ('White Ruthenian') school in October 1915. Training courses for Belarusian teachers got under way in December. This was perhaps the first indication that the rulers of *Land Ober Ost* sought to stimulate and patronize Belarusian culture, as a means of weakening the dominant position of Polish culture.[29]

Minsk, still free of German occupation, boasted the famous *Belorusskaia hatka* [*Belarusian house*] that came to be regarded as a model for cultural and educational activities. In October 1916 the noted Belarusian poet Maksim Bahdanovich arrived in the city and immediately lent his support to cultural and educational work. He later described his experiences in an article entitled 'A Belarusian refugee shelter':

> Not long ago I happened to visit one of the few shelters where the language of instruction is Belarusian. The headmistress of the shelter – surrounded on all sides by children clinging to her dress – gave me the following explanation: "Here everything is Belarusian. We teach in Belarusian, we speak Belarusian, we read Belarusian authors, and we dress children in Belarusian '*vopratki*' (dresses)".[30]

To be sure, not all such initiatives met with official approval. When, in December 1916, Chausov petitioned the vice-governor to allow Bahdanovich to deliver a lecture on what he termed the 'Belarusian awakening', the Ministry of Interior refused permission, even if the military authorities raised no objections, such was the degree of official sensitivity to national self-expression.[31]

In the difficult conditions imposed by war, the attempt to develop cultural and educational programmes was hampered by the limited resources at the disposal of refugee organizations. The activities of the Minsk BASVW, for example, suffered from a constant lack of funds. The Union of Zemstvos and Towns (Zemgor) continued to refuse to provide support throughout 1916. By contrast, the Polish Society for Assisting the Victims of War, the Jewish Society, the Lithuanian Society, the Rezhitsa district zemstvo, the All-Russian Society for the Care of Refugees, and Northern Aid all received generous levels of support.[32]

Educational and cultural work also suffered from a lack of qualified personnel. Few people could find time to work for the BASVW. Recollecting a meeting with her friends in Minsk, Zos'ka Veras quoted the brave yet somewhat desperate words of one local activist by the name of Ales' Smolicz, who proclaimed the duty of Belarusians to leave the backwaters, in order to assist in the task of educating the refugee population: 'And you think you could stay there [in Al'hovniki, Grodno province] as if we had no work to do here! Here every Belarusian is worth his weight in gold!' In his letter Smolicz mentioned that he had helped to set up a branch of the BSAVW in Minsk, but that he had struggled to turn it into a fully fledged agency.[33] Nevertheless a small group of people did their best to boost its activities. 'Small deeds' mattered in this context. Since Belarusian refugees originated mainly from rural areas, the section organized courses in agronomy; lectures were delivered in the Belarusian language, and at the end of the course participants had to pass an exam.[34] Clearly the teachers attached a great deal of importance to Minsk as a centre for Belarusian cultural and educational work, and as the basis for developing additional networks of activists.

The national press too developed apace during the war years. In October 1916 two newspapers in the Belarusian language began to be published in Petrograd, *Dziannica* [*The Morning Star*], edited by the publicist Tishka Gartny,[35] and *Svetacz* [*The Torch*], under the editorship of Eduard Bud'ko.[36] The future of Belarusian refugees and their homeland emerged as the main theme in both periodicals. The inaugural issue of *Dziannica* opened with the verses *Uciakaczy* (*Refugees*) by Gartny himself, clearly linking their misfortune to the difficulties encountered by all Belarusians in attempting to forge a sense of national unity.[37] One of the first articles to published in *Dziannica* ended with a rousing appeal to all Belarusians to 'unite and work without respite in order that our voice – the voice of Young Belarus – will be also heard in these grim days when probably the very future of the country is decided'.[38] Although only seven issues of *Dziannica* and five issues of *Svetacz* appeared, the journalists claimed to have begun to make an impact upon the political education of the Belarusian population.[39]

Taken as a whole, the visibility of the relief organizations should not be exaggerated.[40] The chief factor accounting for this state of affairs is that many Belarusian refugees were looked after by non-Belarusian organizations, which had been able to establish a much firmer footing in the world of late imperial Russian politics. No tsarist officials were prepared to countenance the creation of autonomous Belarusian organizations, and this was reflected in the allocation of resources.[41] Belarusian societies had practically no independent sources of income and semi-official bodies were unwilling to step in. As Viaczeslav Grinewicz recalled later: 'People of various nationalities received material and moral support from their brothers – only we Belarusians could not count on it. Our people had to enrol in Russian and Polish committees.'[42] The Polish refugee committee in Irkutsk rubbed salt in the wounds by announcing that Belarusian refugees had asked to place their children in Polish orphanages and schools. The Petrograd Belarusian society was forced to acknowledge that Belarusian refugees had to take what help they could, from whatever source.[43] Pavlina Miadzelka later remembered how she had been invited to work in a Polish committee that housed some 360 Belarus refugees from Grodno province. Its chairman told her that the majority of children in the orphanage were Belarusians who could not understand Polish.[44]

Cultural work among Belarusian refugees produced a small yet important body of personal testimony. Of particular significance were the stories collected by the Belarusian ethnographer Fedor Kudrinskii (1867–1933), who wrote under the pseudonym 'Stepanets'. A friend of Jakub Kolas, the noted Belarusian poet, Kudrinskii witnessed wartime population displacement at first hand from his home in Rogachev, Mogilev province. He wove this testimony into a 'documentary tale', first published in Petrograd in 1917.[45] In similar vein Evgenii Kancher (Kanczer) (1882–1979), an eye-witness of Belarusian refugee settlement in Central Asia, drew upon his observations to suggest that contemporary Belarusians had been reconnected by their wartime experiences with their forebears who 'in the course of hundreds of years have been condemned to wander the earth ... fertilising the land of other peoples'.[46] All this activity helps to explain why, according to Zmitruk Zhilunowicz, 'working for the cause of Belarus (*belorusskaia deiatel'nost'*) was the exclusive preserve of the refugee committees'.[47]

Thus the lack of a secure network of Belarusian organizations forced many refugees to turn for help to other nationalities who shared the same religious confession. Orthodox Belarusians turned to Russian refugee relief committees, and Catholics appealed to Polish societies for assistance. Naturally, Belarusian activists at the time bemoaned the various obstacles that stood in their way. But one way of approaching the issue is to suggest that the very lack of a dedicated and secure national welfare organization strengthened the Belarusians' assertion that they had no less of a 'right' than other non-Russian minorities to a distinctive organization that they could call their own. In all likelihood the fact that this gap was frequently filled by Polish committees helped to sharpen a sense of distinct national identity amongst Belarusian patriots. However, the constant litany of complaint about the lack of national consciousness among the bulk of the Belarusian population suggests that non-refugees did not share these sentiments.

REVOLUTION AND BELARUSIAN REFUGEEDOM DURING 1917

After the February revolution Belarusian relief organizations became much more heavily politicized.[48] Initially the most significant developments took place in Minsk. Here the BSAVW, under the chairmanship of Rygor Skirmunt, proclaimed a 'provisional national committee'. Between 25–27 March 1917 the BSAVW convened a congress of nationalist organizations, which established the Belarusian National Committee (BNC).[49] Elections to its executive committee confirmed the status acquired by refugee welfare organizations in Minsk, leading members of which included Skirmunt himself (a prominent landowner, and former member of the Russian Duma), Pavel Aliaksiuk (a lawyer), Ales' Smolich (an agronomist), Vsevolod Fal'skii (an actor), Ales' Burbis (a bank employee) and Vincent Gadlevskii (a Catholic priest). Other members of the executive included an engineer, teachers and an architect.[50] However, the authority of the BNC was undermined, both by its remoteness from many Belarusian refugees on Russian soil and by the chilly reception it received from the Provisional Government in Petrograd, whose leaders were unwilling to concede much autonomy at this stage.[51]

The self-appointed patriotic leaders in Minsk prepared new guidelines for relief work among refugees, and these were approved by another congress of nationalist organizations in early July 1917. Particular attention was devoted to the arrangements for orphanages and schools. Yet again, financial difficulties reared their head, this time as a consequence of the unhelpful stance taken by Russia's liberal politicians. When the Belarusian People's Hramada (BNG), formed in March 1917, and by summer 1917 a force to be reckoned with in Minsk, asked the Union of Zemstvos and Towns to transfer to itself the administration of the institutions assisting Belarusian orphans, it met with a negative response.[52] Other groups – some with an explicitly religious profile – also emerged and attempted to speak on behalf of the scattered Belarusian communities in Russia and in Belarus itself.[53]

Tensions between the Belarusian intelligentsia in Minsk and more radical elements became more acute during the autumn of 1917. In this respect an important role was played by the Hramada. Led by the lawyers Jazep Vasilevicz and Ales' Cvikeviecz, the BNG convened a congress in September 1917. Its leaders asked that the BNG be affiliated to the Moscow-based Central Section on Refugee Relief, hoping thereby to improve the credibility of the Hramada. Other proposals included the creation of a network of Belarusian refugee organizations and the election of community elders (*starosty*). The congress also called for a resolution of Belarus's 'territorial status' after the war, in the expectation that this would secure the basis for socio-economic reform. The discussions revealed that the 'refugee issue' had become a cornerstone of the BNG political platform. The establishment of a national system of refugee relief was meant to create political support for the BNG in the localities, while its proposed system of welfare aped the structure and principles of the public organizations.[54]

In a subsequent convention, in December 1917, again inspired by Cvikievicz, the BNG managed to assemble a total of 74 delegates to discuss refugee affairs.[55] In his memoirs, PM Kraskovskii, attending on behalf of the Petrograd branch of the Hramada, vividly conveyed an image of his fellow delegates:

> History repeats itself. Shapeless, disorganised, just arrived from their villages, peasant, purely Belarusian masses ... reminded us of the times when the ancient Belarusian *vecze* [assembly] convened in Polotsk – the times entirely forgotten but very dear to us all.[56]

This rhetoric suggests the hopes that members of the patriotic intelligentsia invested in the new 'assembly', which evoked the distant 'origins' of Belarus. In this national narrative it was not difficult to see how wartime population displacement might be deployed as part of an historic tradition. Sure enough, the refugee issue emerged as one of the main problems to be discussed. The delegates to the Moscow congress agreed to establish a central administration for refugee relief, which would be affiliated to the Hramada. In an important statement of intent, the congress stipulated that Belarusian nationals should henceforth be given preference when posts were being filled by agencies that provided aid to Belarusian refugees.[57] The growing involvement of refugee activists in politics also revealed itself in the decision to include Belarusian refugees in the lists of candidates to the forthcoming Constituent Assembly.[58] Attempts were clearly being made to link refugee concerns to a new national politics.

It fell to Cvikeviecz to defend the interests of Belarusian refugees at the First All-Belarusian Congress that took place in Minsk between 12 and 17 December 1917. Nearly 1,900 delegates attended, an impressive total. Cvikeviecz had already prepared the ground by establishing a special refugee commission under his leadership. He insisted that the refugee issue be given priority at the December congress, stressing the need to reorganize all institutions responsible for refugee relief according to democratic principles and to place them on firm national foundations.[59] In an obvious display of national assertiveness, delegates opposed the transfer of Belarusian refugee relief organisations to non-national institutions.[60] Delegates also devoted particular attention to the issue of returning displaced Belarusians to their homes. This raised the question of Belarus's relations with Russia. However, the debates were cut short when, having entered Minsk, Bolshevik troops dispersed the congress, in a foretaste of what would happen a month later at the Constituent Assembly in Moscow. Thus, for a brief period over the new year, Minsk found itself in Bolshevik hands.

Belarusian politics took on a fractured appearance during 1917. Particularly troubling for the patriotic elite was the sudden emergence of local soviets on the territory of Belarus. Their membership swelled rapidly during the late summer months, and particularly after the Second All-Russian Refugee Congress held between 19 and 27 November 1917. The soviet institutions, at district and town level, dealt with all local refugee affairs. They often included national sections that claimed the right to direct cultural and educational activities.[61] Developments during 1917 also suggested that the leaders of Belarusian refugees on Russian soil articulated a more radical programme than their counterparts in Minsk. The national patriots in Minsk forfeited any claim to speak on behalf all Belarusian refugees. The situation was complicated still further by the broader radicalization of society in the unravelling Russian empire.[62]

POPULATION DISPLACEMENT AND POLITICAL UNCERTAINTY IN BELARUS AFTER OCTOBER 1917

The October revolution had profound consequences for Belarus. In the first place, it galvanized Belarusian refugee organizations in Russia, encouraging them to link their aspirations for greater national autonomy with the broader movement for political change. In the second place, the revolution inaugurated negotiations between Soviet Russia and Germany that culminated in the Treaty of Brest-Litovsk, whereby German troops extended their occupation of Belarusian territory. This paved the way for a declaration of Belarusian independence. On 25 March 1918 an Executive Committee of the Council of the All-Belarusian Congress proclaimed the Belarusian People's Republic (BNR). The declaration stated that 'the peoples of Belarus themselves, through their own Constituent Assembly, will decide upon the future relations between Belarus and other states'. This dramatic move appears to have taken the governments of Poland, Lithuania, Russia, Ukraine and Germany by surprise.[63]

As in other states that emerged from the wreckage of the Russian empire, the issues posed by population displacement acquired acute political importance for the fledgling Belarusian polity. Did the new state have the ability to look after the interests of the displaced population and, more importantly, to organize their return home?[64] To this end, one of the first acts of the 'People's Secretariat' of the BNR was to form a Central Belarusian Refugee Committee.[65] The Refugee Committee in turn encouraged the creation of local committees that were now charged explicitly with the task of 'awakening and boosting national identity among Belarusian refugees'. Existing welfare organizations were urged to get in touch with the Refugee Committee in order to co-ordinate their activities. The new Belarusian government also began to make plans for the repatriation of refugees.[66]

One key task for the BNR was to establish contacts with the numerous refugee settlements beyond Belarus, particularly in Ukraine and in the Baltic region. Some of these had developed a fairly sophisticated operation. The Belarusian society in Odessa, 'Gai' (Garden), boasted around 800 members and had reasonable financial resources. Like other such societies, Gai concentrated upon cultural and educational activities. By 1918 it had registered more than 10,000 Belarusian refugees and had found employment and housing for most of them. This was a remarkable success story, given the difficult economic conditions that prevailed at this time. In an important shift of emphasis, Gai also promoted the organized repatriation of refugees.[67] Other provincial and local refugee organizations in Russia also expressed some support for the government of the BNR. Refugee groups in Khar'kov and Ekaterinoslav each formed a local Belarusian council (Rada), demonstrating that the BNR gained popular backing from some groups.[68] The BNR appointed plenipotentiaries for refugee affairs, who attempted to spread nationalist agitation among refugees beginning to congregate in places such as Orsha and Smolensk.[69]

The conditions in which Belarusian refugees found themselves in the aftermath of the October revolution left a great deal to be desired. The well-known ethnographer and activist Evgenii Kancher, who made a close study of the subject, reported that 'if, during the war, the care of refugees left a lot to be desired, in 1917 and especially in 1918 it became impossible'. He painted a picture of 'persecution' by local people, who denied refugees work and food. Much of Kancher's anger was directed at local soviets, whose leaders (he said) did nothing to counter the hostility of the residents.[70] A refugee by the name of Roman Bagrovskii recalled of his sojourn in Riazan' province that 'before the revolution both refugees and the locals lived well ... The local residents brought us food and clothing, and we got 35 rubles each month in financial support ... After the revolution everything changed for the worse. Famine took hold. The shops had no salt, matches or kerosene'.[71] Belarusian refugees in Moscow doubted that administrative changes would make any difference; only speedy and practical assistance with the return journey home offered the prospect of a real improvement in the condition of those whom Kancher described as Belarus's 'forgotten citizens'.[72]

Belarusian refugees were of course fully aware that they would be returning to a land occupied by German troops. Soviet propaganda tried to exploit their anxieties. In April 1918 the refugees of Grodno province protested that

> during the peace negotiations the Austrian-German delegation declared that the peoples of the occupied territory expressed a wish to be transferred from Russia to Germany. In this way many Belarusian lands will be seized from Russia and turned over to Germany, and we, Belarusians, will have to become German subjects and the slaves of German masters, landlords and capitalists, in the same way as before we have been under the yoke of our own landlords and capitalists ... The native population of Belarus would never make such a statement'.[73]

Belarusian refugees from Saratov, 'after hearing a report about the situation in occupied Belarus, where German bandits looted and assaulted hard-working Belarusian people, [decided] to protest strongly against the partition of Belarus by German imperialists that takes place almost every day with the purpose of handing out separate parts to its servile neighbours.' However, although many Belarusian refugees did not support the terms of the treaty of Brest-Litovsk, it was precisely this document that gave them hope in returning back home.[74]

The BNR was not the sole agency dealing with issues of refugee repatriation. Following the dissolution of the All-Belarusian Congress by the Bolsheviks in December 1917, Sovnarkom approved the formation of a Belarusian National Commissariat (Belnatskom). Belnatskom maintained bases in revolutionary Petrograd, Vitebsk and Smolensk, although its headquarters moved to Moscow in the spring. It was subordinated to the newly established People's Commissariat for Nationalities (Narkomnats).[75] Belnatskom got off to a shaky start. Proponents of the 'refugee soviets' that had emerged in late 1917 opposed any extension in the powers of national committees. In Moscow, for example, members of the regional soviet for refugee affairs informed Belnatskom that there should be no question of transferring refugee issues to 'national commissariats', and that all efforts should instead be directed towards organizing refugee soviets 'where they currently do not exist'. Systems of refugee relief structured along ethnic lines should be suppressed.[76] This stark warning was reinforced when the Moscow regional soviet refused Belnatskom permission to take control of orphanages and hostels in which Belarusian refugees were housed.[77]

Belnatskom continued unabashed, concentrating in the first instance upon educational and cultural work among Belarusian refugees. It published its own version of *Dziannica*, with a print run of 3,000, and distributed it on German-occupied territory as well as in Soviet Russia. Teaching materials were translated into the Belarusian language. In Moscow in July 1918, it convened a conference of Belarusian writers, who discussed the prospects for the restoration of schools and colleges in Belarus. Distinguished scholars such as the historian Vladimir Picheta (1878–1947) and the literary scholar Z Zhilunovicz (1887–1937) gave impromptu lectures. Belnatskom arranged instruction in Belarusian for the children of Belarusian refugees.[78] Apart from this publishing and educational activity, Belnatskom also maintained separate sections devoted to legal, statistical, military, employment, propaganda and refugee matters. The refugee section focused upon three tasks: collecting information on the number of refugees, dealing with enquiries from Belarusian refugees, and preparing for the re-evacuation of refugees from Russia.[79] Belnatskom engaged in a publicity drive, issuing books, newspapers and pamphlets, not only to inform refugees of the current situation in the 'homeland', but also to instruct them in the history and culture of Belarus. The newspaper *Czyrvony szliach* (*Red road*) published an article entitled 'Belarusians, Call yourselves by your own name', in which the author enjoined refugees to be proud of their title.[80]

Belnatskom thus developed *de facto* an administrative apparatus, becoming a kind of Belarusian civil service on Soviet territory. In the summer of 1918 it despatched officials to Orsha, Tambov, Kaluga and Saratov, and subsequently to Orel, Simbirsk and Samara. Belnatskom also trained some workers in Bolshevik Party schools before sending them to occupied Belarus, where they engaged in underground activities.[81] By the end of 1918, as a result of negotiations at a high level involving both Narkomnats and the Soviet Central Collegium on the Affairs of Refugees and Prisoners of War (*Tsentroplenbezh*), Belnatskom was given full responsibility for the registration and welfare of Belarusian refugees.[82] Most members of Belnatskom were affiliated either with the Belarusian Social Democratic Party, with the Left SRs, or with the Belarusian section of the Bolshevik Party. They were, of course, opposed to the establishment of a bourgeois Belarus, and had no affection for either the BNR or the German army of occupation. Accordingly, its officials devoted some effort to detecting 'counter-revolutionary' opinion among the refugee population, lest such attitudes bolster the status of the BNR.[83]

Meanwhile, the creation of a Refugee Commission by the BNR signified the next stage in addressing the 'refugee issue'.[84] The commission, which came into being on 1 May 1918, concentrated mainly on organizing the repatriation of Belarusian refugees from Russia. In order to achieve this objective the commission had to enter into negotiations with the German administration in the occupied territories. A sub-commission attached to the German Commissariat on Refugee Affairs began to operate in Orsha in July 1918. Its officials registered Belarusian refugees in the surrounding camps and issued them with certificates permitting their return to their original place of residence.[85] The infant Belarusian government also attempted to organize relief work among refugees in Russia, but with limited success.[86]

One of the ambitions of the BNR was to establish jurisdiction over refugees in Vilno and Grodno provinces. The Lithuanian government cautiously gave its approval to the creation of Belarusian schools as well as a range of cultural societies and other associations. The Lithuanian cabinet also found room for a Minister for Belarusian Affairs, who had originally been a member of the Vilno Belarusian Rada. The BNR, particularly its conservative leaders, found this arrangement unacceptable, but their intransigence provoked a political crisis that was not resolved until the German withdrawal convulsed Belarusian politics.[87]

Matters were more complicated so far as Soviet–German relations were concerned. On 21 April 1918, the German Ministry of Foreign Affairs informed the Soviet government about the conditions of repatriation for Polish refugees. The German government declared that it was not yet possible to open the border. Instead the German authorities suggested allowing a limited number of people to return to the territory of the German-administered 'Eastern Headquarters' and the Warsaw General-Governorship, provided they had sufficient quantities of food and that housing was available. (Only Polish re-emigrants could enter the Warsaw General-Governorship.[88]) These conditions were extremely difficult to meet, given that *Tsentroplenbezh* prescribed tight limits on the food supplies that refugees could take with them.[89]

Significantly, the German military authorities made a careful note of the ethnic background of those who requested entry to the territory they controlled. At a conference arranged by the western district of *Tsentroplenbezh*, Borkiewicz – head of the border checkpoint at Polota railway station – noted that 'in admitting refugees through the demarcation line, the Germans grouped people using their own discretion and paying great attention to the national background of persons in question.'[90] The German authorities sought to organize refugees into teams according to nationality. They gave preferential treatment to ethnic Germans, and to those with a command of the German language, thereby excluding almost all Belarusians. Borkiewicz reported that 'at present [16 September 1918] a large crowd has formed at the Polota checkpoint, including around 150 Belarusian refugees whom the Germans refuse to allow through ... The German authorities let in about 100 persons every other day, but only Lithuanians are allowed to enter Lithuania, and only Poles are allowed to enter Poland. They do not let Poles, Belarusians or Jews into Lithuania.'[91] On top of these problems, refugees passing through Polota railway station were faced with a form of institutionalized robbery; the Iur'ev soviet of peasants' deputies confiscated gold coins and other items except wedding rings and pince-nez, all fabrics and brand new goods from those who crossed the demarcation line at Polota.[92]

Of course the Soviet authorities sought to impose their own restrictions on population movement. As Kancher put it, 'the refugee question had its own politics'.[93] Permits to leave Soviet territory were issued in the first place to peasants, the unemployed and to others in need. Using class slogans the Soviets were in effect getting rid of excess mouths to feed. More prosperous people, such as merchants and landlords, had to submit a certificate of their reliability issued by a local soviet. As V Baranov, a refugee from Belostok, recalled, when his family decided to return home the Bolsheviks refused to let them cross the border until they had obtained a certificate signed by the head official at the railway station.[94] Males between the age of 18 and 45, factory workers and technical specialists were kept behind. As a representative of *Tsentroplenbezh* in Olonets noted, 'some refugees working at the Murmansk railway are not allowed to be discharged and turn to us for assistance. We have to refuse them in order not to leave the railway without a labour force'.[95] This practice became widespread.[96]

In sum, the return journey was invested with great difficulty and even trauma. One of the leaders of the Belarusian national movement, Jazep Voronko, bitterly remarked, 'out of a million Belarusian refugees one half has already found their way back to Grodno and Vilno provinces aided only by God, leaving behind a new city of Orsha next to the old one – the Orsha of the dead – made of Belarusian graves dating from 1918.'[97] A Belarusian refugee by the name of Semen Onishchuk subsequently recollected the consequences for his relatives of their journey home: 'When we left the village of Rusaki we were eight, but only three of us returned.'[98]

REFUGEES AND THE FUTURE OF BELARUS

Given the climate of uncertainty described above, what views did Belarusian refugees hold of the political future of Belarus? A key indicator of the popular mood among the displaced population was a series of speeches made at an All-Russian Congress of Belarusian Refugees, convened in Moscow by Belnatskom between 17 and 21 July 1918. This was an important occasion attended by more than 200 delegates, most of whom were either representing Belnatskom or the Belarussian section of the Bolshevik Party. The majority came from Tambov, Penza, Saratov, Tver', Tula and Kazan' provinces. One after another they protested in the name of the 'toiling Belarusian people' against the partition of Belarus at Brest-Litovsk. A series of resolutions emphatically opposed the authority of the BNR: 'the Congress does not recognise the recently created Peoples' Republic of Belarus represented by the self-proclaimed Von Skirmunts and Aleksiuks, and protests energetically against their attempts to arrange the affairs of Belarus.' Delegates demanded the 'reunification' of the country and its incorporation into the new RSFSR. Only then would refugees be free to go 'home'.[99] This revealed a growing perception of the BNR as the enemy, collaborating with the occupation regime and against the interests of the Belarusian people. As one of the delegates put it, 'There is no doubt that upon our return home we will be subjugated to the German rule ... The struggle with Germany is an indisputable fact.'[100]

Several speakers made the point that the process of repatriation involved more than technical issues, such as registration of personal details and transport arrangements. Attention had also to be given to the political education of the returnees. In this respect the congress provided an opportunity to bemoan the low level of politicization of Belarusian refugees. Delegates acknowledged that 'hitherto we did not know that we were Belarusians', a lack of consciousness that was attributed partly to 'inertia' on the part of the 'dark masses' and partly to the absence of a fully fledged patriotic intelligentsia. In the short term, the welfare of Belarusian refugees suffered from poor organization and inadequate finance, especially when compared to other national minorities such as Latvians and Poles. Belnatskom itself came in for criticism from the delegates.[101] Without proper support, it was difficult to engage with the masses who lacked (as one of Belnatskom's emissaries to Saratov put it) 'civic and national consciousness'.[102] Much therefore remained to be done to disseminate 'progressive' opinion among the Belarusian narod. As if to prove the point, many refugees, when asked by Belnatskom officials to complete registration forms, entered their religious affiliation in the box marked 'nationality'.[103]

Many Belarusians, of course, simply wanted to get home. Viaczeslav Griniewicz emphasized that refugees, worn out with starvation and cold, displayed very little interest in the political affairs of both Germany and Russia. They were mostly interested in finding out when they could get back to their own homes.[104] Economic difficulties in Russia hampered the cultural aspirations of Belnatskom. One of the speakers at a conference convened by the western district of *Tsentroplenbezh* acknowledged that 'the question of cultural and educational activities is directly related to the issues of food supply ... Until the refugee masses are supplied with bread, we are bound to encounter difficulty with our educational programmes.'[105]

Throughout 1918 Belarusian refugees demonstrated a propensity to make their own arrangements to return. In part this reflected the difficult economic conditions referred to above, and to which refugees of all nationalities were subject. Belnatskom prided itself on having created a series of 'committees that, in view of the impending evacuation, will deal not with spontaneous masses (*stikhiinaia massa*) but only with orderly groups.'[106] But 'spontaneous' movement was also prompted by rumours, following the Brest-Litovsk treaty, that Belarusian refugees were to be given just four months to claim the property they had abandoned, lest they forfeit it for good.[107] In April 1918 thousands of Belarusian refugees crowded into Petrograd during the so-called 'Refugee week', hoping to receive travel permits to return home. According to Kancher, the German authorities refused to cooperate, leaving the refugees stranded.[108] The return process proved to be a protracted and complex affair, which requires fuller investigation. Belnatskom's own records suggest that it oversaw the repatriation of 40,000 Belarusian refugees between July and October 1918. Another 60,000 refugees had signalled their intention to return, and steps were taken in the new year, and again following the German withdrawal, to enable them to do so. Cultural assets and educational facilities were also returned to Belarus.[109]

The evidence presented above suggests that Belnatskom had achieved a great deal, in a short space of time and with limited resources, to prepare the ground by alerting Belarusian refugees to the need to publicize their existence and to work together. Statistical materials collected by Belnatskom found its way into the hands of *Tsentroplenbezh*, whose officials handled the arrangements for repatriation during the difficult years of 1919 and 1920.

After the Belarusian Soviet Socialist Republic proclaimed its independence for the second time on 31 July 1920, the re-evacuation process became the responsibility of the Belarusian Administration for the Evacuation of the Population (Belevak) – later renamed the Belarusian Committee on Evacuation – and subordinated to *Tsentroplenbezh*. Belevak had a staff of around 450 officials responsible for registration and welfare of refugees, including those in Nagoreloe, Bobruisk and Slutsk, as well as Minsk.[110] At the outbreak of the Soviet–Polish war re-evacuation came to a virtual standstill. The organized return of refugees started only after the war ended and the peace treaty was signed between Russia, Ukraine and Poland on 18 March 1921. According to the treaty, ethnically Belarusian territories were partitioned, with Poland receiving the largest part.[111]

Most Belarusian refugees found that their former homes were located in the newly independent states of Poland, Lithuania and Latvia. To give some idea of this tendency, Table 1 provides data on the traffic of refugees. This shows that around half of those who went to Poland were Belarusians.

In practice the governments of the newly independent states tried to prevent the return of those who would constitute themselves as ethnic minorities. Thus, for example, the report of the Belevak office at Vitebsk railway station for the year 1922 emphasized that

> the major obstacle for the liquidation of the phenomenon of refugees has been a negative attitude of the representatives of the neighbouring states towards admitting to their territories refugees of a certain background. Such an attitude is related only to the ethnicity of refugees. Poles admit Poles, Latvians admit Latvians. Lithuanians are even more sophisticated – they return the documents of non-Lithuanian refugees that have already been approved by their own immigration office'.[112]

For their part, the Polish authorities were loath to issue permits to Belarusian refugees, whereas Polish refugees did not encounter any problems in entering Polish territory.[113]

The repatriation process came to an end by 1925.[114] Some 700,000 refugees, many of them ethnic Belarusians, did eventually make their way from Soviet Russia to Polish-held western Belarus between 1919 and 1924.[115] A variety of factors must have been at work in persuading refugees whether to return or to stay in Soviet Belarus. One astute refugee, an employee of the postal service from

TABLE 1: Ethnic background of refugees registered and re-evacuated by the Belarusian Administration in 1921

Ethnic background of refugees	Repatriated to															
	Belarus				Poland				Lithuania				Latvia			
	Belarus	Polish	Jewish	Other	Belarus	Polish	Jewish	Other	Lithuanian	Jewish	Polish	Other	Latvian	Jewish	Polish	Other
February	424	9	115	3	—	13	62	27	132	288	19	43	27	—	13	—
May–June					—	1000	484	153	349	374	87	9	4	—	1	2
July	4378	144	314	44	1752	1880	615	340	16	4	—	1				
August	10452	998	766	196	11492	2138	2188	193								
October									274	119	177	59	3	5	7	9
November	5833	240	202	10	1765	493	407	71								
December	2438	340	1472	15	1252	560	325	7								

Source: NARB, f. 40, op. 1, d. 84, l. 1–203.

Grodno province, took a considered view of Soviet nationality politics; in his petition to Belnatskom for help in returning he wrote that 'even if in the Soviet republic all people have equal rights, and the Great Russians are equal to Belarusians, still I have a great desire to return to my native Belarusian land.'[116] But the future would demonstrate how complex were the meanings that could be attributed to 'native Belarusian land', divided as it had been between bourgeois Poland and Soviet Russia.

What became of some of the activists who had developed such a close concern for Belarusian refugees during the war years? A key figure was Ales' Cvikievicz. A graduate of the Law Department of St Petersburg University, Cvikievicz initially earned his income as an attorney in Pruzsany. In 1916 the 27-year old lawyer was forced to leave Belarus and to join the ranks of the displaced. Settling in Tula, he joined a group of dedicated professionals who sought to improve the conditions of Belarusian refugees. Cvikievicz soon became a prominent member of the Belarusian Society for Assisting the Victims of War. He took part in the work of the various congresses that met to discuss the needs of refugees. As happened in other instances, war and refugeedom helped to launch a career on the national stage. After the proclamation of independence, Cvikievicz consolidated his reputation by joining the independent Republic (BNR). As one historian remarks, 'it was by no means certain that Cvikievicz would have become a politician if fate had decreed differently and he had not faced a major disaster experienced by his people, a disaster as immediate and soaring as an open wound.'[117]

Other activists likewise remained in the public eye, in one form or another. Anton Luckiewicz (1884–1946?), whose unilateral declaration of Belarusian independence in Vilno in February 1918 so incensed his counterparts in the Minsk Belarusian National Republic, subsequently became director of the Belarusian Museum in Vilno, whose collections owed a great deal to the donation made by his brother, Ivan Luckiewicz. Vaclav Lastowski (1893–1938) had, like Luckiewicz, been a member of the Belarusian Socialist Union. He settled briefly in Lithuania, where he became head of the government-in-exile of the Belarusian Democratic Republic and attempted to relax the tough policies being pursued by Polish officialdom in western Belarus. He was to die in a Soviet prison. Vaclav Ivanowski became Minister of Education in the short-lived BNR.[118] Reflecting the bitter political divisions over the future of Belarus, some of the figures mentioned above (such as Kancher) were content to settle in Soviet territory. Countless officials who enlisted in the Belorussian Soviet Socialist Republic had a background in refugee relief, including of course those who were stalwarts of Belnatskom. Fedor Kudrinskii, for example, became a noted historian, ethnographer and pedagogue, who settled in Leningrad. During the

1920s he was entrusted with establishing the Belarusian national museum and archives in Russia.[119]

CONCLUSIONS

World War One was a time of great upheaval in Belarus, over which Russian and German troops fought more or less continuously. The western portion of Belarus was wrenched from tsarist control. Tens of thousands of civilians sought sanctuary either in the eastern part of Belarus or in the Russian interior. Of course not all of them were ethnically Belarusian; they included large numbers of Jews, Poles, Lithuanians and others. But the displacement of Belarusians had a particular resonance. As in other instances, the war afforded patriotic elites an unparalleled opportunity to establish closer contact with members of the displaced 'nation'. In the case of Belarus the patriotic intelligentsia faced two obstacles. One was official tsarist intransigence to the formation of specifically Belarusian relief organizations, particularly on Russian soil. This meant that Belarusian activists frequently had to relinquish the welfare of refugees to Polish organizations. Where Belarusian organizations were able to flourish, as they did in Minsk between 1915 and 1916, the local leadership focused mainly on educational activities. There they struggled to confront a second obstacle in the shape of a low level of national consciousness among the local population. It may be that the very scale of civilian population displacement helped to instil a greater sense of national identity, by giving refugees some degree of access to specifically Belarusian welfare provision and by reminding them that the alternative was continued subordination to Russian, Lithuanian or Polish authorities. However, none of the nationalist leaders exercized real authority among the bulk of the population, few of whom at this time considered themselves to be 'Belarusian'. The end of the war brought renewed complaints from patriotic spokesmen that Belarusians were for the most part 'inert' and lacking in national consciousness.

The policies pursued by the German occupation regime, and later on by the BNR, had only a limited impact. Ironically, in view of the delicate relationship it enjoyed with the Bolshevik-dominated regional soviets, Belnatskom probably did more to develop a sense of national identity among Belarusian refugees, by virtue of its educational and cultural initiatives.

The Soviet government took no concerted measures regarding refugees until the formation of *Tsentroplenbezh* in spring 1918. For the most part Belarusian refugees were left to fend for themselves. They organized around the institutions that were already been in place or (as in the case of refugee soviets) recently endorsed by the new government. Notwithstanding the efforts of

Belnatskom, this state of affairs resulted in a rather haphazard definition of structures and goals, contributing to the difficulties that stood in the way of refugees' return to their native land. For its part the Soviet state did not stand in the way of Belarusian refugees, particularly if they were peasants (it was a different matter if they were technical specialists or potential military conscripts). Nor did Poland's policies make the plight of refugees any easier. The Polish state took an interest almost exclusively in the repatriation of ethnic Poles. Although most Belarusian refugees managed to make their way home between 1918 and 1922, they faced great difficulties.

No Belarusian representatives were invited to attend the negotiations that led to the peace treaty signed between Poland and Soviet Russia at Riga in March 1921. The treaty led to the inclusion of several million Belarusians in the Polish state and paved the way for the formal establishment of the Belarusian Soviet Republic (BSSR). Belarusian leaders, above all Zhilunovicz, appealed to refugees to stay in Soviet Belarus, and not to leave for Poland. However, refugees preferred to return to their original homes, even though they were now located on Polish territory.[120] As recent work emphasizes, the delimitation of borders had important implications, encouraging Soviet leaders to offer 'ostentatiously generous treatment' of national minorities on Soviet territory, in the hope of garnering support among their 'ethnic brethren' in the successor states. One scholar summarizes this as an 'attempt to exploit cross-border ethnic ties to project political influence into neighbouring states.'[121] There took place a concerted effort at *korenizatsiia* ('indigenization'). Belarusian exiles returned from Poland and Lithuania to the BSSR.[122] *Korenizatsiia* represented a kind of Soviet-style legitimation and extension of the cultural and educational activities so energetically pursued by national refugee organizations during World War One. Yet *korenizatsiia* carried with it political risks. According to one Soviet official who reported to Stalin in 1929, more than a decade after the Revolution party leaders in Belarus 'played around with the nationalists far too much'. Interestingly, he offered as an explanation – although not as a justification – their wish to compensate for a sense of national insecurity. In some respects this echoed the problem that Belarusian activists wrestled with during the war, when they bemoaned the widespread cultural 'backwardness' of Belarusians relative to other minorities but refused to accept defeat and to renounce the nationalization of refugee politics. By the late 1920s, the more readily a new generation of Soviet Belarusian leaders tolerated and even encouraged the return of exiled co-nationals, the more they exposed themselves to the challenge that it was time to choose between nationalism and socialism.[123]

* Parts of Valentina Utgof's original paper have been developed by Peter Gatrell in consultation with the author.

4
In Search of a Native Realm: The Return of World War One Refugees to Lithuania, 1918–24

TOMAS BALKELIS

INTRODUCTION

In this chapter, I explore how population displacement operated in one part of the former Russian Empire. In 1918 the disintegration of the old imperial polity led to the emergence of an independent Lithuanian state.[1] Having emerged from the cauldron of World War One, the new state quickly found itself immersed in new conflicts with Polish, Soviet and White Russian armies. These conflicts continued until the end of 1920. Beyond the field of battle, the struggle to maintain the independence of Lithuania was characterized by an intense process of state and nation-building, led by a young and ambitious nationalist elite. All this hectic activity was accompanied by population displacement on a scale first witnessed in Lithuania during 1915 and 1916.

Unlike the military campaigns, these state-building efforts did not come to an end in 1920. My argument in this chapter is that population displacement presented the Lithuanian authorities with an opportunity to claim and to establish Lithuanian refugees as potential members of a new nation-state, thereby defining its spatial boundaries, its demographic composition, and its cultural attributes. Newly formed Lithuania offered a potential political homeland for tens of thousands of war refugees from various ethnic groups (Lithuanians, Poles, Jews, Russians, Belarusians, Gypsies, Tartars) who had lived in the former north-western provinces of Kovno (in Lithuanian, Kaunas), Vilno (in Lithuanian, Vilnius) and Grodno before 1914, but who were displaced by war. According to rough estimates, the total number of refugees from Lithuania who settled in the Russian interior stood at 550,000 at the beginning of 1918.[2] What was their fate in the immediate postwar period? What policies did the new Lithuanian state adopt towards them?

The emerging contours of Lithuanian nationalism implied that the itinerancy of the displaced had to be replaced by their sedentarism: only those who would adopt 'homeland' as opposed to 'exile' could be construed as loyal citizens of the new state. The need to domesticate the refugees also implied that they had to be registered, examined, classified, quarantined, screened and, if necessary, rejected as 'undesirable elements' by the state institutions responsible for their repatriation. Such an approach appears to suggest that refugees occupied the role of an historical object rather than being the subjects of their own repatriation. In order to avoid such reductionism, I also seek to consider Lithuanian refugees as a specific socio-cultural category continuously shaped not only by growing state repatriation strategies, but also by refugees' own experiences of displacement. What motives prompted them to return to Lithuania? What kind of personal choices did they face as a consequence of their exile in Russia? How did those choices affect the formation of their postwar identities and self-awareness? Did their perceptions of a Lithuanian 'homeland' correspond to those articulated by the state authorities, or did they try to develop their own meanings of it?

THE CHRONOLOGY OF REPATRIATION

The most intensive burst of repatriation took place in the years 1918 and 1920–21.[3] The return of refugees from Russia to Lithuania began shortly after the signing of the peace treaty of Brest-Litovsk in March 1918.[4] The first refugee trains reached Lithuania in April 1918.[5] Their return was an irregular process, which was interrupted by the outbreak of fresh hostilities in 1919 between the newly formed Lithuanian army, German troops and Bolshevik forces, who occupied most of eastern Lithuania. But for some refugees (especially for those who were stranded in areas adjacent to Lithuania) the shifting and often fluid military boundaries presented an opportunity rather than an obstacle to their return home. Under the brief Bolshevik occupation, which lasted until their expulsion in August 1919, thousands of war refugees found their way from Belarus and Russia to eastern parts of Lithuania and Vilno.[6] In all, around 245,000 refugees returned to Lithuania in 1918 and 1919.[7]

The state-organized return of refugees became possible only after the conclusion of the Lithuanian–Soviet Russian peace treaty on 12 July 1920.[8] The treaty confirmed the border between Lithuania and Soviet Russia and made repatriation the business of state officials. This treaty, as well as a Lithuanian–Soviet Russian refugee return agreement (signed on 30 June 1920), marked the end of the 'spontaneous' repatriation of refugees.[9] Official registration of those refugees willing to return to Lithuania continued until the end of 1922.[10] By

1924 most of the refugees who expressed the desire to return to Lithuania had left Soviet Russia. The best estimate is that around 350,000 refugees found their way to Lithuania during 1918–24.[11] For a state with a total population of approximately 2.2 million, this meant that one in six citizens was a refugee. Moreover, about 185,000 refugees either chose not to, or could not, return to Lithuania.

Repatriation in 1918 until the beginning of 1920, and from mid-1920 until 1924, occurred under differing political conditions. Consequently, we can identify distinct features both in the strategies of state officials and the behaviour of refugees. The essential difference between these two periods was the degree of Lithuanian state efforts to control, select, screen and, if possible, to 'fix' the returning masses of refugees.[12]

THE FIRST PHASE: 1918 TO MID-1920

According to Martynas Yčas, the Chairman of the Lithuanian War Relief Committee (LWRC), formed in 1914, his staff laid the foundation for an independent Lithuanian state among the Lithuanian war refugees.[13] Although its role as 'maker of the nation' subsequently became official orthodoxy, and tended to drown out the voices of ordinary refugees, the LWRC played a crucial role in the early stage of repatriation. Its activities were instrumental in shaping the fragile national identities of the Lithuanian refugees in exile. The committee was dedicated not only to securing the political or cultural loyalties of the refugees but also to acting as the guardian of their values. As Yčas claimed:

> The Committee provided care for hundreds of thousands of the Lithuanians and protected their dispersed masses from moral degradation. ... Those who lost their national consciousness and had been transformed into live corpses of our nation, joined in the common work with a new impulse of love for our nation.[14]

The ideological guidelines of the LWRC included the goal 'to strengthen the ties of refugees with Lithuania and Lithuanian culture, and to maintain among them a strong desire to return to their homeland.'[15] Not surprisingly, the committee was in the forefront of attempts to return refugees to Lithuania after the Brest-Litovsk treaty at the beginning of 1918. At this time given the weakness of the Lithuanian government, which had yet to resolve its relationship with the German authorities, the LWRC was the only institution capable of such a task. It possessed a large network of around 250 local offices, which attended to the needs of more than 100,000 Lithuanian refugees. The committee immediately started the registration of refugees through its local offices in the former Russian empire.

The task of making contact with potential returnees was easier where refugees formed tightly knit communities or belonged to various charitable organizations, orphanages, hospitals and schools, as in Moscow, Petrograd, Voronezh, Khar'kov and Minsk. In these instances it was relatively straightforward to register individuals. The Ukrainian Relief Committee proceeded with the repatriation of 150 mentally handicapped patients, who had been evacuated from Vilno in 1915.[16] Where appropriate, Lithuanian leaders negotiated with the German authorities. Thus the representative of the Georgian war relief committee, Pranas Dailidė, secured the permission of German officials to send Lithuanian refugees from Tbilisi back to Lithuania.[17]

However, many refugees, having heard news of the peace treaty, proceeded to organize their return to Lithuania spontaneously. In Ekaterinoslav they elected a committee (mostly from the ranks of the intelligentsia) and entrusted it with the task of securing the necessary permits and transportation.[18] In Minsk, a local relief committee chose from its ranks five representatives responsible for repatriation. The first trainload of Lithuanian refugees from Ekaterinoslav had to bribe various Ukrainian and Russian officials eight times before it reached its destination.[19]

The motives that prompted refugees to return to Lithuania were diverse and complex. Their 'emotional' attachment to their native environment and to family 'roots' was only one of the dominant motives among the complex pressures to which they were exposed and the adverse political and economic circumstances in which they found themselves. Other motives included an ideological attachment to the cause of independent Lithuania, an expectation of better career and livelihood prospects, and a concern for basic safety and survival. If a sense of patriotism was more persistent among groups of the displaced intelligentsia, the fear of starvation was widespread among the majority of refugees. But in any event, the meaning of patriotism was itself subject to shifts in interpretation.

The experience of 'exile', revolution and enemy action forced some refugees to redefine and re-evaluate their notions of 'homeland', helping to reinforce their cultural and ethnic identities and to set them apart from local populations. Thus, Veronika Janulaitytė, a German-educated doctor working among Lithuanian refugees in Minsk, wrote in her memoirs:

> There was a revolution in Russia. Lithuanians became eager to return to their homeland. They travelled by train, in horse carriages or by foot. Minsk fell into the hands of Germans. The Lithuanian refugees were not allowed to return to Lithuania. (But) nobody wanted to stay in Russia.[20]

Significantly, Janulaitytė complained that 'nobody was waiting for us in Lithuania.' It was no surprise that many felt the same way, having lost personal contacts with their relatives for several years.

The surviving evidence reveals something of the kaleidoscope of emotions that refugees experienced as they weighed up the choice between returning to the newly reconstituted homeland or staying in Russia or Ukraine. Many, totally disoriented by the hectic pace of events, felt unable to make a clear-cut choice. A deserter from the Tsarist army, Švaistas-Balčiūnas, expressed his uncertainty and doubt in the following terms:

> When I return to the time [of 1918], I see more darkness than light in my soul ... It was a kind of chaos, neither peace, nor war; of revolutions in Russia and in Germany; of the consolidation of an independent Lithuanian state. ... On the other hand - corruption and exploitation were common everywhere...[21]

Nevertheless, after some hesitation Švaistas-Balčiūnas chose to return to his native land, but confusion and insecurity were common among those refugees whose every day in exile was a struggle for survival. Another Lithuanian soldier, having spent time in a German prisoner-of-war camp in Latvia before going back to Lithuania, decided differently:

> And what am I going to do here? I'm not going to stay in Lithuania. I'm bored and shackled here. Things are totally different there (and he pointed to the East): a vast expanse and endless opportunities await us there!'[22]

His enthusiasm for revolutionary adventure demonstrates the powerful appeal of Bolshevik propaganda that continued to make inroads amongst Lithuanian refugees in Russia. As early as 1918, the Lithuanian refugees faced attempts by both Bolshevik authorities and representatives of the LWRC to secure their political loyalties. The ideals of the proletarian revolution seemed to promise to many Lithuanian war refugees a bright future as citizens of the first Soviet state. Numerous Bolshevik organizations vigorously conducted socialist propaganda among the Lithuanian refugees, and in some cases curbed the activities of rival Lithuanian refugee organizations. For example, a local Lithuanian Bolshevik committee in Voronezh, led by Zigmas Angarietis, sought to prepare refugees to operate illegally in independent Lithuania.[23] Pro-Bolshevik Lithuanians formed the most powerful element among the ranks of the Soviet militia in Voronezh in early 1918, and proceeded to arrest members of the local Lithuanian relief committee, eight of whom were jailed. The Lithuanian Bolshevik Commissariat in Moscow coordinated action such as this, both in Voronezh and elsewhere.[24] Nor were the Bolsheviks alone in vying for the political sympathies of the refugees. Stasys Raštikis, subsequently a general in the Lithuanian army, recalled that Polish and Georgian officers in Tbilisi tried to enlist him in their armed forces.[25]

Lithuanian patriots made their own efforts to secure the political loyalties of the refugees. The future Lithuanian Minister of the Interior, Rapolas Skipitis, himself a refugee, managed to return to Kovno from Voronezh via Moscow and Riga in April 1918. Before his return he travelled extensively to different communities of Lithuanian refugees in Russia, promoting the idea of a 'new' Lithuania. In his memoirs he claimed, '... I was passionately urging all our refugees and those Lithuanians who had lived there before to come back to their fatherland Lithuania.'[26] Apparently, his main argument was that 'an independent Lithuanian state is going to be revived.' Although the Lithuanian Bolsheviks in Moscow were about to arrest him, Skipitis managed to bribe a Lithuanian Bolshevik commissar and secure a separate train coach for his relatives.[27] Other members of the elite, such as Veronika Janulaitytė, who exploited her German university acquaintances, were able to do likewise.[28] Not surprisingly, Skipitis later wrote that 'the mood of all of them [refugees] was heightened, but each felt depressed by the uncertainty as to how and when they would be able to return home.'[29]

The new Lithuanian government also intervened, primarily in order to recruit technical specialists and other members of the intelligentsia among the refugees whose skills were in short supply. As a result, provincial welfare committees in Russia compiled lists of doctors, students, teachers, technicians, lawyers, priests, land-surveyors and university professors.[30] This exercise took no account of the ethnicity of the displaced population: the young state desperately needed professional expertise. Thus in 1918 the government approved the admittance of Lithuanian Jewish bankers, industrialists, merchants, doctors and teachers.[31] In their applications for Lithuanian citizenship most of them indicated that they knew the Lithuanian language and had worked in Lithuania before the war. It is striking that many of them expressed a willingness to work as civil servants for the time being, if need be without any salary.

By contrast, other refugees had only a limited number of options if they decided to embark on the return journey to Lithuania. Those who tried to return by rail found this was a hazardous undertaking. In 1918 refugee trains were often caught in the crossfire between Bolsheviks trying to requisition stocks of food, and armed bands of 'bread-seekers'. There were numerous cases of shot and wounded refugees.[32] Many refugees had to rely on the goodwill and knowledge of the local population, or upon bribes to corrupt Soviet officials or black marketeers. No wonder that, under such harsh conditions, the journey home could take months. A former Tsarist officer, Jurgis Jakelaitis, recollected that:

> There were more than a hundred of us, Lithuanians, in four train coaches, mostly soldiers with families and little children. In our cargo car the temperatures dropped below 20 degrees every day. There was a metal stove in the middle, heated constantly, because we were always able to steal some coal in train stations. It took us one month to get from Voronezh to Vilno.[33]

The worst enemy was not the threat of violence but the ever-present fear of starvation. Refugees travelling in large groups were more fortunate in securing food than were individual families. They tended to congregate according to their places of origin. For many refugees the fact that there was no famine in Lithuania betokened a brighter future. Upon arriving in Lithuania, Jakelaitis expressed his bewilderment that people were not starving there and that food was available in great abundance.

The safety of refugees was not guaranteed even after having entered Lithuanian territory. Jakelaitis and several of his friends who tried to get from Vilno to Kovno with a help of a Jewish black-marketeer were first robbed by the Bolsheviks and then arrested by Germans as 'Red agitators'. German, Lithuanian, Bolshevik and Polish troops threatened refugees with arrest or even execution for having no official papers, accusing them of espionage or desertion.[34]

Refugees' first encounters with Lithuanian troops in Kovno testified to their surprise, confusion and incapacity to comprehend the new political realities of 1918. They could not readily confront the new military signs and power symbols of the Lithuanian state as somehow 'native' or representative of the 'homeland'. Instead these symbols had to be read and interpreted anew:

> At dawn my eyes noticed a strange view: a simple country fellow with wooden shoes, padded coat, similar pants and with an emblem of the Lithuanian tricolour on his sleeve. On his shoulder rested a Russian rifle. Later I noticed more such fellows: one with shoes, the other with wooden clogs. All them had very strange hats on their heads. And all of them had the same flag-shaped triangle on their sleeves. ... I sneaked in closer and said, 'Are you a Lithuanian?' He was surprised and replied, 'Of course, are you blind?' I said, 'I'm very sorry. I just returned from Russia this evening, I know nobody here. What is the meaning of this triangle on your sleeve? ... Why do Germans allow you to carry the arms?' And the soldier said, 'Man, did somebody just kick you out of heaven? All these lads are volunteers of the Lithuanian army. ... Germans are only our guests.' ... After this conversation with the soldier, I became more courageous.[35]

Perhaps this experience was untypical. However, for many Lithuanian refugees the new symbols represented an unfamiliar and challenging political reality, yet to be integrated into their sense of identity.

Thus the early return of refugees was conditioned by their ability to organize themselves into small groups, to arrange means of transportation (often by bribing officials), to avoid the dangers of a Civil War, and to get through the still porous political and military borders of states. At this stage the Lithuanian government gave priority to specialists of various kinds rather than to 'ordinary' refugees. Once in Lithuania, refugees tended no longer to preserve their organizational patterns, instead submitting to the role of Lithuanian citizens being prepared for them by the government. Only in some cases when entire refugee organizations such as hospitals, schools and orphanages, returned intact, did they continue in their earlier form.[36] But relatively few refugee organizations continued to operate in independent Lithuania. In other words, after their return many refugees were left to their own devices.

Lithuanian refugees represented a great mixture of ethnic and cultural groups, united mostly by their common geographic origins and their experience of displacement. Living in Russia had forced some of them to adopt new languages and to accept non-Lithuanians as members of their families. These encounters with non-Lithuanians were reinforced during the return journey, as one refugee described:

> Among the refugees conversation is conducted in all languages, or to be more precise, in a mixture of all languages. Despite the fact that our train could be called the 'special' train of Lithuanians, because most of the travellers who return to the homeland are Lithuanians, the Lithuanian language is not dominant... And it is easy to understand. Having lived for so long in foreign lands, our countrymen intermarried with the Ukrainians; the majority are bringing their wives from Ukraine to Lithuania... [and they] don't understand a word of Lithuanian. And the entire Lithuanian family speaks to each other in Russian... You would not hear the Lithuanian language in the 'diplomatic' coach of our 'mission', as the refugees called it. Former officials of the Diplomatic Mission of Lithuania are returning in that coach.[37]

PHASE TWO: THE POLITICS OF ORGANIZED RETURN (MID-1920 TO 1924)

The organized return of refugees started only in the autumn of 1920, following the signing of the Lithuanian–Soviet Russian refugee return agreement. The agreement stated that those refugees who expressed a wish to return were to be returned as soon as possible.[38] Both sides agreed to define as refugees those persons 'who had lived on the territory of either side before the war, and who during the Great War in 1914–17 voluntarily left their places of residence occupied by the enemy, under a threat of occupation or were forced to evacuate by orders of the Russian civilian or military government.'[39] Conscripts of the Tsarist army were included in this definition. People of non-Lithuanian descent who had served as government or military officials in the Lithuanian provinces were denied the status of refugee and thus deprived of any right to return. Article 3 of the treaty stipulated that those repatriated had to be registered on special lists and transported through designated refugee transfer centres. The Soviet government agreed to provide transport for those Lithuanian refugees who had to travel from distant Russian territories.

The agreement also introduced a whole set of various rules and regulations regarding the transfer of refugee property. Each head of the household was allowed no more than 130 kg of baggage, excluding hand luggage. Additional members of the family were entitled to a maximum of 90 kg of belongings (children were limited to 30 kg). The rules stipulated that baggage could include only personal items essential to travel: change of clothing sufficient for 6 days per person, no more than 2 pairs of shoes, a teapot, pillowcases and covers. The amount of food allowed to be taken was limited to 12 kg per person of flour or bread, meat, milk products, sugar, and tea. In addition, returnees required special approval to take in photographs, personal documents and printed materials of any kind. No domestic animals, birds, cars, carriages or sledges were allowed unless the refugees travelled by means other than train. They had to leave behind all golden and silver money and precious stones heavier than one carat. They could not bring in more than 2,000 rubles, or any other currencies without a special permit.

Further articles stated that the first to be returned were those who had family members living in their destination country. The treaty also included a special provision that those refugees who had lived in the Lithuanian lands occupied by Poland would be returned home only when those territories would be freed from Polish control. Thus the fate of refugees trying to return to the former Vilno and Grodno provinces remained unresolved until 1921, and served as a source of tension between Poland and Lithuania (see below).

As part of the arrangements for implementing the agreement, the Refugee Division of the Lithuanian Ministry of the Interior sent two representatives to Soviet Russia, who were ordered to bring refugees to Moscow for registration, prior to sending them on to the Lithuanian border.[40] Their instructions were 'to check the papers of every person intending to return to Lithuania and allow only those who qualified under the conditions of the Refugee Return treaty.'[41] Representatives of the Lithuanian Ministry of Foreign Affairs in Russia were responsible for providing trains and establishing local repatriation committees comprising refugees, while the Ministry of the Interior undertook the screening of lists of refugees and the organization of a train schedule to Lithuania.[42]

The mission also sent officials and emergency food parcels to refugees who were scattered across Russia and Ukraine, in order to alleviate their condition until they could be repatriated.[43]

Increased efforts by the Lithuanian government to repatriate refugees corresponded to the stabilization of the political situation in Lithuania and the consolidation of state institutions. Having adopted an 'ethnic' model of the nation-state, the Lithuanian state realized that the return of Lithuanian war refugees could become a significant political and demographic factor in its survival. The increased public awareness of the refugee issue meant that efforts were devoted to securing the return of ethnic Lithuanian refugees. Despite official claims that refugees would not be discriminated against on the grounds of their nationality and political loyalties, state officials gave preference to ethnic Lithuanian refugees who wished to return.[44] To be sure, this did not always have the desired effect. One official commented in despair that:

> In general trains from Ukraine reach us in total disarray. They contain only about 29 per cent of Lithuanian citizens, while all the rest are some kinds of "doubtful elements" ... Given all the circumstances and the instructions with which I was entrusted ... I have no other way out of the situation except the following: to return all Jews, Poles and Russians, despite the visas issued by our Mission [in the Ukraine], or I myself will have to return to Lithuania.[45]

We can see the new policy at work in a proposal (in August 1921) by the Ministry of the Interior to change the rules of repatriation:

> In order to prevent foreigners from coming to Lithuania, we should introduce a new order starting in February. All Lithuanian citizens, whose relatives are still in Russia, have to apply to a local authority, indicating the refugees' addresses in Russia, date of departure and their place of residence before the war. The person in charge, having verified whether the persons are truly Lithuanian citizens, will send the data to the Department of Social Control. The latter will draw up a list of the refugees in three copies: one goes to the Lithuanian Mission to Soviet Russia, the second to the quarantine, and the third to the refugee control in Rezekne. Only refugees from these lists will be allowed to enter Lithuania.[46]

The new rules meant that refugees who had lost or had no relatives living in Lithuania found it increasingly difficult to return to their homeland. This change is reflected in the immigration statistics in 1921. While in May only 25 per cent of refugees who applied for repatriation were refused the right of return, by November this proportion had risen to 61 per cent. Other data confirm the increasing restrictions placed on non-Lithuanian returnees. In May,

Lithuanians made up 27.2 per cent, Jews 29.8 per cent, Poles 4.5 per cent of all refugees. Among those allowed to return, in November, 60 per cent were Lithuanians, but only 11 per cent were Jews, and 9 per cent were Poles.[47] Thus the stricter policy produced a noticeable disparity along ethnic lines.

In 1921 the Lithuanian authorities also toughened their policy towards the immigration of spouses of refugees. The fact that some refugees had conducted only civil, as opposed to church-registered, marriages while in Russia now could be used to prevent their settling in Lithuania. As the Director of the Eastern Department at LMI wrote to the Lithuanian Mission in Moscow:

> In Lithuania we conduct our marriages in church. Therefore, our citizens who stay abroad have to conduct them in church too. Certificates issued to those married by civil authorities do not validate them as married, and, therefore, the wives of such married men do not become Lithuanian citizens.[48]

This regulation was directed in the first instance at Poles, Jews, Gypsies, and others that had married non-Lithuanian spouses in Russia. After 1922, the fact that before the war they had resided in Lithuania and had a legal right to claim Lithuanian citizenship became increasingly irrelevant. As Skipitis recalled, 'it seemed to us that foreigners, and almost all of them were non-Lithuanian, were a danger for the security of our state.'[49]

The two most important institutions that determined the fate of individual refugees were the Refugee Division at the Moscow-based Lithuanian Mission to Soviet Russia and the refugee quarantine facility in Obeliai on the Lithuanian–Latvian border. Moscow was the first destination for thousands of Lithuanian refugees who found themselves scattered all over the plains and cities of European Russia, Ukraine and Siberia. From Moscow their journey continued on cargo trains to the west: through Rezekne, Daugavpils, Kalkūnai to Obeliai.[50]

The procedure to secure the necessary papers for the return involved in the first instance a preliminary screening of refugees by Lithuanian officials in Moscow. Each refugee was required to submit a personal application to the Lithuanian Mission or its regional offices, to fill in special questionnaires and to provide official proof of his place of origin. Only after local verification of these documents could he be issued with travel permits.[51] The desperate attempts by the government in Lithuania to control the flow of refugees were reflected in constant complaints from Kovno that officials in Moscow had issued visas for optants (the descendants of those men and women who had been exiled to Siberia after the revolt of 1863), trans-emigrants and foreign citizens travelling by transit, who travelled not by refugee trains, but on their own.[52]

After being fed by Latvian authorities in Rezekne, refugees had to pass through a Latvian quarantine, where those diagnosed with contagious diseases were isolated and sent onwards by separate train coaches to Lithuania. During the passage across Latvia, armed guards accompanied some of the refugee trains. Those whose eventual destination was the provinces of Vilno and Grodno were forced off the trains and obliged to continue their journey under the surveillance of Polish officials.[53] Neither Latvian nor Polish officials expressed great sympathy for the refugees, who represented a mixture of ethnic groups, languages and cultures.

Quarantine facilities had already been established by the German military authorities, who maintained a quarantine in Kalkūnai as early as 1918. Its purpose was both to filter out Bolshevik spies from the ranks of refugees and to prevent the potential danger of epidemic disease. Švaistas-Balčiūnas wrote that:

> The quarantine was located far from the town ... Here I met people of different nationalities. All were displaced by war, on their way to native places: Lithuania, Poland, Latvia and Belarus ... One had to spend here two weeks or longer until there was a sufficient group of refugees or a train. It was like in prison. Armed sentries and barbed wires were everywhere. Nobody could leave without a permit ... Nobody was told when they would be freed ... The food was just enough to survive. For the first time in my life I tasted such disgusting bread and coffee.[54]

Refugees were forced through 'something resembling a sauna'.[55] Then they were soon taken by train to Vilno and Kovno, from where they were allowed to travel to their native places. Their freedom, however, was constrained, since the permits allowed them only to travel within their native district.

The new quarantine centre at Obeliai played a decisive role in Lithuania's efforts to 'fix' the refugee population. It documented and screened refugees in a variety of ways. Women and children were taken directly into quarantine, while men had to unload their luggage into special barracks for disinfection. Being rewarded with two pieces of soap per family, they had to proceed to a sauna, supervised by Lithuanian doctors. After this cleaning and scrubbing, the refugees were subject to political screening by a Commission of Refugee Control. Officials registered them according to age, nationality, profession, point of arrival, destination and date of repatriation.[56]

The quarantine commission was made up of representatives from the Department of Social Security, the Ministry of Defence and the Department of

Municipalities.[57] Significantly, it also included officials from the Department of Intelligence and from the Lithuanian military. They were instructed to 'gather information about political views of refugees ... and to control their civil and political loyalty.' The commission censored letters and telegrams of refugees, and had the right to search their personal belongings. The decision to allow an individual refugee to enter Lithuania had to be accepted unanimously by all members of the commission. Those whose documents appeared insufficient, loyalties suspicious or past doubtful were transferred to a refugee detention camp, where they had to spend weeks or even months until police departments verified their attachment to an intended residence. Those who failed to qualify for citizenship were deported back to Soviet Russia.[58]

The fact that some refugees, having been issued with a visa in Moscow, were then denied one in Obeliai complicated their fate and added to the confusion. Merkys, a Lithuanian army commander, dealt with the consequences of overcrowding in the temporary refugee camps in the following manner:

> The Russians refuse to accept back the persons whom we [originally] acknowledged as our citizens, and these foreign refugees are forced to stay in camps for an unlimited time. .... Bearing this in mind, today I issued an order to the commandant of Eglaitė not to accept the refugees who are to be returned to Russia, and to the commander of camps of prisoners not to accept them into the camps ... Such persons will be returned in care of those institutions, which brought them into Lithuania.[59]

Attempts to deport those who represented a potential political threat sometimes led to tension between the military and the Lithuanian civil service. Nor did it contribute to improved relations with Soviet Russia.

Having secured her independence, Lithuania confronted enormous economic problems. The country's economy was in total disarray.[60] The work of the repatriation officials was constantly plagued by a chronic lack of funds necessary for the return of such large numbers of people to Lithuania. In 1921, famine in European Russia and the growing concentration of refugees in Moscow created a humanitarian crisis among the displaced. The Lithuanian authorities were not capable of dealing with it on their own. In October 1921 the Lithuanian Mission in Moscow applied for urgent help from the Moscow City Soviet to secure the basic minimum for Lithuanian refugees in the capital city. Lithuanian orphans who sought refuge in Moscow were described as being 'in a horrifying condition: half-naked, exhausted by starvation and travel fatigue; many of them having lost their relatives on the road and, therefore, in an extremely depressed state'.[61] Unable to provide sufficient financial means for helping the starving refugees, officials appealed to the Lithuanian Red Cross, which assumed full responsibility for feeding the Lithuanian refugees in Russia after February 1921.[62]

The government's difficulty in financing the return was also reflected in its quarrel with Latvia, which accused it of failing to keep to the financial terms of the refugee return agreement signed by Lithuania and Latvia in early 1921.[63] This agreement stipulated that Latvians should provide refugee trains from the Soviet border to Daugavpils as well as food, paid for by Lithuania. However, Lithuania's failure to keep up its payments led to the virtual suspension of the agreement thereby, producing an immediate humanitarian crisis among the Lithuanian refugees on the Soviet–Latvian border. The Director of the Eastern Department tried desperately to find a solution for more than 1,500 refugees 'who are suffering from disease, frost and dying of starvation'. He urged Skipitis to arrange to pay Latvia 326 tons of grain instead of cash, an offer that was gladly accepted. Thus, in effect, the Lithuanian refugees were exchanged for grain.[64]

The government tried to find other solutions to the problem of funding by levying substantial travel fees upon returnees who, while not qualifying as 'refugees', expressed a desire to return to an independent Lithuania. This applied to the so-called 'optants', the descendants of those men and women who had been exiled to Siberia after the revolt of 1863.[65] Their designation as 'Lithuanian colonists' testified to the unwillingness of officials to assign them the same status as refugees. It is difficult to establish, however, how many abandoned their plans to return due to a lack of funds. The state was barely in a position to meet the costs of those whom it considered worthy to be included in the category of refugees, let alone the costs of anyone else.

SHIFTING BORDERS AND POLITICAL LOYALTIES: REFUGEES FROM VILNO AND GRODNO

The return of displaced people implies that there should be a defined space that can accept and accommodate them as permanent residents. In independent Lithuania this was complicated by the confusing shifts of borders in the early postwar years. New state boundaries were far from the so-called historical boundaries of the Grand Duchy of Lithuania (which included most of Belarus), as well as from the 'ethnic' boundaries in which Lithuanian speakers resided. The fact that Poland occupied the south east of Lithuania created problems for the government in trying to deal with the Lithuanian refugees returning to their native former Vilno and Grodno provinces. Did government officials try to find any solutions to this problem? Did they consider the east Lithuanian refugees as foreigners, or as potential citizens of independent

Lithuania? How did international rivalries between Poland, Lithuania and Soviet Russia affect the re-evacuation of this group of refugees?

In April 1919, Polish troops occupied Vilno and the surrounding region, forcing the government to evacuate the capital to Kovno. Although the Lithuanian army managed to stabilize the Polish–Lithuanian front in the middle of 1920, the Polish army retook Vilno in October. For thousands of Lithuanian refugees from the former provinces of Vilno and Grodno the stalemate provided a chance to return home. Some of them tried to return with other Lithuanian refugees through Latvia and Obeliai. However, many (including those returning to independent Lithuania) attempted to reach their native provinces through Belarus and Vilno. In 1920–1 the urgency of their return was most of all dictated by the worsening economic and humanitarian situation in Soviet Russia.

In 1920 Lithuanian authorities faced a serious border control problem: they had to respond not only to manoeuvres by Polish forces, but also to thousands of Lithuanian refugees trying to cross the demarcation line without any official sanction. The authorities regarded this as a challenge to the future political and economic stability of the state. A report from Skipitis to the Minister of Defence, E Galvanauskas, in February 1921 stated that:

> We should enlarge our border guards' contingent by several times, because in the area of Vievis separate crowds of refugees returning from Poland are able to get through on a daily basis. In the area of Obeliai our border troops are so weak (30 soldiers for 60 miles) that not only can people travelling by foot or in horse carriages avoid our border guards, but even a train can cross the border without any supervision.[66]

Finally, in February 1921, unable to cope with the flow of illegal refugees through the demarcation line with Poland, the government had to issue an order forcing all refugees to enter Lithuania only through the quarantine in Obeliai.[67] However, this measure did not improve the situation, but instead created a chain of new problems. The quarantine became blocked with the refugees travelling to Vilno and Grodno provinces, while the illegal migration through the demarcation line still continued. In October the Director of the Department of Social Security, Kubilius, urgently reported that the quarantine was flooded with 300 refugees travelling to the Vilno region, and their prolonged stay in Obeliai was too costly for the state. He urged the government to send them to the occupied lands as soon as possible.[68]

Besides the financial constraints and the concern that 'undesirable residents' could enter the country, there was also a fear that refugees might bring into Lithuania an outbreak of cholera (see below).[69] An additional factor stimulating the government's reluctance to accept the Lithuanian refugees was the critical shortage of available housing in Lithuania.[70]

Thus, due to a variety of reasons, by summer 1921 the Lithuanian refugees returning to the Vilno and Grodno provinces suddenly found themselves uninvited guests in their own homeland. This inevitably led to their worsening condition and another humanitarian crisis both in the successor states and the former Russian empire. Gradually the crisis became an international issue, which demanded the intervention not only of Lithuanian, but also of Polish, Latvian and Soviet authorities. The desperate situation of the refugees trying to move across borders threatened the stability of all these states, already severely tested by war and economic chaos. The worsening situation in which refugees found themselves called for at least limited cooperation between the different belligerents. Soviet Russia, Lithuania and Poland tried to solve the issue by trying to determine which state should assume responsibility over the repatriation of the Lithuanian refugees. However, the ensuing international negotiations also meant that the refugees would be examined and demarcated in political as well as ethnic terms.

Lithuania tried to solve the problem by attempting to persuade the Polish government to transport the Vilno and Grodno refugees from Kalkūnai to their native places in the occupied territory.[71] However, Poland agreed to accept no more than a small number. Lithuanian officials complained that the Polish authorities would allow 'only those refugees whom they like, despite the fact that they originated from the Vilno and Grodno provinces. Jews are not accepted altogether, and, therefore, we don't know where to place the refugees.'[72] The worsening situation on the Latvian – Lithuanian border prompted Skipitis to issue an urgent request to the Foreign Minister on 12 July 1921:

> Due to the fact that Poles are not allowing the refugees, who are returning from Soviet Russia, to enter the occupied territories, I ask you to urgently notify the Lithuanian Mission to Soviet Russia to stop the return of the refugees travelling to the occupied zone.[73]

However, he added that 'I think that the Lithuanian specialists, who could contribute to the common work of rebuilding the state, should be returned to Lithuania, despite the fact that they come from the occupied territories.'

Although totally overwhelmed by the flow of the displaced, the Lithuanian authorities continued their work of segregating and selecting the refugees. The educated refugees and various specialists continued to be in high demand by state agencies. After 1921 the Lithuanian male refugees came to be increasingly treated as a potential source of recruits for contending Lithuanian, Soviet Russian and Polish armies. In early 1921 the Soviet authorities became increasingly concerned at the possibility that Lithuanian men could be drafted into the Polish army. The Lithuanian Foreign Minister, J Purickis, reported that:

> The Russian Consulate to Lithuania in a personal conversation asked the Foreign Ministry what to do with young males, who can be recruited by Zeligowski into his army. Should not they be sent to Kovno and mobilised there? The Russian consulate is expecting an answer as soon as possible. So far the Russian authorities are not allowing any males aged 18–40 through the Polish border into the Vilno province.[74]

Despite all official efforts, the Lithuanian refugees continued to stream into Moscow, and to gather at the Lithuanian borders in a desperate attempt to leave Soviet Russia as soon as possible. Under pressure from the Soviet authorities, the Lithuanian cabinet agreed to accept all Lithuanian refugees coming from the occupied territories. Some of them later returned through the demarcation line with Poland to their native Vilno and Grodno provinces.[75]

Official documents shed little light on the emotions, moods and political views of refugees originally from Vilno and Grodno. Nevertheless, Lithuanian officials in Moscow betrayed great anxiety about their questionable political loyalties. Begging the authorities in Lithuania to review their decision to stop repatriation, one of them pointed out that 'after selling their last rags, our citizens' condition becomes so horrible that they die, and those who remain alive are cursing the Lithuanian government.' He added that their situation entailed political risks, because 'in those lice-ridden refugee transfer centres they shout that the Lithuanian government wants only the land of Vilno and Grodno provinces, and it does not care about living people.' He noted alarmingly that some of the refugees had already, out of a sense of bitterness at their treatment, expressed their hatred of independent Lithuania. Alarmingly, the Poles were already conducting propaganda among them.[76]

The case of the Vilno and Grodno refugees exemplified the limitations and inconsistencies in the Lithuanian policies of repatriation. Faced with the prospect of increasing economic costs, the danger of epidemics and, most importantly, potential political instability, the government tended to abandon its nationals, despite their critical situation. The shifting political borders and hostile interstate relations dictated their own practical policies towards the refugees. For thousands of Lithuanian-speaking refugees it meant that they were at the mercy of state bureaucrats, and could be excluded as potential citizens of the new state. Ethnic markers, otherwise so essential in the selection of 'potential citizens', occasionally had to be abandoned for the sake of more practical reasons of state. In such situations, as the case of the Vilno and

Grodno refugees, the new politico-spatial arrangements served to delineate different categories of refugees.

REFUGEES' ETHNICITY AND THE 'JEWISH QUESTION'

Public attitudes towards the displaced population were most directly expressed in relation to Jewish refugees, and in particular to the policies adopted by the Minister of the Interior, Rapolas Skipitis. In his memoirs, Skipitis devoted a substantial chapter to rebutting public criticism of his 'anti-state' immigration policies during 1921 and 1922, when he was repeatedly accused of 'filling Lithuania with Jews'.[77] He was criticized and ridiculed not only in the press, but also by both right- and left-wing political figures and institutions. His rival Jonas Vileišis, former Minister of the Interior and a prominent figure in the Lithuanian prewar national movement, personally reproached him for allowing 'too many' Jews from Russia into Lithuania.[78] Even The Social Democratic newspaper *Darbininkas* [*The Worker*] voiced the same criticism:

> We have to note that the majority of the refugees who returned are Jews. Having illegally brought gold and various properties from Russia, they conduct their 'business' here in Lithuania. And, we have to say, very successfully.[79]

Predictably, similar criticism was echoed in the conservative *Tėvynės sargas* [*The Guardian of the Homeland*]:

> Due to the peculiar geographic, political and economic conditions of our country, it became 'the Promised Land' for many foreigners. They are streaming to our country from all places and bringing with them many different dangers and unhappiness to the true citizens of our country and to the state itself.[80]

The issue was picked up not only by the press, but also by some members of the artistic intelligentsia, who publicly ridiculed the stereotypical 'new Lithuanians' who had no grasp of the language. In 1921 the satirical theatre company 'Vilkolakis' staged a play entitled 'The Quarantine of Sheep', which received notable public acclaim for publicizing the corrupt immigration policies in Obeliai and for simultaneously satirizing Jewish refugees.[81] Skipitis, a former member of the company, regretted that:

> My former colleagues from 'Vilkolakis' showed on stage how a Ukrainian Jew, who had never visited Lithuania, hurriedly learned the geography of Lithuania and, after sneaking past border controls, showed up in Kovno ... The jokes of 'Vilkolakis' had a serious effect on public opinion, setting it against the return of Jews from Russia.[82]

Public discontent became sufficiently strong to demand a debate in the Parliament in January 1922. *Tėvynės sargas* berated Skipitis for showing 'mercy to the members of other nations'.[83] The official *Lietuvos žinios* [*Lithuanian News*] published statistics showing that Jewish refugees outnumbered the settled Jewish population by a factor of three, far higher than the corresponding figure for Polish, Latvian and German refugees. The editorial concluded that 'perhaps the return of "refugees" means the colonisation of Lithuania, which is harmful to us.'[84] The fact that Jewish refugees included large numbers of anti-Bolsheviks cut little ice with many Lithuanian politicians. The sharpest political attack against the liberal immigration policies of Skipitis came from the Christian Democrats, who adopted a special resolution urging the government to curb the numbers of Jewish refugees.[85]

Official immigration policies supported the recruitment of different specialists among the refugees as early as 1919. Thus it is quite understandable that some Jews saw the new Lithuanian state as fertile ground for starting their professional careers. In the aftermath of the Revolution and Civil War, 'famous engineers, merchants, doctors, and talented artists' from Russia flooded into Lithuania.[86] Some of them saw Lithuania as a springboard for their further immigration to the West. The fact that most of the Jewish intelligentsia was concentrated in a few Lithuanian towns made them more visible to the public, who became increasingly dissatisfied with the growing share of Jewish businesses in the country. Skipitis pointed to shortages of food in the Lithuanian countryside during 1920–1. He defended those Jewish refugees who could not assimilate.[87] He added that right-wing political groups should be exposed when they tried to rally public support by exploiting the issue.

Skipitis did not survive the onslaught. He was replaced in February 1922 by the Christian Democrat K Oleka. Oleka immediately introduced tougher refugee controls in Obeliai by strengthening the border police and cracking down on the black market.[88] Politicians complained of returnees who could not name even one acquaintance in Lithuania or a part of the city to which they were travelling, using this as support for tougher controls on immigration. The new policy was reflected in the Ministry's refusal to employ a Lithuanian Jew as representative of the Lithuanian Jewish Committee, despite the strong support that he received from the Minister of Jewish Affairs of Lithuania.[89] By 1922 repatriation policy became much more conservative and exclusive. Observers greeted this change of heart, noting that 'it is sad that our government responded with strict measures only now, when in our capital Kovno one may notice great numbers of these foreigners on every street corner ... But it is better late than never.'[90]

REFUGEES AND CONTAGIOUS DISEASE

The risk of cholera and typhus in Lithuania presented government officials with a fresh challenge. In July 1921 the Department of Health warned Skipitis that the mass return of refugees carried a risk of cholera from Russia and recommended limiting the number of refugees in Obeliai to 1,200 per week, vaccinating them and keeping individual refugees at least five days in quarantine.[91] His deputy refused to accept such changes, noting that 'such limitations would disrupt their return, which would be harmful to the refugees themselves and to the state which pays for the apparatus of the return.'[92] Mass repatriation continued unabated until the issue of epidemics spilled out into the Lithuanian press. In May 1922 *Lietuvos žinios* wrote:

> The government announced the civil mobilisation of doctors to fight contagious diseases. Well, we will mobilise against the diseases, which can kill more than a battlefield. But we will ask the medical authorities for one thing: don't infect us with contagious diseases ... Refugees are returning. They are bringing to us directly from Russia or from quarantine in Obeliai infectious diseases.[93]

Similar press stories not only helped to form a negative public image of the refugees, but also vilified them in the eyes of the Lithuanian society. The refugees found it increasingly difficult to counter their image as bearers of disease, which undoubtedly further limited their integration and contacts with local communities. Official correspondence demonstrates the close association that was made between the 'threat of epidemic disease' and 'refugees'. In fact, both terms came to be used almost interchangeably. One report that landed on the desk of Skipitis read:

> Please find attached a separate report with regard to the typhus epidemic in the Obeliai quarantine. We ask you, sir, to urgently undertake strict measures to battle this approaching and dangerous misfortune of our nation ... A Jewish hospital alone contains 50 infected patients. Due to the fact that spotted fever is increasingly spreading among refugees, doctors tend to think that the source of infection is the quarantine in Obeliai.[94]

The Ministry of the Interior tried to limit the consequences of the epidemic by temporarily suspending further transportation of the refugees from Moscow to Obeliai in December 1922.[95] At the same time the government responded to the public outcry by introducing a number of modest reforms in the process of repatriation. It further limited the freedom of refugees by imposing stricter controls not only on their identities, but also on their bodies.

The weakest link in the repatriation system was its central institution, the quarantine in Obeliai. As Sutkus recalls, 'refugees of one or another brand, all of them had to become submissive sheep in the quarantine, if they wanted to find a home in Lithuania. Some of them were "cut with scissors", others "shaved with razors", while some were "left without their tails".'[96] Obeliai became not only a major refugee-processing centre, but also the place where those who arrived in their thousands attracted scores of local black-marketers, who traded in refugees' belongings and offered to exchange currency.[97]

In the middle of 1921 the Ministry was forced to undertake several inspections of the quarantine, which revealed serious deficiencies in its internal organization, funding and administration as well as the style of work of some officials. In June the head of the Sanitation Department of the quarantine, Juškys, reported that 'disinfections do not reach their purpose here.'[98] The shortage of necessary facilities and the great numbers of arriving refugees (often more than 1,000 people at a time) made disinfections a symbolic gesture only. It was impossible to isolate sick families or refugees from the healthy ones. He suggested leaving in Obeliai only a refugee transfer centre and proposed to establish a separate quarantine without any additional functions of political control.

In July the Ministry sent its representative to Obeliai to clarify the situation. He reported:

> I have to say that misunderstandings here became customary from the very beginning. ... I think the reason is that until now there were no clear instructions established on the limits of the competency of the director of quarantine and the personnel of the sanitation department ... Because the director was not a doctor, he didn't think it is a matter of greater importance to provide refugees with water, boiled water, washstands and laundries ... In Obeliai now there is no quarantine in the true sense of the word. It is rather a refugee transfer point with a hospital, barracks and dispensary. At the moment it does not protect the country from contagious diseases, and its significance is more political than sanitary.[99]

These problems continued into late 1921. The sauna stopped working, was repaired, burned to the ground and rebuilt for a second time in the fall. The disinfection chamber was out of action for an entire month because there were no thermometers, while 'there were several cases in which clothing was taken from the chamber infected with live lice'. The carcasses of slaughtered cattle were not buried properly, but instead dumped into a local lake serving as a source of drinking water for many refugees.[100] There were numerous cases of refugees stealing unattended personal belongings of others. One barbed-wire fence was not sufficient to prevent illegal trading in the quarantine (Skipitis objected on humanitarian grounds to the erection of a second fence). Finally, the LMI came to the conclusion that the only way to stop the outbreak of epidemics was to disinfect the quarantine itself between: old wooden beds were to be 'ripped out and washed with disinfecting substances.'[101]

Thus the Lithuanian authorities found themselves increasingly overwhelmed by the flow of refugees. This was especially evident in government's inability to provide at least basic medical services to the ailing bodies of the refugees, due to different administrative divisions between various state institutions as well as to a chronic shortage of necessary resources. The outbreak of epidemics across the borders of the region's successor states hampered the work of officials and contributed to the negative image of refugees as 'bearers of contagious diseases' in Lithuanian society. The fact that in 1921–2 the percentage of non-Lithuanian refugees increased in comparison with the early period of repatriation served as an additional reason for the government to tighten its immigration policies. At the same time the refugees felt increasingly vulnerable not only to political, but also to sanitary state control. The quarantine in Obeliai exemplified state efforts of 'fixing' not only the political or national loyalties of refugees, but also their bodies.

CONCLUSIONS

Between 1918 and 1924 approximately 350,000 refugees, originally from Lithuania and comprising diverse ethnic and social groups, made their way to independent Lithuania. The repatriation of Lithuanian refugees from the former Russian empire should be interpreted not only in the immediate context of civil and interstate wars but also in the context of different processes of state-formation. The continuing frontier wars meant that the population displacement did not stop in 1918 but continued until and beyond the refugees' return to their new political homeland. Government repatriation policies thus primarily reflected the political need to create and shape the category of the 'Lithuanian refugees' according to the will of the repatriation officials. Generally, after a brief period of 'spontaneous' repatriation, beginning in 1922, the official policies with respect to non-Lithuanian refugees assumed an increasingly rigid character. This reflected not only the nature of the political change in independent Lithuania, which from 1923 was ruled by the right-wing Christian Democratic government, but also the increasing nationalizing attempts of the state bureaucracy to rid Lithuania of the heritage of the multi-ethnic Russian empire. It also testified to the changing nationality policies of the government, which from 1923–4 increasingly came to believe that those liberal rights that had been secured for national minorities in 1918 should be rescinded.[102]

The logic of the homogenizing national state required that the refugees had to be persuaded or forced to abandon their divergent and multiple identities born in exile and to become 'rooted' in the exclusive space of the national homeland. Nevertheless, the spatial pattern of the 'homeland' was still in flux, due to the border wars between Lithuania, Soviet Russia and Poland in 1918–20. As a result some refugees, such as those from Vilno and Grodno, were excluded from the ranks of the Lithuanian citizenry. Their difficult situation was further aggravated by famine in Russia in 1921, which resulted in at least limited international cooperation between Soviet Russia, Lithuania, Poland and Latvia. Thus, on the one hand, the refugees served as a focus for the propaganda of the belligerent states, while on the other hand their uncontrollable movement compelled governments to cooperate internationally.

If the early official policies of the Ministry of the Interior were relatively liberal, after mid 1922 they became more conservative and rigid, reflecting the general tendency of interwar Lithuanian politics. In 1922 the outbreak of contagious diseases, inefficiency and corruption of the repatriation system, together with an unstable economic situation, contributed to the tendency that certain non-Lithuanian groups of refugees (mostly Jews) became vilified in the eyes of the public and some political groups. The refugees, increasingly perceived as a harmful foreign element, were seen as a potential threat to the country's stability. This was reflected in the government's tougher repatriation policies, based predominantly on the ethnic background of refugees, and led to decreasing numbers of non-Lithuanian – as opposed to ethnic Lithuanian – refugees arriving in Lithuania.

For many refugees their first encounters with the symbols and institutions of an independent Lithuanian state were crucial in shaping their 'fixed' national, as opposed to 'itinerant' multicultural, identities. However, refugees still read and interpreted those symbols of state power in the light of their experience of displacement. Further work is required to establish to what extent the refugees were assimilated into Lithuanian society or remained marginalized and excluded.

TABLE 1: Population displaced from Lithuania to Russia during World War One

Population displaced from Lithuania to Russia during World War One		Displaced persons who returned from the former Russian empire to Lithuania after World War One		Displaced persons who did not return to Lithuania from the former Russian empire
		1918–19	1920–1	
Lithuanians	250,000	150,000	65,000	35,000
Jews	160,000	35,000	45,000	80,000
Russians	90,000	30,000	5,000	55,000
Poles and others	50,000	30,000	5,000	15,000
Total:	550,000	245,000	120,000	185,000

Source: Rapolas Skipitis, *Nepriklausomą Lietuvą statant* [Building an Independent Lithuania], Chicago, Terra, 1961, p. 265.

Table 2: Return of refugees and others to Lithuania after World War One

Year	Refugees from the former Russian empire	War prisoners from Western Europe	Refugees from England	Hostages	Total number
1918	60,000	–	–	–	60,000
1919	32,000	8,000	–	–	40,000
1920	34,000	4,000	3,900	60	41,960
1921	69,728	–	–	–	69,728
Total:	195,728	12,000	3,900	60	211,688

Source: 'Tremtinių grįžimas' in *Lietuvos žinios* [Lithuanian News], Kaunas, (25) 28 March 1922, p. 3.

5
Population Displacement and Citizenship in Poland, 1918–24

Konrad Zielinski

This chapter deals with Polish emigrants, repatriates and refugees in Russia who after 1918 sought to settle or resettle in their newly independent 'homeland' during its first years of statehood. It also considers the non-Poles, displaced by revolution, war and shifting borders, who sought to make their home in the independent state. The main focus is on policymaking in the new Poland, its underlying principles and implementation at both central and local level. I approach the question of Polish policy towards displaced persons from the perspective of their claims to citizenship, and examine the circumstances under which newcomers were or were not granted citizenship and thus membership of the new national community. The first section examines aspects of nationality politics, drawing attention to an emerging Polish nationalist hostility towards non-Polish minorities. In the second section of the chapter I consider the legal framework that was developed to define rights to citizenship and residency. In section three I turn to issues of interpretation and implementation, demonstrating that the resettlement of population in independent Poland was especially bound up with political considerations relating to the Bolshevik revolution. The final section offers some preliminary remarks on the Russian presence in the eastern borderlands, which increased significantly as a result of population movements following World War One.

MIGRATION AND NATIONALITY POLITICS IN THE NEW POLAND

According to the first Polish census of 1921, which strongly overstated the relative predominance of Poles, the territory of the new state totalled 388,200 square kilometres and was inhabited by 27.2 million people.¹ Even according to these figures, the country was far from ethnic and national homogeneity: Poles made up 69 per cent of the total population, Ukrainians 14 per cent, Jews eight per cent, Belarusians four per cent and Germans four per cent. The remaining one per cent comprised Russians, Czechs, Lithuanians and others.² In the eastern voievodships,³ especially in the rural areas, the majority of the population were Ukrainians and Belarusians. In the Silesia and Poznań regions, there was a substantial number of Germans. Taking into consideration the new state's ethnic diversity, it is no wonder that nationality issues occupied such an important place in the political discourse of its leaders. The new Polish elite was divided into two main political camps, headed by Roman Dmowski and Józef Piłsudski. Dmowski, the leader of National Democracy (*Narodowa Demokracja*, or so-called *Endeks*), favoured incorporating areas inhabited by eastern Slavic peoples into the territory of a unitary Polish state. While he believed that the assimilation of Belarusians and Ukrainians was desirable, he rejected the notion of assimilating Germans (in the western provinces) and Jews. By contrast, Piłsudski and the Left envisioned a broad, federal Poland incorporating the eastern territories of the historic Polish–Lithuanian Commonwealth, which would 'grant their incipient nationalities wide autonomy, and encourage them to develop their national individuality – all as buffers against Russia.'⁴ By the early 1920s, Piłsudski's federal proposal had been nullified by the establishment of an independent Lithuanian state and the partition of Belarus and Ukraine. Dmowski's assimilationist ideology and nationalizing approach prevailed.

Here, I consider both the great return of refugees from the former Polish territories of the Russian Empire following World War One and the immigration of newcomers fleeing west from the Bolshevik revolution and Civil War. A study of the Lublin voievodship during the first few years of independence allows us to make certain generalizations about the relationship between Poland's emerging nationalities policy and contemporary migrations. Lublin voievodship represents a valuable case study because of its great ethnic and religious diversity (many Ukrainians and Russians in particular lived in the Chełm and Podlasie regions of this province). In addition, Lublin voievodship was the area most strongly affected by war and population displacements in the years 1914–18. In other ways, however, Lublin may be taken as representative of all Polish provinces. After the end of World War One many people – Poles, Ukrainians, Russians and others – returned, or tried to return, to Poland and to secure citizenship of the new state. Official actions such as those undertaken in administrative sub-units of the Lublin voievodship, and those registered by the central administration in Warsaw, took place across all voievodships of the new national state, and the legislation, regulations and procedures for registration were the same everywhere.

Before November 1918, virtually no one was refused permission to enter the territory of the Kingdom of Poland. This relatively open and liberal policy was governed by several assumptions. First, although not yet independent, Poles sought to assert themselves as the real rulers of their country, to recruit these people to serve the Polish cause, and to distinguish themselves from the German occupying authorities, who did not want to accept a mass influx of poor refugees and repatriates to the Kingdom of Poland. Second, Polish anti-Bolshevism had not yet become the overwhelming national preoccupation. Finally, the Polish authorities of the Kingdom and the autonomous authorities in Galicia and the Poznań region were too weak to counter the mass influx of newcomers.

However, as Polish officials became stronger and less dependent on the Germans and Austrians, they began to introduce restrictions and conditions on resettlement. Already by the end of 1918 they were openly discriminating against Jews. Jews were now perceived as the 'pioneers of Communism', and every Jewish returnee or immigrant as a potential traitor, saboteur or partisan.[5] This attitude drew upon a deep well of anti-Semitism. In addition, the fact that a small number of Jews had made fortunes by supplying the Central Powers' armies during 1915–18 caused considerable resentment towards them within Polish society.[6] Of course, only a tiny minority of Jews had profited from the occupation, while the vast majority had been subjected to the same hardships and inconveniences as the rest of the population.[7] The economic crisis following the war intensified competition between Poles and Jews in trade and business; this, compounded by the Polish–Soviet war of 1920, produced a marked rise in anti-Semitism in Poland.[8] This, in turn, influenced the attitudes of the Polish authorities towards Jewish emigrants from Russia. Greeted with open hostility, large numbers of Jews regarded their stay in Poland as purely temporary while they waited for entry visas to Canada, the United States, Palestine and other countries.[9]

By the terms of the Polish–Soviet Peace Treaty, signed in Riga in March 1921, certain non-Polish citizens of the former Russian Empire could opt for Polish citizenship, provided they did so in the presence of a high-ranking official of the Polish state. This applied mainly to Russians, Lithuanians and 'Ruthenians' (the term sometimes used for Ukrainians and Belarusians in eastern Poland) returning to their former homes or seeking refuge in Poland during these years. Although these groups provoked much less hostility than Jews, they still attracted a good deal of police surveillance, in particular those who could not prove that their stay in Russia was unconnected with supporting the Bolsheviks, but was rather caused by personal matters or difficulties in contacting Polish diplomats or refugee organizations. In principle, people who had lived in the Kingdom of Poland before 1914–15 faced no difficulty returning to Poland, although Russians had to prove they had harboured no anti-Polish views during the tsarist period (see below). However, as we shall see, many found it difficult – in many cases impossible – to reclaim their abandoned homestead or employment. In practice, much depended on the attitude of the local authorities.[10]

Apart from Petliura's soldiers, allies of Poland in the war of 1920,[11] Ukrainians also faced increasing problems in obtaining the right to remain in Poland. This was especially difficult for people who had been active in nationalistic parties and organizations in Eastern Galicia or the Chełm and Podlasie regions (which Germany and Austria had planned at Brest-Litovsk, in 1918, to transfer from Poland to Ukraine). Generally, the authorities did not create special obstacles for Czechs, Germans or Lithuanians who planned to settle in Poland, although the situation was quite different for Lithuanians in Vilna and Białystok voievodships. Nor did the Polish government hinder the return and settlement of people declaring themselves to be Belarusians. Indeed, many Polish officials denied the existence of a Belarusian nationality and considered Belarusians to be 'almost Poles', and suitable for assimilation into the Polish national community.[12] Of course, the Poles only granted such liberal treatment to people without a 'suspicious political past'.

THE LEGAL FRAMEWORK

Although Poland fell into the hands of the Central Powers between 1915 and 1918, this did not prevent its national leaders from considering the question of who would be granted citizenship of a prospective independent Polish state after the war.[13] Their deliberations on this issue, however, took place in the context of the significant wartime displacement of population from occupied Poland to the interior of Russia.[14] In 1917, the Polish Temporary Council of State (*Tymczasowa Rada Stanu*), which laid claim to the status of a national government during the German and Austrian occupation of the Kingdom of Poland, issued a draft law on citizenship. This proposed conferring automatic Polish citizenship on all those who had left the Kingdom of Poland after 1 August 1914, and who either returned to their former place of residence within a year after a future armistice, or notified the communal authorities of their intention to do so. Different regulations applied to those who had left the territory of the Kingdom of Poland before 14 August 1914, mainly comprising Poles born and living in Russia, such as political deportees and their families (the so-called *Sybiracy*), as well as the non-Polish spouses of those who were Polish citizens: these categories would have to apply for citizenship.[15] This draft legislation was but one of several attempts by the Temporary Council of State to resolve the issue of citizenship. However, neither the Temporary Council nor the Regent's Council (*Rada Regencyjna*) had introduced a citizenship bill to the National Assembly by the time the war ended.

As might be expected, the question of Polish citizenship aroused a great deal of controversy and confusion in the initial phase of independence. Most significantly, the borders of the new state had yet to be secured. In this period, the country faced genuine external threats to its independence, in particular with the Red Army's invasion in the summer of 1920. It was beaten back from the very gates of Warsaw, and a Treaty signed on 18 March 1921, but there was no definitive resolution of the border question until 1922.

In addition, the structure of the new state was far from uniform, not least because three different legal systems coexisted on its territory. These were a legacy of partition, and posed considerable challenges for codifying a new national law. Moreover, the Treaty of Versailles and subsequent military action in Lithuania (the so-called Żeligowski revolt)[16] led to the incorporation of ethnically non-Polish territories into the new Polish state, and the Polish authorities trod extremely cautiously when it came to granting citizenship to people of non-Polish origin.[17] Right-wing politicians, notably those associated with the National Democrats, gave vent to fears that certain national groups were inherently disloyal towards the new Polish state.[18] Neither centrist nor leftist politicians had definite views on the subject. The issue first arose in respect of non-Poles, who as a result of the Armistice of 11 November 1918 and the subsequent border settlement of 1922 found themselves living on Polish territory. But it also concerned non-Polish repatriates and refugees from Soviet Russia, who wished to obtain right of permanent residence in Poland.

The entire process of codification of the legal system was delayed by recurrent political instability between 1918 and 1926, during which more than a dozen cabinets came and went.[19] After the end of World War One, the government presented several immigration regulations to parliament. The first of these, introduced in January 1920, was the most controversial.[20] It granted Polish citizenship to people who possessed no other citizenship, and were currently living on Polish territory. A person was regarded as a resident of Polish territory if he or she satisfied one of the following conditions:

1. they had been registered or had been entitled to be registered in the registrars' files of permanent residents of the Kingdom of Poland (i.e. before the Russian evacuation in 1915);

2. they had enjoyed the right of *swojszczyzna*, i.e. had been a member of a community (not necessary Polish) formerly incorporated into the Austrian Empire;
3. they had lived permanently in those parts of Polish territory which before the war were within Prussia, as holders of German citizenship before 1 January 1908 (this referred to residents of Silesia and the Poznań region);
4. they had belonged to a community or class organization (*stan*) in territories of the former Russian Empire that now formed part of the Polish state.[21]

The interpretation of this bill gave rise to many problems, and created numerous opportunities for unfair practice. It implied that the Polish government had no interest in granting citizenship to certain national and religious groups, notably Jews and Ukrainians and, in some parts of the country, Lithuanians and Germans. Whether or not the Polish legal authorities deliberately set out in 1920 to exclude these minorities, it is clear that the restrictive definition of persons entitled to Polish citizenship failed to meet the needs of many potential claimants. Despite all controversies, this bill became law (as the Citizenship Bill, enacted by the Sejm on 20 January 1920).[22]

By way of illustrating the bias inherent in this legislation, let us consider the clauses relating to permanent residents of the former Kingdom of Poland and the Russian Empire. If a new-born child was registered with a considerable delay or not registered at all–something not uncommon, particularly among Jews and peasants, people who would have been entitled to citizenship as categories 1 and 4 went unrecorded and were therefore excluded. To make matters worse, many registrars' files had been lost or destroyed during World War One. This caused immense problems for a great number of immigrants who needed to prove that they had been permanently resident in the defined territories before 1918. If we also bear in mind the antipathy of some Polish civil servants towards certain ethnic minorities, it is plain to see how difficult it could be to prove an individual's right to Polish citizenship.[23] As one might expect in the case of lost registrars' files, it was very difficult to claim Polish citizenship for persons who were not of Polish ethnic origin.[24] Unsympathetic Polish officials could all too easily call into question such claimants' rights to citizenship and frequently discriminated against their applications because they were believed to be 'unsuitable'.[25] The new Poland, as Rogers Brubaker writes, 'was conceived as the state *of* and *for* the ethnolinguistically (and ethnoreligiously) defined Polish nation, in part because it was seen as made *by* this nation against the resistance of Germans, Ukrainians, and Jews. A clear distinction was universally drawn between this Polish nation and the total citizenry of the state.'[26] However, practices varied sharply. For example, as I have already mentioned, the assimilation of Ukrainians (especially those living outside Galicia) was viewed as desirable, and Belarusians were also considered as potential candidates for membership of the Polish nation and for Polish citizenship.[27] On the other hand, very few spoke in favour of the assimilation of Jews.

German diplomats pointed out that in many respects this legislation contradicted the Treaty of Versailles.[28] According to the Treaty, every person of German citizenship living permanently in any part of Polish territory was entitled to Polish citizenship. German authorities argued that the 'place of residence' of eligible applicants should not be restricted to the former Prussian territories (Silesia and Poznań), as the Polish law of 1920 stipulated. Many German citizens, after all, lived in the great industrial centre of Łódź, but they were to be excluded from citizenship by the provisions of the law. These controversial provisions, and their relationship to the Treaty of Versailles, could not be resolved by Polish and German diplomats, and the case had to be decided by the League of Nations and the Permanent Court of Justice in The Hague. The argument was only settled in 1924 by the so-called Viennese Convention. According to the Convention's regulations, and in accordance with German demands, Germans and Poles currently living in Germany who claimed domicile (that is, permanent residence) on any part of the territory of Poland could claim Polish citizenship. The Convention also allowed applicants to claim two places of permanent residence. It was sufficient to declare one of them in Poland in order to obtain citizenship (remarkably, it was unnecessary for the claimant even to be living in Poland at the time of making the application). In the Vienna Convention, Germany and Poland established 1 July 1926 as the deadline for making applications for Polish citizenship. After that date the Polish government could deport people of non-Polish citizenship. The implementation of these regulations proved to be a constant source of controversy during the interwar period.[29]

A different solution of the problem was adopted in the Polish–Russian Treaty signed in Riga on 18 March 1921. According to point 2, part IV of the Treaty, former citizens of the Russian Empire who were at least eighteen years old on the date the Treaty was signed, and who stayed in Russia at the moment of ratification of the Treaty, but who were registered or had the right to be registered in the registrars' files of residents of the Kingdom of Poland, were to be regarded as Polish citizens. The Treaty gave them until April 1922 to apply for Polish citizenship, but their application was only valid if a Polish diplomat, ambassador, consul or other representative of the Polish state had approved it.[30] Thus, a diplomat was 'the first instance': every application required his signature and approval, and the declaration was then sent to the relevant department in the Foreign Office (*Ministerstwo Spraw Zagranicznych*).[31]

In practice, however, the Polish government discriminated vigorously against certain categories of people and favoured others, especially in the eastern voivodships (Volynia, Polesie and Eastern Galicia). In these regions, home to many non-Poles, the complex ethnic differentiation and the proximity of the Polish-Soviet border posed acute difficulties for Polish nationalist opinion. The government and local authorities often issued temporary regulations that supplemented legislation. Quite often, because of the tense domestic political situation, those regulations had a more restrictive character. Indeed, as we shall see, in conditions of growing nationalist sentiment they invariably tended to acquire permanent form.[32]

REGULATIONS AND PRACTICE

The re-emigration and immigration of both Poles and non-Poles from Russia continued throughout the occupation of Poland by Germany and Austria. Despite this, in 1918 huge numbers of Polish soldiers, POWs and refugees still found themselves on Soviet-held territory.[33] Although it is unlikely we shall ever find precise figures for the total of returnees and immigrants to Poland in subsequent years, it is clear that the pool of potential Polish citizens remaining abroad was considerable.

From March 1918, when Soviet Russia withdrew from the war, the number of these individuals returning to Poland grew so great that the occupying forces issued special decrees to regulate it. Nevertheless, the mass influx continued. According to official Polish statistics, during the period 1918–22, 1,198,043 people arrived in Poland from the lands of the former Russian Empire. Of this total, 40.1 per cent declared themselves to be Belarusians; 37.1 per cent, Poles; 10.1 per cent, Ukrainians; 10.0 per cent, Russians; and 2.7 per cent, Jews.[34] It is very likely, however, that in fact there were far fewer Belarusians and a far larger number of Jews. According to the historian Jerzy Kumaniecki, 1.1 million Polish citizens returned to Poland between April 1921 and April 1924 (including about 15–25 per cent Poles and about 65 per cent Ukrainians and Belarusians), and by 1925 the total number of Polish citizens who had been repatriated from the Soviet Union stood at 1,265,000.[35] It is clear from these figures that the precise number of immigrants cannot be determined with any accuracy. For one thing, not all of those who were either returning to their former homes in Poland or escaping from revolutionary Russia were ever registered. To be sure, some Poles and others reached Warsaw and other large towns, where they were probably counted by immigration officials. But many migrants crossed the border illegally. This practice became more extensive after November 1918 as, on the one hand, increasing numbers of Poles in Russia, disillusioned with Soviet reality, decided to leave Russia, while, on the other hand, the Polish government sought to stem the inflow of re-emigrants by refusing to issue them with entry visas.[36]

How easy was it for these returnees to undertake the long journey to the new Poland? Both the territorial immensity of the Soviet state, as well as continuing military operations, made it impossible for all of those who wished to travel to Poland to reach Polish border posts, consulates or welfare and repatriation committees in the interior of Russia. Some migrants, of course, could scarcely have heard of the Treaty of Riga, not to mention its regulations on citizenship. We can also assume that in many cases local Bolshevik officials made it impossible for potential citizens of Poland to declare their intention to seek citizenship, as described above.[37] Besides, many people who had been affiliated with anti-Bolshevik organizations and military formations were afraid to disclose their identities for fear of Bolshevik repression. On the other hand, to cross the border illegally was a risky venture that was certain to arouse the suspicion of the Polish authorities.

The Polish government itself created difficulties for returning migrants. Officials deliberately raised procedural objections, for example by finding petty errors in the application forms that some people submitted. In some cases, the authorities threatened these unfortunate applicants with deportation. Heedless of the fourth clause of the 1920 law, some people still encountered problems with obtaining citizenship. As late as August 1926, the Ministry of Internal Affairs issued a circular to voievodship governors, stating that although the borders of Poland had been demarcated, the citizenship of the majority of inhabitants of the Białystok, Brest Litovsk, Łuck, Nowogródek and Vilno regions remained unresolved. The 'explanation' offered was that communal registrars' files from those regions had either been taken to Russia or lost, making it impossible for prospective applicants to present the necessary documents for validation of their claim. The only course of action open to them was to embark on a prolonged and tedious attempt to prove their *bona fide* origin. This applied to a few thousands of people of non-Polish origin, Orthodox clergy, Russian landlords, tsarist officials and military officers, mainly Russians and Ukrainians. In the long run this situation proved awkward for the state itself: for example, these people and their sons, as non-citizens, could not be called up to serve in the Polish army. Finally, although the 1925–6 special decrees (which were, in effect, supplementary to the 1920 regulations), created provisions for summarily granting Polish citizenship to categories of people who could prove that they had been permanent inhabitants of a given community, the final decision belonged to the voievodship governors, who could exclude some persons (such as well-known anti-Polish activists or criminals) from the scope of these decrees.[38]

Polish practice towards refugees and emigrants was not, of course, always in harmony with the legal principles upon which it rested. It is clear, for one thing, that the authorities discriminated in favour of certain categories of people. After 1918, tens of thousands of people, fearing Bolshevik repression, sought refuge in Poland. Initially, the Polish authorities looked favourably upon them, issued them with so-called 'emigrant passports' and admitted them to Poland. Holders of emigrant passports intended in the main to stay in Poland only briefly, in transit to other countries, for example, the United States, Canada, Argentina or Palestine (many of these emigrants were Jewish), so the Polish government believed there to be no danger that these people would remain indefinitely in Poland. Such passports were issued until July 1921, when the Polish-Russian border was closed.[39] At this time, however, the situation changed, as the United States and other countries introduced quota systems and other measures to limit immigration.[40] In response, the Polish government refused to issue further emigrant passports and tried to deport those individuals holding this status whom it regarded as undesirable.[41] Despite these actions, people continued to escape across the border from Bolshevik Russia. The plight of refugees in Poland immediately became a *cause celèbre*. In Poland, several newspapers (mainly the Jewish and leftist press) loudly criticized the government's attitude towards refugees. In the West, emigrants' organizations similarly condemned the new Polish policy. The following month, a League of Nations conference held in Geneva on 22–24 August directed the Polish government to cease its practice of expelling refugees from its territory, passing a resolution stating that 'refugees from Russia cannot be forced to leave Poland and sent back'. The Polish government, however, refused to implement this resolution, and the deportation of refugees continued.[42]

Which categories of people were regarded as 'undesirable', and what methods were used to force them to leave Poland? First of all, each and every newcomer from the Soviet side of the border was obliged to register either in the place of their former residence (if he or she had previously lived or had been born on Polish territory) or in their place of destination. The local authorities were instructed to inform the police if any unregistered individuals were found to be staying in the community.[43] Meanwhile, those refugees who registered had to surrender their passports and were issued with temporary identity cards, which made travelling very difficult for them. This practice contravened the law, and foreign diplomatic representatives in Poland sometimes appealed to the Foreign Ministry on behalf of their citizens.[44] The local authorities were also responsible for submitting to the police monthly reports on every newcomer. These assessments placed particular stress on 'the individual's political views and loyalty /disloyalty towards the Polish state.'[45] People who had 'voluntarily' enlisted in a foreign military service (meaning in this instance, of course, the Red Army), who had assumed foreign citizenship and had concealed the fact from the authorities, or who had left the Polish Army, were refused the right to apply for Polish citizenship. In practice, Jews were most likely to fall foul of the last provision, being labelled deserters.[46] The authorities were more lenient towards holders of foreign citizenship, however, acknowledging in particular that many Poles and other nationalities in Soviet Russia had been coerced into adopting Russian citizenship by the Bolshevik authorities. Many of these migrants were allowed to renounce their foreign citizenship in writing and then to apply for Polish passports.[47]

Registered immigrants were obliged regularly to report to the local police station or to the local authorities; those who failed to present themselves at the appointed time were also subject to deportation.[48] In practice, deportation could be postponed to allow for an appeal to be heard. For instance, Nansen on occasion appealed to the Polish authorities on behalf of Russian citizens.[49] Such interventions often proved to be effective.

As mentioned above, the Polish authorities before the end of 1918, at least formally, made no real distinction among immigrants of different nationalities. To be sure, they were much more willing to assist Polish repatriates and re-emigrants than they were to help former tsarist officers, Orthodox peasants or Jews. However, after November 1918 newcomers from behind the eastern border were informally divided into two categories, as we can infer from special instructions and circulars. The first category consisted of Poles who had migrated to Russia before or during the war and who wished to return. Poles who had been forced to leave the country during the Russian retreat in 1915 also fell into this category. With certain exceptions (such as criminals), such persons could settle freely in Poland. Sometimes the military authorities or the border guard suggested to the local police a place of settlement where a person could be more easily put under surveillance (this particularly applied to political refugees). Such individuals usually reported to the police every three days; they also had to inform officials about every change of address and job, and about every journey they wished to undertake (since they needed special passes). The term of surveillance varied: from weeks to 2–3 years.[50]

The second category consisted of Jews, Ukrainians and Russians (Belarusians were sometimes also included in this category). This category was divided into sub-categories. The first sub-category comprised people who were entitled to hold Polish citizenship because of their place of residence before the war; the second concerned those who did not have that right. Those belonging to the first sub-category were allowed to settle, but were put under surveillance. Those belonging to the second were suspected of crossing the border illegally, and were discouraged from settling in Poland. The authorities usually applied for such persons to be expelled.[51] People threatened with deportation tried to bribe officials, and sent individual or collective appeals to high-ranking officials and governors or to the Sejm. Sometimes it helped, but more often the authorities were deaf to such efforts.[52]

In order to avoid discrimination, many Jews attempted to register themselves as Russians.[53] The Polish authorities, however, did their best to thwart this practice. In September 1921 the local council in Siedlce learned from the Government Commissioner of Warsaw (*Komisarz Rządowy*, at this time the highest authority in Warsaw) that 156 Russian citizens, 'all of them Jews', planned to arrive in Siedlce under instruction from authorities in the capital (most of them were waiting for United States or Canadian visas). The local councillors protested on the grounds that their town was already overpopulated. They added that 'Russian Jews did not know Polish and paid with Russian roubles'. They urged that those who had not yet been granted their American or Canadian visas should be deported back to Russia, to wait for their new visas there.[54]

Sometimes international Jewish organizations such as the American Joint Distribution Committee helped these groups with obtaining visas or getting funds for the journey. Thanks to this aid, about 80,000 Jews left Poland before 1922, mainly for North America.[55] However, as we read in a report of Conjoint (The Anglo–American Jewish Committee) of 1922, 'there are over 35,000 Jews who have illegally crossed the borders into Poland, many of them with no possible chance of entering Canada or the United States, or of returning to Russia.'[56] Sooner or later these people left the territory of Poland, but some of them were forced to live a life of uncertainty for years.[57]

Emigrants or refugees from Russia who wanted to settle in Poland had to declare either that they had sufficient funds to support themselves or that they could count on the help of relatives in Poland.[58] The local authorities checked the veracity of these statements, but this was a complicated and time-consuming procedure. Besides, the legacy of war made it less likely that refugees could truthfully claim to be self-sufficient. The farms they had suddenly abandoned during the war had always been small, but now the refugees found their property diminished further – during their absence, buildings had been burned down and the military had requisitioned the livestock. This applied especially to homes situated close to the front and in regions where the Russian army had adopted scorched-earth tactics during its retreat in 1915. Often whole villages had been evacuated, with the peasants leaving no one to look after their farms.[59] It was possible also that a Polish neighbour or a new settler had already taken over a farm that had originally belonged to the returning migrant. In these cases the new occupant might exert pressure on the local authorities to undervalue the farm. If they did so, the farm could not be regarded as a source of income sufficient for the needs of the original owner, and the authorities were entitled to sell the farm to the usurper. However, these situations were rare, and despite the propaganda being spread by certain groups (especially by Ukrainian and Belarusian nationalists and Bolsheviks), there is no reason to believe that the Polish authorities made particular efforts to expropriate Ukrainian or Jewish farmers.[60]

THE 'CHARACTER' OF THE REFUGEE

The new Polish state carefully scrutinized the character of its potential citizens. On 13 February 1924, the Ministry of Interior Affairs announced and published in the official press its Citizenship Regulations (*Przepisy o obywatelstwie*). According to these regulations, to obtain Polish citizenship and secure the right to permanent residence in Poland, emigrants from the former Russian Empire had to satisfy four conditions:

1. A 'spotless' political reputation;
2. A 'spotless' moral reputation;
3. A 'proper' attitude towards Poles during the era of tsarist rule and during the period of occupation by the Central Powers (in particular, this applied to military and administrative officials);
4. Funds sufficient for living in Poland.[61]

All four conditions had to be met without exception by all those intending to return and settle and those seeking refuge in the territory of Poland, regardless of their nationality or religion. However, Poles and people of Polish origin were preferred. As I have mentioned above, ethnic non-Poles who had never lived in the territory of the Kingdom of Poland, Galicia or the Poznań region, had no right to Polish citizenship. They could only secure the so-called emigrant passport, which gave its holder the right of transit in Poland. To be sure, it was possible to extend the period of transit or even to change one's status. In practice, however, this was difficult to achieve.[62]

The first condition, a 'spotless' political reputation, meant having no Bolshevik sympathies and no connections with socialist and communist parties (and sometimes also having no connections with national Ukrainian movements). Anyone with known leftist views could encounter discrimination.

Polish antagonism towards Bolshevism is easy enough to understand. This, after all, was a period of hostility and tension between Poland and Soviet Russia. Even after the Polish – Soviet War of 1920, emergency powers remained in force in some districts of the eastern voievodships in order to deal with espionage and potential anti-Polish activity. The tense relationship between Poles and Ukrainians in Eastern Galicia (developing even before the hostilities erupted in Lvov in November 1918) also forced the authorities there to retain a state of emergency. Endless attacks on Polish manors and military settlers' colonies by Ukrainians and, on the other hand, the frequent 'pacification' of Ukrainian villages by Polish troops, worsened the situation. Soviet Russia, for its part, welcomed and strove to intensify this lack of stability and atmosphere of uncertainty in Poland's eastern borderlands.[63] Indeed, throughout this period the Bolsheviks pursued an active policy of destabilization in these territories, despatching agents to conduct illegal agitation and espionage and to recruit and aid local underground communists.[64]

Jews, in particular, fell victim to the widespread spy-mania in Polish society; their itinerant occupations especially exposed them to accusations of espionage. It is true that many Jews, particularly in eastern Poland, did join the Red Army or Soviet administration during the war of 1920.[65] However, because of anti-Semitism in Poland, to which the severe economic crisis gave added impetus, the Polish police subjected almost all Jews without exception to close scrutiny.[66] In correspondence between the voievodship and local authorities of the provincial town of Tomaszów Lubelski, one reads that: 'In truth, we have no reason to suspect our Jews of Bolshevism; however, we must still be very careful with them.'[67]

Did the Polish authorities, then, favour immigrants with established anti-Bolshevik credentials? At first, many Russian and Ukrainian refugees considered their stay in Poland temporary. They wanted to create an anti-Bolshevik army that would in due course liberate Russia and Ukraine from Bolshevik rule. With this objective, they maintained contacts with other emigrants' organizations in Europe, organized paramilitary formations and tried to set up an intelligence service inside Soviet Russia. Initially, the Polish authorities tolerated such organizations and, in general, looked favourably on the Russian émigré community in Poland, which was wealthy and conservative and was unlikely to be 'contaminated' with left-wing sympathies.[68] Towards the end of the 1920s, however, when Poland's relations with Soviet Russia began to normalize, the government took measures to limit or ban anti-Bolshevik activities based on its territory. In any case, once the émigrés stopped believing in the possibility of any restoration of 'Great Russia', their political and social activity decreased significantly. For Russian émigrés such as the prominent intellectual

Boris Savinkov, Poland was transformed from merely a temporary place of refuge at the beginning of his exile to a second homeland.[69] Besides, the economic crisis after World War One forced the émigrés to deal with financial rather than political matters. By the time of the Polish elections of 1928 and 1931, the Russian émigré population in Poland had all but ceased any cultural or political agitation.[70] During the 1930s, a stricter political regime and renewed economic crisis ensured their activities remained low-key.

The formal powers of the Polish police to monitor the activities of immigrants were augmented by a growing network of informal surveillance. Thus, in order to meet the first two conditions (a spotless political and moral reputation) a newcomer needed the evaluation of a neighbour and/or of the local authority as to their moral condition and political views. Only then could the individual obtain either permission for permanent residence in Poland or citizenship. If an applicant had previously been found guilty of some criminal offence and imprisoned or fined, his prospect of securing permission for residence or citizenship was significantly reduced. It appears that in such cases the Polish authorities did not apply the criterion of nationality. If this criminal past were detected, the individual was discredited automatically, regardless of his nationality or religion, increasing his chances of being deported.[71]

The local authorities paid particular attention to Russians who had been civil servants in the Kingdom of Poland before or during the world war. On their return to the independent Poland, these tsarist administrators, military officers, teachers and Orthodox clergy had to prove that they had always demonstrated a 'proper' attitude towards Poles before being permitted to apply for citizenship. However, many of these former officials still enjoyed high social status; many also were bound by family ties to Poland: some of them came from mixed marriages, others were the offspring of Polish exiles, who in the course of time had become russified.[72] So, at times even those who were known to have been anti-Polish before the war could often use acquaintances and business or social connections to obtain a positive assessment of their 'correct' attitudes towards Poles and Poland. If this turned out to be impossible, they would usually get a temporary or even permanent permit to stay in Poland. On the other hand, it might be difficult for them to find employment. For instance, in the district of Biała (Lublin voievodship), only two of a total of 22 teachers who were of Russian and Ukrainian origin and who had formerly taught in Russian schools in Poland were still employed in education in 1926. These former teachers, when asked why they were no longer working in their profession, most often answered that the local authorities did not allow them to do so.[73] The situation in other voievodships was quite similar. At least refugees who had been associated with the former tsarist government, education or military administration could count on significant aid from the Russian émigré community and from Petliura's organizations in Poland.[74] From the Polish point of view, the most important thing was that they did not pose any 'Bolshevik' threat. Still, they were usually forbidden to engage in political activity and were sometimes subjected to police surveillance.[75]

The fourth condition for citizenship stipulated that prospective Poles had to have sufficient funds to be able to maintain themselves in their new homeland. Given the dire economic circumstances that prevailed at this time, it is not difficult to understand why this condition was imposed. But this created an excellent opportunity for the practise of prejudice and discrimination. Many Ukrainians and Jews, for example, were unable to prove that they had a reliable and sufficient current source of income, even though they might have a professional qualification which gave them assured prospects for the future. Russian Jews seeking to settle in Siedlce were refused permission even for temporary residence, since they were deemed to lack sufficient funds. In this instance, the economic condition was no more than a pretext for prejudice: the local authorities urged the authorities in Warsaw to agree to the immediate expulsion of the Jews before 'they find a source of sufficient income'.[76] By contrast, Poles were less likely to face difficulties of this kind, although after the 1922 border settlement and with progressively deteriorating domestic economic conditions, even native Poles were sometimes unable to obtain permission to settle in Poland – even those who had established a 'politically and socially spotless reputation' – on the grounds that they had insufficient personal wealth and could not find relatives who might support them in Poland.[77]

Sometimes, however, the economic crisis could have the opposite effect. Thus, on occasion, the local Polish authorities would appeal for a non-Pole to be granted the right of abode (provided he had a 'spotless' political reputation), if his services were likely to be of use to the community. Refugees who worked as tailors, blacksmiths or millers could benefit from these provisions. Yet these situations were the exception rather than the rule.[78]

Russian POWs constituted a separate category. About 300,000 Russian POWs remained on German territory at the end of World War One. As the German authorities did nothing to hinder the departure of these prisoners, the Polish authorities had to deal with the problem of their transfer to Russia. Poland was a 'land of passage' for those people.[79] When they arrived in Poland, Russian POWs were helped by the Soviet Red Cross Mission, the Polish Red Cross and by the Committee for Protection of POWs.[80] But the outbreak of the Polish–Soviet War brought with it a fresh influx of Russian POWs, this time captives from the Red Army. They were sent to several prison camps, where the most severe problem was to ensure appropriate medical care and sanitary conditions. In November 1919 about 23,000 Soviet POWs (including more than 16,000 Ukrainians) were confined to these camps. By the end of the war there were still around 110,000 Russian POWs on Polish soil. The attitude of the Polish authorities towards POWs appears to have been relatively proper and no acts of cruelty were reported.[81]

Influenced by Polish agitation, some of these prisoners joined the Ukrainian troops of Semen Petliura and the anti-Bolshevik formations of Boris Peremykim and Stanisław Bułak-Bałachowicz.[82] The authorities planned also to recruit some of the POWs to the anti-Bolshevik troops which were being organized in Poland to fight alongside the Polish Army.[83] After the Red Army counteroffensive of summer 1920, the majority of these formations found themselves back on Polish territory where they were interned. Living conditions in the camps where these soldiers were kept were hardly better than in the camps for Red Army POWs. At the beginning of October 1920, as negotiations for a Peace Treaty were being finalized in Riga, Poland still held over 40,000 White Russian soldiers and Cossacks as internees. Soviet Russia attached great importance to the issue of anti-Bolshevik military formations existing in Poland, as is clear from Article II of the Polish–Bolshevik armistice signed on 12 October 1920. Under this paragraph, the Polish authorities were obliged to renounce their treaty with the Ukrainian People's Republic and to annul military and political agreements with other allies. Under pressure from the national parliament, Polish military authorities fixed 2 November 1920 as the deadline for non-Polish detachments to leave the territory of Poland. Finding themselves expelled in this way, these troops launched their own campaign against the Red Army in Ukraine and Belarus, but were rapidly beaten back by the Bolsheviks and retreated towards the Polish positions.[84] After their return, some of these anti-Soviet forces decided to leave Poland but not to go back to Soviet territory (many of them subsequently migrated to Czechoslovakia), having been indoctrinated in an anti-Soviet spirit by the Polish authorities and the Russian emigrant organizations.[85] Others resolved to remain in Poland. Some of the Soviet POWs also decided to settle in Poland, a problem that requires further and more detailed research.[86]

RUSSIANS IN POLESIE: AT HOME OR IN EXILE?

Before concluding this study, I wish to draw attention to the Russian minority in Polesie, one of the so-called eastern borderlands (*kresy*), and how its members sought to adjust to conditions in the newly independent state. The total population of Polesie in 1931 was 1,131,939. In the census of that year, the national composition of the population (native language being used as the determinant of national identity) was as follows: speakers of Polish, 14.5 per cent; of Ukrainian, 4.8 per cent; of Belarusian, 6.7 per cent; of Yiddish or Hebrew, ten per cent; of Russian, 1.4 per cent; and of a 'local' language, 62.4 per cent; the tiny residual population claimed German, Czech or other languages as their mother tongue.[87] There was a large number of native Russians in Polesie, but interwar Polish statistics made no distinction between the native Russian minority of the region and Russian re-emigrants and émigrés, who included officers and soldiers of the former tsarist army and members of the White Army.[88]

There were, however, marked differences between local Russians and Russian emigrants and refugees in their political sympathies and cultural and religious attitudes. The key to understanding the difference lay in a Russian saying: '*ia iz rodnoi zemli ne uezhal, eto ona ot menia uekhala*' ['I have not left my motherland, it is she who has left me'].[89] Indeed, although it is impossible to assess accurately the proportion of native Russians versus immigrants, many sources, including the Russian press and fragmentary Polish statistics on the populations of administrative units in this voievodship, implied that the majority of Russians in Polesie had not moved home. They had stayed where they were (apart from temporary dislocations during the war years) but found that the border had moved instead.[90] They represented the more quiescent part of the Russian population. On the other hand, the Russian émigrés were very active in social and cultural undertakings (establishing schools, cultural and economic societies, charity organizations, newspapers, etc.), and also became involved in local politics.[91] In the opinion of the Polish authorities, Russian émigré welfare organizations, schools, cultural and educational societies, political associations, secret youth and monarchist circles often became 'centres of Russian nationalism and chauvinism'.[92]

The situation in the Polesie voievodship aroused concern in Warsaw for another reason. As the census data shows, Polesie was home to an ethnically mixed native population, relatively few of whom had a clearly articulated sense of their 'nationality'. This population, mainly rural, was the object of indoctrination simultaneously by the Polish authorities and by Russian émigré organizations. Both sides were interested in the assimilation of the local population (which manifested little national consciousness of its own), in order to expand their influence in this territory.[93]

At the same time, the Polish authorities regularly pointed out that Russians in Polesie were to be found in large numbers amongst those who supported pro-Communist political movements in the region. Although many of them were actually Ukrainians and not Russians, this state of affairs prompted the Poles systematically to arrest and imprison local Russians.[94] However, we have to remember that Polesie region, which had a very significant number of non-Poles and bordered directly on the Soviet state, was a special case. The Poles feared, not without reason, that Bolshevik agitation was much easier here than in other regions (as we have already mentioned, the Polish authorities acknowledged that the Russian population of Poland as a whole, being relatively wealthy and conservative, posed no political danger). Against this background, Russians in Polesie found it extremely difficult to negotiate their place within the new social and political reality of postwar Poland. More work is needed to trace emerging forms of national identity and self-organization amongst the Russian-speaking population, their cultural and educational activity, political movements, participation in the local and parliamentary elections, and the collaboration between Polesie Russians and the Orthodox Church.[95]

CONCLUSIONS

During the period 1918–24, the new Poland embarked on the systematic 'nationalization' of the state, its administration and military forces, leaving few opportunities for non-Poles to participate.[96] In so doing, it was forced to accommodate, both physically on its territory and figuratively in its national community, numerous different categories of returnees and migrants, who in turn were impelled by different motives to seek to settle in the newly independent state.

Many non-Polish refugees, and those who were not entitled to hold Polish citizenship because of their prewar places of residence, offered as the reason for coming to Poland their 'fear of Bolsheviks' or their affiliation with anti-Bolshevik organizations.[97] However, many others (especially Jews and Ukrainian peasants) decided to return to Poland only after the end of the Polish–Soviet War, suggesting that they had initially welcomed aspects of the Bolshevik regime. Police reports confirm that many of them had served in the Red Army after October 1917. In the course of time disillusionment with the system in Russia had changed their minds, and they had decided either to return to Poland or to seek refuge there. The same gradual process of disillusionment can be observed in the case of Soviet POWs, some of whom decided to join anti-Bolshevik military units organized by Russians in Poland.[98] Meanwhile Polish re-emigrants and inhabitants of the Polish territories before 1914–15, all of whom were entitled to Polish citizenship, gave as reasons for wishing to return their fear of Bolshevism, the deserted farms and houses in Poland and a desire to be reunited with their families in Poland.[99]

The Polish government, for its part, was not at all interested in strengthening the non-Polish nationality element in independent Poland, particularly in the eastern borderlands. This explains why Polish officials did not like having Ruthenians and Ukrainians settle there, and why the presence of Russians in Polesie gave rise to such anxiety. As already mentioned, attitudes towards Jews were determined by World War One, the economic conflict and the suspicion that they favoured Bolshevism. All this strengthened existing anti-Semitism. In addition, many Ukrainians coming from the East, as well as a significant proportion of the former tsarist officers now serving in the Polish Army, also had strong anti-Semitic views.[100]

The economic crisis in Poland played an important part in shaping the attitude of the authorities towards the mass of newcomers from Russia, many of whom were in desperate need of medical care and attention. As we have seen, the assessment of a newcomer's personal means and of his ability to support himself often depended on the attitude of the local officials. This constituted a convenient and informal mechanism for the regulation of migration. These tactics were applied most frequently with regard to the non-Polish population, Jews being the most common target. Jews who had lived in the Polish territories before 1914 or 1915 and who did not possess sufficient funds or landed property, or who lacked a recognized professional qualification, were deemed unable to provide for themselves (indeed, even some Jews who did have professional qualifications were frequently disqualified). The fact that they could provide for their families by working as travelling salesmen, brokers, tradesmen or craftsmen was often ignored by government officials. By these means the Polish apparatus of control over migrants was able to put into effect its inherent anti-Semitism.

What of Polish state-building? National exiles who had been active during World War One in the national relief committee and its subordinate affiliates established in Russia might have been expected on their return to have actively participated in constructing the new state apparatus. No doubt, some of them did reinforce the Polish administration. However, this seems to be less true of Poland than of Lithuania and Latvia. Many Poles from the former Austrian and Prussian annexed territories had some experience in local government and even in parliament. Poles from Galicia had autonomous institutions (the most important of them being the *Sejm Krajowy*, the regional Parliament in Lvov). Their experience was much more extensive than that of Poles living under Russian rule. In the case of the Kingdom of Poland, relatively independent local authorities dated only from the time of the Central Powers' occupation.[101] All in all, interwar Poland did not lack people with administrative experience. The problem was to work out the rules of common policy, to make different traditions and experiences more compatible, and to codify the different legal systems that functioned in the territories of the three former states.[102]

We have emphasized the legal framework and the regulations that governed migration, and the ways in which they were implemented by officials to control the movement and settlement of displaced persons. In this connection it is worth remembering that Poland was by no means alone in regulating migration and imposing immigration quotas. Like the other new 'successor states' in central and eastern Europe, Polish policy towards re-emigrants, repatriates and refugees from the lands of the former Russian Empire during these turbulent years was governed primarily by its uncertain future, threatened as it was by a resurgent Germany and the looming danger of Bolshevism.

6
The Repatriation of Polish Citizens from Soviet Ukraine to Poland in 1921-2

KATERYNA STADNIK[*]

INTRODUCTION

This chapter examines the repatriation of Polish citizens from the newly Sovietized Ukraine to independent Poland after the conclusion of hostilities between Poland and the Soviet state. It deals, first, with the institutional arrangements that governed this process. However, much more was at stake than purely technical and administrative issues relating to repatriation. The two states concerned were ideological opponents, and until recently had been at war. Thus their relationship was characterized by suspicion and hostility. The second part of the chapter shows how this mutual distrust affected the process of repatriation. Ideological divisions were manifested in the distinctions that the Soviet authorities drew between different 'categories' of evacuees, some of whom, it was believed, were likely to agitate against Soviet power, while others (including orphaned children) might be 'saved' for the revolution. The final section of the chapter identifies the steps taken by Polish evacuees to make their way to Poland against a background of severe economic deprivation and uncertainty.

The Soviet-Polish war of 1919-20 dominated all other episodes in Ukrainian-Polish relations during the period from the collapse of the tsarist empire to the Treaty of Riga in March 1921. But it was not the only instance of conflict. Other instances of discord concerned Polish participation in the first government of the Ukrainian People's Republic in 1917, the Polish-Ukrainian war for the possession of Eastern Galicia in 1918-19, and the anti-Bolshevik Polish-Ukrainian alliance under the Treaty of Warsaw signed in April 1920.[1] The territorial partition of Ukraine between Soviet Russia and Poland in March 1921 did not bring to an end the tense relations between the two states, and the alternating skirmishes and armistices between successive Ukrainian governments and the Polish authorities were a prelude to even more dramatic political developments that lie outside the scope of this chapter.[2]

As Norman Davies has observed, the Polish–Soviet campaign was 'a fast war of movement [when] up to a million men on either side marched the best part of a thousand miles and back in six months.'[3] In the aftermath of this campaign large numbers of Polish soldiers and civilians found themselves on Bolshevik-held territory, including the Left-Bank Ukraine.[4] The Donbass region, which for geographical reasons did not form part of mainstream political discourse and was not threatened during the Soviet–Polish war, nevertheless had its share of social and political problems. These resulted in the first place from the wreckage of abrogated agreements.[5] Problems also arose in consequence of the fact that large numbers of prisoners of war, refugees and emigrants were scattered throughout the region.[6] As we shall see, this made it difficult to establish a clear picture of the size of the displaced population, including those who expressed a willingness to return to Poland.

THE INSTITUTIONAL FRAMEWORK

Following the end of hostilities with Poland, the Soviet leadership instructed local Party and government authorities 'to prepare and to carry out the re-evacuation of citizens of the Polish Republic from all provinces (*gubernii*), and to organize the readmission of prisoners of war and citizens of the Ukrainian Soviet Socialist Republic from Poland to their homeland.' The administrative framework was designed to regulate legal, technical and ideological provisions for the repatriation campaign in each province, as provided for by the Soviet–Polish Agreement on Repatriation. Early in 1921 the Central Committee of the Communist Party of Ukraine (CCCPU) created a network of Provincial Re-evacuation Committees (*Gubevak*).[7] Each provincial committee consisted of three plenipotentiaries (the so-called *Revakotroika*): one from the Political Department of the Provincial *Guberniia* Committee, one from the 'Extraordinary Commission', that is the Secret Police (*Gubcheka*) and one from the Polish Bureau (*Polbiuro*), which was accountable to the Provincial Committee (*Gubkom*).[8] Each *Gubevak* was subordinated to the Central (All-Ukrainian) Re-evacuation Committee, which was in turn affiliated to the Central Committee of the Communist Party of Ukraine and required by the latter to submit regular reports on the progress of 're-evacuation'.

Each *Revakotroika* had as its overall mission three responsibilities: first, establishing political control over re-evacuated persons; second, monitoring the technical organization of the re-evacuation; and third, supervising agitation among repatriated persons. Clearly, political considerations were of paramount concern. We shall see later on how these calculations operated in the classification of the displaced Polish population on Ukrainian territory, and in making calculations about the effectiveness of the propaganda effort.

The *Gubevak* supervised the whole complex of material, technical and ideological issues associated with the process of re-evacuation. These included matters of food supply, health and medical supplies, the maintenance of order and security in the railway carriages, the inspection and surveillance of the passengers and – last but not least – the recruitment of activists from among the evacuated population to work in new 'monitoring commissions' for mobilizing resources. Under the new regime all questions relating to refugee relief relied heavily on Party officials or rank and file communists from among the refugee population. By the same token, potentially less 'reliable' refugee leaders, such as from among *zemstvo* workers or Polish clergymen, were excluded from the process.[9]

Within this framework a Party worker (*politrabotnik*) was assigned to each contingent of refugees, with responsibility for 'the proper supply of refugee needs' (*pravil'noe snabzhenie bezhentsev*), including food, medical care and personal security.[10] Party workers also had a duty to maintain a vigilant watch over the entire group. They were supposed to determine its social composition, to ascertain its origins and destination, to monitor refugees' attitudes and to look out for any sign of discontent (and note the issues over which discontent arose), and finally to note signs of counter-revolutionary agitation among the contingent.[11] Obviously, this workload presupposed a high level of surveillance and inspection of refugees before and during their journey to the Polish border. The arrangements placed a huge burden on the entire provincial system. Shortages of transport and of facilities, combined with the threat of typhus and the rapid spread of other infectious diseases, made the situation even more difficult than it seemed at the outset.[12]

One way of dealing with the problem of surveillance was to empower refugees' own representatives to assist the *politrabotniki*. This implied that the refugee population had among their number sufficient class-conscious workers sympathetic to the cause of the revolution, who could be expected to get involved in political life of the Soviet Republic, while working alongside Party members. These 'delegates', as they were styled, assisted in maintaining order, distributing rations, monitoring refugees' health, disseminating literature and convening any meetings that might be needed.[13]

Thus the Soviet regime deemed it a matter of special concern to maintain close supervision of these contingents. Party officials paid careful attention to the composition of the refugee trains, scrutinizing the lists of people who were due to be re-evacuated from various towns and cities.[14] Once re-evacuation got under way, the representatives of the Polish Bureau stressed the need to monitor the process more thoroughly, because the *Gubevak* agencies had been negligent in doing so.

However, the Polish authorities also had their own agenda, and were no less interventionist in this regard. The crucial matter of selecting people for the 'echelons' was discussed at regular meetings of a Joint Soviet–Polish Commission for Repatriation.[15] Polish representatives of the Joint Commission began to reject applications from poor peasants of Eastern Polish descent and also from Jews who were originally from Central Poland. Jews were considered to be a particular 'security risk' for the bourgeois Polish state, on account of their alleged pro-Bolshevik orientation, something that the statistics of Communist Party membership were believed to confirm.[16] They were simply crossed off the lists.[17]

The Polish members of the Joint Commission made no secret of their selective attitude towards the list of candidates for re-evacuation submitted by the Soviet side. The military consulate attached to the Polish Embassy in Moscow was responsible for making enquiries about suspicious applicants who might be Bolshevik agents. It was a matter of special concern to remove them from the lists straight away, before they got on to the trains, let alone before they entered Poland. This laborious activity left little time for other important business.[18]

Soviet authorities attempted to mitigate this discrimination by referring to the appropriate clauses of the Polish-Soviet Repatriation Agreement. They also drew attention to the need to accelerate the re-evacuation process in light of the worsening food supply crisis in Ukraine and Russia during 1921. Regardless of these efforts, the Polish members of the Joint Commission continued to block all doubtful candidates, whether they were regarded as Bolsheviks or as people whose claim to Polish citizenship was contentious.[19]

LABELLING RETURNEES

The institutional framework thus contributed to a situation in which Polish and Soviet officials alike drew distinctions between displaced persons. The Soviet Ukrainian authorities distinguished between different categories of returnees on grounds of social origin, political affiliation and current biographical aspirations. The Polish authorities likewise discriminated, but on grounds of ethnicity as well as political persuasion.

One of the first issues in defining the displaced population was discussed at the Fourth All-Russian Conference of the Bolshevik Party in September 1920.

'Comrade Merezhkin', representing the Jewish section, submitted a special report 'Concerning Emigration', primarily to address the needs of Jewish refugees. In July 1921 this text was sent to each of the national minorities' departments (*natsmenotdeli*) of the provincial committees, and formed part of the instructions for the forthcoming re-evacuation campaign. The document distinguished between three types of the so-called 'emigrating contingent':

(a) 'ex-capitalists and ex-landowners who are not willing to adopt the Soviet way of life and work, and who are eager to emigrate in order to maintain their capitalist way of life';
(b) 'the general, terror-stricken public, which anticipates finding shelter in the capitalist countries from the consequences of the Civil War';
(c) 'people who have ties of kinship in the countries to which they wish to migrate. These are predominantly wives and children who seek to be reunited with their husbands and parents, or else they are disabled persons who need assistance from their relatives'

The Bolsheviks regarded the first category as clearly counter-revolutionary. The Instructions glossed this as follows:

> In respect of the first of the mentioned group the policy of Communist party members must be the same as that applied to deserters, enemies of the economic revival of the Soviet Republic, and potential collaborators of the capitalist countries that are fighting against the Soviet Republic. So far as this group is concerned, *war should be declared against any aspirations for emigration* [my emphasis].

At the same time, this stark warning was coupled with the suggestion that the end of the era of 'War Communism' had brought about an entirely different economic regime:

> In addition, it must be emphasised for this group that Soviet power offers a wide range of possibilities for taking private economic initiatives within the programme of the New Economic Policy (NEP).

Clearly, the Bolsheviks were not averse to holding out an olive branch to potential economic 'collaborators' who might be willing to join cooperatives, or to become farmers of one kind or another now that restrictions on the marketing of grain and the use of hired labour had been lifted.[20]

They had some success, since the transitory liberalization of Bolshevik economic policy in the early 1920s triggered off a tendency to re-immigration.[21] Among these were several hundred labour migrants who took up jobs in the coal mines of the Donbass. However, many of them soon fell victim to the campaign against 'socially unreliable types'.[22]

So far as the second category – 'the general, terror-stricken public' – is concerned, it was important for Party workers to explain Soviet policy to aspiring emigrants, and in particular the belief that the flames of revolution would be fanned beyond Soviet frontiers. As a result, they would be exchanging one newly stabilized country for an uncertain future in another. In the words of the 'Instructions':

> For the second group, it is a duty of each communist to fight against the nationalist and petty-bourgeois trends which sow the seeds of mistrust towards in the creative potential of the Soviet Republic. It is a duty of each communist to explain to the exhausted public that their hopes of finding a quiet life in the capitalist countries are vain because the up-coming imminent socialist revolution there will be accompanied by acute Civil War... with all the typical characteristics such as lawlessness, pogroms, slanders, expulsion and exile, etc.

Again the document allowed for the possibility that some people would insist on making the journey west:

> Those elements in this category that are *totally unsettled psychologically* and are not able to be conscripted into military or labour services in the Soviet republic should not be confronted with any obstacles in realising their aspirations for emigration. In order to deliver them from the hardships and save them from smuggling rings, their departure should be legalised [my emphasis].

Thus there seems to have been a clear distinction drawn between 'class enemies' (members of the old elite in category one) and the 'psychologically unsettled' (category two). 'Enemies' were to be rounded up, incarcerated, and if necessary shot. Those who were 'psychologically unsettled' required sympathetic consideration and (so far as was possible) an untroubled passage home.

Within the second category, class distinctions were also significant, because people's response to calamity was determined by the economic resources at their disposal. This was well understood by the member of one *Revakotroika* who reported on attitudes among refugees in this category. He emphasized that, among Polish refugees at least, individual 'push' factors generally varied according to the household's social status. The 'petty bourgeoisie', possessing some property, never took an 'impetuous' decision to return to their homes but instead carefully considered the living conditions in Poland before reaching a decision. On the other hand, poorer 'elements' of the refugee population were desperate to leave, perceiving escape as the only way of getting away from their desperate plight. Since the largest part of the re-evacuated population belonged to relatively deprived social groups, this was an important observation.²³ This argument drew on a familiar distinction between 'spontaneous' displacement and 'rational' migration.²⁴

The third and final category of emigrants deserved to be treated much more favourably, 'because it has a *right of departure* from the Soviet Republic through having family ties with the recipient countries' (my emphasis). As the Instructions made clear:

> [For those with ties of kinship] the route for emigration must be facilitated by all possible means. Among matters of special concern are the preparation of legal documents, arrangements for a safe departure, and the creation of normal conditions of passage. A network of institutions, responsible for instruction, information, housing, provisions and medical care during their journey should therefore be established.

Other measures provided for the extradition of Polish citizens who had been accused of criminal activity by the Soviet authorities. In April 1921 the People's Commissariat of Justice suspended all sentences on Polish citizens and agreed to cease all legal, administrative and other proceedings against 'civilian prisoners, internees, hostages, refugees, emigrants and prisoners of war'. Under the arrangements for extradition, 'if a person announces his unwillingness to return, or the Polish side rejects his application, he is liable for a further term of imprisonment in the Ukrainian Soviet Socialist Republic'.²⁵ The extradition procedures were implemented through a bilateral exchange. Those who had already been repatriated were asked to provide information about potential candidates for mutual extradition. This effectively extended the period of repatriation beyond 1925, when the last branch office closed down. After mass repatriation came to an end, in June 1924, and the last repatriation office went into liquidation, the diplomatic corps monitored these extradition arrangements.²⁶

The Polish government was principally concerned to reclaim Catholic clergymen, secret-service agents, representatives of the erstwhile 'Polish legion' and other 'class enemies' of the Bolshevik state²⁷. On the Soviet side, Communist Party members, having been extradited to the Soviet Union, took the opportunity of returning to Poland with forged documents in order to undertake 'party work'.²⁸ Although it is difficult to assess how many Polish citizens were liable for extradition under this programme, not to mention how many Ukrainian Communists were unwittingly 'imported', it is clear that most evacuees from the Donbass were workers and peasants.²⁹ This was something of a disappointment, in so far as the Polish government hoped to give priority to those who, for various reasons, were under threat of repression in the Bolshevik-held territory and who might contribute at a higher level to the development of the

Polish state. Meanwhile, the Bolsheviks were keen to retain precisely these skilled Polish workers, many of whom displayed little enthusiasm for emigrating to Poland, where they did not expect an easy life, and who met the requirements for Soviet citizenship.[30] Whether they stayed in Russia or not, they were subject to sustained ideological influences.[31]

COUNTING RE-EVACUEES

How many people were caught up in these exercises in classification and political persuasion? Put another way, how large was the potential pool of re-evacuees? The Soviet authorities were anxious to know the answers to these questions. Instructions issued by the Central Committee of the Russian Communist Party in September 1921, and signed by its secretary, Viacheslav Molotov, required *Guberniia* Committees to prepare reports on the activities of their national minorities' sections and bureaus. The reports were to focus on their achievements and shortcomings. Molotov called for an indication of the size of the population of the national minority groups in *guberniias* and *uezds* (the next administrative tier downwards), the percentage of the national minority population that had little or no Russian language proficiency, and the number of colonists, prisoners of war, refugees and emigrants located in each *guberniia*.[32] This information was to be used to compile at regional and national level all the data needed to break new ground in the state-building strategy.

TABLE 1. Estimated number of Poles on the territory of Soviet Ukraine expressing a wish to leave for Poland (as of 18 April 1921)

Guberniia (province)	*Number of persons*
Chernigov	25,000
Donetsk	11,000
Ekaterinoslav	16,800
Kiev	37,000
Khar'kov	16,500
Kremenchug	14,350
Nikolaev and Kherson	8,550
Odessa	6,700
Poltava	9,200
Total	145,100

Source: Data from the All-Ukrainian Re-Evacuation Committee, cited in T. Eremenko, 'Politichni ta dyplomatychni vidnosyny radians'koi Ukrainy z Pol's'koju Respublikoju (1921–1923)', *Ukrainian Historical Journal*, 1998, no. 4, pp. 61, 62.

There are various estimates of the displaced population in the different provinces of Soviet Ukraine in the early 1920s. So far as the Poles in Donetsk province are concerned, there are three main sources of data. These are, first, the records of the All-Ukrainian Re-evacuation Committee (*Ukrevak*), second, reports of the Polish Bureau of the Guberniia Communist Party Committee (*Gubkom*), and finally the information assembled by the Guberniia Re-evacuation Committee (*Gubevak*).[33] These estimates put the Polish population of potential evacuees at anything from 11,000 to 20,000. The fragmentary and unsystematic nature of the records makes it difficult to assess at all accurately the number of Poles re-evacuated from the eastern borders of Soviet Ukraine during the early 1920s, and the number of those who stayed.[34]

TABLE 2. Number of Poles registered for re-evacuation in the uezds of Donetsk province (as of 28 June 1921)

Uezd	Number of persons
Bakhmut	1,200
Debaltsevo	2,500
Grishin	1,556
Lugansk	2,100
Mariupol'	2,300
Slaviansk	1,220
Starobel'sk	600
Shakhtinsk	600
Taganrog	1,545
Yuzovka	3,000
Total	16,621

Source: 'Report of the Polish Section of the Dongubkom, 28 July to 1 September 1921', GADO, f. 1, op. 1, d. 837, ll. 8, 9.

The absence of statistical accuracy during the re-evacuation campaign in the region was largely a function of the frequent administrative redivisions of Soviet Ukraine, because changes to the internal borders frequently disrupted the record-keeping system.[35] As a newly established administrative unit, Donetsk *guberniia* had only just started to develop a statistical department. It took many months to develop a proper information network, linked with the personnel departments of trade unions and enterprises.[36] For this reason, as the re-evacuation campaign got under way the local agencies remained notorious for the bad quality and inaccuracy of their data. Official records were further undermined by 'spontaneous' mass migration of a kind that was anathema to officialdom.

THE DECISION TO MIGRATE

Amongst the many factors that prompted Poles to attempt to leave Soviet territory the deteriorating economic outlook was of greatest significance for those employed in Ukrainian industry. As a result of the precipitous industrial decline and food-supply crisis in the region, many employers laid off their Polish workers on the grounds that they were liable to be repatriated in any event.[37] As the system for hiring and firing workers was poorly coordinated, many unemployed Poles who had never been registered with the authorities migrated to other provinces, particularly to those in Right-Bank Ukraine, which was known for its substantial Polish population. Others travelled long distances straight to the Polish border, attempting to facilitate their return to the homeland by all available means, including illegal crossing.[38] At the same time, it is perfectly understandable that many other unemployed people, particularly those with families, were deterred from taking the risk of migrating to Poland. Stories reached them of refugees who had been menaced by gangs, and of the terrible grip that cholera and typhus had on the population of the borderlands.[39] To minimize these problems, the Soviet authorities warned people not to risk a hasty departure and not to sell their property before they got permission to leave.[40]

There was another reason why the Soviet authorities hampered refugees' efforts to re-emigrate. Potential evacuees made up of highly qualified workers were often held back because they could help to restore declining industries in the Donbass. For example, one of the instructions sent to the provincial *Gubevak* in April 1921 urged that all measures be taken to retain the foreign workers, 'whose mass departure would have painful consequences for the local coal-mining industry.'[41] This was an accurate observation. Foreign professionals were badly needed to substitute for a lack of technical personnel and skilled workers. In March 1921 foreigners made up 30 per cent of all engineers, 25 per cent of mining deputies (*shteigery*), 14 per cent of face workers, and 10 per cent of other qualified workers.[42] It is equally clear that the Polish authorities were eager to encourage the return of professional people and skilled workers.[43]

If qualified workers sometimes encountered difficulties in navigating the Soviet bureaucratic procedures for emigration, much more serious was the plight of Polish Jews, whose departure was by contrast usually impeded by the Polish side.

Ethnic Poles were much more successful in negotiating the barriers to exit. Two hundred Polish families whose members had been selected for re-evacuation as part of the first group finally departed from Bakhmut (Ukraine) to Zdolbunow (Poland) on 27 August 1921. These were peasants from Volyn and Grodno provinces who had fled to the Left-Bank area during World War One and had settled temporarily in the districts of Mariupol', Lugansk and Iuzovka. The majority were elderly men and women, and mothers and their children.[44] There was no information on the missing adult men who might have been conscripted into the tsarist army or might have enlisted as combatants in subsequent conflicts.[45]

ABANDONED CHILDREN

The Instructions issued by Molotov in 1921 (see above) made no specific mention of abandoned children. But this was one of the most pressing and troubling social policy issues in post-Civil War Russia.[46] The available sources give little clear indication of the numbers of Polish children either repatriated to Poland or remaining in Ukraine.[47] The only extant data for the Donbass appeared in a report describing the '*Dekad* (ten days) of Assistance to the Starving Children of the Donbass', which was organized in March 1922. During this event the Polish Bureau helped to distribute funds (288,000 rubles) and foodstuffs (beans, salt etc.) among 242 Polish refugee children who were awaiting re-evacuation at the railway station in Bakhmut.[48]

The issue of abandoned Polish children was specifically addressed in January 1922, in a top-secret document sent by the Party committee of the RCP to the Polish Bureaus. This document drew attention to the efforts made by the Polish bourgeoisie to inveigle children to leave Soviet territory. The sensitivities of the Soviet authorities are clear:

> Data received from different localities indicates that some attempts have been made and the ground prepared to remove Polish children from the Soviet Republic to Poland. Some of the best endeavours are being made by the most ossified elements, such as Polish teachers. Members of the teaching staff are trying to make off with Polish children from elementary, boarding and reformatory schools and other educational institutions, which are then just abandoned. Even some communists look with tolerance on these projects having, perhaps, forgotten what fates might have been sealed for those children in Poland where in the clerical-nationalist environment they are doomed to be brought up as enemies of communists and the proletariat.

According to the Soviet–Polish Agreement on Repatriation (24 February 1921), only those children whose parents or grandparents planned to leave for Poland were eligible for repatriation. Thus, 'orphans and those children whose fate can only be decided by social welfare institutions can under no circumstances be removed from the Soviet Republic to Poland.' The secret document went on to emphasize that children were not capable of taking their own independent decision: 'any wish to go to Poland apparently expressed by children, as well as their claim to have parents or relatives in Poland, do not constitute grounds for repatriation.' Relatives who were already resident in Poland could only initiate the repatriation of children by applying to the Polish diplomatic corps.

Polish children who remained on Soviet soil were to receive full maintenance allowances and be provided with education by Soviet–Polish educational institutions, under the supervision of the Polish Bureaus. The document concluded that

> the Central Polish Bureau [that is, in the Central Committee of the RCP] should be informed by Provincial Polish Bureaus of any instance in which there are clear difficulties (such as a poor harvest, hunger, a dearth of schools or insufficient children to support separate Polish educational institutions) in facilitating children's care so that they may immediately arrange children's transportation to a more appropriate locality.[49]

These efforts demonstrate that the Soviet authorities showed great concern for the fate of orphaned children who were expected to be brought up as loyal citizens of the Soviet state. Consequently, relief work with children was not left to ad hoc agencies but kept firmly within the network of Soviet organizations and movements under the aegis of the Communist party.[50]

WELFARE, POLITICS AND DECISION-MAKING BY REFUGEES

The actual process of re-evacuation was accompanied by scenes of desperation and squalor. Whatever the precise number of those who sought to leave, the Soviet authorities faced serious problems relating to the nourishment, protection and control of thousands of emaciated, disoriented and embittered people, many of whom congregated close to the Soviet frontier. According to the available documentary evidence, the conditions under which most refugees were living in Soviet Ukraine often plunged them into a mood of despair. In January 1921 the refugees of Iuzovka submitted the following application to the Central Re-evacuation Committee:

> We have no means of support. We suffer from starvation and cold. All the well-off people received departure permits and left. But we, the poor, are not able to pay our way (*a nam, bednym bezhentsam, ne s chego davat'*). If you do not introduce order in Iuzovka, we shall all die of starvation. We will also write to the consuls [that is, in Khar'kov where the Polish Embassy was located at this time, KS] to say that we have been prevented for more than six months from leaving.[51]

As the Polish chargé d'affaires, Zygmunt Stefanski, explained to the Minister of Foreign Affairs of the RSFSR, Georgii Chicherin, on 10 January 1922, the facilities for Polish repatriation deteriorated sharply during the winter months. The living conditions of refugees in the Soviet-held territories also got much worse.[52] It was not only making adequate provision for refugee communities that proved to be a challenging task for the Soviet authorities. The departure of the first echelon of Polish refugees in August 1921 revealed a number of weak points in the organization of the Provincial Evacuation Committee in the province. The Polish Bureau reported that, apart from financial difficulties, 'a lack of political work and shortage of administrative system' were the main shortcomings at the beginning of the repatriation campaign. The Bureau prepared a series of further instructions for the Soviet representatives who escorted the various parties or echelons of re-evacuees. Of particular concern was the need to maintain a clear division of responsibilities between Soviet political officials, on the one hand, and administrative personnel on the other. Only then could re-evacuation proceed smoothly. The Polish Bureau regarded political work as needing urgent attention. Political officers were expected to:

(a) explain to refugees the 'real' state of events in Poland, making use of easily accessible information from the foreign media
(b) clarify the tasks likely to confront refugees if and when they returned to 'bourgeois' Poland
(c) provide *Guberniia* evacuation units with sufficient numbers of political and administrative workers capable of speaking Polish
(d) make political literature in the Polish language widely available to refugees, facilitating newspaper circulation and arranging for leaflets to be printed in cities close to the evacuation units (principally in Bakhmut).
(e) organize ceremonial departure meetings, with music and revolutionary hymns.[53]

The tasks placed an onerous responsibility on the communist personnel at the disposal of the Polish Bureau. They were hardly sufficient in number to address the task of political 'education'. According to a report dated November 1921 Donetsk province could muster barely more than 50 Polish communists, including 17 in Bakhmut, 18 in Iuzovka, 2 in Slaviansk and 5 in Grishin.[54] Set against the refugee population this was a drop in the ocean – the total Polish population in Donetsk province numbered at least 15,600.[55] Thus the ratio of Party members in the whole population amounted to a mere 0.3 per cent. Such a thin layer of Party activists was hardly sufficient to spread extensive Communist propaganda among the Polish 'contingent'.

In practice, the two main dimensions of Soviet work during the re-evacuation, one of mere 'managerial' and the other of purely political design, had the same purpose. Both were intended to affirm the superiority of the socialist state in the eyes of potential members of an ideologically alien society. Critical reviews of the Polish press were widely distributed among the Polish population. These reviews painted a depressing picture of the 'bourgeois reality that was in store for the repatriated contingent'. Each summary usually consisted of several items, covering the following issues: the devaluation of the local Polish currency, the catastrophic national budget deficit, the gross inflation of bread prices in Warsaw, the low quality of life, and the stranglehold of the Catholic Church over the education system. (One review described a pupil's schedule at one of the Catholic schools that 'starts at 6 a.m. lasts for 17 hours'). Other negative comments were made about a wave of labour unrest, as well as the Polish Socialist Party (PPS, *Polska Partia Socjalistyczna*), which was in the throes of a deep organizational crisis. A favourable comparison was drawn with the recently established Polish Communist Workers' Party (KPRP, *Komunistyczna Partia Robotnicza Polska*).[56]

The Polish population, on hearing of re-evacuation elsewhere, was eager to know more about recent events in Poland. From a Soviet point of view this offered a relatively favourable opportunity for political agitation prior to their departure, provided Party organizers could be found. Meetings, discussions, performances, leaflets and brochures all had a part to play in mounting something akin to a propaganda offensive.[57] Typically, an event was held in a factory courtyard or in a club assembly hall, and included an oration devoted to 'current events in Poland and conditions of the re-evacuation campaign' which was followed up with some entertainment programme, designed to make people more appreciative of Soviet life and their prospects under Soviet rule. Political work in early 1921 among the Polish population in Khar'kov, including 4,000 Polish employees in local factories, took the form of meetings attended by 2,000 people, as well as a discussion forum (200 people participated), and 12 lectures (with around 500 people taking part). Concerts and other musical events took place. On average these drew audiences of 100 adult workers and 200 youngsters. On the 'Day of Youth' initiated by the Gubkom in April 1921, Polish children and teenagers watched a ballet, listened to a concert recital and attended a choral concert. They also had lunch followed by tea and sweets.[58]

On the other hand, propaganda would be doomed to failure if it were not supported by a careful and rational approach to the urgent needs of the refugees for food, medical care, personal security and so forth. A bewildered mass of refugees, who neither collectively nor individually demonstrated any capacity to withstand the hardships of the journey, required the regular assistance of reliable and trustworthy officials. A Soviet political worker who could neither speak nor understand Polish would not be recognized as a reliable guardian and would not have been given any opportunity to propagandize amongst the re-evacuees. There are frequent references in the archives to cases in which units were poorly equipped and in which the staff were unable to deal with basic sanitary problems. Fewer still were the staff capable of persuasive advocacy on behalf of the Soviet regime. To be sure, those native speakers and compatriots who did represent the Soviet authorities (most of whom were former Polish front-line soldiers) could minimize public animosity towards the Soviets and contribute to a more trusting attitude on the part of the refugees. Yet it remains the case that, during the entire period of re-evacuation, the achievements of the Soviet tactic of mass political involvement were quite limited in scope.[59]

Many Polish refugees were indeed much more concerned about basic material conditions than they were about the content and purpose of political agitation.[60] Numerous accounts testify to the ragged and destitute appearance of the displaced Polish population. As the Polish Bureau reported in March 1922:

> Attitudes among the Polish refugees are rather depressed, mainly because of their plight and the troubles they suffer continually. For instance, in the state-owned factory of Petrovsk in Enakievo, all Polish workers were dismissed in August 1921. They caught cold living in the railway carriages until February 1922, during which time they had no assistance or supplies of any kind. Although the head of the Polish Bureau visited the factory in December, nobody informed him about this matter. It is impossible to present to the refugees the claim that Soviet power is superior to that of bourgeois regimes, when they have been kept for half a year without any help whatsoever. The whole process of re-evacuation is characterised by total disorder: in Mariupol there have been a lot of aged people, disabled persons, abandoned children and people with large families (with up to twelve family members) who are doomed to starvation.

The report went on to accuse the staff of the provincial re-evacuation committee of corruption: 'a majority of financially independent people and single persons had already left for Poland in the previous autumn. One must confess that this smacks of bribery. Notwithstanding the fact that previous heads of the Gubevak are being held under arrest by the DOPR [*Dom prinuditel'nykh rabot*, or 'House of Forced Labour'], this experience clearly has had a negative influence on the refugees' attitudes to Soviet power. We must keep Gubevak under close surveillance.'

The same source offered further confirmation of this point. An instructor from the Polish Bureau described the departure of the third party of Polish evacuees, and revealed how difficult it was to offer parting words of comfort to these exhausted and frustrated people:

> Since the echelons were overcrowded and because of the cold (the refugees are half-clothed) there was no possibility of organising a general meeting before they departed. Some literature was distributed among the echelons and some farewell words were uttered. But refugees berated us, blaming us for their deprivation and expressing outrage at the delay in their departure. They asked who was responsible for the negligence in carrying out re-evacuation procedures. It was explained to them that this escape might be not their last, because a new bourgeois war is possible that could cast them to other side of Europe. Consequently they have been told to strive for the overthrow of all bourgeois regimes and to work towards a transfer of power to the working class and peasantry in their homeland.[61]

The political worker who escorted the sixth contingent of refugees from Bakhmut to the Polish border also touched upon the 'political attitudes of the Polish contingent' during the journey and upon the arrival. He too painted a depressing picture:

> Some members of the group showed their discontent with the Polish government and were curious to get more information on the current situation in Poland. Yet the Agitprop centres had been closed all along the line. Some political literature was bought from the Kazatin Regional Party Committee. Because of the lack of the agitators it was impossible to organise a farewell meeting, although this should have been arranged because the echelon was approaching the Polish border. Having arrived in Poland some refugees ventured to sing 'Jeszcze Polska ne zginela' ['Poland has not perished yet'].[62]

The overwhelming majority of the refugees 'were desperate to arrive in Poland as soon as possible and cared only about their final destination'.[63] On the other hand some *troika* members offered a more upbeat assessment of the attitude of refugees towards Soviet efforts, particularly once the displaced persons had reached their destination. One member by the name of 'Comrade Schliumi' noted in his report that for most of the journey refugees did not show as much confidence in Soviet plenipotentiaries as did they on the border, 'where in the exchange terminal they were driven onto the platforms, each escorted by two Polish gendarmes. After having seen this incident many refugees said good-bye to us and thanked us for all our efforts.'[64] It is worth noting that, in addition to 'refugees', the Polish Bureau readily assisted and gave priority to individual applications for departure 'initiated from above'. Typically, comments in support of these applications emphasized the motive for the journey as a desire to work in the underground Polish Communist Workers' Party.[65]

The behaviour of the Polish authorities suggested to the refugee population that Soviet officialdom was not so odious or ineffective after all. Thus another *troika* member, known only as 'Comrade Wasplebakt', who reported on the arrival in the Polish town of Zdolbunow of the first Polish contingent of evacuees, recalled that in the exchange terminal:

> ... [they] were forced by the Polish gendarmes to show how they could pray and cross themselves just to confirm that they are true Polish Catholics. A Polish Jew who dared to address a Polish colonel without using his title was immediately whipped for his blunder. For a chance to get to Poland thousands of refugees have gathered on the border and have waited for several months. Bourgeois Poland chooses from this contingent for entry those who are better off, while the poor often wander around the border. There has been one case in which a refugee has returned from Zdolbunow to Shepetovka in Ukraine.[66]

These various difficulties and drawbacks persisted during the whole period of repatriation from Donetsk province, and help to explain the slow rate of re-evacuation (see Table 3).

TABLE 3. Number of Poles resident in and re-evacuated from Donetsk province, between summer 1921 and spring 1922

	Number of Poles in Donetsk	Numbers re-evacuated
Summer 1921	20,000 (July)	900 (1st echelon, August)
Autumn 1921	15,591 (November)	500 (2nd echelon, October)
		1,500 (3rd echelon, November)
Winter 1921–2	9,000 (February 1922)	280 (4th echelon, December 1921)
Spring 1922	10,000 (March)	1,000 (8th echelon, May)

Source: Reports of the Dongubkom Polish Bureau (July 1921–May 1922), GADO, f. 1, op. 1, d. 837, ll. 7, 8, 20, 21, 24, 28, 37, 52, 54.

On 30 May 1922 the eighth – and presumably the last – contingent of refugees departed.[67] This echelon consisted of around one thousand refugees, mainly from Mariupol' and Slaviansk, the majority of them originally from the eastern area of Poland. Most were peasant farmers and their families. In the course of revisions to the re-evacuation list for the seventh party, 126 persons were crossed out. Not surprisingly, perhaps, the bulk of them were Jews.[68]

What can be said about the overall results of this re-evacuation campaign? According to the data of a Joint Soviet–Polish Commission for Repatriation, around 1.1 million people returned from the USSR to Poland between April 1921 and June 1924.[69] At a rough estimate, 200,000 of these were repatriated from

Soviet Ukraine alone. The Polish authorities meanwhile calculated that 1.5 million Poles remained on Soviet territory in 1924.[70] In August 1924 the Polish population in Soviet Ukraine numbered 350,000.[71] The estimated size of the 'Polish minority' living in the Donbass by the end of the mass re-evacuation campaign in 1924 was just 6,300.[72] Most of them, as we have seen, were employed in the coal mining industry. During the next couple of years, reports speak of a 'spontaneous' repatriation.[73] The scale of movement had gradually been reduced by the restrictions mentioned above. A report in June 1924 concluded that 'Polish refugees, having got permission to leave, are refusing to do so'. In all likelihood the Soviet authorities attempted to hinder further departures of refugees, in the hope of involving more of them in economic reconstruction.[74]

CONCLUSIONS

The consequences of postwar population displacement were far-reaching. From the point of view of Soviet Ukraine, including the Donbass, a large number of migrants appeared in the region either forcibly or voluntarily during World War One. This chapter has shown how Soviet officials elaborated a rigid classification scheme for the displaced population, particularly those people who wished to return to their homeland. The re-evacuation programme developed and supervised by the Central Committee of the Communist Party of Ukraine was implemented by agencies that were specifically designed to regulate the repatriation process.

A number of instructions and reports relating to the legal, technical and ideological issues of the re-evacuation campaign were issued between 1920 and 1924. These reveal the substance, extent and importance of the 'refugee problem' for the Soviet state. The Bolshevik authorities looked upon re-evacuated persons as potential members of a bourgeois society. This explains why Soviet officials took such deliberate attempts to shape the political attitudes of the evacuees before their departure to Poland. Attempts were also made to induce refugees to adopt the communist doctrine and participate in the socialist state-building in the Soviet Union. Officials hoped to choose the most advanced fellow travellers to export the proletarian revolution to Poland and other countries.

The characteristic features of the repatriation campaign in Donetsk province – a newly fledged unit created in one of the administratively least developed areas of the former Russian empire – were largely shaped by local conditions. The under-developed administrative network, lack of resources and a shortage of qualified staff, among other problems, hampered the re-evacuation programme and made it difficult for revolutionary ideology to make much headway amongst the refugee population. On a more basic level, although the Soviet authorities made some attempts to moderate their plight, these efforts were hardly sufficient to meet the needs of the destitute and exhausted migrant population.

The desperate economic situation in most Soviet territories, and particularly in industrial areas, which suffered from a considerable drop in manufacturing output and a food supply crisis, made it extremely difficult for small minority groups to survive. Eventually, the majority of Polish refugees returned to their homeland during the periodic re-evacuation campaigns described above. Those who for various reasons ventured to stay or were simply not successful in their exodus, had to find their place as best they could in the fledgling Soviet state. Many individuals and families moved to the Right-Bank provinces, where the local Polish population was considerably greater in number and where national-administrative units could be developed. Overall it was a miserable fate for a population that had endured eight years of war and revolution.

* This study is based on material held by the Donetsk State Regional Archive (*Gosudarstvennyi Arkhiv Donetskoi oblasti*, GADO). It draws on reports, instructions, minutes, working materials, etc. contained in the hitherto closed collections of the Donetsk province Communist Party Archive (*Dongubkom*).

7
'Sybiraki': Siberian and Manchurian Returnees in Independent Poland

ŁUCJA KAPRALSKA

INTRODUCTION

The sociologist Robin Cohen has enumerated important general characteristics of diaspora, including shared memories and idealized conceptions of home, group involvement in activities supporting the 'homeland', awareness of group separateness and solidarity with the members of one's own group living abroad.[1] In a collective work devoted specifically to the Polish diaspora, Adam Walaszek argues that it consists of 'victims', 'fighters', and 'workers'.[2] This chapter sheds light on a key moment in the history of the Polish diaspora.[3] It finds evidence for each of these characteristics and categories.

In what follows I focus upon those elements of the Polish diaspora that returned to independent Poland from Siberia and Manchuria in the years following World War One. The displacement of Poles in the Russian empire began long before 1914. Polish subjects of the Tsar who challenged tsarist rule, as in 1830 and 1863, were deported to far-flung corners of the empire, where many of them lived out their lives in exile, normally in Siberia and the Far East. Their descendants often remained on Russian soil. Other Poles had migrated eastwards voluntarily, in search of better economic prospects during the late nineteenth century. Many of them settled permanently in Russia.[4] World War One unleashed fresh population displacements of Polish civilians, soldiers and prisoners of war, and these remote regions became once again the site of diasporic settlement.

The first section of this paper looks in more detail at the fate of Polish exiles, refugees and prisoners of war in Siberia and the Far East, and considers arrangements made for their repatriation following the end of World War One and the establishment of an independent Polish state. The next section discusses the activities of the postwar Polish Association of Siberian Deportees, which dedicated itself to keeping alive the memory of deportation. The third section is devoted to the Association's house journal *Sybirak* [*The Siberian Exile*], whose contents shed important light on the positions and attitudes of returnees in the Polish homeland. Throughout this chapter attention is given not only to practical aspects of population settlement and re-settlement, but also to exploring the significance that Polish deportees and returnees attached to displacement. As we shall see, displacement gave rise to multiple meanings, in which ideas of place loomed at least as large as ideas of personal sacrifice and (mis)fortune. Such connotations were severely tested in the crucible of independent Polish statehood. While some veterans of exile and deportation found a warm welcome in postwar Poland, others found homecoming much more troubling. Yet others developed a sense that the Far East, and perhaps Siberia too, could serve as the focus of potential and enriching economic interaction with Poland. In short, as recent historical and social science literature reminds us, we must not assume that population displacement can be reduced to a single tidy construction.[5]

POLES IN SIBERIA AND THE FAR EAST BEFORE AND DURING THE RUSSIAN REVOLUTION

It is difficult to establish the size of the Polish diaspora in the Russian interior with any precision. Around 600,000 Poles were living in Russia proper (that is, excluding the Polish lands) at the outbreak of World War One. The likely number of Poles who lived in Siberia and Manchuria before 1914 totalled around 70,000. They comprised various social classes and occupations, including peasant farmers, workers, members of the intelligentsia and clerical workers. Included among their number were Polish deportees, successive generations of whom had been sentenced to permanent exile or state service in various parts of Siberia. Their fate is well documented in the abundant memoirs, diaries and descriptions of Siberia written by those who managed to return. Many remained in Russia, being 'eternally settled', i.e. having no right to return to Poland. Some of these settlers described themselves as having 'grown into' Siberia, where they helped to develop the region, and praised its unique, scenic beauty.[6] Towards the end of the nineteenth and early twentieth centuries, the character of these exile communities began to change, as a result of a new wave of migration. Poor peasants and workers from the less industrialized parts of central Poland looked upon Siberia as a land of tremendous potential. As a modern Polish historian has written, Siberia was home to 'engineers, physicians, administrators, military people, and even merchants, petty officers and clerks, those who hoped for riches ... Polish fortunes were often made there.'[7]

World War One multiplied the number of Poles in Siberia as well as in Russia as a whole. The largest group comprised Polish men conscripted into the Russian army. Poles were also conscripted into the armed forces of Austria-Hungary. If captured, the Russian authorities incarcerated them in prison camps or other settlements, often in Siberia and the Far East.[8] In addition, important settlements of Polish civilian refugees were scattered throughout Russia, including 11,000 in Siberia. Moreover, approximately 3,000 political prisoners sentenced for plotting against the authorities were deported during the war to settlements deep in the heart of Russia or in Western Siberia. Following the orders of tsarist military authorities, Polish peasants from Lublin, Chełm, Łomża, and Siedlce provinces were also forced to move eastwards. Some of these established contact with Polish settlers in Siberia. Indeed, given the long history of 'economic migration' from Poland to western Siberia, many peasant families evacuated during the war could now join their families beyond the Urals.[9] By 1917, Polish deportees, evacuees, prisoners of war and soldiers serving in the Russian army numbered around 1.5 million.[10] These population movements were frequently chaotic and took place with little concern for public health or the supply of food and clothing.

During the late nineteenth century, many Poles also migrated beyond Siberia to the Far East in pursuit of better economic conditions. They found work building the Far Eastern Railway and remained behind to help operate the line. In 1903 the Polish community in Manchuria consisted of 7,000 people, most of whom worked for the railway company. Others were employed as physicians, engineers, bankers and lawyers. Unlike other Polish diaspora communities, this group largely comprised wealthy and educated individuals. The number of Poles in Manchuria increased after the Russo – Japanese War, when tens of thousands of soldiers from the Kingdom of Poland were sent to fight in the Far East: at the end of hostilities, some of them settled in the hope of improved prospects. The main Polish settlement was in the city of Harbin, which thanks to a rapid influx of migrants from throughout the Russian Empire had expanded to a population of 55,000 by the eve of World War One. The Polish community in Manchuria was highly organized and boasted numerous social, cultural and educational associations, including a school that provided tuition in the Polish language at both elementary and lower-secondary levels. As in most Polish settlements, the Catholic Church played an important role.[11]

During World War One and the Russian revolution, Manchuria attracted additional Polish immigrants. These comprised, successively, evacuated railwaymen of the Warsaw–Vienna railway, groups of refugees and prisoners of war from Austrian and German armies previously interned in Siberia. They were joined by a group of so-called Trans-Amurians, minor members of the Polish nobility, settled by the tsarist authorities beyond the Amur River in 1910. After 1917 they managed to get to Harbin, hoping to make their way to Australia.[12]

The last group to arrive in this region were soldiers of the Fifth Siberian Division of Fusiliers, a unit that is closely associated with the history of returnees from Siberia and the Far East. Polish military units in Siberia began to form in late 1917, when prisoners of war from the Austro-Hungarian and German armies, as well as soldiers from the disarmed Polish Corps and local Polish civilians all mobilized of their own accord to fight the Bolsheviks. By the end of the year these units numbered 8,000 men.[13] The Polish War Committee (*Polski Komitet Wojenny*), established in 1918 'for matters of a political nature', signed an agreement with the Czechs (at that time the only major military power in the area) to organize a Polish force within the Czechoslovak army.[14] The agreement stipulated that the Polish army was to receive weapons, clothes, money and food, while the PKW could commandeer 'volunteers', form units and establish officers' schools. PKW officials were expected to care for conscripts' families and to look after disabled soldiers. As Biegański writes, the Fifth Siberian Division was unusual in that it was accompanied by a large number of family members: 'The reasons for this are to be sought in the fact that a certain percentage of soldiers came from the depths of European Russia and Siberia (approximately twenty per cent of officers and ten per cent of the lower ranks) and were usually married. Another reason was the long duration of the war and revolution that encouraged marriage on the part of former POWs from Austrian and German armies as well as the soldiers of the 1st and 2nd Corps, and even the Russian army.'[15]

A detailed analysis of the armed effort of the unit would go beyond the scope of this chapter. After three expeditions against Bolshevik forces approaching Novo-Nikolaevsk, the Fifth Division covered the evacuation of Allied forces along the Trans-Siberian Railway. In December 1919 Polish troops fought near the station of Taiga, where they suffered heavy losses. Continuing to cover the retreat of the Czech forces, Polish troops found themselves surrounded by Bolshevik forces. The Poles were forced to surrender in January 1920 at Kliukvennaia railway station. Most were taken into Soviet captivity; just under two thousand escaped.[16]

Thus the Russian revolution and Civil War completed a pattern of longstanding Polish migration, forced and voluntary, to Siberia and the Far East. How this considerable population might be enabled to return to Poland – in

RETURNING HOME

After the capitulation of the Fifth Division, the Red Army transferred the captured Polish soldiers to prison camps in Krasnoiarsk. Some officers were subsequently deported to camps in Omsk, and later to Tula in the central industrial region. The Soviets formed the so-called Enisei Labour Brigade out of those who remained in the camp. The Polish prisoners frequently escaped. Some initially joined local guerrillas fighting the Bolsheviks. Most strove by any means to return to their newly independent homeland. 'Some tried to go west across Russia, others headed for Irkutsk and the Republic of the Far East, to reach Vladivostok, from where they went by sea to Trieste or Marseilles. Yet another group went down the Enisei river to the Arctic Ocean, hoping for a passing English ship ... Most of the refugees [i.e. fugitive Fifth Division soldiers], however, chose the least expected option, making their way across the Mongolian border through the Sayan Mountains and Uryan-kchai to Urga.'[17] A few of them managed to enter China, from where they were able to cross the steppes of Kirgizia and Turkestan to reach Persia, Afghanistan or India, whence where they returned to Europe. Most did not return to Poland until the autumn of 1921.

The 1,800 soldiers of the Fifth Siberian Division who had avoided Soviet capture at Kliukvennaia station tried to get through to Harbin, a journey that was fraught with particular hardship, because Bolshevik troops had captured all the major towns on their route, such as Taishet, Irkutsk and Verkhneudinsk (Ulan-Ude). The Siberian winter took a dreadful toll. In March 1920 they reached Harbin, where they were cared for by Polish settlers and the Polish Military Mission. A month later, they were collected from Harbin by General Baranowski, who had been sent from Poland specifically to organize their rescue. The long road home followed a route via Vladivostok, Southeast Asia, the Indian subcontinent, Suez, the Mediterranean, the Atlantic, London and Copenhagen. The troops finally reached Gdansk on 2 July 1920, after a journey that had taken two and a half months.[18]

Yet another road to Poland was taken by those soldiers who remained in Soviet prisoner of war camps. Some 3,200 stayed in Krasnoiarsk, as members of the 9th and 10th battalions of the Enisei Labour Brigade, as mentioned above. Their fate was closely related to the Polish–Soviet talks which resulted in the Repatriation Treaty on 24 February 1921. The area covered by this Treaty was enormous, extending from Omsk to Irkutsk (a distance of 2,350 kilometres), and from Eniseisk to Abakan (600 kilometres). The Polish repatriation delegation arrived in Moscow on 26 April 1921. Firstly, it negotiated the return of around 80,000 Poles who were concentrated near the western border close to their homeland. They were soon permitted to return to Polish territory. The Polish delegation was especially concerned to secure the release of the Polish Fifth Division prisoners of war. Knowing that the Soviet authorities were reluctant to liberate these troops, the Polish representatives sought out former soldiers arriving in Moscow and entrained them together with other prisoners and exiles heading westwards. Some travelled to Minsk, from where it was hoped to arrange special transports back to Poland. Negotiations relating to Polish officers of the Fifth Division (now in Tula) eventually led to their release in September 1921, following the direct intervention of the Polish government.[19]

An official Polish mission travelled to Siberia in September 1921 as part of the Siberian Committee of the Joint Commission established to implement the Repatriation Treaty; its president was Kazimierz Gintowt-Dziewałtowski. The committee intended to concentrate Fifth Division prisoners of war in the Krasnoiarsk camp, from which they could be evacuated later. The Russians approved the Polish plan for repatriation: first, in July, the evacuation of invalid prisoners of war from camps, then three further transports (of prisoners of war, all prisoners over 40, and those with a family accompanying them) in August, and finally four transports of all remaining prisoners in September.

It should be noted that the former Polish soldiers had already been transferred out of the custody of the Soviet military to the Soviet Central Committee for Prisoners of War and Refugees (*Tsentroplenbezh*), in accordance with the Polish–Soviet Repatriation Treaty. Lists of those to be repatriated were prepared by special commissions consisting of representatives of *Tsentroplenbezh*, of the Polish communist section, and of the so-called Workers' and Peasants' Inspection (Rabkrin). These lists were then submitted for approval by the provincial secret police (*gubcheka*), who removed the names of those they considered dangerous oppositionists, before being returned to the Polish communist section for further vetting. Those who were not permitted to depart remained in Soviet captivity.[20]

However, the Soviets did all they could to obstruct the departure even of those whom they had approved for repatriation. The documents reveal many cases of Soviet officials delaying transports, removing individuals from trains just before departure, interfering in registration procedures, as well as of the security police making threats against Polish committee members. This prompted an ultimatum by the Polish Government and retaliatory measures, such as the suspension of transports of Soviet prisoners of war from the territory of Poland.²¹ The return transports, many including large numbers of family members, were sent between the middle of August 1921 and the beginning of May 1922.

The road home differed from one transport to the next. It took the first one a month to reach Poland, the next two reached home in eight weeks, and the fifth one took three months. Following the conclusion of the peace treaty between Poland and Russia, it took eighteen months for all the soldiers of the Fifth Siberian Division to be returned to Poland. Conditions were very difficult: hungry returnees were crammed in dirty railway wagons and suffered mistreatment at the hands of Russian officials. Aid from the Polish Delegation did little to improve this situation, since its resources were limited. The Russian Red Cross intervened to provide some food parcels and other kinds of assistance.

The repatriation of Polish civilians followed a different pattern. Numerous organizations sprang up throughout Russia to provide for their needs. Since 1918 Vladivostok had been the base of the Polish War Committee. Although the Committee was a military organ, one of its first initiatives was to claim liberation from Soviet citizenship of all Poles in Siberia and the Far East, and the establishment of 'national freedom'.²² Similar developments took place in other parts of Russia wherever Polish communities were located. During World War One, Ignacy Sobieszczański, one of the most influential Poles living in Irkutsk, had formed the Committee for Assisting the Victims of the War (*Towarzystwo Pomocy Ofiarom Wojny*) and a Citizens' Committee, while similar organizations had sprung up elsewhere in Siberia. Later on, as foreigners found their lives in increased danger, the Polish Civic Organization (*Polska Organizacja Społeczna*, or 'Kapos') was established. In collaboration with the PKW, 'Kapos' established a 'Legitimacy Commission', which issued 'Polishness Certificates' (*świadectwo polskości*), which the Allies recognized during the years between 1918 and 1920.²³ The First Congress of 'Siberian Polonia', which was held in Harbin on 18 March 1918, was the brainchild of these organizations, although it was convened under the aegis of the Polish Political Council of the Far East and Eastern Siberia. In October 1918 the Central Polish National Committee (*Polski Komitet Narodowy*, or PKN) was established in Harbin. It agreed to cooperate with the PKW in Vladivostok. The two centres began to muster their forces in various parts of Siberia and Manchuria, their main task being to arrange for the liberation of Poles from Russian sovereignty, to secure them the status of foreigners in Russia, and then – after the establishment of the Polish state – to grant them Polish citizenship.²⁴

Faced with the constantly changing political situation, the PKN and PKW jointly elaborated a number of 'principles for liberating Poles from Russian sovereignty' (20 March 1920), which they communicated to the government of General Kolchak at Omsk. These principles remained in force until overtaken by the Treaty of Riga in 1921. Stanislaw Lubodziecki, a member of the PKW, describes in his memoirs how PKN–PKW Joint Political Bureaus in Harbin, Vladivostok and other towns quizzed applicants on details of their Polish relatives, family ties and their city of origin, and checked their papers. The Political Bureaus in each location, of course, already knew members of their local Polish communities, so their interviews were primarily concerned to verify those who had recently arrived as refugees or aspiring re-emigrants to Poland. Lubodziecki recounts episodes when the interrogators refused to believe the stories told by applicants. It should be remembered that many of the re-emigrants in particular spoke little Polish, or spoke it badly, which was hardly surprising after so many years spent in Russia. After their verification, successful applicants were expected to sign a declaration to the effect that they 'feel Polish' and that they and their family wished to renounce Russian citizenship. Two independent witnesses had to sign this declaration. The person's details were then registered, together with a photograph, and their Russian passports were exchanged for new interim documents, which were printed in Shanghai under the control of the representative of the PKW. Personal data were entered in these passports in Polish, Russian and French. Both the PKN and PKW also took steps to prepare for the repatriation of these civilian groups and provided considerable help for those in need. But increasing conflict between the two committees after 1919 undermined their efforts to liaise with the local White Russian and Allied authorities and weakened their position as representatives of the Polish communities.[25]

The fall of Kolchak's government and the changing political situation in the Far East (in particular, the establishment of the Far Eastern Republic and the Japanese occupation of areas south of Vladivostok) resulted in a drastic deterioration in the living conditions of Poles in this region. Contagious diseases, including bubonic plague and cholera, had a disastrous impact on public health. Civilians who had hoped to return home along with the Fifth Siberian Division became extremely despondent:

> Poverty and hunger were pervasive. Polish families who gathered along the Trans-Siberian, Amur, and Baikal railways, in the hope of transport back home, were now dying out ... Robber bands multiplied, especially in the Far Eastern Republic. Whole trainloads of people froze to death ... No-one can reckon the loss of human potential.[26]

Despite the activities of numerous Polish welfare committees the situation did not improve. To be sure, the Polish Rescue Committee (PKR) managed to secure the safety of Polish children.[27] The Polish–Soviet War in mid-1920 further worsened the plight of Poles in Siberia and Far East. In 1920 Polish officials visited Manchuria. Autonomous local Polish organizations were abolished, and only those (such as the PKR) which looked after Poles scattered over the entire region remained. Meanwhile, those who could afford to do so left Russia at their own expense, on ships leased by the Polish government from China and Japan. The publicity given to the PKR's activities galvanized the Polish diaspora in the USA to collect money for Polish children dispersed across the Russian interior; a small sum was raised towards the repatriation of the remainder of the Siberian Fifth Division marooned in Harbin. Eventually, the Treaty of Riga enabled repatriation to proceed more easily. As a consequence, around 1,000 individuals left Irkutsk and twice as many quit Krasnoiarsk. This still left 2,000 Poles hoping to return home from Chita and 10,000 in Transbaikal. The Siberian Committee of the Polish–Soviet Joint Repatriation Commission operated in western Siberia (Omsk), but the area of the Far Eastern Republic was beyond its jurisdiction. Poles living outside its reach made their own attempt to return. The problem of repatriation was finally resolved on 14 December 1924, when Poland and Soviet Russia signed a further agreement according to which Russia permitted Polish repatriates from the territory of the former Far Eastern Republic to be transported across central Russia. In return for this, Poland at last agreed to recognize the Soviet Union. The long process of repatriation was completed only in 1924, when most of the remaining Poles living in Siberia and Manchuria returned to their newly independent homeland.[28]

THE ASSOCIATION OF SIBERIAN DEPORTEES (ZWIĄZEK SYBIRAKÓW)

The Polish constitution (adopted in 1921) permitted all citizens freedom of organization, provided that it did not pose any danger to the state. This provided the basis for the establishment of numerous civic groups in the new democracy. Among these were various organizations established by Polish veterans during the 1920s to assist former comrades and to help integrate them into postwar society. One such organization was the Association of Siberian Deportees, the activities of which offer us some insights into the role of shared experiences of displacement and diaspora in forging community ties and creating social interest groups in new states.

Several years elapsed before the return of Polish exiles from Siberia led to the creation of an organization dedicated to bringing them together on the basis of collective experience. The origins of the Association of Siberian Deportees are to be found in a decision taken in February 1926 to establish a local Silesian organization in Katowice for veterans who had returned from Siberia to Poland. In 1928 a nationwide returnee organization came into being. The founding statutes declared that the Association undertook to 'unite former military, political, and civic and social activists for whom Siberia was a site of the struggle for independence or the place where such activity was to be punished.'[29] The Association was to dedicate itself both to current political and welfare concerns and to sustaining the memory of exile, undertaking to promote the publication of historical works as well as contemporary publications of a 'national' character, and to encourage solidarity and reciprocal support among returnees.

The Association was divided into sections devoted to history, economic activity, propaganda and publishing, and intermittent fundraising. A mutual aid section offered poorer members benefits, legal and medical advice and help in looking for work. The Association also established meeting places and libraries. Veterans of the Fifth Siberian Division had their own separate club. A youth section was established to cater for the needs of 'Polish Youth of the Far East', supporting people who had returned to Poland from Manchuria in their childhood years. The Association also sponsored groups reuniting Poles who had lived in particular towns and cities in Siberia. One such group brought together the former Polish residents of the city of Orenburg, south of the Urals, who confidently announced that 'the steppes of Kirgizia have always counted as Siberia'.[30] Polish settlement in Russia had been spread widely, but it is clear that Siberia had assumed a particular role in the memory of the repatriated refugees and re-emigrants, not only as a land of exile and loss but also of diasporic solidarity and national rebirth.

The programme of work undertaken by the Association's Economic Section was especially interesting, aiming as it did to 'propagate the idea of economic expansion to Siberia and Far East among the Polish people.'[31] An article describing its activities in 1935 stated that 'the Section is exploring real possibilities for such expansion. Contacts are being established by the Polish consular agency in Harbin. Samples of products are being sent. Large-scale activity is under way.'[32] As far as Siberia was concerned, the objective of promoting Polish trade and investment was of course wishful thinking. Relations between Poland and the Soviet Union had become increasingly tense since the early 1930s, and (as some in Poland recognized at the time) 'each and every Pole in Soviet lands is a potential suspect and liable to be found guilty of sabotage and/or espionage, which renders cooperation impossible.'[33] In the Far East, on the other hand, prospects were better. Harbin was at this time in Chinese hands, and cooperation with the small Polish community which had remained in the city was feasible.

By 1935, the Association of Siberian Deportees had 5,211 members, of whom 1,504 were paid-up members. It had branches in nine major Polish cities, and three clubs in smaller towns.[34] The Association was managed by an executive comprising the President and two Vice-Presidents, the Treasurer and his Deputy, and the Commander-in-Chief of the club of former soldiers of the Fifth Siberian Division. Other sections included a Board of Control and a Court of Arbitration.[35] One of the members of the Association was the Head of State, Józef Piłsudski, who had spent the years between 1887 and 1892 as a deportee in Siberia: he was frequently referred to as the 'Great Siberian Exile' (*Wielki Sybirak*). Most Poles did not question his authority, and the Association proclaimed its loyalty towards Piłsudski and promised to support his policies. Another important figurehead was Wacław Sieroszewski, who enjoyed a varied career as a writer, as a soldier in the Polish Legion, as an anthropologist working among the peoples of Siberia, and as President of the Professional Union of Polish Writers and of the Polish Academy of Literature. Sieroszewski had spent twelve years in exile in Siberia during the years 1880 to 1892.[36]

From its inception the Association sought to distance itself from formal politics, instead seeking to foster a sense of shared experience and communal solidarity among former deportees. In practice, organizing the 'Sybiraki' into an association sharing similar values and goals posed major problems. Though bound by the common experience of exile and memory of the diaspora, the 'Siberian exiles' were a highly disparate group both socially and in terms of their experience – some had been born in Siberia and lived there all their lives, some had spent all their adult lives there, others had resided only a short time in exile, as wartime refugees or as prisoners of war. Many of the older Siberian deportees, of course, scarcely knew Poland at all and spoke Polish very badly. Some had been prosperous individuals in Siberia, but had lost their property to the revolution and arrived in Poland destitute. Undoubtedly, the reality of the new state for many repatriates was quite different from the image of their homeland which they had cultivated and nurtured while in diaspora. As a consequence, many found it hard to adjust to the new social and cultural environment they encountered.

Some indication of the difficulties that deportees faced can be found in adverts placed in the journal *Sybirak*, asking for assistance on behalf of the unemployed members of the Association. Occasionally such appeals bore fruit. For example in 1936 a Polish film studio decided to make a film based on the history of the Fifth Siberian Division. The script consultants had belonged to the Division and were active in the Association of Siberian Deportees. Unemployed members of Association were given walk-on parts in the film – these men, who had fought on behalf of Poland and covered thousands of miles returning to their homeland after long years of Siberian exile, now found themselves reduced to accepting bit-parts in a semi-mythic account of their own deeds.[37]

The Association of Siberian Deportees was but one of many veterans' organizations that were active in interwar Poland. Others included the Association of Soldiers of the First Eastern Army, the Union of Jewish Participants in the Struggle for Polish Independence, the Union of Soldiers of Kaniowski and Żeligowski (names of two famous Polish generals), the Union of Legionnaires, the Union of Members of the Polish Organization of Freedom, the Union of Invalid Soldiers of the Polish Republic and the Union of Defenders of the Eastern Borderlands.[38] Over thirty such organizations, embracing a wide range of political views and social constituencies, came together in February 1929 under the umbrella of the Federation of Polish Associations of Defenders of the Fatherland (*Federacja Polskich Związków Obrońców Ojczyzny*, or FPZOO). By 1938 the Federation boasted around 600,000 members. Significantly, Piłsudski became its Life President (following his death in 1935 this role was taken over by Marshal Edward Rydz-Śmigły). The Federation's leadership proclaimed its belief in 'everything for the State, its development, its security, and its claim to be a world power.'[39] Initially, the Association was occupied mainly in promoting mutual aid activities among its members, but in the years leading up to World War Two it began to engage in civil defence training and political education for the wider population.

THE ROLE OF *SYBIRAK*

One of the self-proclaimed tasks of the Association was to preserve the Siberian exile tradition, so that future generations of Poles would never forget the history of the Polish diaspora in Siberia. To this end it supported the publication of the quarterly journal *Sybirak*. An analysis of the contents of the eighteen issues that appeared between 1934 and 1939 sheds light on the Association's ideology and activity, as well as on the social, civic and political stance of its members. Its ideological stance, in particular, is evident in every issue. The Association believed in total obedience to Piłsudski. In the case of Siberian exiles, the connection with Piłsudski was reinforced by the fact that he had shared their experience.[40] In addition, many of the Association's members had a military background and strongly supported the cult of the 'Chief'. For these reasons each issue of *Sybirak* contained information about the 'Great Siberian Exile' and numerous extracts from Piłsudski's speeches and writings. The Siberian deportees could support no other political line. As Gintowt-Dziewałtowski said, 'As with our predecessors who had been deported to

Siberia, the only objective for us all was the regaining of independence by Poland; the greatest vision is the idea of a Poland that is strong and just.'[41]

The historical section devoted itself to gathering material and publishing scientific and literary works on Siberia, including the tribulations of Poles in its hostile territory. It arranged exhibitions on Siberian themes in various Polish cities, usually on the occasion of the anniversary of Poland's independence. Another task was to collect the reminiscences of Siberian exiles in order to preserve this testimony for future generations. Each new issue recounted stories of Polish deportees, their descendants, and former prisoners of war.[42] The history of the Fifth Siberian Division and the long journey home of its soldiers was another recurrent theme. These accounts recur in *Sybirak*, both in the memories and diaries of its members, and in reviews of relevant works that appeared in Poland, France and Czechoslovakia. By cultivating and developing a mythology of national exile and rebirth in diaspora, these Siberian recollections could be made to serve the purpose of sustaining the Polish national project.

The themes of veterans' experience and personal martyrdom were not the only ones represented in the discourse relating to Siberia. One of *Sybirak*'s regular contributors wrote that 'the Association of Siberian Deportees would not be a living organisation if it concentrated solely on the post-partition trauma experienced by the nation, if – as representing the last line in successive generations of Polish prisoners and exiles – the Association became dedicated only to the cause of preserving the sacred memories and traditions of those bygone times ... Such a programme is insufficient ... During the mighty development of our revived statehood, when Poland is faced with various choices in the field of international relations - the Association should be a lively centre of attention devoted to the future prospects that result from our closeness to the vast expanse of Russia and Siberia.'[43]

Increasingly hostile Polish–Soviet relations and the prevailing anti-Bolshevism meant that this vision was never fully articulated, still less realized. Nevertheless, the journal continued to debate Polish perceptions of Siberia. One notable contribution took the form of an analysis of an article by Feliks Gross, entitled 'Siberia, Deportation, Learning', published in the monthly periodical *Droga* [*The Path*]. Gross claimed that Siberia had thus far been treated largely as a political issue, in which far too much attention was devoted to deportation and the suffering of Polish exiles. He maintained that there was another side to the Polish experience, namely the Poles' contribution to the development of Siberia. This contribution reflected the fact that most deportees had been educated and highly motivated people. The free time at their disposal enabled Polish exiles, such as Wacław Sieroszewski, to study the indigenous peoples of Siberia as well as its flora and fauna. This research had been recognized by Russian and Polish science, and even internationally.[44] The editors of *Sybirak* endorsed the view that these achievements should be recorded in order to encourage a new perception of Siberia.[45]

Mieczyslaw Lepecki's important book, *Syberia bez przekleństw* [*Siberia without Curses*], was written in a similar spirit:

> [Poland] is free and the younger generation no longer remembers the years of enslavement. Siberia, much like Russia is but a geographic name for us ... Today we may think and speak freely of that country ... we are also free to describe the natural beauty of Siberia not from a politically-biased point of view, of national hatred, but with the eye of an unbiased spectator, just as if we looked at exotic American or African lands. For those of us who are lucky to live in a time of freedom, Siberia is no longer the destination of exile – we no longer have to love it or hate it.

Lepecki produced a collection of reports on contemporary Siberia seen with the eyes of one who perceived the exotic beauty of the country and considered it a future tourist destination.[46] Works of this type encountered the criticism of those who saw Siberia solely as the place of suffering. For these critics, such as Włodzimierz Bączkowski, Siberian deportees had a duty to preach the 'truth' about the eternal rivalry between Poland and Russia, rather than about the scenic beauty of Siberia.[47] Similarly, Artur Zabęski criticised Lepecki's optimism on the grounds that it was too soon to discount the 'scars' that Siberia had left on the mind of many Poles.[48]

Others claimed that Siberia had something of a sacred connotation, and that this was in danger of being 'turned into a bazaar by young Poland', for whom Siberia was nothing more than a land of economic opportunity. Others disagreed, arguing that this 'bazaar' would do just as good a job of bringing nations and peoples closer together as a 'museum of martyrdom'.[49] In fact, each issue of *Sybirak* contained proof of a lively discussion of the meanings that attached to Siberian diaspora and the landscape of displacement. The dispute went beyond the milieu of Siberian deportees and became something of a national debate. In the literary annual, *Rocznik Literacki* [*Literary Yearbook*], Kazimierz Wyka, an eminent literary critic, remarked that '"revisionism" is a fashionable word in literary matters. If one could relate "revisionism" to travel literature, then surely one of the most revisionist books is Lepecki's *Siberia Without Curses*. For the average Pole, Siberia has an age-old emotional association. It is high time to break the sorcerer's evil spell. We can assume that there is no more suffering. What Siberia is like today has not been described until Lepecki wrote about it ... He has described how its beauty – the uniqueness of the *taiga* and of Lake Baikal, the beauty of its inhabitants – accustomed the exiles to Siberia ... We can fully believe his reports.'[50]

The themes articulated in *Siberia Without Curses* were also present in *Sybirak*. They involved more than straightforward recollections of personal experience. Each issue of the journal contained a section entitled 'Soviet current affairs', a regular column containing assorted economic and social (and occasionally also political) news from Soviet Russia. In addition, readers could find detailed information about Soviet festivities, such as events celebrating the two hundredth anniversary of the founding of Cheliabinsk. In the last issues that appeared before the journal ceased publication in July 1939, the magazine began to publish ethnographic works devoted to the peoples of Siberia and the Far East including Yakuts, Giliaks, Nantsy, Buriats and others whom Polish settlers had encountered. To judge from the popularity of this material, readers who were suffering serious economic deprivation in Poland entertained a great nostalgia for the lands they had left behind.

This material demonstrates an ambivalence in the treatment of Siberia by the returnees. Despite the many differences among their life histories and experiences, returnees constituted a special group for a variety of reasons. They had all had an extraordinary personal trajectory, consisting of deportation, exile and a determination, longing and striving to return home. Their lives were marked by a division between the time before and after their return to Poland, a division that resulted in problems adapting to new circumstances. As we have mentioned, by no means everyone found the 'new Poland' a pleasant place to settle. As well as economic hardship, Siberian returnees often found their formative experiences largely ignored by state and society, especially by a young generation preoccupied with the present and future. Despite the cult of the soldier and officer, and the widespread admiration for 'freedom fighters', in practice the life of the former exile or refugee now mattered little for Polish society. The former deportees spoke somewhat sadly of 'young Poland', describing the new generation that had become influential. Polish youth treated the old folk with disdain. There are a few instances in which returnees even decided to make their way back to Siberia or to the Far East. For example, in the biography of Kazimierz Grochowski, a Polish engineer from Harbin, we read that '... even rich people from the Polish colony in Harbin, who elected to go to Poland without financial support from Polish organisations, found it impossible to find work in Poland. They returned to Harbin after several months, very disappointed.'[51]

Faced with this new reality, the Siberian deportees took one of two stances. Some actively joined in the construction of the reborn Poland, using their experience and education as best they might for the new state. Unfortunately, it is difficult to chart this commitment very extensively. But some of it comes across, indirectly at least, in the obituary columns of *Sybirak*. These short biographies tell of individuals who had demonstrated enormous courage, not only by surviving Siberia but also in managing to fight their way back home. In later life they had served independent Poland as engineers, soldiers, railway administrators and teachers. Many of them had assumed high political office or senior administrative posts. About the lives of the second group, *Sybirak* had nothing to say. Their character was beautifully portrayed by Zofia Lech in her intriguing work entitled *Syberia Polską pachnąca* [*The Scent of Poland in Siberia*]:

> More than a few people were torn in two. Living in Poland they missed the boundless expanses of the taiga, the tundra, and the "holy" Lake Baikal. They recollected bear-hunting, encounters with the Giliaks, and fishing for salmon in the Amur River. These Poles, true denizens of Siberia, never cursed Siberia but rather loved the land for what it was. And it was indeed an infinite space, a haven for bird and fowl, the source of vast deposits of fossil fuel, fertile soil, and a place where friendships were born. With the passage of time all the cruelty resulting from Russian rule stopped haunting the hearts and minds of these Siberian deportees. They gathered into groups to reminisce and to discuss the bygone times. They understood that a land that had provided them with employment, food, clothing – and even hope – should not be cursed.[52]

Another example is in the famous novel *Cudzoziemka* [*The Stranger*], by Maria Kuncewicz.[53] Its heroine returns to Poland from Russia. She complains that in Russia she was Polish, in Poland she is called 'Ruska', and everywhere she is treated like a 'foreigner'. Finally, in Igor Neverly's novel *Wzgórza Błękitnego Snu* [*The Hills of Blue Dream*], based on the true story of Bronisław Najdarowski, a member of the Polish political party 'Proletariat' exiled to Siberia for an attempt on the Tsar's life in 1906, we read about the difficulties he faced in Poland after he returned in 1923. The novel recounts how 'very often people from the milieu of Siberian deportees visited him. Old-aged, in better or worse financial situation, they couldn't make themselves at home in their homeland. A little shamefully, they still pined for Siberia.'[54] For people such as these, the Association of Siberian Deportees and its journal constituted a kind of surrogate life. It was in particular an association of Siberia and its landscape with the dreams and hopes of youth, with a sense of future possibilities for the Polish nation and, paradoxically for a land of exile, with a spatial openness and spiritual freedom which, contrasted with the grim realities and responsibilities of contemporary life in the new Polish state, encouraged the emergence of this Siberian nostalgia.

CONCLUSIONS

The Polish diaspora in Siberia and the Far East was internally differentiated. Some Poles found themselves in Siberia and the Far East against their will, either because of their previous anti-imperial activity in the tsarist state or because they were deported during World War One. Others established labour settlements, hoping as 'economic migrants' to find a better life than they would otherwise endure in the poorest parts of Poland. Yet others enlisted in Polish military detachments during the revolution and Civil War, in order to contribute (as they hoped) to the eventual liberation of Poland.

At the same time, these disparate elements of the Polish diaspora shared many common characteristics. Recalling the key elements of diaspora enumerated by Robin Cohen, we can see that they seem to be valid for the Polish population of Siberia and the Far East. Each generation retained a memory of 'homeland', a memory that was at times illusory and constructed in and through the experience of exile. In Polish literature this syndrome is called *mit szklanych domów* ['the myth of glass-houses'], by which is meant a beautiful illusion, all too easily shattered. The term was coined in Stefan Żeromski's famous novel, *Przedwiośnie* [*Before Springtime*]. The father of the protagonist had been an engineer in Baku before the Revolution. Travelling by train from Tsaritsyn to Poland via Moscow, the father talks to his son, who had been born in Russia, about the 'new Poland', a country of justice and civilization, where 'even the houses were made of glass'. The reality which his son faced after returning was far from this idyllic image, as the novel proceeded to demonstrate.[55]

Generations of deportees and settlers subscribed to this myth of the Polish national homeland, which reinforced a yearning to return, a dream that the Russian revolution made a reality. Many Siberian and Far Eastern Poles certainly migrated to the 'new Poland'. But the process of adjustment to new conditions was little different to problems of 'assimilation' faced by non-national immigrants. The history of Siberian returnees demonstrates just how difficult the process of adaptation could be. In many it bred a sense of nostalgia for the lands of their exile. In some cases it ended in tragedy.

The members of the group shared two additional features that played a crucial role in the construction of their civic identity in postwar Poland. Firstly, they shared a common experience of a time of exile, during which they had cultivated idealized collective memories of the 'homeland'. Secondly, on return they constructed a sense of solidarity on the basis of a common identification with the landscapes of the diaspora, be it Siberia or the Far East. These core elements of the returnees' identity were at the same time a cause of ambivalence. For this group, Siberia and the Far East were more than geographical regions; these physical places were at the same time mythic spaces, and as such critical factors influencing their behaviour, emotional states and attitudes. By investing 'space' with meaning – meaning that changed as their experiences of exile and diaspora receded into the past and became elements of a new and equally idealized collective memory – the returnees strove to define their social identity, status and role in the new Poland.

8
Refugees in the Urals Region, 1917–25

GENNADII KORNILOV*

INTRODUCTION

In contemporary Russia, the refugee problem has become especially acute. As is well known, incessant military conflict and political instability in a number of regions have provoked huge displacements of population. But the problem is not new. At the beginning of the twentieth century, Russia already experienced forced migration on a massive scale as, in rapid succession, World War One, the Civil War and then a catastrophic famine acted as catalysts prompting vast outflows of refugees from the most populated regions. The causes and consequences of these waves of population displacement are only now beginning to receive due attention.[1]

However, many dimensions of these displacements have yet to be researched. For one thing, these migrations were largely spontaneous and disorganized, so that in a majority of cases it was impossible to register the origins, numbers and destinations of displaced persons. Where officials did strive to formulate a statistical account of displacements, as, for example, they did for prisoners of war, these were rarely successful. Archival materials on forced migration, therefore, can offer only sparse, partial information, which in turn demands painstaking and imaginative analysis on the part of historians. The State Archive of Sverdlovsk Region (GASO) contains a number of materials that cast light on the refugee problem in one important region.[2]

Through a close analysis of surviving archival materials, this chapter sets out to investigate the dynamics of refugee movements and numbers, to describe the process of their registration in the Urals region, to ascertain the major places of origin of immigrants and their main areas of local resettlement, and to follow their subsequent re-evacuation to their homelands. I devote special attention to the so-called 'famine refugees' (*golodbezhentsy*).

THREE PHASES OF MIGRATION AND THE INSTITUTIONAL CONTEXT

The Urals region was one of the primary destinations of forced migrants, owing to its favourable climatic conditions, its thin population density (which enabled it to accommodate large numbers of new settlers), its distance from the major war zones and its relatively abundant food supply. It was also a region of transit for migrants travelling eastwards towards Siberia, a proportion of whom chose – or were forced by circumstances – to remain in this region. In the period between 1915 and 1925, the Urals witnessed three main waves of population displacement. The first major influx consisted of refugees of World War One. These were mainly non-Russians (Lithuanians, Poles, Latvians and others), who had quit their homes following the German occupation or because the tsarist authorities ordered them to leave. This wave peaked in 1919–20, when huge numbers of refugees, impelled by a dream of returning to their homelands, passed through the Urals in transit back from Siberia and the Far East towards the western border. These returnees ran into large numbers of national migrants who had settled in the region earlier on, and were also now intent on returning home. The spontaneous arrival of migrants ignoring official re-evacuation plans placed the carrying capacity of the railways under great strain and resulted in dreadful congestion at all major junctions. By 1920 there were up to 200,000 foreign citizens on the territory of the Urals region, all of them intent on leaving Russia as soon as possible. Their condition was critical: the meagre supplies of food, clothing and other necessities, as well as the lack of accommodation, made the refugees' desire to return to their homeland ever more urgent.

During 1920 this first wave of involuntary migrants merged with the second influx, produced by the tumult of the Russian Civil War. The majority of these refugees were formerly residents of central, southern and eastern regions in flight from the depredations of White and Red forces alike. From this time on, the evacuation authorities began to take account of both categories of forced migrants in their reports. This second wave reached its peak in 1920 when Ekaterinburg province (*guberniia*) alone registered about 10,000 displaced persons. Most of these refugees, however, did not stay in the Urals but moved on to Siberia and the Far East, where they dispersed and resettled. Only relatively small numbers of these migrants subsequently returned to their places of birth.

In 1921–2, a third wave of refugees flooded into the Urals, seeking to escape the terrible consequences of the famine which had affected some of Russia's most fertile regions. These involuntary migrants were not only more numerous than their predecessors but were also physically the most stricken. They brought with them typhus, starvation and poverty. At the same time, the Urals region witnessed huge internal population movements provoked by a series of peasant uprisings against Soviet power.

From 1921, these three waves of forced migrants began to merge, creating a crisis of proportions beyond the management capabilities of the evacuation authorities. In such a catastrophic situation, officials found it impossible to register the 'famine refugees', who moved through the region in huge numbers by railway, on carts or on foot. For this reason, contemporary reports offer in place of statistics such vague phrases as 'floods of refugees', 'many unorganised refugees', and so on. The situation was further complicated by the fact that a large number of forced migrants were not settling in the Urals but travelling through the region in transit. In 1922, for example, 3,700 people passed through the Cheliabinsk resettlement point on their way eastwards, and another 29,200 migrants returned through the resettlement point on their journey back towards the western regions. It should be noted that before 1924 we do not find the term 'famine refugees' used in official Cheliabinsk resettlement point reports to describe those migrants who had been forced to leave their homes because of sparse food supplies.[3] Previously, various terms had been used to describe this category of migrant, including 'those arriving from famine-afflicted localities' (as in *gubevak* reports for 1919), 'resettlers from famine-afflicted regions' (reports in 1921) or 'individuals suffering from starvation' (*golodaiushchie*) (as in reports submitted by the Cheliabinsk resettlement point in 1921).[4]

It is difficult to define or distinguish with great precision the chronological limits of each of these three waves of forced migration, since groups of refugees moved across the Urals territory throughout this period, intermingled and became caught up in other flows. For this reason, I have demarcated the three main categories of migrant not chronologically but according to the reasons that compelled them to change their place of residence. Thus, military action during World War One produced the first wave; the Civil War the second wave; and the famine of 1921–2 the third wave. The process of re-evacuation lasted until 1925–6, by which time each group had the opportunity to return home, and the Soviet government had launched a policy of planned resettlement to the Urals. Thus, the first wave of forced migration extended from 1914 to 1925–6; the second from 1918 to 1925–6; and the third from 1921 to 1925–6.[5]

From 1918, the Soviet governmental institution with responsibility for overseeing the movement and welfare of refugees was the Central Committee for Prisoners of War and Refugees (*Tsentroplenbezh*, renamed *Tsentrevak* in February 1920) and its subordinate field offices. *Tsentroplenbezh* planned and operated transports for all categories of migrants except military contingents, and organized the re-evacuation of prisoners of war and refugees alike.[6] It issued a steady stream of directives to regulate all migrant traffic under its remit, although these were frequently violated or ignored by local officials. *Tsentroplenbezh* also established regional departments and field stations at major railway and river junctions. These offices serviced migrants' needs so far as accommodation, sanitary facilities and food were concerned. They also offered advice and information. In 1921, the Urals region had three base stations (in Perm, Ekaterinburg and Cheliabinsk), which as well as carrying out their own organizational tasks supervised the activities of eight subordinate line-service stations. Thus the Perm Regional Administration for Evacuation (*Gubevak*) oversaw the Perm, Viatskii, Kotel'nich and Glazov stations. The Ekaterinburg *Gubevak* managed field operations in Ekaterinburg, Sarapul and Krasnoufimsk. The Cheliabinsk *Gubevak* had responsibility for the Cheliabinsk line station.[7] At lower levels, each *uezd* (district) also had its own evacuation administrations. Within Ekaterinburg province, for example, such organizations existed in Shadrinsk, Kamyshlov, Krasnoufimsk and Kamensk *uezds*, and evacuation plenipotentiaries in Verkhotur'e, Irbit, Nizhnii Tagil, Nadezhdinsk and Alapaevsk *uezds*.[8] On 13 November 1922, the government of the Russian Soviet Socialist Federal Republic (Sovnarkom RSFSR) issued a decree reorganizing this network of evacuation offices as the scale of their activities began to diminish.[9] All responsibilities of the Central Evacuation Administration were transferred to the People's Commissariat of Agriculture (Narkomzem). The activities of the regional and local base and line-service stations were to be wound up by 1 January 1923. Also from this time, the State Political Administration (GPU, that is, the political police) and foreign representatives had to authorize all refugee transports organized by local evacuation offices.[10] Narkomzem's resettlement offices in the localities took over responsibility for the technical details of evacuation. On the basis of this experience, these offices took on the main tasks of organizing planned resettlement to the Urals region later in the decade.

THE FIRST PHASE AND ITS IMPLICATIONS

According to AN Kurtsev, refugees from Russia's western front began to arrive in the interior on a mass scale in July–August 1915, with their numbers reaching a peak in September–October and beginning to decline from November–December of the same year.[11] By the middle of September there were about 750,000 refugees in central Russia, including all those who had fled the front since the start of the war. During the next three and a half months, over two million people travelled eastwards on scheduled through trains alone. We may derive an impression of the dynamics of this traffic from the regular information reports on 'the daily passage of refugees through fifty-four registration points within European Russia': 148,900 people travelled through these stations during the second half of September alone (when mass railway transports of refugees began); another 111,800 during October; 8,600 in November; and 1,700 in December. The special refugee trains *(eshelony)* first began to arrive in Siberia, Central Asia and the Far East at the end of September; the last contingents arrived at the same time as refugees began to depart for other destinations.

Using data from the localities, Kurtsev has put the number of registered refugees in the summer of 1917 at 3,800,000 people. In the war zone of European Russia there were 744,800 refugees (19.4 per cent of the total number). These were geographically distributed as follows: 396,500 on the northern and western fronts (above all in Lifland (170,500), and in Minsk (145,200); the remainder were to be found in Vitebsk province and the territory of Vilno province, which was still in Russian hands); and 348,000 on the south western front. The vast majority of wartime refugees (2,600,000, or 67.9 per cent of the total) remained in the territories of European Russia behind the front lines. The largest proportion was to be found in the provinces of Ekaterinburg (234,700); Moscow (212,000, including 170,784 in the city of Moscow); and Samara (173,000). Some 114,600 refugees (three per cent of the total) travelled as far as Asiatic Russia (Siberia, the Far East, Central Asia), most of whom settled in Akmolinsk region (31,900) and Tomsk province (30,000). Finally, there were 373,500 refugees in the Caucasus and Transcaucasus (9.7 per cent of the total). By December 1919, according to *Tsentroplenbezh* data, about 759,000 of these refugees were still registered as being in Russian territory (see Table 1).

In 1917, the provinces of Viatka, Perm, Ufa and Orenburg were merged into a single unified Urals region. The information in Table 1 thus establishes that there were approximately 135,000 forced migrants in the territory of the Urals region (according to government data, which probably understates the real number), equivalent to 17.8 per cent of the Russian nationwide total. At the end of 1919, the Soviet authorities in the Urals, having re-established their power in the region, implemented a new territorial-administrative division, forming five provinces: Ekaterinburg, Perm, Cheliabinsk, Ufa and Tiumen. However, this did little to improve the efficiency of communications between the periphery and the centre. Poor connections among territorial units (a consequence of the military situation), a lack of state officials and other factors meant that the Soviet authorities in the centre failed to receive much of the information collected in the regions. Thus, Tiumen *Gubevak* compiled a report in 28 May 1921, according to which '... the uprising of White Guard bands in the prov-

TABLE 1: Distribution of refugees in Russia (*Tsentroplenbezh* data, 1 December 1919)

Province	Number	%	Province	Number	%
Astrakhan	23399	3.1	Orel	34715	4.6
Vitebsk	3833	0.5	Penza	18407	2.4
Vladimir	9298	1.2	Perm	50000	6.6
Vologda	1063	0.1	Petrograd	282	0.03
Voronezh	59360	7.8	Pskov	698	0.09
Viatka	647	0.1	Ryazan	10000	1.3
Dvina	821	0.1	Samara	88889	11.7
Ivanovo	1254	0.2	Saratov	123338	16.3
Kazan'	46426	6.1	Simbirsk	10805	1.4
Kaluga	14009	1.8	Smolensk	24072	3.2
Kostroma	3575	0.5	Tambov	36405	4.8
Kursk	31775	4.2	Tula	25000	3.3
Moscow	21024	2.8	Tver	6367	0.8
Mogilev	1783	0.2	Ufa	67548	8.9
Nizhegorod	15981	2.1	Yaroslavl'	7435	1.0
Novgorod	1733	0.2	Cherepovets	2045	0.3
Orenburg	16912	2.2	Total:	758903	100

Source: GARF f. r-3333, op. 4, d. 604, l. 13.

ince, primarily in Ishimsk and Ialutorovsk *uezds*, makes it impossible to send out documents.'[12] Many localities were similarly cut off or embroiled in conflict, so information on the number of refugees in the Urals in these years is necessarily incomplete.

However, it is possible to attempt a provisional calculation on the basis of an analysis of the materials gathered by hard-pressed local officials. In order to establish the number of foreign refugees (of the first wave) on Russian territory, the evacuation authorities tried to register them in their localities of settlement. Thus in 1920, *Tsentrevak* issued an Instruction setting out procedures for registering and compiling lists of refugees.[13] This noted that 'in view of the imminent re-evacuation of Polish refugees, to take place in connection with the conclusion of the Treaty with Poland, all registrations of refugees carried out to date should be considered cancelled, and a new registration of all refugees is immediately to be implemented on Russian territory.' The same Instruction defined refugees as 'all citizens who can proffer adequate and genuine documentation and proof that before 1 August 1914 they resided permanently outside Russian borders and left their places of birth during the World War of 1914–1918, or the Russian–Ukrainian–Polish war, or the Civil War, as a consequence of enemy occupation or the threat of attack, or who were forcibly evacuated (*vyslannye*) by civil or military authorities.' The registration of refugees might be carried out on the basis of the following documents: a passport, issued in the previous place of residence before evacuation; a refugee's book (*bezhenskaia knizhka*), issued by the former Tatiana Committee, Union of Zemstvos, Union of Towns or other similar institutions under the imperial regime; certificates or copies of directives attesting to the individual's evacuation or expulsion from his place of residence, issued by appropriate authorities; a refugee's registration card (*registratsionnaia bezhenskaia kartochka*), issued by the relevant national department of the People's Commissariat for Nationalities before 1 January 1919; or other documents proving beyond doubt that the person in question had lived in a specific place before evacuation.[14] The Instruction emphasized that under no circumstances could the testimonies or guarantees of other refugees or certificates attesting to the loss or destruction of documents be accepted as proof of refugee status.

Registration cards were intended to include comprehensive information about their holder (surname, first name, patronymic, age, nationality, religion, family status, current place of residence, original place of residence, occupation). The registered (adult male) refugee could co-register and be accompanied in his re-evacuation by members of his family, which included his wife (so long as they were currently living together), his mother, his father (if he was too old or infirm to work), grandchildren, foster-children (*pitomtsy*) or wards (*vospitanniki*), and other dependent household members (*domochadtsy*). Refugees who received a place on the lists of departing contingents but who refused to leave lost the right of departure and were given lowest priority in future re-evacuation schedules. The right to evacuation by road, with a cart, livestock and horses, could only be granted to those refugees who could offer proof that they had brought this same livestock with them from their homeland. Refugees also received the right either to sell their property or to take it with them under a number of restrictive conditions. The total weight of baggage, other than hand luggage, could not exceed eight *puds* for the head of the family (or for one unmarried person), five *puds* for each family member and two *puds* for children under ten years of age.[15] Items which refugees could take with them as hand luggage included: personal linen, clothing and footwear (no more than two items or a pair of each), one fur coat and up to six pairs of underwear. In addition to this, they were permitted to take enough travelling items (pillows, blankets, sheets, tea-kettles, etc.) to meet their needs on the journey. The following items were prohibited: printed matter and documents without appropriate authorization, weapons and military equipment, manufactured or other goods for trading, more than thirty pounds of food, locally bred or bought livestock and poultry, automobiles, precious metals, antiques, more than one piece of soap per person, and so forth.[16]

However, despite these precisely formulated instructions on procedures for registration and for forming and despatching groups of refugees, local authorities immediately encountered a range of problems. On 15 March 1921, for example, the Ekaterinburg Regional Administration for Evacuation (*Gubevak*) reported that

> the re-evacuation is proceeding according to *Tsentrevak*'s orders, but in order to establish and carry out our orders we need to have exact information on the number of refugees within our province, with an indication of their place of origin and the current place of residence from which they are to be evacuated. However, in spite of *Gubevak*'s directive no. 241 setting out the procedure for registering this group and the procedure for submitting relevant information on its members, many *volost* (parish) executive committees (*volispolkomy*) are failing to carry out their tasks. This unfortunate fact precludes any accurate registration of refugees, for one thing. Secondly, it disrupts the refugees' planned re-evacuation.[17]

A further, equally troublesome problem which the evacuation authorities encountered was the tendency of refugees, as soon as they heard that a re-evacuation was imminent, to depart independently for their homelands in disregard of official plans. In a report on its activities, *Tsentrevak* noted that 'in relation to the refugee phenomenon, spontaneity (*samotek*) signifies a chaotic movement of refugees, predominantly towards the state border, manifesting all the characteristics of an endless flow of large groups. As a rule, any spontaneous movement of human masses grievously undermines the territorial evacuation plan.'[18] A telegram despatched to the Urals from Moscow on 19 May 1920 reported that 'despite the Centre's repeated prohibition on issuing travel permits to refugees and prisoners of war without corresponding orders from the People's Commissariat of Railways and *Tsentrevak*, there has recently been a sharp increase in unorganised movements of people from various places on the authorisation of executive committees, officials of the political police [known at this time as the Extraordinary Commission, or *Cheka*] officials and other institutions.'[19] The Ekaterinburg Department of the Regional Administration attributed this behaviour on the part of local personnel to 'the refugees' stubborn persistence in making demands, and the desire of local authorities to be rid of them as quickly as possible.'[20] Indeed, groups of refugees continued to be granted travel permits without formal authorization from the appropriate evacuation administrations, causing great damage to the latter's attempts to plan departures and itineraries. The migrants found themselves in a terrible predicament. Usually they were travelling with their families and children. They were forced to remain for long periods waiting in various towns until their turn came for departure. The stations where they were billeted often lacked sufficient accommodation and sanitary facilities; they also suffered from a paucity of food. The railway system itself had insufficient capacity to cope with the massive influx of refugees, which produced great congestion at major junctions. The regional administrations coped little better. Tiumen *Gubevak* reported on 28 May 1921 that 'in view of the food crisis in Tiumen province, which has ruined the refugees of the imperialist war and driven them from their places of temporary residence, it is necessary to make provisions for the immediate relief of the region'.[21] They estimated that there were 25,000 refugees in their region (20,000 of these were Poles, the remainder being Latvian and Lithuanian citizens). To make matters worse, most of them had already sold their property, and found themselves in terrible poverty. About 16,500 foreign citizens had congregated on the territory of Ekaterinburg province (not counting prisoners of war).[22] The Kamensk Department of the Regional Administration reported that 'refugees of the imperialist war residing in our province find themselves in a desperate impasse. Hunger, infectious diseases, mortality, crime and so on are all rife. We cannot offer any aid locally because we have inadequate resources for this. We insist that arrangements are urgently made to issue orders for the departure of refugee groups – at the very least, for the 7,000 people who were granted travel permits in November 1921 but who are still waiting to leave because no railway carriages have yet been officially requisitioned.'[23]

In order to overcome these problems, in particular to put a stop to unorganized, independent departures, the People's Commissariat of Internal Affairs (NKVD) issued a directive on 30 March 1922 altering procedures for the registration of refugees. From now on, repatriates had to present documents attesting both to their identity and to their place of employment. Information taken from the documents presented (number, name of document, issuing agency) was entered into the repatriate's registration card or ticket. At the same time, all documents were amended to indicate that their holder had been registered. When the departure lists were compiled, all the documents noted in the registration ticket were taken from the refugee, who instead was given a single certificate serving as a residence permit valid until departure of the group.[24] Without his own documents, the refugee was obviously discouraged from setting off independently. This directive was therefore largely successful in reducing the phenomenon of spontaneous migration.

But there was still another problem. For diverse reasons, many refugees did not have all the documents necessary for re-evacuation. In particular, many foreign migrants could offer no proof of their national citizenship. Lack of adequate documentation also made it impossible for many refugees to obtain residence permits in their places of sojourn. Therefore in 1923, the Ekaterinburg *Gubispolkom* issued a directive initiating yet another re-registration of refugees.[25] All foreign citizens above the age of sixteen who were still awaing official re-evacuation to their homes and were yet to be granted a residence permit were subject to this procedure. The directive noted that

> it is necessary to carry out this registration in order to set a deadline for establishing the citizenship of all individuals of foreign origin who do not hold documents indicating their nationality and who wish to receive the appropriate documentation by means of a direct petition to the authorities. At present, individuals in this category are not officially recognised as foreign citizens, yet there are frequent instances when, contrary to the law, they are removed from the register for military conscription and are granted various privileges and given preferential treatment by Soviet authorities as if they were foreign citizens, officially recognised as such by the Foreign Departments of Gubotuprav or NKVD.[26]

Registration was also necessary to establish the number of people claiming the right to Polish, Lithuanian, Latvian and Estonian citizenship who had failed to leave Russia before the deadline fixed by the Sovnarkom RSFSR decree of 29 August 1921 (which had also granted them the right before this deadline to apply for Soviet Russian citizenship).[27] In December 1924, the NKVD launched a fourth re-registration of foreign citizens in order to expedite the final removal of those individuals claiming foreign citizenship but refusing to depart.[28] All persons of this category who within two weeks had not either voluntarily left or submitted an application for Soviet citizenship would be subject to forcible deportation by the political police (that is, the Unified State Political Administration, OGPU).

It is difficult to establish precisely how many refugees of the first wave resided within Urals territory at various times because numbers registered in various places fluctuated as the re-evacuation progressed. Table 2 has been compiled on the basis of an analysis of the available archival materials.

TABLE 2: 'First wave' refugees on the territory of Ekaterinburg province in 1920

Uezd	03.06	23.06	06.07	15.07	31.07	15.08
Ekaterinburg (city)	5401	5429	5686	5757	5817	6007
Ekaterinburg	3399	3399	3399	3434	3455	3455
Kamyshlov	3700	3700	3771	3771	3771	5890
Irbit	820	820	832	832	832	722
Verkhotur'e	440	440	440	440	0	582
Krasnoufimsk	282	282	396	403	405	410
Shadrinsk	1944	1251	1946	1946	1960	1971
Total	15986	15321	16470	16583	16240	19037

Source: Compiled from data in GASO f. r-511, op. 1, d. 199, ll. 50, 51, 55, 56, 62, 64, 71, 75.

THE SECOND WAVE JOINS THE FIRST

At this time there was a significant influx of Civil War refugees into the Urals. Since the evacuation authorities distinguished between the two categories of refugees it is possible to compare their numbers. Table 3 offers an indication of the numbers of refugees residing within Ekaterinburg province, based on data drawn from the protocols of a meeting of the heads of the regional evacuation administration on 27 April 1921.

TABLE 3: Refugees within Ekaterinburg province, April 1921

Uezd	Civil War Refugees (Number of persons)	World War Refugees (Number of persons)
Ekaterinburg	4400	
Kamyshlov	4552	
Irbit	790	756
Verkhotur'e	438	192
Krasnoufimsk	266	–
Shadrinsk	708	1910

Source: Compiled from data in GASO f. r-1646, op. 1, d. 2, l. 91–91 ob., 92; f. r-511, op. 1, d. 199, l. 20.

As a result of *gubevak* activities the numbers of refugees steadily diminished throughout 1921. Table 4 indicates the scale of transports organized during this year in Ekaterinburg province by the regional evacuation administrations.

TABLE 4: Refugee transports (data from 1 January to 1 September 1921)

Gubevak	Arrivals	Departures	Balance	Notes
Perm	43169	35057	8112	Information for February
Viatka	120065	2209	117856	No information after April
Ekaterinburg	190145	67735	122410	Information for January
Cheliabinsk	160752	149155	11597	January, February
Tiumen	114893	114893	–	

Source: Compiled from GARF f. r-3333, op. 2, d. 236, l. 1.

At this time, the *gubevak*s were dealing with widely diverse migrant populations, including industrial workers, agricultural settlers, Russian and enemy prisoners of war, and demobilized Red Army soldiers. However, the administrations' primary task was to organise the transportation of World War and Civil War refugees. These two categories, according to official data, comprised 50 per cent of all migrants whose transport was organized by the evacuation authorities in July 1921: 36.4 per cent in August, 57.9 per cent in September and 68.2 per cent in October.

As already mentioned, a great number of refugees travelled through the Urals in transit. Up to the beginning of 1920, most were moving eastwards (towards Siberia and the Far East), but from 1920 the re-evacuation of foreign refugees towards the former empire's western borderlands initiated a strong migration flow in the opposite direction. The majority of refugees from the World War were heading, in the first instance, towards Petrograd (specifically to the Narva railway junction, where the exchange of foreign citizens – that is, refugees and prisoners of war – took place). We can trace these movements through the daily reports on refugee traffic at the Ekaterinburg railway station.[29] Thus from January to the end of March 1922 approximately 74,000 people passed through the Ekaterinburg *gubevak* offices, and 11,000 through offices of the *uezd* evacuation administrations.[30] The number of refugees steadily decreased. Among these groups, more than half were travelling towards a destination outside Soviet borders. However, the process of re-evacuating these refugees to their homelands was somewhat slowed down by a range of factors. A report of the Ekaterinburg line-service station for the period from 1 April to 1 October 1922 yields the data presented in Table 5.

TABLE 5: Refugees passing through Ekaterinburg train station, 1 April–1 October 1922

Destination of refugees	Registered	Evacuated	Still registered on 1 October
Poland	2680	1322	1358
Lithuania	149	84	65
Latvia	48	23	25
Total	2877	1429	1449

Source: Compiled from GASO f. r-1646, op. 1, d. 15, l. 68.

It is clear from Table 5 that the Urals' evacuation authorities were despatching fewer refugees in this period than they were registering in their books. The main reasons for the slow rate of departure were delays on the part of foreign diplomatic representatives in Moscow in issuing passports and the returnees' refusal (in a few cases, their inability) to leave their current places of residence.

The extant archival materials therefore permit us to establish approximate numbers for both the World War forced migrants and Civil War refugees who found themselves in the Urals region in the early Soviet period. These data, of course, are by their very nature inconstant and fluctuating, owing to the continuous movement of the human masses they describe, which rarely corresponded to the authorities' careful but often futile planning. Ekaterinburg data give us the most complete picture we have found of these phenomena. Thus, in 1920 there were 19,000 foreign (World War) refugees and 4,200 Russian (Civil War) refugees on regional territory.[31] By 1921 their numbers had fallen to 16,500 and 1,900 respectively.[32] In 1922, the Ekaterinburg line-service station reported that about 3,000 foreign refugees remained on its territory.[33]

'FAMINE REFUGEES'

The third wave of migration to the Urals occupies a special place in the history of this region. As mentioned earlier, in 1921–2 the majority of Russia's central regions were affected by severe famine.[34] *Tsentrevak*'s end-of-year report on its activities during 1921 stated that

> for the first time in the history of our organisation we have had to carry out the planned re-evacuation [sic] of refugees at the same time as carrying out relief operations in localities from which people are spontaneously fleeing. The majority of these new refugees come from the famine-struck Mid-Volga regions, where, being Russia's former granary, many Polish, Lithuanian and Belarusian refugees had settled at the start of the imperialist war. After living for six years in this area, a significant proportion of these refugees had already become acclimatised and had established themselves on the fertile land which, since the October revolution, they had cultivated as their own. Now, however, a natural disaster – famine – has sharply changed the course of their lives. The spontaneous emigration of these refugees from this region at the forefront of the fleeing masses has seriously undermined our capacity to relieve the famine bottleneck in a planned and painless manner. These spontaneous migrants, knowing only one slogan – "Onwards, regardless! Straight onwards!" – have thrown into confusion our best laid plans for implementing relief operations in the region and have obstructed the free movement of the starving local population who are pressing behind them in order that they too can escape.[35]

Local reports confirmed this picture. One report noted that

> the spontaneous migrants offer a terrifying picture. Dragging with them the diverse, unbelievably dirty remains of the property they have sold, the disordered crowds move on foot towards the railways, leaving in their tracks the usual signs of transient and nomadic hordes. As soon as they come across an oncoming empty train they cram themselves into it, well beyond its capacity. Disregarding the highest-level administrative prohibitions, local authorities permit endless queues of trains to depart without any plan or order in the face of this inescapable necessity. These trainloads of forty to fifty people in each wagon leave the famine belt without any attempt having been made to account for numbers or to prepare for their reception on the part of the localities through which they are travelling. This signals the beginning of a period in which the consequences of the famine begin to affect more prosperous regions. There is no question, of course, of even the most elementary sanitary

provisions for these people. Their railway wagons, their clothes and their own bodies are encrusted with dirt. Each stopping place quickly takes on the appearance of a field freshly strewn with manure. This is the general picture. The nightmare is in the detail: children in the pastures eating grass and any roots they can dig up, regardless of whether they are edible or not, people lying for days in railway wagons next to covered corpses, and so on. It is hard to imagine better conditions for an outbreak of infectious disease, and any such outbreak occurring in these trains produces a high proportion of mortality since the human organism exhausted beyond all measure loses all capacity to resist.[36]

This, however, described only one phase. Another phase followed, consisting of further special trainloads of 'spontaneous' migrants. From this time on, the evacuation authorities began to provide more regular assistance to carry out the registration of the refugee masses and to plan the more rational allocation of wagon space.

The poor condition of refugees who fled spontaneously (i.e. the majority) was exacerbated by the fact that in 1921 the Siberian railway administration ceased to accept refugee contingents on its lines, given the network's low traffic capacity and the impossibility of accommodating all those who wanted to travel in the special trains.[37] Moreover, various localities began to refuse to accept forced migrants. Thus, the Ekaterinburg evacuation authorities reported on 13 November 1921 that they would agree to the resettlement of no more than 11,000 people (of whom Irbit *uezd* would accept 3,000, Kamyshlov 2,000, and Shadrinsk 6,000).

The notice concerning the region's limited capacity was accompanied by a warning that all refugees had to have sufficient clothes and footwear, since they would be distributed among local villages which themselves suffered shortages of these items. The same report noted that Krasnoufimsk *uezd* was closed to refugees because of a typhus epidemic, and Verkhotur'e *uezd* was closed because of lack of food supplies. Nevertheless, it conceded that the latter could accept between three hundred to one thousand refugees. The city of Ekaterinburg was unable to take in new refugees, although as a transit point it would be required to accommodate some of them on a temporary basis.[38]

The accumulation of huge numbers of these 'famine refugees' at junction stations more or less paralysed the railway network. On 1 June 1922, the Perm railway authorities reported that

> Tiumen and Cheliabinsk provincial executive committees are despatching refugees who have left the famine-stricken regions by special warrant of the evacuation committees but without authorisation from the centre. In view of this, the railway is refusing to entrain them, and they are not moving on from

their stopping points. In Tiumen 48 railway wagons have been stranded because of this problem, and 140 in Cheliabinsk. It is vital to take immediate measures to organise the departure and passage of these contingents of refugees. It is necessary to add that in Tiumen refugees are also arriving on their own initiative by water transport.[39]

On 28 July 1921, the Presidium of the All-Russian Central Executive Committee (VTsIK) published a decree 'On the Planned Evacuation of the Population from Famine-Afflicted Regions.'[40] This document prohibited the authorities from carrying out planned resettlement operations in order to stem the spontaneous exodus of people from these localities. Several days later, on 1 August, it was announced that 'working elements' of the population would be evacuated 'who because of the crop failure had already lost their vital connection to their native soil.' This operation would resettle 105,000 people, including 5,000 from Astrakhan province, 5,000 from Tsaritsyn, 15,000 from Saratov, 10,000 from Marksshtadt (Marxstadt), 15,000 from Samara, 10,000 from Ufa, 15,000 from Simbirsk, 15,000 from the Tatar republic, 5,000 from the Chuvash region, 5,000 from the Mariinsk region and 5,000 from Viatka.[41] Table 6 gives us an insight into the scale of these transports in autumn 1921.

TABLE 6: Refugee traffic through Ekaterinburg train station, September 1921

Date	Destination	No. of Wagons	No. of People	Place of origin
09.09	Ekaterinburg	9	262	Famine-stricken regions
14.09	Ditto	15	453	Famine-stricken regions
18.09	Ditto	1	–	Children from famine-stricken regions
23.09	Ditto	8	260	Famine refugees and World War refugees
27.09	Ditto	7	178	Famine-stricken regions

Source: GASO f. r-1646, op. 1, d. 29, l. 4, 6, 8, 14, 23.

However, the Urals population itself did not escape famine. A report by the Ekaterinburg Regional Committee for Aid to Famine Victims (*Gubkompomgol*) indicated that one hundred local volosts suffered bad harvests in 1921, affecting 665,000 people, of whom 334,600 were badly afflicted by starvation (not counting families who had alternative sources of food or urban populations suffering shortages of food supplies).[42] The population of *uezds* directly hit by the famine found themselves in appalling conditions. A telegram sent by the Mikhailovsk volost executive committee (in Ekaterinburg *uezd*) reported that 'the famine is assuming monstrous proportions, the starving are feeding themselves on cats, dogs and even skin and wool. Entire families are dying one by one. In panic, people are fleeing their homes, leaving their children to the mercy of fate. Localities have no resources to cope with this famine.'[43] Other areas submitted similar reports. In Kamensk *uezd* one case of cannibalism was recorded. Of course, the desperate situation made it impossible to carry out any precise statistical investigation of the numbers of famine victims and refugees. The data presented in Table 7 are therefore necessarily approximate.

TABLE 7: The scale of famine in Ekaterinburg province, 1921

Uezd	No. of victims	No. of refugees	Contemporary descriptions
Ekaterinburg	89,600	'Floods of refugees'	'Typhus arising from malnutrition'
Kamyshlov	32,800	No data	–
Irbit	3,700	5,000	'Typhus'
Verkhotur'e	No data	'Many unorganized refugees, abandoning their children'	'Typhus brought by refugees'
Krasnoufimsk	72,100	No data	'Increasing numbers of children being abandoned; between 50 and 100 on market days'
Shadrinsk	49,400	No data	'60% of the population has no alternative food sources.'
Nizhnii Tagil	6,400	No data	–
Nadezhdinsk	No data	'About 10,000 in a critical condition'	–
Kamensk	108,000	'1,200 refugees from the imperialist war'	'The refugees are unclothed, barefoot, in a critical condition.'

Source: Compiled from GASO f. r-512, op. 1, d. 1, l. 50–8.

We can establish some idea of the aggregate scale of the Urals famine from Soviet data recently published in a collection of documents. Contemporary statistical reports indicate that up to 795,300 people in Ekaterinburg province suffered from the famine, 469,800 in Perm and 420,000 in Cheliabinsk provinces.[44]

The Ekaterinburg provincial executive committee, recognizing the human consequences of crop failure throughout three regional *uezds* and in numerous *volosts* in other areas, as well as the vast numbers of starving people among the local peasant population, the flood of refugees from other afflicted regions and the Siberian railway's refusal to transport further shipments of refugees to the east, issued a decree suspending the levy of food tax in the localities most affected by poor harvests. It hoped this measure would ease starvation and halt the widespread slaughtering of livestock.[45]

In Cheliabinsk the food situation was even worse. A regional summary report dated 6 July 1921 noted that Spasskii *uezd* had recorded an instance of death by starvation, and in Verkhne-Ural'skii *uezd* the factories were experiencing mass walk-outs by starving workers, while the rural localities were being abandoned by whole families heading for more fertile areas.[46] Other Urals regions were also witnessing huge outflows of population. The Chair of the Kamensk *uezd* executive committee VM Balandin reported in July 1921 that

> the political situation in the volosts is extremely tense, almost wholly as a result of the food crisis. All the leaders of volost executive committees, with the exception of two, have expressly refused to take any responsibility for the future progress of their work in the event of their not receiving any food relief. There is no thought of any constructive work at this time. For example, I have received reports that the following numbers are fleeing the volosts: 2,500, 1,300, 1,696, 2,700, 2,280 persons, etc., etc. Of course these enormous numbers are terribly worrying and should indicate in what a dreadful condition the *uezd* finds itself.[47]

Not all peasants fled their home villages. Some became embroiled instead in the Urals – Siberian uprising, moving with the rebel forces within the borders of the Urals region (a form of internal migration). Compiled on the basis of official Soviet summary reports, Table 8 presents present some data on the composition, number and activities of these so-called 'bandit groups'.

In general, however, the situation in the Urals was a good deal better than in many other Russian regions at this time. For this reason, the central authorities considered it feasible to open a wide network of children's homes in Ekaterinburg to receive homeless or orphaned children from the Mid-Volga region. This ambitious plan, however, remained merely a plan: there were insufficient materials and equipment to construct most of these homes, and many *uezd* authorities simply ignored the instructions given to them by the Regional Committee for Aid to Famine Victims. By 22 November 1921, the few new institutions that had been opened in Ekaterinburg province could accommodate only 715 children.[48] Most of the children from the famine-stricken Ufa province were forced to remain in their home regions. Indeed, the centre decided it was more economical to transport food supplies into these areas than to evacuate its children to other regions. Thus Ufa formally despatched only 200 of its children to the Urals. Most places in the new children's homes were filled by children from the Mid-Volga region, a product of so-called 'spontaneous' migration (*samotek*).

Famine refugees flowed into the Urals from all sides. In 1922, 3,700 people

TABLE 8: The scale of operations of Urals' 'Bandit Groups'

Date	Province	Size of group	Notes
23.03.21	Tiumen	8,000 men	Attacked in Mokrousov *uezd* (s-w of Ishim) and moving n-w. Has 2,000 rifles.
31.03.21	Tiumen	Up to 10,000 men	Active in Ishim and Ialutorovsk *uezds*. Partially destroyed, some escaped.
26.05.21	Ekaterinburg	About 1,000 men	Numerous different gangs.
28.05.21	Cheliabinsk	Up to 2,000 men	Active in Troitsko-Poltavskii, Verkhne-Ural'skii, Kurgansk *uezds*.
03.07.21	Cheliabinsk	–	In e. part of Troitskii *uezd*, assaults on grain-collecting stations. Powerful 'People's Army' operating under leadership of Mazepa.
18.10.21	Cheliabinsk	500 men	The Bulatov group moved from Ialutorovsk (Tiumen province) to Kurgansk *uezd*. Mainly active in Korkinsk and Mokrousov.
18.10.21	Tiumen	–	Peasants complain: 'The communists are robbing us and forcing us into banditry.'

Source: Compiled from data in *Sovetskaia derevnia glazami VChK-OGPU-NKVD. 1918–1939: Dokumenty i materialy*. Volume 1, 1918–22, Moscow, Rosspen, 2000, pp. 396, 400, 443, 445, 450, 512.

fleeing the famine passed through the Cheliabinsk resettlement point on their way eastwards, and 29,200 passed through westwards.[49] The following year, 1,500 refugees travelled through to the east, 20,300 returned towards the west.[50] In 1924, a further 8,600 journeyed back from Siberia to European Russia, according to the records of the Cheliabinsk authorities. The place of origin of these migrants was varied. The largest proportion of them had been inhabitants of Samara province (41 per cent of the total number of famine victims); the remainder came from Kazan' (13 per cent), Saratov (9.5 per cent), Simbirsk (6.9 per cent), Riazan (5.9 per cent) and other regions. The most popular destinations for these refugees were the regions of the Altai (28.4 per cent), Semipalatinsk (12.1 per cent), Omsk (25.9 per cent), Novo-Nikolaevsk (8 per cent), Enisei (5.8 per cent) and Tomsk (6.9 per cent).[51] The main factors impelling the active return movement of refugees' were, firstly, the refugees' own desire to return to their homes and, secondly, the state's policy which sought to relieve particular regions of heavy overpopulation caused by the exodus from famine areas. In 1924, Narkomzem proposed to launch a full-scale evacuation of the famine refugees from 1921–2, to be finished by 1 October 1925.[52]

COMING TO TERMS WITH POPULATION DISPLACEMENT

It will be clear from our discussion that it is impossible to establish the precise number of refugees in all three waves of migration in the Urals, given the incompleteness of the archival record. For one thing, the critical situation in which the region found itself, as a result of military conflict, famine and other factors, meant that many documents did not survive these years. For another, there was never any accurate statistical registration of even the organized flows of refugees – most of the data we possess on these groups derives from estimates made by contemporaries. Third, a huge number of migrants travelled on their own initiative and are therefore entirely absent from all official records. Large numbers of other refugees avoided official registration procedures because, for various reasons, they did not wish to be evacuated to their former homes. To be sure, there are means of resolving these statistical difficulties. In 1926 the Urals Region *oblast'*, formed in 1923, launched a policy of planned resettlement. The regional administration conducted a registration of all independent migrants who had settled on its territory in previous years. Rabkrin (the Workers' and Peasants' Inspectorate), the Soviet governmental agency responsible for supervising the activities of central and regional bureaucracies, reported that 'most of the independent migrants (*samovol'tsev*) settled in the Urals during the imperialist and Civil Wars and during the famine years. Having failed to receive any information about measures regarding plots of land, they have been living without a formal allocation of land and now find themselves in an extremely impoverished condition.'[53] The 1926 procedure registered 18,065 of these migrants, who were subsequently provided with land. According to the 1926 Soviet All-Union Census, 165,000 people settled in the Urals between 1917 and 1920 (including World War and Civil War refugees), and a further 246,600 from 1921 to 1923 (the years of the famine). Another 364,400 individuals arrived between 1924 and 1926, by which date the government programme of planned resettlement had already been launched. (It should be remembered that there was a parallel out-flow of population from the region during this period.[54])

We can find evidence of regional population movements from the censuses conducted in 1920 and 1926. These shed some light on nationality issues. Between these dates, the number of Poles shrank by 2.3 times (from 15,600 to 6,900), Latvians by 3.5 times (from 7,000 to 2,000), Estonians by 1.3 times (from 2,800 to 2,200), while the number of Germans was halved (from 13,000 to 6,000). This sharp reduction in the number of non-Russians in the Urals was of course a result of the re-evacuation policies described above. Contemporary census data also indicate changes in the ethnic and social composition of the indigenous population in these years, further testifying to the existence of vigorous migration currents.

Of particular interest to historians is the process of household formation and distribution by refugees in their places of settlement. Despite the efforts of the regional Soviet authorities, the plight of refugees remained very difficult. They were initially accommodated in any vacant buildings, regardless of whether these were suitable for long-term habitation. In the city of Ekaterinburg, one of the first buildings used for this purpose was the Kharitonov House. After completing a sanitary inspection of this house, a local medical officer wrote in October 1919:

> these premises are being used to accommodate both prisoners of war and refugees, who entirely occupy one of its wings as well as an outbuilding. On the top floor there are mainly captive soldiers, about one hundred and fifty men. On the ground floor and in the outbuilding live the refugees, mostly family people, about 200 in number. All premises occupied by these people are extremely dark and so small that the volume of air hardly suffices for all the living beings therein. There are a few plank beds available for sleeping, but far too few for the number of inhabitants, so most of them sleep on the floor, while some have pulled wardrobes over onto their sides and sleep on top of them. The dirt is everywhere and is appalling, with rubbish and human debris strewn all over the floor with no attempt being made to clean up. A few of the refugees have begun to mend shoes and boots or have started basket-weaving, whch only adds to the amount of rubbish and further spoils the air. The refugees have many children of all ages, who run around and litter the floor. Despite the thick dirt in the building, the refugees are beginning to prepare cabbages for the winter, cutting and chopping it up. If all this wasn't bad enough, dogs are running around everywhere as well. The volume of air is utterly insufficient for the number of living beings, and it is not unusual for the unhygienic state of the rooms to produce an outbreak of typhus among the residents. On top of all this, various immoral scenes are played out right in front of the eyes of children and adults, which I too was forced to observe.[55]

Subsequent years brought no improvement; indeed, refugees were actually displaced from their accommodation. In 1922, a certain Inspector Ganich wrote to the Director of the Regional Investigation Department (*Gubrozysk*): 'I hereby report that the building occupied by *Gubevak* on Voznesenskii Prospect, no. 44, the former Kharitonov House, which is meant to accommodate refugees, is in fact sheltering homeless and unemployed individuals (*litsa bez opredelennogo mesta zhitel'stva i professii*) and, frequently, criminal elements, who, benefiting from this night refuge, are carrying out robberies throughout the town. They become acquainted with each other overnight in this doss house, conspire to commit robberies together, etc.'[56]

Not surprisingly, refugees suffered from a dearth of food. The food ration established by *Tsentroplenbezh* by a decree of 1 January 1920 was in any event meagre, and insufficient for normal adult calorific requirements (see Table 9).

TABLE 9: Food rations, established by *Tsentroplenbezh* decree, 1 January 1920

Item	Basic ration (grams)	Famine ration (grams)
Bread	410	410–310
Grains	136	77
Meal	136	102
Fish	170	102
Vegetables	204	204
Potatoes	408	408
Fats	20	20
Salt	13	13
Sugar	26	26
Tea	0.8	0.8
Erzatz products	4	4
Onions	4	4
Soap	100 per month	
Tobacco	200 per month	

Source: Compiled from GASO f. r-1159, op. 1, d. 39, ll. 5, 5ob., 6.

Fruit compote, *kissel* (a drink made of fruit juice and starch), and eggs were available but only by doctor's prescription. Other items were frequently unobtainable. The year 1920 brought further difficulties in food supply. On 8 May, Ekaterinburg *Gubevak* sent the following written request to the Regional Food Agency (*Gubprodukt*): 'The lack of potatoes, cabbages, of any foodstuffs whatsoever for cooking, forces those living on our rations to subsist in foul conditions. We hereby request you to issue any possible substitutes.'[57] In a sign of desperation, the Ekaterinburg evacuation administration resolved no longer to allocate food rations to refugees settled within its territory.[58] From now on, refugees and their families were no longer eligible for aid – lodging, food or clothing – provided by *Tsentrevak* and its regional agencies. Infirm and non-working refugees would henceforth be served by the regional social welfare administrations. Within a week of the publication of this directive, all refugees were removed from their places of residence. In order to receive any food at all, or other forms of aid, they had to submit an application for a food ration card and for housing on the same basis as the local civil population.

These difficulties only confirmed the wishes of refugees to return to their homelands. The archives contain texts of appeals and requests written by refugees, either to be sent to their former place of residence or to more fertile lands on Russian territory. The Ekaterinburg *Gubevak*, for example, received an application on 3 March 1922 from a refugee from the Birsk *uezd* of Ufa province, who was currently living in the village of Krutikhinsk in Shadrinsk *uezd*. His letter stated that 'in 1921 our village suffered a terrible harvest of grain, and we were forced to leave our homeland and go, or rather run, towards richer areas in order not to starve to death in our homeland. We beg you now to resettle us to another place, to Shchuch'e lake, as the famine has now reached us here. We are being forced to eat dead cattle and all sorts of harmful substitutes.'[59] Such requests were not always granted. Another refugee, originally from Grodno province and now living in Verkhotur'e, wrote that all their documents and applications for the journey homewards had been lost by the *uezd* evacuation committee and that 'already seven months have passed, but we have had no news and now we do not even have any solid documentation. Now wherever we go, we're asked "And who might you be?" We say "Refugees." They ask for our documents. We have none, nor even any certificates proving that someone else has them. It's impossible to get work without refugee documents. We ask you, as refugees of the German war, to evacuate us to our homeland.'[60]

CONCLUSIONS

This chapter has distinguished three phases or 'waves' of refugees in the Urals which followed closely upon one another within a single decade. It has also described the terrible conditions in which refugees were forced to live, the procedure of their registration, their geographical distribution and the attempts made by local authorities to provide them with minimal welfare. The arrival of these migrants, their accommodation, assignment to work and the provision of rations for them, of course, only served to exacerbate the intolerable conditions in which the local population already lived.

We have seen how regional authorities in the Urals struggled to come to terms with the magnitude of the refugee movement. The scale of displacement in this region was partly a function of its location, which made it a major place of transit between European Russia and Siberia. As an area of sparse population, which generally enjoyed adequate food supplies, it also attracted peasants and others who desperately sought to escape from parts of the country devastated by famine in 1920–2. However, this new mass influx of population aggravated the already growing food problem in the region, and inflicted further hardship on the displaced populations which already found themselves in the Urals. This was an unprecedented combination of circumstances.

The Soviet authorities had no prior experience of dealing with these problems. Some of their mistakes and miscalculations made the distress of refugees even worse. Administrative errors were compounded by the fact that there were no clear lines of communication between the centre, where new state agencies formulated policies of population settlement, and the regional authorities which were expected to implement policy. Continuing military engagements account in part for this administrative deficiency, but it remained a problem even after the Civil War had come to an end.

The frustration of regional and local officials was evident in the choice of words they used to describe population displacement in the Urals. The more the authorities attempted to impose control, the more they complained of 'spontaneity' on the part of refugees. The choice of words was not, of course, accidental. The rhetoric of Soviet officialdom was strikingly reminiscent of the vocabulary used by tsarist officials. It drew attention to the familiar metaphorical distance, as it were, between a settled bureaucracy made anxious by surveying vast, unsettled populations.

Further research is required to examine important questions that have only been hinted at here. Prominent among these is the relationship between refugees and the local populations. Evidence thus far suggests that this relationship is more likely to have been conflicting than constructive, not least because of the prevailing shortages of basic goods and the competition for scarce resources. How this relationship was affected by, and itself contributed to, the emerging system of local and regional bureaucracy is worthy of further study. More work is also needed to explore refugees' own sense of community. It is clear that some parties of refugees had travelled together to the Urals and were resettled as national groups. How much solidarity there was, and how it translated itself into plans for returning to the homeland, are questions that need to be explored more fully. Other potential bonds may have been forged between refugees who 'belonged' to the different phases of migration that are the subject of this chapter.

* This paper was translated by Nick Baron.

9
Armenia: the 'Nationalization', Internationalization and Representation of the Refugee Crisis

PETER GATRELL AND JO LAYCOCK*

INTRODUCTION

As other contributions to this book have demonstrated, World War One and its aftermath in Europe generated involuntary migration on a massive scale. In this chapter we focus upon the displacement of the Armenian population that inhabited extensive parts of the Transcaucasus and eastern Anatolia. Armenians living in this region had come under Russian or Ottoman jurisdiction prior to the dissolution of these empires. During the war countless Armenian subjects of the Ottoman empire fell victim to organized deportations carried out by Turkish troops and police in 1915. Many of those who escaped massacre managed to flee to neighbouring lands. Virtually uninterrupted military conflict and continuing political uncertainty thereafter deprived these refugees of any speedy or straightforward resolution of their status and security, and indeed added to their number. In the 1920s, Armenian refugees came to symbolize the condition of statelessness, serving to remind the more fortunate citizens of postwar Europe of their entitlement to protection by 'their' sovereign nation-state.[1] No-one expressed this condition of loss more powerfully than Hannah Arendt: 'Once they had left their homeland they remained homeless, once they had left their state they became stateless; once they had been deprived of their human rights they were rightless, the scum of the earth.'[2]

The wreckage of empire not only magnified the scale of the 'refugee problem', but also exposed bitter disagreement over the future status of Armenia itself. At one extreme, Armenian patriots demanded the establishment of a large nation-state whose territory corresponded to 'historic Armenia', a vision that could only be realized at the expense of the fledgling Turkish republic. At the other extreme, radical Turkish nationalists denied the right of Armenia to exist as a distinct entity. Nor were these disputes confined to the region. Partly because of the existence of a vocal (and at times disputatious) Armenian diaspora, and partly because of a long history of international involvement in the 'Near East', population displacement and resettlement became matters of diplomatic concern and a focus for intervention by new transnational organizations.[3]

Here we seek to show the ways in which international agencies, foreign governments, religious groups and private individuals alike intervened to sustain the welfare of Armenian refugees after 1917. Most of our evidence addresses British involvement, although this is not meant to imply that other countries played a minor role. We suggest that such intervention was accompanied by the dissemination of powerful images of 'national' hurt, one important aspect of which was a gendering of the prevailing discourse. In common with other contributors to this volume, we are struck by the way in which those who attempted to relieve the suffering of Armenian refugees allowed them little scope to articulate their own sense of self. (We acknowledge, in this regard, the need for more work on how Armenians experienced displacement.) Finally, we demonstrate how the refugee crisis came to be internationalized, first in terms of humanitarian activity and later in terms of resettlement programmes. Intervention by the League of Nations in Armenia did not have its counterpart in either Poland or the Baltic. There, newly constituted states seemed sufficiently strong to address the issue of population displacement – albeit with a good deal of emergency assistance from overseas – whereas Armenian refugees lacked a stable or well established sovereign authority that could speak on their behalf. As a result, the League of Nations became actively involved. We examine the calculated rhetoric and imagery that its representatives deployed.

WORLD WAR ONE, 'GENOCIDE', AND THE MOBILIZATION OF INTERNATIONAL OPINION

European governments became embroiled in the 'Armenian Question' during the second half of the nineteenth century, as part of an international preoccupation with the widely perceived decline in the viability of Ottoman rule. A key moment was the Treaty of Berlin in 1878, following the Russo–Turkish War, which called for administrative reforms in the Ottoman empire.[4] In Britain, several leading politicians (William Ewart Gladstone being the best-known) had taken up the Armenian cause, seeking to overturn Britain's traditional support for the Sublime Porte. However, international intervention was limited and ineffective in respect of the Armenian minority. A small yet vociferous pro-Armenian lobby in Britain denounced the failure of the British government to intervene decisively on Armenia's behalf following the massacres that took place in 1895–6, and again in 1909.[5] As Ottoman repression of Armenians intensified, societies such as the Anglo–Armenian Society and the Friends of Armenia came into being. These bodies held public meetings and issued pamphlets in order to raise funds and public awareness. They maintained that Britain had a legal and moral responsibility towards the Ottoman Armenians, and played upon the sentimental attachment to Armenia and the Armenian population that developed in the UK and France during the later nineteenth century. These Armenophiles, who included scholars, travellers and government officials, constructed an image of Armenia as a 'cradle of civilization'. Armenia was treated as 'European', being Christian and 'cultured', in stark contrast to its Ottoman overlords. It was also sufficiently 'different' to retain a romantic and exotic appeal.[6] Meanwhile, in the USA, a sustained period of immigration in the two decades before 1914 created a sizeable American Armenian community that retained close links with their counterparts in the Ottoman empire and in Russia. Here, too, was a constituency willing to mobilize in defence of Armenian interests.[7]

In tsarist Russia, government officials, lawyers, writers and others had traditionally evinced a strong interest in the internal politics of the Ottoman empire and its Armenian minority, as well as in the 'Armenian Question' in Russia itself. Even more than in western Europe, the Caucasus exerted a powerful fascination on Russian writers and scholars, a tendency fostered by a belief in the civilizing role of those Armenians who had settled in the Russian empire. By the later nineteenth and early twentieth centuries, however, the tsarist state demonstrated much less sympathy for the Armenian cause, partly because it did not wish to concede any measures of autonomy to its own substantial Armenian population, which by 1914 amounted to some 1.5 million. The formation during the 1890s of radical Armenian political parties, the Dashnaktsutian (Dashnaks) and the Hnchaks, whose leaders were unwilling to accept continued subordination to non-Armenian authority, reinforced these misgivings by equating Armenians with terrorist conspiracy rather than with Christian suffering.[8] At the same time, an emerging group of diplomats and lawyers attached to the Russian Ministry of Foreign Affairs had begun by 1913–14 to formulate a new reform programme on behalf of Ottoman Armenians. This envisaged the creation of a single administrative unit for the Christian inhabitants of the empire, affording a greater degree of legal protection than was currently extended them. The European conflagration put paid to this scheme.[9]

Against the background of this combustible politics, the Ottoman empire entered the war on the side of the central powers in November 1914. Six months later, Russian troops crossed the border with Turkey. Held up by a Turkish counter-offensive, Russian commanders ordered troops to withdraw from the region around Van. In chaotic circumstances, some of the local Armenian population managed to flee to the relative safety of the Caucasus; others were left behind in the hasty Russian retreat. Worse still, youthful Turkish radicals blamed Armenians for the defeats already suffered by the Ottoman army in the winter of 1914 and early 1915, and charged them with having instigated uprisings against Turkish rule. By April 1915 Armenians had already become the target of organized violence.[10] Still worse was to befall them. Armenians who remained on Ottoman-controlled territory in July 1915 suffered a terrible fate. Using as a pretext events at Van, and in accordance with emergency legislation ordering the deportation of communities suspected of espionage or treason (or whose presence was not conducive to military effectiveness), the Turkish authorities rounded on the Armenian population. Hundreds of thousands of Ottoman Armenians were disarmed, arrested and deported, being forced to endure long and humiliating marches to the south from which many never recovered. Many were simply butchered. One contemporary graphically likened this concerted action to a 'Bartholomew's Day massacre' on a 'national' scale. André Mandelstam, the renowned Russian international lawyer, proclaimed it a crime against humanity. Controversy rages to this day about the magnitude of the catastrophe and where responsibility for it rests.[11]

The more fortunate victims managed to escape to safety, either to Syria or to the Russian-controlled Transcaucasus. By the beginning of 1916 at least 105,000 ex-Ottoman Armenians had sought refuge in Erevan alone, which became even more of an 'overgrown village' during the course of the war (its population in 1914 barely reached 30,000). The total number of Armenian refugees in Erevan trebled during the following twelve months.[12] In further retaliation against the Armenian population of the Ottoman empire, their abandoned farms were hastily assigned to 750,000 Turkish refugees from western Thrace. This appears to confirm the suggestion that the 'Young Turks' had embarked on a process of 'national homogenisation'.[13]

Stories of the deportation and annihilation of Armenian subjects of the Ottoman empire filtered through to Britain, France and the USA, via diplomats, American missionaries in Turkey and Armenians who had escaped the killings.[14] With the publication of the famous 'Blue Book' in 1916, news of the massacres reached a wide audience. In France and the USA, the Armenian diaspora began to mobilize public opinion.[15] Books, articles, photographs and even feature films portrayed the suffering of Armenian victims of Turkish violence, and called upon a shocked public to give funds in support of homeless and frightened Armenian refugees. As a result of these initiatives, donations began to pour in.[16]

Public concern was accompanied by an assertive new rhetoric. Armenian patriots argued that the diaspora was transcended in wartime: 'Armenians, scattered throughout the entire world, are becoming a solid and strong unit, before which the cruel enemy trembles'. What began as 'national tragedy' thus had the potential to culminate in national survival and revival. Within the Russian empire, Armenian activists organized national committees that promoted a sense of Armenian 'national' identity among the refugee population, and trained a new generation in the techniques of government.[17] The onslaught against the Armenian population in the Ottoman empire, and the plight of Armenian refugees on tsarist Russian territory, drew attention to the claims of Armenia for political recognition and 'freedom'. The form this took would largely be determined by military events and international diplomacy.[18]

TERRITORIAL RECONFIGURATION AND POPULATION DISPLACEMENT, 1918–20

The difficult months that followed the Russian revolution of October 1917 spelled further danger and uncertainty for the Armenian refugee population. A renewed Turkish offensive in February 1918 led to the recapture of Erzinjan and Erzerum, and culminated in the fall of Kars in April.[19] Dramatic political changes followed hard on the heels of these military developments. Georgia, Azerbaijan and Armenia came together in a new Transcaucasian Federation, but this experiment was rapidly aborted. Where Georgia could count upon the temporary patronage of Germany, and Azerbaijan upon the diplomatic overtures being made by Turkey, Armenia found itself in a highly exposed position. Armenian political leaders, many of them based in the Georgian capital Tbilisi, established an independent Armenian Republic in May 1918.[20]

Against the background of continued military and political conflict, the displacement of population continued almost without interruption. Around 300,000 refugees from Anatolia settled in the provinces of Erevan and its environs during 1918–19.[21] They struggled against dreadful odds. During the harsh winter of 1918, tens of thousands were exposed to typhus and famine. When typhus abated, malaria struck. There were insufficient supplies of quinine and too few doctors to cope with the fresh health crisis.[22] In overcrowded Erevan, violence erupted between the Christian Armenians and Muslim Azeris. The Armenian authorities – mostly Dashnak in their political affiliation – sought to attend to the needs of the large displaced population, which became the responsibility of a 'Refugee Committee' formed by the new parliamentary assembly.[23]

Turkey's decision to seek peace with the Allied powers in October 1918 offered the prospect of a brief respite. As a result, tens of thousands of Armenians now began to return under French or British supervision to their homes in Anatolia and Cilicia. This would prove to be a high-risk venture.[24]

In fact peace negotiations complicated the situation still further. Divisions between Armenian politicians over political strategy came to the fore, although they were temporarily masked by the decision to send a single delegation to the Paris peace conference.[25] There the Armenian delegation tabled grandiose territorial plans. In February 1919, filled with optimism, political exiles from Turkish Armenia met in Erevan to prepare for a 'United, Free Armenia'.[26] In this diplomatic maelstrom, it sometimes appeared as if refugees were pawns in the game of realizing the vision of 'Greater Armenia'. Meanwhile the new Armenian republic staked its own claim to look after the interests of Armenian refugees in Cilicia, northeastern Anatolia and other parts of the former Ottoman empire.[27] Diplomatic representatives of the victorious great powers grew nervous. The more that the 'friends of Armenia' called upon the Allies to make a concerted attempt to repatriate Armenian refugees to an enlarged polity, the more western governments backed away from becoming further embroiled in Near Eastern politics.[28]

Many of the Armenian refugees from the Ottoman empire took a sceptical view of the claims of the government in Erevan to speak on their behalf. They objected to the 'Russianist' tone of the so-called 'Araratian republic', arguing that the natural centre of gravity for a new state lay in 'historic' Armenia, not the 'peripheral province' of Erevan.[29] In the words of the leading scholar of independent Armenia:

> With mounting impatience they awaited the opportunity to turn homeward, to lands extending into the western horizon. Consequently, the refugee population persisted in maintaining its distinct militia, clustering around compatriotic societies bearing the names of Western Armenian districts, and evading, whenever possible, the obligations of citizenship in the Erevan republic.[30]

These difficulties were temporarily masked by the 'Act of United Armenia', read to a large and enthusiastic crowd in Erevan by Prime Minister Alexander Khatisian on 28 May 1919. Khatisian took the line that 'the refugee population was surging homeward. As nothing could stop this unbridled movement, the establishment of a *government of all Armenia* could be delayed no longer.' This optimistic vision, coinciding with the recapture of Kars, proved short-lived. In truth, the new Armenian republic exercised only modest territorial jurisdiction. Its weakness was further exposed by the continued manifestation of a severe refugee crisis that the constant threat from Turkey's armed forces only served to exacerbate.[31]

What of the practical measures taken to deal with the consequences of population displacement in Armenia? During these critical years, and against the background of immensely difficult circumstances, Armenian officials managed to create an embryonic state structure on the small territory over which they had any kind of control.[32] One important step was the formation of a Department of Repatriation and Reconstruction in July 1919. Part of the republic's new Ministry of Welfare, it organized the distribution of food and established workshops for refugees. Officials divided refugees into three categories: the prosperous, who received no government aid; wage earners and some peasants, who were entitled to buy food from government shops; and the destitute, who received free supplies. Public works projects (such as canal repairs) were supplemented by new enterprises, owned and administered by refugee entrepreneurs in Erevan and Etchmiadzin, an interesting indication that the government was prepared to accord refugees a role in economic reconstruction.[33]

The task was one of immense proportions. According to one report in the autumn of 1919, 'the state of the city of Erevan is indescribable. Nearly everybody is suffering from or recovering from disease, and I saw two men lying dying of hunger. Long continuance of this misery has had a demoralising effect.'[34] Several months later the situation had still not improved. An American observer of the scene in Erevan painted a picture of:

> thousands and thousands and thousands of dirty, lousy, half-clad sick and diseased, cringing and suffering unfortunates of humanity. Old gnarled grandmothers and grandfathers are here who seemingly never had the right to survive; then there are the young men who should be strong but their strength has gone in the struggle simply to live; but the thing that grips you is the women and little children who will haunt you with their mute appeal, and force you to think very tenderly of those who are near to you and for whom you will die a hundred deaths rather than have them ever reach this condition.[35]

Practical efforts on the part of the Armenian republic met with a sceptical response on the part of some refugee agencies and foreign observers. The American James Harbord loftily – and unfairly – dismissed all governments in the region as 'thoroughly inefficient, without credit, and undoubtedly corrupt.'[36] He might have been closer to the mark had he pinpointed the often intractable political divisions that affected the conduct of government, as well as the difficulties in establishing a resource base upon which to support a government bureaucracy. Economic activity in town and country alike was limited and fragile, and internal communications left much to be desired.[37]

As indicated earlier, Western Armenian politicians and refugee activists hoped that the 'refugee question' could be settled by an organized programme of repatriation to Anatolia. They rejected any initiatives that implied the permanent settlement of Western Armenian refugees in Erevan, and took comfort from the London Conference, convened in February 1920 to discuss a proposed peace treaty with Turkey. According to one estimate, around 800,000 Armenians were thought likely to resettle in the former Ottoman empire, once eastern Anatolia had been handed over to a 'new Armenia'. This figure comprised 300,000 Western Armenians in the Caucasus, 100,000 survivors of the genocide still in Turkey, 240,000 desperate Armenians in Georgia and Azerbaijan, 30,000 from the Balkans and several thousand more from America, Persia, Egypt, the Sudan, and Ethiopia.[38] The Turkish government had other plans. The reoccupation of Anatolia by Turkish troops in 1919 was followed by a fresh offensive in the autumn of 1920, culminating in the capture of Kars on 30 October and Aleksandropol a week later. These military developments led to a renewed influx of Armenian refugees to Erevan and its environs. Many of them had only recently returned to their former homes.[39]

The resolution of Armenia's status remained unclear while neither Russia nor Turkey was in a position to intervene decisively.[40] But Soviet victory over the Whites in the Russian Civil War brought the Red Army to the border of the Armenian republic. Soviet Armenia came into being in December 1920 as a result of a power vacuum caused by the ultimate inability of the leaders of the independent Armenian republic to create a viable state. Khatisian and his colleagues went into exile, leaving behind a rump of Left Dashnaks to conclude terms with the Red Army. There followed several months of further bloodletting and the seizure of privately owned assets by the Bolsheviks, culminating in the final rout of the Dashnaks in March 1921.[41]

International diplomacy had done little to assist the infant Armenian republic. True, Armenia had received favourable treatment under the Treaty of Sèvres in August 1920, whereby Turkey was obliged to recognize its independence. But by then it was evident that the grandiose vision of an enlarged Armenia, including Cilicia and Western Armenia, had evaporated. Turkey had already challenged Allied forces in Anatolia without any serious retaliation, and since the Allied governments did not commit themselves to back the Treaty's provisions with military force it remained a dead letter. The new Soviet state wished for peace with its neighbour and was prepared to agree terms with Turkey on behalf of Soviet Armenia. By 1923 Mustafa Kemal (Atatürk) was sufficiently strong to negotiate the Treaty of Lausanne (24 July), which validated Turkey's occupation of Anatolia.[42] During the negotiations, Atatürk proclaimed that the 'Armenian Question' had been 'liquidated'.[43] Grandiose hopes of a new Armenia at Turkey's expense had finally been dashed. Turkey having washed its hands of the refugees, it was left to international agencies to deal with the crisis.

The new sovietized Armenia itself had an important part to play in dealing with the consequences of population displacement. Having settled immediate questions of national security, the Soviet leadership turned its attention to issues of public health, housing and education. Against a background of economic liberalization, in line with the adoption of the New Economic Policy by the Bolshevik regime in 1921, the Soviet republic of Armenia became a 'haven of Armenians displaced by the wars and political changes in the rest of the world'. They came in large numbers from Georgia, Egypt, Greece, Iran, France and elsewhere, assisted by special permits issued by the Soviet authorities.[44] The government took decisive steps to combat the continuing health crisis, including emergency measures (for example, in July 1922 it imposed a complete embargo on population movement in and out of Aleksandropol) as well as investment in infrastructure. Faced with desperate poverty, many refugees reportedly turned to crime in order to survive.[45]

In July 1921 the Soviet authorities created a 'Main Administration for Resettlement', which distributed agricultural inputs to refugee farmers, allocated land and levied a special 'refugee tax' on the settled population. According to Ronald Suny, the Soviet administration by means of such measures succeeded 'in turning a land of refugees into a stable, growing society'.[46] As a description of the first years of Soviet rule, this assessment is probably too sanguine. Other sources speak of continued poverty, backwardness and political instability. Settlements that housed refugees from Turkey were believed by the Soviet government to be a particular hotbed of counter-revolution. Relations between the government and Armenian refugees were not helped by the belief that radical Dashnak exile communities in Persia exploited the uncertainty created by population displacement, in order to foment rebellion against Soviet rule.[47]

The magnitude of the challenge posed by population displacement in Armenia was not lost on Fridtjof Nansen, who alluded to recent upheavals when summarizing the situation in 1925:

> Without aid for the development of her great latent natural resources, it is impossible for Armenia to receive any considerable number of refugees and to settle them in a satisfactory manner. The country is really developing steadily under an apparently stable government, the situation is quiet in the interior and on the frontiers, the population is industrious and hardworking, the land rich in soil, water power and mineral wealth. But the country is also

to an impressive extent ruined by invasions, massacres, revolutions, and civil wars of the past. At the present moment it has therefore a greater population than its present conditions reasonably allow; it is suffering from a severe lack of capital, and especially the fertile soil cannot be sufficiently utilised without irrigation and in some parts drainage.[48]

At the same time Nansen encouraged schemes to resettle Armenian refugees overseas (see below). His underlying strategy can be summarized in terms of the simple formulation: irrigate or emigrate. In the following sections we explore the ways in which displaced persons were depicted at the time by those who advocated or engaged in humanitarian intervention.

HUMANITARIAN INTERVENTION, 1918–25

Longstanding supporters of the Armenian cause in Britain led the chorus of anger in the aftermath of the massacres. Societies such as the Friends of Armenia intensified their fundraising efforts. New societies also came into being, such as the Armenian Red Cross and Refugees Fund.[49] Although small groups did continue to raise money independently (for example, the Armenian community in Manchester operated a refugee clothing fund), it was clear early in the war that the scale of the crisis required a larger, more coordinated effort. To this end a national appeal, 'The Armenian Refugees (Lord Mayor's Fund)' was launched in October 1915, rapidly becoming the best organized of all British relief agencies.[50] Raising funds through public subscriptions, the Lord Mayor's Fund continued to operate into the 1930s, when the British government invited it to organize resettlement programmes for Armenian refugees. Many of the figures involved in the Lord Mayor's Fund (for example Noel Buxton, Harold Buxton and Aneurin Williams) were also involved with the British Armenia Committee. This Committee petitioned Ministers, published articles and made contacts with Armenians and their supporters abroad.[51] To its members, the long-term future of Armenia, preferably as an independent state, seems to have been as important as providing immediate relief.[52] Its practical work closely overlapped with that of the Lord Mayor's Fund. Harold Buxton was director of relief for the Lord Mayor's Fund, which organized work schemes for Armenian men in Erevan and maintained orphanages and feeding stations.[53] The Lord Mayor's Fund cooperated with other agencies, such as 'Miss Robinson's fund', which employed Armenian women refugees in lace making in order to raise funds. When Harold Buxton visited the region in the winter of 1921 he could point to a plethora of British relief agencies, including the Society of Friends (Quakers).[54]

That the Armenians fought on the British side was often evoked in appeals for aid for the Armenians. Aneurin Williams, chairman of the British Armenia Committee, suggested that its members should produce a pamphlet on the 'fighting qualities and virtues of the Armenian race'. Armenians were portrayed as having fought throughout history against 'barbarians' and Islamic invaders. Its geographical position meant that Armenians stood on the frontline of the Christian and 'civilized' world, defending its values and surviving despite waves of invasion and conquest.[55] During the war British supporters of the Armenian cause stressed that Armenians continued to fulfil this role. As Emily Robinson put it, 'very many thousands of Armenians are fighting in this war with the armies of the Allies. Many hundreds have laid down their lives in the cause of the European powers.'[56]

British agencies worked in conjunction with the American Near East Relief, which Harold Buxton described as the largest committee at work in the Caucasus. As a neutral power, the USA was particularly active in dealing with the aftermath of the genocide.[57] Formed in 1915, Near East Relief (initially named the American Committee for Armenian and Syrian Relief) established orphanages, schools, hospitals and industrial workshops throughout Anatolia, Greece, Lebanon and the Caucasus. Between 1915 and 1917 funds were channelled to American missionaries via the US embassy in Constantinople. This activity continued beyond 1918.[58] By February 1923, following an agreement with the new Soviet republic of Armenia, Near East Relief became responsible for some 25,000 orphaned children, although the Armenian authorities increasingly sought to bring them into the care of Soviet institutions.[59]

To illustrate something of the ways in which the humanitarian effort was shaped from a British perspective, we focus upon Dudley Stafford Northcote, a British volunteer relief worker in the Near East, who left behind a graphic account of his work at Baqubah refugee camp in Mesopotamia between 1919 and 1925. Northcote was not the only British volunteer in the region. Indeed, unlike some of his compatriots, he approached the task of looking after Armenian refugees with no prior knowledge of Armenia or sympathy towards the movement for Armenian self-determination.[60] He took it for granted that the Armenians would be repatriated to their former homes in Anatolia or Cilicia, because the Allies had a right to divide up conquered territory. Northcote's experiences of the 'concentration camp' at Baqubah turned him into a staunch supporter of the Armenian cause. He developed a deep concern, not only for the fate of 'his' refugees but also for the future of the Armenian nation as a whole.[61]

In his letters home, Northcote indicated that his work at the camp gave him time to 'study' the Armenians. He began to learn the Armenian language. His new-found enthusiasm for ethnography led him to observe the 'traditions' that displaced Armenians sought to maintain whilst at Baqubah. Northcote located Armenian customs and traditions in a framework that was recognizably Christian, yet sufficiently 'alien' to distance the Armenians from western 'civilisation'.[62]

The sense of a looming refugee crisis in the region also emerged from the reports prepared by Harold Buxton on behalf of the League of Nations. Buxton noted that 200,000–300,000 Armenian refugees had converged upon the region, and that it was impossible for them to return home. This problem was compounded by the Turkish presence in Kars, Ardahan and other parts of eastern Anatolia, which Buxton termed an 'enemy' occupation. This bleak picture was not made any better by the weight of Armenian 'tradition'; in Buxton's view, the population of rural Transcaucasia retained backward agricultural techniques and was unlikely to generate resources to support the refugee population. His conclusion, that Armenian peasants were 'far from having the ferocious character which romantic writers attributed to them', leant additional support for the argument that external agencies should intervene on their behalf.[63]

In 1921 the British government decided to close the refugee camp at Baqubah, on the grounds that 'it is quite impossible, with financial constraints as they are at present, to find any more money from public funds for these refugees'.[64] The government declared that responsibility for the welfare of Armenian refugees lay instead in the hands of private charity. In response to this abrupt change of policy, Northcote resigned. He maintained that Armenian support for the Allies during the war imposed upon the British government an obligation to support the Armenian refugees. He protested that abandoning them in Mesopotamia would lead to 'the end of them as a community.' This represented a clear departure from his initial attitude, in which Northcote appeared willing to stand by while the Great Powers divided up the land and decided the Armenians' fate.[65]

The proposal to close the refugee camp attracted the attention of the British public. Letters were sent to *The Times* in protest at the government's statement and in support of Northcote. One writer, styling himself 'Armenus', tellingly argued that it was mistaken to believe that there were numerous wealthy Armenians living in Europe who could afford to assist the refugees. Most of the 3,000 Armenians living in Britain, he argued, lived in very humble circumstances. Private charity was not a realistic option, contrary to the opinion of the British government. Archbishop Gore, another leading figure in the Armenian cause, evoked the Armenians' ancient past, their 'tenacity in holding on to their faith' and their artistic, industrial and commercial gifts, concluding that the British government had a duty to assist another civilized Christian country.[66] Such arguments, emphasizing Armenia's Christian tradition and ancient past, were by this time familiar rhetorical devices.

Gore and others proposed the establishment of an Armenian colony in Mesopotamia that would keep together and protect at least a portion of an 'ancient people'. Support for the establishment of 'colonies' was not uncommon. In 1920 the British government had itself proposed a scheme to resettle Armenians on farms in Iraq. Evidently, because the creation of an Armenian nation-state no longer suited the international agenda, other ways to meet Armenian national aspirations had to be sought. A colony was one such solution.[67] In practice, however, it proved difficult to promote enthusiasm amongst Armenians themselves in such schemes. According to Northcote, Armenian refugees resisted the idea of permanent settlement in Syria: in October 1921 he reported that Armenians in the Mesopotamian camps 'have categorically declined to colonise that country on any condition. They desire to join their compatriots in Armenia'.[68] This did not stop such schemes from being promoted. According to one enthusiastic advocate:

> No element could ever be more suited to colonisation in this country [Syria] than these young Armenians with all the energy of their race tingling in their veins, acclimatised and accustomed to the village life among the Arabs. The colony would attract them in thousands and enable them to become Armenian again under the most favourable conditions, with a prospect of future prosperity before them, utilising that which seemed the greatest obstacle, their "arabisation", to build a strong and thriving peasantry fit to understand and be understood by the native population.[69]

Although the economic development of Mesopotamia entailed Armenian colonization, the future relationship between Armenians and Syrians remained as yet unarticulated.

Although Northcote left for Britain in the autumn of 1921, he soon agreed to an invitation from the Lord Mayor's Fund to travel to Armenia in order to continue his work with refugees. During this time Northcote gathered additional information that he would subsequently incorporate in a projected history of Armenia. He arrived in the Caucasus in December 1921 in the company of Harold Buxton. From January 1922 onwards Northcote submitted a series of reports in which he outlined his programme of work and the general situation in Erevan. Whilst Northcote awaited the arrival of a group of refugees being repatriated from Mesopotamia (where they had refused to form a colony), he and Buxton became aware of the dire refugee crisis in Transcaucasia. Armenian refugees had settled around the Etchmiadzin monastery, home of the head of the Armenian Church (the Catholicos), and in Erevan, whose population had increased dramatically in size. Northcote detailed the type of work carried out by the Lord Mayor's Fund along with other agencies. Given the scale of the crisis, the relief effort had to be spread thinly. It consisted of food rations, feeding stations and schools and orphanages for children, who formed a high proportion of the refugee population.[70]

Reports of conditions in refugee camps elsewhere painted a picture of degradation and despair. A refugee described the camp at Belgaum (modern-day Karnataka) as 'very hard for the people who are more or less accustomed to a higher standard of life'.[71] More to the point, some camps took on a semi-permanent form, and their residents became institutionalized. By 1925 it was said of camps in Syria that they were:

> ... now tending to become regular settlements ... All Armenians who have not attained a certain degree of economic independence wish to be members of groups consisting of their own countrymen, as they derive a sense of security from the existence of groups of this kind.

According to the author, it was 'natural' that Armenian refugees should find solace in group solidarity, because they 'have always lived surrounded by hostile elements. Their dwellings, however primitive, constitute a small capital'. Their readiness to settle on the land was a welcome departure for an ethnic group that had hitherto been more noted (and not always favourably) for its capacity to trade. If agriculture were encouraged instead, 'a final and permanent solution of the Armenian problem [might] be found'.[72] In pursuing this option, a member of a League of Nations' commission commented that Armenian refugees from Greece and Constantinople had already been assisted by local peasants:

> These peasants have for some time been accustomed to receive refugees in their houses, which gives good grounds for hoping that the newcomers, to whom fortune has been so unkind, would find initial assistance and would be placed in a position to provide themselves with a home in the near future.[73]

As we saw earlier, this rested on a rather sanguine appraisal of social relations and cultural contacts. It also implied a transformation in the way in which Armenians were conventionally represented, namely as urban dwellers. More conventionally perhaps, TF Johnson, Nansen's deputy commissioner, bemoaned the conditions in refugee camps, and implied that Armenians preferred an urban milieu, however squalid, to rural life:

> The Beyrouth [sic] camp, constructed mostly of petrol cases and tins, presents the appearance of a town of cards or at best of match boxes; the streets, or rather alleys, are so narrow as to make it difficult for two persons to

pass each other, and are the receptacles for the draining and refuse of the houses.[74]

Whichever view of their future settlement outside observers espoused, the Armenian refugee population had become an established category of concern.

INTERNATIONALIZATION: THE LEAGUE OF NATIONS, AND THE RESETTLEMENT OF REFUGEES

The author of a study of Hungarian refugees after World War One has written that '[The] relative immunity of domestic politics to international affairs ended with World War 1 and subsequent territorial changes.'[75] The situation in Armenia shows up similarities. As the previous section has shown, British public opinion mobilized more aggressively in defence of beleaguered Armenians during the war than it had done hitherto. In the immediate aftermath of war, new agencies for international cooperation engaged in humanitarian projects to assist displaced persons. The welfare of Armenian refugees, including issues of property restitution, attracted considerable attention, not least by virtue of exile organizations in France and elsewhere.[76]

The League of Nations High Commission for Refugees was created under Nansen in August 1921, with the initial task of looking after Russian refugees. Nansen held the post of High Commissioner until 1924. Many members of the League hoped that the refugee 'problem' would be solved by repatriation. These hopes were soon dashed, and they were instead confronted by the consequences of upheaval in the disintegrating Russian and Ottoman empires.[77] Initially, Nansen had been reluctant to intervene on behalf of the Armenians, fearing that this would simply encourage the Great Powers to stop sending them aid. Eventually he agreed to do so, because Armenians formed one of the largest bodies of people displaced during World War One. His hand was also forced by the refusal of the Allies to accept long term liability for the welfare of the Armenians by admitting them as prospective citizens. However, the League of Nations Covenant placed no obligation upon the League to intervene, and it had no funds of its own to spend on the relief and resettlement of refugees. The refugee organization played a supporting and coordinating role instead, relying where possible on intermittent financial grants from national governments and voluntary bodies. But funds were always limited, because the refugee organization was (in the words of the official historian of the League of Nations) 'an unpopular institution', and national governments refused to dig deep in their pockets.[78]

Grandiose schemes for the resettlement of Armenian refugees emanated both from the councils of the League and (having had to give up on Anatolia) from the Armenian diaspora. In 1923 the Armenian National Delegation proposed the creation of a settlement on the Sardarabad plain. In 1925 Nansen himself advocated investment in the vicinity of Erevan itself, where 50,000 Armenian refugees could settle, an initiative supported by Armenian refugee organizations abroad. In Nansen's words, Erevan lay at the heart of 'a wonderful land which needs only one thing, and that is water to become a garden of Eden'.[79] In the same year the League sponsored a mission to South America where, it was hoped, refugees would find work and where economic development could stimulate market opportunities for European industry.[80]

The League of Nations devoted particular attention to the task of 'reclaiming' Armenian women and children. At the time of the deportations in 1915 some women and children escaped massacre, but they faced the obliteration of their Armenian identity by virtue of being compelled to convert to Islam, to adopt Islamic names and to be brought up as Turks. As a consequence, according to Armenian authorities, half of all children in Turkish orphanages were in fact Armenian.[81] The Young Turks believed that a person's ethnic identity as Turkish or Armenian was not innate but could be changed by forcible conversion to Islam or by the indoctrination of children. We take up these points in the following section.

THE IMAGE OF THE ARMENIAN REFUGEE

Ever since news of the massacres first reached Western Europe and America, both the media and those campaigning on behalf of the Armenians had focused on the fate of Armenian women and children. Missionaries and relief workers during the conflict became involved with their 'rescue' and rehabilitation and after the conflict there appears to have been an effort to seek out and identify 'hidden' Armenians. This work was framed in both religious and racial terms, in that Christian women and children could be saved from the spiritual and moral 'corruption' of Islam, and that the Armenian race could be prevented from 'dying out'.

Armenia's political leaders themselves deployed ideas of sacrifice and loss, as well as envisaging the recovery of Armenia on the basis of established virtues of enterprise and vigour among its people. In important respects they drew upon the same prevailing images of Armenia that became entrenched in the discourse both of the diaspora and Armenophile opinion. Armenian politicians endorsed the claims of 'martyrdom' and of 'biblical Ararat'. The Armenian prime minister spoke on the second anniversary of the Republic of his people's 'vitality, creativity, industriousness, and indefatigability'.[82] Western Armenians, in particular, spoke of 'shattering the door' (blocked by Turkey), and of 'taking possession of our homeland, which has been irrigated by the blood of countless martyrs and heroes'. It is not clear if refugees counted as 'heroes'; but they were clearly numbered amongst the 'martyred' population.[83]

Public opinion in North America and western Europe was exposed to a constant litany of despair from the Caucasus, reinforcing the idea that external action offered the best prospect of improving the plight of refugees. An American visitor in the spring of 1919 penned a graphic description of the effects of famine and typhus on the children of Aleksandropol and Erevan. In Aleksandropol he encountered:

> children, but I really mean wizened and ancient dwarfs... [In Erevan] we found the children, such as they were, inhabiting an orphanage wherein one sickened at putridity's horrible odour, ... In those young, yet grotesquely aged faces, we seemed to see a long lifetime of tragedy packed into eight or ten childish years. ... Those gaunt faces, those attenuated bodies clad in a shagginess of filthy rags, seemed centuries removed from civilisation. You felt that you had stumbled into prehistoric man's den during some great famine year.

In this account the privileged tourist conveyed to his readers a sense that time itself had been effaced.[84] By implication, American relief would not only relieve suffering (and restore sanity to 'crazed' refugees); it would also restore civilization. The same doctrine operated amongst the personnel attached to Near East Relief, struggling to cope with displaced persons in Syria in 1919, prior to their return to Cilicia.[85]

This appeal to a common 'civilization' also commended itself to those who addressed themselves to public opinion in Britain. Dudley Northcote carefully constructed an image of the Armenian refugees that appealed to the charitable instincts of the British people, in terms that emphasized Armenia's Christian 'heritage' and the population's capacity for hard toil. Evidence of this was their survival in such hostile territory and also the progress the Armenians had made, as indicated by their adoption of Christianity, their own alphabet, religious and literary traditions, and the religious architecture that closely resembled that of the West. Armenians shared with the British a strong work ethic, bravery and desire for progress. Had not Viscount Bryce in 1876 described them as 'the most industrious and energetic race in that region', unlike the stereotyped 'lazy and sensual' Islamic peoples that surrounded them? By 1918, even those characteristics of the Armenians that had earlier been seen as negative, such as their role as traders, were now deployed to support the idea of a hardworking race.[86]

Northcote coupled this characterization with an insistence upon the responsibilities of the British government towards the refugees. In a Memorandum of

July 1921, he pointed out that Armenian refugees found themselves in refugee camps because they had fought with the Allies. The refugees 'have already had more than their fair share of suffering as a direct result of their having taken the Allied side during the Great War.' Any suggestion that Armenians took advantage of British generosity was hotly contested. If Armenian refugees lacked employment, no blame could attach to them, because they simply found it impossible to obtain work:

> The government have only succeeded in finding work for a few hundred, and as the men themselves have been discouraged from looking for it on their own, it cannot possibly be considered the fault of the refugees that they have remained a burden on the shoulders of the British taxpayers for so long.

Northcote emphasized that the refugees suffered real hardship. He described in detail what fate would befall them, should the refugee camp at Baqubah be closed, as the British government was proposing at the time. Penniless people would have to find their own transport, at the hottest time of the year. Deaths from heatstroke and starvation, especially amongst women and children, would certainly follow. Even if the refugees survived the journey from the camp, Northcote believed that their successful resettlement in the region was highly unlikely. The Arab population of Iraq was hostile, and few of the Armenians could speak Arabic. There was no demand for unskilled labour and no 'respectable' work for women. Thus, in Northcote's words, the proposal 'certainly means the end of them as a community and the complete abandonment of them to the Arabs.'[87]

At the same time, the discourse of suffering and national deprivation continued to be associated with feminine vulnerability and masculine incapacity, at least so far as the Armenian diaspora was concerned. Violation of the female subject served as a metaphor for the traumatic invasion of territory by Turkish troops. Armenian victims of Ottoman atrocities attracted a great deal of sympathetic comment. 'Armenian women have, against their will, become victims of the animal instincts of men who pursue them without any shame, like a hunter in pursuit of its prey.' Contemporaries asked their readers to understand why, in these circumstances, some Armenian women should commit suicide: 'this is not surprising when one takes into account the religious and moral upbringing of Armenian womanhood. The outrage inflicted on her honour and dignity is not just a huge crime but an earthly catastrophe', to which death was the only response. At the same time, national security and integrity required a more robust and 'manly' response. Armenian males were called upon to avenge crimes against womenfolk, to deploy real prowess and thus to demonstrate their readiness to embark upon the epic task of national reconstruction.[88]

From the end of World War One, notwithstanding continued conflicts such as that between Turkey and Greece, foreign relief agencies took steps to identify and rescue refugee women and children. As late as 1924 British Members of Parliament expressed concern in the House of Commons about Armenian women who 'are being retained in Turkish harems'.[89] Women were heavily involved in this work, whether on behalf of the League or of charitable agencies in Armenia and the Near East. Emily Robinson, who had long been involved in the Armenian cause in Britain for 'moral' reasons, campaigned for the 'release' of these women, on the grounds that the armistice terms with Turkey provided for the release of all prisoners of war.[90] The Danish social worker Karen Jeppe (1876–1935) played a prominent part in working with Armenian women in Aleppo between 1922 and 1927.[91] Emma Cushman, of Robert College, an American missionary foundation, pressed the League of Nations to back what she described as a 'neutral house' in Constantinople, whose managers aimed to determine the nationality of children taken from Muslim houses, where they had developed a 'distorted mentality'. In these 'American' houses, rescued children once more learned the Armenian language and sang Armenian hymns.[92] Caring for refugee women and children seems to have been a sphere in which European and American women claimed particular expertise and earned plaudits in the West.[93]

More was at stake than the assertion of feminine duty. Cultural stereotyping about Islam and the East was closely bound up with these humanitarian initiatives. Reports to the League of Nations regularly asserted that the 'Orient' was, on the one hand, savage and barbaric, and on the other sensual and morally corrupting. Thus, Armenian female refugees were 'brutalised by degrees, blows and caresses; opium, persuasion and threats are used in turn'. They became 'desecrated virgins'. To be sure, there were reported instances where women wished to remain in Muslim families. For non-Muslim contemporaries, this was a fresh tragedy. It was inconceivable that Armenian women chose this fate; rather it was assumed that they had been 'tricked' into it in some way. 'There are cases, but thank God they are rare, where these unhappy women return voluntarily to their bondage. All Turks are not wicked and often they treat their victims with cruel gentleness.'[94] The emphasis here is on female vulnerability, moral and physical, and an assumption that women played a passive role. All the same, in describing her efforts to 'rescue' Armenian women from the clutches of their lascivious Turkish captors, Karen Jeppe adopted a somewhat different perspective:

> The rescue always required a special effort on the part of the persons rescued; they had to decide for themselves whether they would leave the houses where they were detained or not, and they often ran a considerable risk in doing so ... *They always felt that the responsibility rested with themselves*; we only had helped them to carry out their own intentions.

But Miss Jeppe carefully contrived her description to place the emphasis upon the 'trust' that Armenian refugee women placed in her and her colleagues, as well as the increased mutual respect between 'Arab' men and European volunteer workers: 'now most of these [Arabs] are our friends.'[95]

Somewhat different considerations applied in the case of Armenian children, many of whom had been seized in 1915, either by Turks or Kurds. Turkish orphanages were filled with 'a great number of children who are said to be Kurds but who, in reality, are all Armenians. Rape, violence, fraud, the force of inertia, bad faith, all are employed by men who manifest a particularly odious form of fanaticism in carrying off women and children to captivity and degradation.'[96] Finding those who were now 'nomad' proved particularly troubling. Karen Jeppe pinned her hopes on the ineradicable 'Armenianness' of even the youngest refugee:

> In the beginning this filled us with despair, but we soon learned that they would be sure to return to us again. After all, they could not forget their people and their faith and the whole spiritual atmosphere that was their birthright.[97]

In this regard it is also worth drawing attention to the curious case of Aurora Mardiganian who found herself starring in a film of her own life. Aurora's life was of interest in so far as it supported claims of Turkish cruelty and depravity. However, in re-enacting her experiences for the benefit of a cinema audience in the USA she was clearly being exploited on behalf of the producers, in whose publicity brochure we read that:

> The chaste figure of Aurora is seen, not acting, but living again through the horrors of those two years of captivity.[98]

In other words, what appears on one level to be an instance of a female refugee who claimed the right to tell her own story emerges on closer inspection less as an example of human agency than the appropriation of the refugee by a new authority, in this case the film industry.

CONCLUSIONS

Even more than in Poland or the new Baltic states, Armenia became a kind of canvas on which external observers – on the basis of an authority conferred upon them by being eyewitnesses – portrayed the 'new' land. The dominant narrative was that of a dismembered nation, beset by tragedy that inflicted physical and mental scars upon the Armenian population. This narrative expressed itself in a language that underscored refugees' helplessness, as when an American relief worker spoke of 'cringing and suffering unfortunates'.[99] Other images also surfaced. For example, the new Soviet authorities depicted refugees from Turkish-held territory as socially and politically dangerous – harbingers of crime or, worse, of political disloyalty to the Bolshevik project.[100]

Yet an important aspect of Armenia for the British relief worker Dudley Northcote was not only its history of invasion, occupation, but also its capacity for survival. That history took on a new significance following World War One. As described earlier, Northcote was at pains to point out that the Armenians had fought hard for the Allies. Their valour received pride of place in the culminating words of his unpublished history of Armenia:

> I do not think the Armenians, when they are well led and when they are fighting for a cause in which they believe, are in any way inferior as soldiers to the other nationalities and races by whom they are surrounded. Their principal undoing has been their most unfortunate geographical position, their land for centuries has been a source of contention between rival great empires.[101]

The image of a brave but exposed 'race' was shared by other observers, who spoke of their 'free spirit'. 'You may kill them, but you cannot kill their spirit', said one of the founders of the British–Armenian Chamber of Commerce in 1920.[102] Their depiction as strong, courageous survivors who were prepared to fight seems to have been cultivated by western supporters who appealed to British values, interests – and wallets. This racialized discourse extended, of course, to the non-Armenian population as well, as in one account of the American relief effort which was 'felt by the wild, ragged Kurd, the plausible Georgian, the suspicious Azerbaijan, the able Armenian, and the grave Turk with equal seriousness.'[103]

Armenian resistance to conversion to Islam was also important, and also helped to define the racial characteristics of the entire population. In Northcote's words, 'the fire-worshipping Persians quickly embraced the new religion, but not so the Armenians who still stuck to Christianity'. Armenians had been 'always the very first to receive the full shock of the various onslaughts that have been made on our civilisation in times past'. Armenia, Northcote emphasized, was part of Europe and had played an important role throughout history in defending Europe's borders.[104]

Particular attention was focussed on the need to 'reclaim' Armenian women and children. The aim here was in part to reunite families and restore shattered communities. But it was also to smash the 'bondage' brought about by forced conversion to Islam, and to save the female from moral and spiritual 'corruption', since she could perish 'either from the soft languor of eastern harems, or from savage treatment which is inflicted upon her.'[105]

All the same, imagery and rhetoric were susceptible to revision, and many Armenian survivors ended up in refugee camps, a legacy of the failure to find a durable diplomatic solution to their plight. It was widely believed that their ultimate salvation lay in their readiness to substitute agriculture for trade, even if – paradoxically, for some outside observers – this implied a dilution of traditional identity. This is a background against which schemes for their resettlement must be understood. (In the medium term, their 'conversion' to agricultural occupation may have been sustained in Soviet Armenia by the New Economic Policy and programmes for economic reconstruction.)[106]

From one point of view, the very dispersion of most 'able' Armenians contained the seeds of survival, because it imposed serious responsibilities on the part of the Armenian diaspora. As we have seen, more than a territorial entity was at stake, important though it was to define the frontier and political form of the Armenian polity. But 'Armenia' might be preserved beyond as well as within the boundaries of the new state. This implied a duty of care on the part of Armenians overseas, whose financial support helped to some extent to soften the blow of displacement. Dispersal also levied a duty on Armenian 'colonists' in Syria and elsewhere, who ran the risk of 'de-nationalization' or 'Arabization'.

By means of such rhetorical devices, Armenia's past became a resource to be deployed in order to justify external humanitarian intervention, whether by non-governmental organizations or by enthusiastic individuals. Armenia's present difficulties served to buttress claims to the authority of the expert professional, whether it be the lawyer, doctor, agronomist or social worker. Past and present alike, embodied in the person of the Armenian refugee, sustained the ambitions of the short-lived independent Armenian republic as well as the Soviet state that succeeded it. As in other instances, however, these powerful currents allowed little scope for human agency on the part of the displaced population.[107]

* Our thanks to Nick Baron and Peter Holquist for their comments on an earlier version of this chapter.

Conclusions: On Living in a 'New Country'

PETER GATRELL AND NICK BARON

The contributions to this book have all addressed a crucially important, but hitherto neglected historical problem: the nexus of population displacement, state building and social identity in eastern Europe following World War One. We have drawn attention to the ways in which the experience of wartime exile influenced the emergence of nationalism and national movements in the territories of imperial Russia's western periphery; the role of refugees in promoting and propagating ideas of 'homeland' and ambitions for statehood; and the impact of the mass postwar return of refugees on processes of state-construction in the newly independent polities of the region. We have also shown how persisting conflict after 1918, both civil wars and foreign interventions, continued to destabilize the entire region, giving rise to vast new movements of population. Numerous claims to statehood were raised in these years across the lands of the former Russian empire. Some successor states succeeded in consolidating themselves; other incipient national or revolutionary polities sprang into existence but then just as quickly disappeared from the stage. Population displacement played a powerful role in all these histories, in some cases underwriting, in other instances undermining the ambitions of those who aspired to forge statehood out of its constituent elements: territory, population and a collective idea.

By the early 1920s, eastern Europe was fractured: the October revolution had established a fault line between the Bolshevik state and its bourgeois rivals. And yet border-crossings between these two worlds persisted, as several of our chapters have shown. In particular, the continuing repatriation of wartime refugees to their new 'homelands' created complex dilemmas for state authorities in regions of transit, such as the Urals, as well as at the border itself, where both sides sought to register, sort and filter contingents of returnees according to their own ideological criteria and notions of state interest. This combustible politics of population, which contributors to this volume have traced from the highest levels of decision-making to that of local implementation, was fundamental to momentous shifts in economic power and social relations which were evident on both the national and international scale. In the postwar era, the moorings of community, work and income were even less stable than they had been during wartime. Economic deprivation and social upheaval were exacerbated by the spread of contagious disease, such as cholera, typhus and influenza, and, in Russia, by a devastating famine. Fears of further catastrophe lay close to the surface. Throughout all this, there was a profound awareness, on the part of politicians, officials and the public, of the significance of displaced populations: of the need to accommodate and provide welfare for returning soldiers, repatriated refugees, new immigrants and émigrés, but also of the dangers and challenges posed by unsettled and itinerant people. As this volume has demonstrated, the desire of the displaced to return home was inseparably, and in many different ways, implicated in the process of defining the limits, attributes and qualities of the new post-imperial 'homelands'.

All of the contributors address the politics of population displacement, as well as issues of legal definition and international diplomacy. However, they have taken the discussion a step further than previous historical literature on forced migration. In the first place, they have highlighted the close connection between population movements and state-building, demonstrating how population displacement created opportunities for the crystallization of power by new political authorities and for bureaucratic intervention. We now know much more about the patriotic elites who arranged welfare provision and who helped organize programmes for the repatriation of displaced persons. We also understand better the connections between, on the one hand, the new states' spatial policies – not only defining territories and demarcating external borders, but also establishing internal regional structures and regulating centre – periphery relations – and, on the other, the attitude of state officials towards displaced populations, whose movements transected state borders and internal boundaries, and whose attempts to settle came into frequent conflict with administrative directives or political priorities. This reciprocal relationship between population displacement and the construction – both physical and cultural – of political space constitutes a core theme of all chapters of the present volume.

Secondly, many of the contributors acknowledge the insights offered by cultural history. Cultural history brings to the fore those ways in which contemporaries represented the consequences and implications of population displacement. Consider, for example, the attempt to attribute 'refugeedom' to an entire population, as in the following remarks of a statistician from Saratov, writing in 1922: 'We have lived through so much these past seven years that it is a rare citizen of the [Russian] Republic who has not felt like a refugee, at least for a short while'.[1] This striking verdict lends itself to the depiction of displacement as a universal experience in Russia, the result not only of war, captivity and repatriation, but also of revolutionary turmoil. Yet a moment's reflection suggests that it effaces the specific experiences of refugees, the multiple practices to which they were subject (such as registration, documentation, labelling, and creating a welfare regime) and the distinctions that were frequently drawn between the refugee and the non-refugee population. Our authors have drawn attention to commonalities among refugees' experiences but also have not neglected to consider the particular experience of individual refugees.

Cultural history reminds us that language matters, whether by virtue of the legal terms that were (and continue to be) applied to displaced populations, or the rhetoric used to characterize the perception or experience of displacement. It is impossible, of course, to capture the precise semantic or affective connotations of contemporary terminology across this considerable chronological distance, all the more so as for the purposes of coherence and consistency we have translated into English the various terms used in at least six languages (Latvian, Lithuanian, Belarusian, Ukrainian, Polish and Russian). Nevertheless, all the contributions to this book have drawn attention to some of the most pronounced characterizations of refugees, including the polarities of 'disease–health', 'spontaneity–order' and 'friend–enemy'.

Many refugees certainly suffered from infectious disease, of which typhus was the most distressing. All the successor states to the Russian empire devoted considerable efforts, as described, for example, in Tomas Balkelis' chapter, to screening the refugee population, with the short-term aim of creating 'a permanent system of sanitary defence ... on the border zone forming the bridge between Poland and Russia'.[2] The Soviet state, too, expressed alarm about the 'unlawful and disorderly movement of refugees' during the summer of 1921, because of the threat of epidemic disease.[3] This rhetoric was linked to issues of public order and national security: the contributions by Konrad Zielinski and Kate Stadnik have demonstrated how the 'screening' of refugees was also motivated by the conviction that ideologically suspect individuals or groups could 'contaminate' society and the body politic.

The opposition of 'spontaneity–order' recalls World War One official language in which refugees were likened to a raging torrent that threatened to undermine bureaucratic attempts to monitor and manage their movement. In chapter 8, Gennadii Kornilov has quoted a Soviet official who expressed his frustration with 'the spontaneous movement of human masses [that] grievously undermines the territorial evacuation plan [and] signifies a chaotic movement of refugees, manifesting all the characteristics of an endless flow of large groups.' In using these terms the new authorities of the Russian empire's successor states spoke the language of their tsarist forebears in expressing frustration with refugees' proclivity to 'go their own way'.[4]

The cultural politics of state-formation also articulated careful rhetorical distinctions among displaced populations between friend and foe, which were translated into a range of discriminatory practices implemented through registration procedures, the issuing of visas or passports, and interventions at the moment of border-crossing itself. This was clearly related to the politically divisive impact of the October revolution on the region. As several chapters of this volume have shown, the Moscow authorities put the secret police to work sifting through contingents of Polish, Ukrainian, Belarusian and Baltic, as well as Russian, refugees. Those considered especially hostile were sometimes arrested; politically reliable refugees were sometimes sent abroad to work subversively on behalf of Soviet power in their national 'homelands', or recruited to form national units in the Red Army, to act as political leaders and administrators for national minorities, or to apply their expertise to the task of Soviet economic reconstruction. The newly independent eastern European states were similarly concerned to establish the credentials of refugees and returnees: at border-crossings their officials not only monitored the entry of individuals who might carry infectious diseases, but also policed the entry of those who were politically suspect, because of their former activities, personal contacts or merely their ethnic origin.

The careful categorization of refugees, to which several contributors have drawn attention, also belongs to this set of practices. It carried important implications for ethnic minorities. During World War One the movement of Jewish refugees beyond the Pale of Settlement had been invested with dire consequences. As Aija Priedite has indicated in her chapter, Latvian refugees during the war were frequently mistaken for Germans, and physically or verbally attacked as a result. The postwar return movement of Jewish refugees posed particular difficulties. After 1918 Jewish refugees sought to return to their homes in newly independent states, many of whose leaders made no secret of their unwillingness to support the political rights and economic well-being of Jews. Balkelis has described in his paper how liberal politicians, like the Lithuanian Rapolas Skipitis, observed this exclusionary stance with mounting despair.

Many of the chapters in this volume have demonstrated how these distinctions, and the procedures created to register and record them, formed part of the emerging 'surveillance state', to which several scholars have recently devoted a great deal of attention.[5] It is evident that refugees constituted a 'problem' for new government bureaucracies, military officials and professional or voluntary relief workers. Zielinski has drawn attention to the fact that the Polish authorities made use of informal networks of informants to check how 'spotless' was the 'political and moral' reputation of prospective entrants to Poland, while Stadnik has shown that this intervention had its counterpart in the attempts by Soviet officials to monitor the political beliefs of returnees, in the hope that some of them would contribute to the revolutionary cause across the border in neighbouring states. In this connection it is worth noting the stance in eastern Europe by officials dealing, in the aftermath of the Bolshevik revolution, with the repatriation of prisoners of war. Łucja Kapralska has indicated the priority that Polish officials gave to repatriating prisoners of war from the Siberian Division. The return of such prisoners, however, was not always unambiguously welcomed. For example, Austro-Hungarian POWs who returned from Russia in 1918 found themselves subject to sustained and intensive questioning, lest captivity and Russian propaganda had converted them to an anti-imperial stance. It is worth recalling the chilling words of Max Ronge, head of the Intelligence Bureau of the Austrian General Staff, who anticipated the return of prisoners by saying that 'what awaits [them] is not a jubilant welcome but a thorough examination of heart and conscience'.[6]

No attempt to write refugee history can escape the 'objectification' of refugees that is a consequence of external intervention, whether by governments, professionals or diasporic communities. Refugees frequently came to stand for an entire nationality, as a symbol of potential national renewal, national pride or national suffering. As Priedite and Valentina Utgof have described in their chapters, members of the patriotic intelligentsia used their access to displaced persons, not only to proselytise on behalf of the 'national idea', but also to depict the refugee as an element in the continuing national epic. Thus the Belarusian activist PM Kraskovskii was reminded of 'the ancient Belarusian assembly' when he witnessed a congress of refugees that convened in Minsk in December 1917. Where they suffered from infectious disease, refugees could serve as a reminder of public health as a national responsibility. We recall how a member of the American–Polish Relief Expedition, Captain Howard Jennings Gorman, proclaimed upon encountering displaced persons that 'We can wash Poland' (see chapter 1).

More broadly, the essays in this volume have demonstrated the progressive crystallization of the category of the 'refugee'. A product of World War One, this category continued to resonate and develop further in its aftermath. One far-sighted Belarusian author suggested in 1919 that refugees should be the 'object of study by the sociologist and the political analyst (*gosudarstvoved*) and regarded as an identifiable historical category.'[7] This doctrine requires further research, to establish the extent to which social scientists and others at the time made it operational. It is also evident that the category became established in international diplomacy and law, as well as in cultural discourses. For example, as the chapter by Peter Gatrell and Jo Laycock has shown, British and other European individuals sympathetic to the plight of the Armenians deployed a particular gendered representation of the 'refugee' as a means of drawing attention to the need for coordinated, international humanitarian intervention in particular crises. This, in turn, underlined the need for an international 'refugee regime', a precondition of which was more extensive international cooperation, such as the new League of Nations seemed to offer.

A related point is that – if one looks hard enough or exercises sufficient imagination – one can begin to 'let refugees speak', to demonstrate how they conceived of and articulated their own experiences. Whether the relative lack of refugee testimony is due to the fact it does not exist (perhaps because their voices were rarely registered, recorded or archived, or because their evidence has been lost), or to the fact that historians have not (yet) probed sufficiently deeply, is something on which the contributors to this volume have kept an open mind. We must allow for the possibility that refugees who wished to tell their stories were simply denied an audience, as Kapralska's research into the alienation and nostalgia of Siberian refugees in interwar Poland has suggested. But silence might also indicate that something else was going on. A refugee-interpreter who worked for Near East Relief – and who was interviewed by her employer Mabel Elliott – claimed that much of her experience was impossible to narrate. Perhaps this insistence upon silence enabled her to claim a privileged standpoint of her own. Whatever the validity of this argument, it is also worth pointing out that, despite the relative dearth of first-person testimony, some instances have come to light in which associations were established – the most striking example being the Association of Siberian Deportees in Poland, part of whose purpose was to preserve the experiences of refugees as well as political exiles for posterity.

It can be argued that refugees' actions spoke larger than words. Refugee politics acquired considerable significance. World War One witnessed a remarkable efflorescence of nationally based refugee organizations, enabling the mobilization of non-Russian ethnic minorities in support of refugee welfare and eventual repatriation. These organizations were formed by refugee activists, who brought together co-nationals in relief work. Nor were rank and file refugees simply passive bystanders; the essays in this book have demonstrated the keen interest that Latvian, Lithuanian, Belarusian and Polish refugees manifested in political developments in their 'homeland', including debates about their own status and prospects in the emerging successor states. We have found many instances in which this attentiveness encouraged and enabled refugees to make the arduous journey back home.

We are conscious that important issues remain unresolved. One obvious issue is the way in which gender inflected discussions of population displacement at the time. Careful readers will have noted how many of the names that figured in the process of refugee relief were female, such as those who occupied a prominent position among the Quakers and members of Near East Relief (see, for example, chapter 9). They recounted their experiences in terms of adventure and excitement, and emphasized their empathy with refugees. In other respects, however, gender issues are more difficult to unravel. So far as we can tell from the available record, government officials in eastern Europe paid virtually no attention to the fact that most wartime refugee households would have been headed by women. Only on rare occasions did national refugee organizations or relief workers mention the role that refugee women played in the management of household or community welfare, and in the repatriation process. This silence is conspicuous. On the other hand, issues of gender did surface in the representation of refugeedom in Armenia, as Gatrell and Laycock have demonstrated in their chapter. So far as the representation of Armenia itself was concerned, the plight of 'martyred Armenia' was frequently encapsulated in terms of female adversity, particularly mass rape.

More work is also needed to unpick the cultural meanings that attached to land and to landscapes. Some aspects of the 'land question' are well established. All governments paid close attention to land reform, including not only its more equitable distribution but also related issues of land reorganization and agronomic advice. Even more pressing problems arose in the aftermath of war that had devastated rural land and imposed enormous hardship on predominantly farming communities. Many villagers in the eastern European borderlands had been obliged to supply food and fodder to occupying troops; they also had to negotiate the detritus of battle, such as shell holes, trenches, dugouts, barbed wire, and unexploded bombs. Others were even less fortunate, having seen their farms burned to the ground by troops seeking revenge or for tactical reasons. For the governments of newly independent states this meant the need to divert resources into economic and social reconstruction, and particularly into rebuilding infrastructure. But land was more than a resource to repair. When publicity was given to stories of refugees living in makeshift underground shelters, it served as a reminder of national suffering and loss. More broadly, cultural representations of alien landscapes embodied memories of displacement, diaspora and exile – just as, for refugees, the remembered or imagined landscapes of home had served as metaphors for their present condition and talismans of their future fortunes. In this connection we flag the need for more work on the connections between landscape, ethnic identity and migration. We are aware that this volume has only begun to problematize and deconstruct the rich and diverse connotations of 'homeland'.

Finally, we are aware that there is a 'refugee history' beyond 1924, by which time the process of repatriation was more or less complete. To what extent were the experiences of refugeedom and repatriation obliterated in the public commemoration of war and state-building? How does this relate to the commemoration of other kinds of displacement, such as political exiles and prisoners of war? What measures were taken to support the very young and the very old refugee groups, and with what consequences for national and local budgets and for popular opinion? Did subsequent episodes of population displacement – such as the Soviet deportation of nationalities during the 1940s – prompt any reference to earlier events?

There are thus exciting possibilities for further research, including the use of other kinds of testimony, such as that created by contemporaneous ethnographic and sociological studies, by film makers, artists and others. In the meantime, we can safely assert that demographic and spatial policies were intimately related in building states and remoulding societies, and that refugeedom and repatriation were central to the success or failure of these projects.

Notes

Introduction

1. This argument is developed further in Nick Baron and Peter Gatrell, 'Population displacement, state-building and social identity in the lands of the former Russian Empire, 1917–1923', *Kritika. Explorations in Russian and Eurasian History*, New Series, 4, no. 1 (2003), pp. 51–100. See also James C Scott, *Seeing Like a State: How Certain Schemes to Improve the Human Condition Have Failed*, New Haven, Yale University Press, 1998; George Steinmetz, ed., *State/Culture: State-Formation after the Cultural Turn*, Ithaca, Cornell University Press, 1999.
2. Timothy Mitchell speaks of 'techniques that enable mundane material practices to take on the appearance of an abstract, nonmaterial form', see Mitchell, 'Society, economy, and the state effect', in Steinmetz, ed., *State/Culture*, p. 77. Our argument is that the preference accorded to rootedness simultaneously produces a range of such practices and abstraction at the level of the state. He suggests (p. 90) that the establishment and policing of a frontier as 'mundane arrangements ... help[s] manufacture an almost transcendental entity, the nation-state.' In this interpretation the state is a composite of multiple 'structural effects', and not an entity that is external to the social world. See also Nevzat Soguk, *States and Strangers: Refugees and Displacements of Statecraft*, Minneapolis, University of Minnesota Press, 1999.
3. Liisa Malkki, 'National geographic: the rooting of peoples and the territorialisation of national identity among scholars and refugees', *Cultural Anthropology*, 7, 1992, 24–44.
4. In the scholarship on this period, a milestone was EM Kulischer, *Europe on the Move: War and Population Changes, 1917–1947*, New York, Columbia University Press, 1948. This volume superseded the earlier work of Madeleine de Bryas, *Les peuples en marche: les migrations politiques et économiques en Europe depuis la guerre mondiale*, Paris, A Pedone, 1926. See also Michael Marrus, *The Unwanted: European*

Refugees in the Twentieth Century, New York, Oxford University Press, 1982; Mark Mazower, *Dark Continent: Europe's Twentieth Century*, London, Allen Lane, 1998, chapter 2.

5. Leslie Page Moch, *Moving Europeans: Migration in Western Europe since 1650*, Bloomington, Indiana University Press, 1992; Klaus J Bade, *Europa in Bewegung: Migration vom späten 18. Jahrhundert bis zur Gegenwart*, München, Beck, 2000.
6. The classic text is Hannah Arendt, *The Origins of Totalitarianism*, New York, Meridian Books, 1958. For additional references, see Baron and Gatrell, 'Population Displacement', and chapter 1 of the present volume.
7. Hilary Pilkington, *Migration, Displacement and Identity in Post-Soviet Russia*, London, Routledge, 1998; Neil Melvin, *Russians Beyond Russia's Borders*, London, Pinter, 1995; David Laitin, *Identity in Formation: The Russian-Speaking Populations in the Near Abroad*, Ithaca, Cornell, 1998. For a recent work that identifies concerted population displacement as a key element in 'new' (post-1989) wars, see Mary Kaldor, *New and Old Wars: Organized Violence in a Global Era*, Cambridge, Polity Press, 2001. As will become clear, we question this 'novelty'.
8. See Soguk, *States and Strangers*, for a discussion of the ideological underpinnings of the contemporary relationships between transnational organizations and the nation-state.
9. The League of Nations was established on 10 January 1920. Poland was a founder member of the League. The three Baltic states joined on 22 September 1921. Soviet Russia did not join until 1934, following the withdrawal of Germany and Japan from the League. On post-1918 international initiatives to deal with displaced populations, see Claudene Skran, *Refugees in Interwar Europe: The Emergence of a Regime*, Oxford, Clarendon Press, 1995.
10. See Leo Perutz, *Little Apple*, London, Harvill, 1991 (first published in German, 1928). Perutz's hero, Vittorin, is a former Austrian prisoner of war who, having been freed from a Siberian prison camp, tracks his Russian tormentor across Russia, Italy, Turkey and Austria. The irony is that Vittorin need never have left his home town, because his prey has actually made his way to Vienna.
11. Cited in Mazower, *Dark Continent*, p. x.
12. Peter Gatrell, *A Whole Empire Walking: Refugees in Russia during World War One*, Bloomington, Indiana University Press, 1999.
13. See the essays in Karen Barkey and Mark von Hagen, eds., *After Empire: Multiethnic Societies and Nation-Building. The Soviet Union and the Russian, Ottoman, and Habsburg Empires*, Boulder, Westview Press, 1997; Rogers Brubaker, *Nationalism Reframed: Nationhood and the National Question in the New Europe*, Cambridge, Cambridge University Press, 1996.
14. See chapter 1.
15. Benedict Anderson, *Imagined Communities: Reflections on the Origin and Spread of Nationalism*, London, Verso, 1983. Rogers Brubaker, 'Aftermaths of empire and the unmixing of peoples', in Barkey and von Hagen, eds., *After Empire: Multiethnic Societies and Nation-Building*, pp. 155–80, esp. his remarks on p. 158. On the discourse

of 'elements' in modern Russia, see the remarks of Peter Holquist, 'To count, to extract, to exterminate: population statistics and population politics in late imperial and Soviet Russia', in *A State of Nations. Empire and Nation-Building in the Age of Lenin and Stalin*, eds. Ronald Grigor Suny and Terry Martin, New York, Oxford University Press, 2001, 111–44.

16. Established nation-states might also cast themselves as 'homeland' states promoting or protecting the rights of co-nationals who find themselves (because of border settlements and/or displacement) within another nation-state. Brubaker, *Nationalism Reframed*, pp. 107–47.
17. On physiological metaphors and political space, see Paul Weindling, *Epidemics and Genocide in Eastern Europe, 1890–1945*, Oxford, Oxford University Press, 2000; see also Amir Weiner, 'Nature, nurture and memory in a socialist Utopia: delineating the Soviet socio-ethnic body in the age of socialism', *American Historical Review*, 104, 1999, 1114–45. 'The Reds are sending us typhus now' ... 'Typhus and Bolshevism, it's all the same', as Leo Perutz has two of his characters say in *Little Apple*, p. 165.
18. Renee Hirschon, *Heirs of the Greek Catastrophe: The Social Life of Asia Minor Refugees in Piraeus*, Oxford, Clarendon Press, 1989. An important recent addition to the literature is Pamela Ballinger, *History in Exile: Memory and Identity at the Borders of the Balkans*, Princeton, Princeton University Press, 2003.
19. This term, brought into wider circulation by Rogers Brubaker, *Nationalism Reframed*, was first used by Lord Curzon, according to Marrus, *The Unwanted*, p. 41.
20. For an excellent case study of post-1918 state ambitions in eastern Europe, and the responses they evoked, see Irina Livezeanu, *Cultural Politics in Greater Romania: Regionalism, Nation Building and Ethnic Struggle, 1918–1930*, Ithaca, Cornell University Press, 1995.
21. Baron and Gatrell, 'Population displacement'.
22. Weindling describes how 'desperate German colonists pretended that they were Polish in order to obtain a Polish passport and then switched back to German identity to gain entry into Germany. Others crossed the border on forest paths to evade quarantine', Weindling, *Epidemics and Genocide*, p. 152.
23. Gatrell, *A Whole Empire Walking*, Conclusion.
24. E Valentine Daniel and John Knudsen, eds., *Mistrusting Refugees*, Berkeley, University of California Press, 1995; Liisa Malkki, 'Speechless emissaries: refugees, humanitarianism, and dehistoricization', *Cultural Anthropology*, 11 (3) 1996, 377–404. One might express this prevalent doctrine as follows: refugees cannot pursue a path, instead, they must *be* pursued.
25. These large questions emerge in theoretical work, including the following: Liisa Malkki, *Purity and Exile: Violence, Memory, and National Cosmology among Hutu Refugees in Tanzania*, Chicago, Chicago University Press, 1995; Alistair Ager, ed., *Refugees: Perspectives on the Experience of Forced Migration*, London & New York, Pinter, 1999.
26. Malkki, *Purity and Exile*, p. 16.

27. Sir John Hope Simpson. *The Refugee Problem: Report of a Survey*, London, Oxford University Press, 1939, pp. 3, 5.
28. Joseph Van Gelder, 'Activities of Refugee Department American JDC in Europe during the years 1921, 1922, 1923', Typescript, May 1924, p. 5, copy in JDC Archives, New York.

Chapter 1: War, Population Displacement and State-Formation in the Russian Borderlands, 1914–24

1. SG Wheatcroft and RW Davies, 'Population', in RW Davies et al., eds., *The Economic Transformation of the Soviet Union, 1913–1945*, Cambridge, Cambridge University Press, 1994, pp. 60–2. This picture of massive social upheaval was completed by the exchange of prisoners of war by the former belligerents, by the return migration of hundreds of thousands of those who had been displaced in 1915–17, and by internal population displacement that followed the terrible harvest failure in Russia's main grain-producing regions in 1921–22. According to Volkov, 3.57 million legally registered refugees and 1.41 million prisoners of war remained on Soviet territory on 1 January 1921. Between 1918 and 1921, 3.17 million prisoners returned to Russia from captivity abroad. EZ Volkov, *Dinamika narodonaseleniia SSSR za vosem'desiat let*, Moscow, Gosudarstvennoe izdatel'stvo, 1930, p. 185.
2. Stéphane Audoin-Rouzeau and Annette Becker, *1914–1918: Understanding the Great War*, London, Profile Books, 2002.
3. *Osobye soveshchaniia i komitety voennogo vremeni*, Petrograd, 1917, p. 47.
4. AN Kurtsev, 'Bezhentsy pervoi mirovoi voiny v Rossii (1914–1918)', *Voprosy istorii*, 1999, 8, pp. 98–113; Peter Gatrell, *A Whole Empire Walking: Refugees in Russia during World War One*, Bloomington, Indiana University Press, 1999, pp. 15–32; AIu Bakhturina, *Politika rossiiskoi imperii v vostochnoi Galitsii v gody pervoi mirovoi voiny*, Moscow, AIRO, 2000.
5. SI Zubchaninov, speaking before the Special Council for Refugees, 10 September 1915, Rossiiskii Gosudarstvennyi Istoricheskii Arkhiv (hereafter RGIA) f.1322, op.1, d.1, ll.10b.-2.
6. Rossiiskii Gosudarstvennyi Voenno-Istoricheskii Arkhiv (hereafter RGVIA) f.2020, op.1, d.131, l.184, General Beliaev to General Danilov, 24 July 1915.
7. Memorandum by Prince NL Obolenskii, 30 August 1915, RGVIA f.2003, op.2, d.945, ll.10.
8. Quoted in *Bezhentsy i vyselentsy*, Moscow, 1915, p. 54.
9. Gatrell, *A Whole Empire Walking*, p. 22.
10. Eric Lohr, *Nationalizing the Russian Empire: The Campaign Against Enemy Nationals during World War 1*, Cambridge, MA., Harvard University Press, 2003.
11. Senator A.B.Neidgardt, quoted in Gosudarstvennyi Arkhiv Rossiiskoi Federatsii (GARF) f.651, op.1, d.39, l.25.
12. Gatrell, *A Whole Empire Walking*, pp. 18–19, 52–3; see also Gatrell and Laycock, this volume.

13. Eugene Kulischer, *Europe on the Move: War and Population Changes 1917–1947*, New York, Columbia University Press, 1948, p. 32.
14. Gatrell, *A Whole Empire Walking*, p. 3.
15. Violetta Thurstan, *The People Who Run: Being the Tragedy of the Refugee in Russia*, New York and London, GP Putnam's Sons, 1916; Ruth Fry, *A Quaker Adventure: The Story of Nine Years' Relief and Reconstruction*, London, Nisbet, 1926.
16. Lester M Jones, *Quakers in Action*, New York, Macmillan, 1929; and Joice Mary Nankivell, *The River of a Hundred Ways: Life in the War-Devastated Areas of Eastern Poland*, London, Allen and Unwin, 1924.
17. Gatrell, *A Whole Empire Walking*, chapter 4.
18. Ibid., pp. 162–8 for Russian, Ukrainian, and Belarusian refugees.
19. Quoted in ibid, pp. 156, 159, and Priedite, this volume.
20. Martynas Yčas, *Pirmasis nepriklausomos Lietuvos desimtmetis*, London, n.p., 1955, p. 38.
21. See also the analysis in Mark von Hagen, 'The Great War and the mobilisation of ethnicity in the Russian empire', in Barnett Rubin and Jack Snyder, eds., *Post-Soviet Political Order: Conflict and Statebuilding*, New York, Routledge, 1998, pp. 34–57.
22. As suggested by Utgof, this volume.
23. Vejas G Liulevicius, *War Land on the Eastern Front: Culture, National Identity and German Occupation in World War One*, Cambridge, Cambridge University Press, 2000.
24. See the summary in Aviel Roshwald, *Ethnic Nationalism and the Fall of Empires: Central Europe, Russia and the Middle East, 1914–1923*, London, Routledge, 2001, pp. 95–8.
25. Edward Hallett Carr, *The Bolshevik Revolution, 1917–1923*, volume 3, Harmondsworth, Penguin Books, 1971, chapter 1.
26. NP Vakar, *Belorussia: The Making of a Nation*, Cambridge, MA., Harvard University Press, 1956, pp. 98–105; Carr, *The Bolshevik Revolution, 1917–1923*, volume 1, pp. 294–5; Anthony E Upton, *The Finnish Revolution*, Minneapolis, University of Minnesota Press, 1980.
27. John Wheeler-Bennett, *Brest-Litovsk: The Forgotten Peace, March 1918*, London, Macmillan, 1938; James D White, *The Russian Revolution 1917–1921*, London, Edward Arnold, 1994, pp. 176–82.
28. Wojciech Roszkowski, 'The reconstruction of the government and state apparatus in the Second Polish Republic', in Paul Latawski, ed., *The Reconstruction of Poland, 1914–1923*, Houndmills, Macmillan, 1992, pp. 158–77.
29. Gatrell, *A Whole Empire Walking*, p. 194; T Bartele and V Shalda, 'Latyshskie bezhentsy v Rossii v gody grazhdanskoi voiny', *Otechestvennaia istoriia*, 2000, 1, pp. 18–31; Utgof, this volume.
30. Arno J Mayer, *The Political Origins of the New Diplomacy 1917–1918*, Princeton, Princeton University Press, 1959, chapter 9.
31. CA Macartney, *National States and National Minorities*, Oxford, Oxford University Press, 1934, pp. 192–211; Christian Baechler and Carole Fink, eds., *L'établisse-*

ment des frontières en Europe après les deux guerres mondiales, Bern, Peter Lang, 1996.
32. Quoted in Jocelyn Baines, *Joseph Conrad: A Critical Biography*, London, Pelican Books, 1971, p. 495.
33. S Kutrzeba, 'The struggle for frontiers 1919–1923', in WF Reddaway ed., *The Cambridge History of Poland 1697–1939*, Cambridge, Cambridge University Press, 1941, pp. 512–34.
34. Carr, *The Bolshevik Revolution, 1917–1923*, volume 3, p. 30.
35. Balkelis, this volume; John Hiden and Patrick Salmon, *The Baltic Nations and Europe; Estonia, Latvia, and Lithuania in the Twentieth Century*, revised edn., London, Longman, 1994, p. 39.
36. Richard Ullman, *Britain and the Russian Civil War, November 1918–February 1920*, Princeton, Princeton University Press, 1968, pp. 256–8; Taras Hunczak, '"Operation winter" and the struggle for the Baltic', *East European Quarterly*, 4, 1970, pp. 40–57.
37. Robert Machray, *Poland, 1914–1931*, London, George Allen & Unwin, 1932, pp. 170–2, 271–2.
38. Owen Rutter, *The New Baltic States and their Future: An Account of Lithuania, Latvia and Estonia*, London, Methuen, 1925, p. 30; Macartney, *National States and National Minorities*, p. 199; Zielinski, this volume.
39. Frank Golczewski, *Polnisch-Jüdische Beziehungen, 1881–1922: Eine Studie zur Geschichte des Antisemitismus in Osteuropa*, Wiesbaden, Steiner, 1981, pp. 218–45; Werner Benecke, *Die Ostgebiete der zweiten polnischen Republik*, Cologne, Böhlau Verlag, 1999.
40. Vakar, *Belorussia*, pp. 110–36.
41. Ronald G Suny, *Looking Toward Ararat: Armenia in Modern History*, Bloomington, Indiana University Press, 1993, p. 125.
42. Richard G Hovannisian, *The Republic of Armenia: Volume 4, Between Crescent and Sickle*, Berkeley, University of California Press, 1996, pp. 390–408.
43. James G Harbord, 'The American military mission to Armenia', *International Conciliation*, 151, June 1920, pp. 275–312; Hovannisian, *The Republic of Armenia*, volume 4, pp. 1–44, 322–6.
44. Suny, *Looking Toward Ararat*, pp. 126–7, 130; Richard Pipes, *The Formation of the Soviet Union: Communism and Nationalism, 1917–1923*, second edition, New York, Atheneum, 1964, pp. 231–4.
45. Geoff Eley, 'Remapping the nation: war, revolutionary upheaval and state formation in eastern Europe, 1914–1923', in Peter Potichnyj and Howard Aster, eds., *Ukrainian-Jewish Relations in Historical Perspective*, Edmonton, Canadian Institute of Ukrainian Studies, 1988, pp. 205–46.
46. The phrase 'flood of barbarism' was used by Sir Horace Rumbold, the British Ambassador to Poland, in a letter to Lord Curzon, 24 August 1920, in EL Woodward and R Butler, eds., *Documents on British Foreign Policy*, volume 11, London, HMSO, 1958, document no. 482.

47. Arno Mayer, *The Politics and Diplomacy of Peacemaking: Containment and Counter-revolution at Versailles, 1918–1919*, New York, Vintage Books, 1967, p. 314, quoting Lord Milner's article in *The Times*, 19 December 1918.
48. Evan Mawdsley, *The Russian Civil War*, second edition, London, Allen and Unwin, 2001; Orlando Figes, *Peasant Russia, Civil War: The Volga Countryside in Revolution, 1917–1921*, Oxford, Clarendon Press, 1989; Andrea Graziosi, *The Great Soviet Peasant War: Bolsheviks and Peasants, 1917–1933*, Cambridge, Mass., Harvard University Press, 1996.
49. Cited in JD Smele, *Civil War in Siberia: The Anti-Bolshevik Government of Admiral Kolchak, 1918–1920*, Cambridge, Cambridge University Press, 1996, pp. 369–71, 593.
50. Peter Kenez, *Civil War in South Russia, 1918: The First Year of the Volunteer Army*, Berkeley, University of California Press, 1971; Mawdsley, *Russian Civil War*, chapter 12; Peter Holquist, '"Conduct merciless, mass terror": decossackization on the Don, 1919', *Cahiers du monde russe*, 38, 1997, pp. 127–62.
51. John S Reshetar, *The Ukrainian Revolution, 1917–1920: A Study in Nationalism*, Princeton, Princeton University Press, 1952, pp. 158–9.
52. NS Raiskii, *Pol'sko-sovetskaia voina 1919–1920 godov i sud'ba voennoplennykh, internirovannykh, zalozhnikov i bezhentsev*, Moscow, RAN, 1999, pp. 8–9.
53. Norman Davies, *White Eagle, Red Star: The Polish – Soviet War 1919–1920*, London, Macdonald, 1972, p. 81; Peter Stachura, 'The battle of Warsaw, August 1920', and the development of the second Polish republic', in idem, ed., *Poland Between the Wars, 1918–1939*, London, Macmillan, 1998, pp. 43–59. See also the chapters by Zielinski and Stadnik, this volume.
54. Machray, *Poland, 1914–1931*, p. 175; AP Isaev, *Voina s Pol'shei: Rossiia za liniei fronta*, St Petersburg, Nestor, 1999, pp. 153–6, on Polish refugees in the Central Industrial Region; Utgof, this volume.
55. The Treaty of Riga settled the border between the two states, which was drawn some 200 miles east of the Curzon line. The so-called *kresy* ('borderlands'), inhabited by a large Belarusian population, came under Polish jurisdiction. PN Ol'shanskii, *Rizhskii mir: iz istorii bor'by Sovetskogo pravitel'stva za ustanovlenie mirnykh otnoshenii s Pol'shei, konets 1918–mart 1921 gg.*, Moscow, 1969; Benecke, *Die Ostgebiete*.
56. Joseph Van Gelder, 'Activities of the Refugee Department, American JDC in Europe during the years 1921, 1922, 1923', unpublished (May 1924), JDC Archives, New York, pp. 40–4. See also Zielinski, this volume.
57. Kapralska, this volume.
58. AL Okninskii, *Dva goda sredi krest''ian*, Russkii put', Moscow, 1998 (written in 1924, first published 1936), pp. 140–1. These refugees were originally from Grodno.
59. Kornilov, this volume; Allan Wardwell papers relating to Red Cross Mission and Russian Famine Fund, 1917–24, Bakhmeteff Archive, Columbia University, File 4. Other testimony includes a report by Boris Bogen, who visited Kiev, Zhitomir, and Odessa in the spring of 1922: 'the situation here is the most terrible I have ever seen.

[In Kiev] the refugee concentration camp was a veritable nightmare of horrors.' *Through the Ukraine with Bogen*, publicity pamphlet produced by the American Jewish Relief Committee, April 1922.

60. Archie McDonnell, 'The reaction of the Russian famine on Poland', *The Friend*, 10 February 1922, p. 106.
61. Anna Louise Strong, 'Typhus attacks relief missions in Poland', *The Friend*, 31 March 1922, p. 220. The expression 'White Ruthenian' was used by contemporaries who wished to avoid using the term 'Belarusian'.
62. VS Utgof, 'Reevakuatsiia belorusskikh bezhentsev pervoi mirovoi voiny, nachal'nyi etap, struktury, formy, organizatsiia', in MM Krom, ed., *Istochnik, istorik, istoriia*, St Petersburg, European University, 2002, pp. 396–416.
63. Kornilov, this volume. For the role of *Tsentroplenbezh* see Gatrell, *A Whole Empire Walking*, pp. 188–90. See also IP Shcherov, 'Zapadnyi plenbezh (1918–1920gg.)', *Voprosy istorii*, 1998, no. 9, pp. 130–3.
64. Resolution of the Central Executive Committee of the Union of Communes of the Northern Region, 12 June 1918. Tsentral'nyi gosudarstvennyi arkhiv Sankt Peterburga, f.75, op.1, d.10, l.6. I thank Valentina Utgof for this reference.
65. See the chapters by Balkelis, Zielinski and Stadnik, this volume.
66. Utgof and Kornilov, this volume; Okninskii, *Dva goda*, pp. 141–2, 271.
67. Zielinski, this volume.
68. Paul Weindling, *Epidemics and Genocide in Eastern Europe, 1890–1945*, Oxford, Oxford University Press, 2000, pp. 142–3.
69. Piotr S Wandycz, *Soviet Polish-Relations, 1917–1921*, Cambridge, MA., Harvard University Press, 1969, pp. 60–1.
70. *Pogranichnye voiska SSSR 1918–1928: sbornik dokumentov i materialov*, Moscow, Nauka, 1973, pp. 172–3.
71. Weindling, *Epidemics and Genocide*, chapters 4 and 6; Tytus Filipowicz, 'Russian refugees in Poland', 7 July 1922, British Library, Oriental and India Office Collections (OIOC), L/E/7/1210/537 et seq.; Harold H Fisher, *America and the New Poland*, London, Macmillan, 1928.
72. Gaines M Foster, 'Typhus disaster in the wake of war: the American-Polish Relief Expedition, 1919–1920', *Bulletin of the History of Medicine*, 55, 1981, pp. 221–32.
73. Alfred E Cornebise, *Typhus and Doughboys: The American Polish Typhus Relief Expedition, 1919–1921*, Newark, University of Delaware Press, 1982, p. 15.
74. Captain Howard Jennings Gorman, quoted in ibid., p. 66. Emphasis mine.
75. Wojciech Roszkowski, *Land Reforms in East Central Europe after World War One*, Warsaw, PAN, 1995; George D Jackson Jr., 'Peasant political movements in eastern Europe', in Henry A Landsberger, ed., *Rural Protest: Peasant Movements and Social Change*, London, Macmillan, 1974, pp. 259–315.
76. Goba diary, October 9 1918. I am grateful to Aldis Purs for permitting me to use his translation of the manuscript in his possession.
77. Fry, *A Quaker Adventure*, pp. 272–3.
78. Kulischer, *Europe on the Move*, p. 127.

79. Aldis Purs, 'The price of free lunches: making the frontier Latvian in the interwar years', *Global Review of Ethnopolitics*, 1, 2002, pp. 42–60.
80. Joseph Rosen, *Founding a New Life for Suffering Thousands*, New York, United Jewish Campaign, 1925, pp. 15, 42.
81. Gatrell and Laycock, this volume.
82. Iu A Poliakov ed., *Naselenie Rossii v XX veke*, volume 1, Moscow, Rosspen, 2000, pp. 134–42; Catherine Gousseff, 'L'Europe des réfugiés russes, une géographie explosive', unpublished paper.
83. A Stoupnitzky, 'La condition de réfugies russes en Pologne', ms., January 1938, and Miss Liepmann (sic), 'Statistical notes, Poland', ms., April 1938, both in the archives of the Royal Institute of International Affairs, London. See also Karl Schlögel, ed., *Der grosse Exodus: die russische Emigration und ihre Zentren 1917 bis 1941*, Munich, Beck, 1994, and Kapralska, this volume.
84. From an editorial in the *Morning Post* on Wrangel's army, quoted in Claudene Skran, *Refugees in Inter-War Europe: The Emergence of a Regime*, Oxford, Clarendon Press, 1995, p. 39, emphasis mine.
85. Balkelis and Zielinski, this volume.
86. Quoted in Skran, *Refugees*, p. 103.
87. Marta Aleksandra Balińska, 'Assistance and not mere relief: the Epidemic Commission of the League of Nations, 1920–1923', in Paul Weindling, ed., *International Health Organisations and Movements, 1918–1939*, Cambridge, Cambridge University Press, 1995, pp. 81–108.
88. The American Joint Distribution Committee commenced operations in Poland in February 1919. A brief institutional history is Yehuda Bauer, *My Brother's Keeper: A History of the American Jewish Joint Distribution Committee, 1929–1939*, Philadelphia, Jewish Publication Society of America, 1974, pp. 10–30.
89. Fisher, *America and the New Poland*, chapter 10.
90. Gatrell and Laycock, this volume.
91. Fry, *A Quaker Adventure*; Rufus Jones, *Quakers in Action: Recent Humanitarian and Reform Activities of the American Quakers*, New York, Macmillan, 1929; Joice Loch Nankivell and Sydney Loch, *The River of a Hundred Ways: Life in the War-Devastated Areas of Eastern Poland*, London, Allen and Unwin, 1924.
92. The speaker was M Paon. The conference met from 10 to 12 May 1926. India Office Library, British Library, L/E/7/1434/181.
93. Richendra Scott, *Quakers in Russia*, London, Michael Joseph, 1964, p. 196.
94. Van Gelder, 'Activities of the Refugee Department', p. 27.
95. Quotations from Cornebise, *Typhus and Doughboys*, pp. 15, 123.
96. Fry, *A Quaker Adventure*, p. 160.
97. Paul Weindling describes how 'desperate German colonists pretended that they were Polish in order to obtain a Polish passport and then switched back to German identity to gain entry to Germany'. Weindling, *Epidemics and Genocide*, p. 152.
98. GARF, f.3333, op.1a, d.102, l.86.
99. Okninskii, *Dva goda*, pp. 142–3.

100. 'Suzanne twice a refugee', in Mabel Evelyn Elliott, *Beginning Again at Ararat*, New York, Fleming Revell, 1924, pp. 244–66.
101. 'Poland: refugee problems, conditions, and relief work', in the papers of the Friends' Emergency and War Victims' Relief Committee (FEWVRC), Box 9, parcel 1, folder 3, Library of the Religious Society of Friends, London.
102. Fry, *A Quaker Adventure*, pp. 269–72.
103. See 'Polish thanks', signed Wojt Pozniak and Soltys Jukowicz on behalf of the community, in *The Friend*, 27 October 1922, pp. 746–7.
104. The well-known Latvian pastor, Vilis Olavs, created a 'refugee archive', but it was lost during the Russian Civil War. Personal communication from Aija Priedite. This brings to mind attempts made by the Tatiana Committee in 1916–17 to establish a record of refugees' experiences. See Gatrell, *A Whole Empire Walking*, p. 95.
105. In the following section, I draw on Nick Baron's analysis of the Goba diary in Nick Baron and Peter Gatrell, 'Population displacement, state-building and social identity in the lands of the former Russian empire, 1917–1923', *Kritika. Explorations in Russian and Eurasian History*, vol. 4, no.1, 2003, pp. 51–100.
106. From the diary of Alfreds Goba, 6 March 1918.
107. Ibid., 17 July 1918.
108. Quoted in Jacob Billikopf and MB Hexter, *The Jewish Situation in Eastern Europe, Including Russia, and the Work of the JDC*, Chicago, National Conference of United Jewish Campaigns and JDC, 1926, pp. 15, 18.
109. Elliott, *Beginning Again at Ararat*, p. 246.
110. This phrase is taken from David Bressler and Joseph Hyman, *Report to the JDC on Present-Day Conditions of the Jews of Eastern Europe*, New York, JDC, 1930.
111. The key treaties were those between the RSFSR and Estonia (2 February 1920), Lithuania (12 July 1920), Latvia (11 August 1920), Azerbaijan (30 September 1920), Ukraine (20 December 1920), Georgia (21 May 1921), and Armenia (30 September 1921). Soviet Russia signed a treaty with Poland on 18 March 1921.
112. Malbone Graham, *New Governments of Eastern Europe*, New York, Henry Holt & Sons, 1927; Ivan T Berend, *Decades of Crisis: Central and Eastern Europe before World War II*, Berkeley, University of California Press, 1998.
113. Francine Hirsch, 'Toward an empire of nations: border-making and the formation of Soviet national identities', *Russian Review*, 59, 2000, pp. 201–6; Terry Martin, *The Affirmative Action Empire: Nations and Nationalism in the Soviet Union, 1923–1939*, Ithaca, Cornell University Press, 2001.
114. In the range of its case studies, Kulischer, *Europe on the Move*, remains an unsurpassed treatment. See also Sir John H Simpson, *The Refugee Problem: Report of a Survey*, Oxford, Oxford University Press, 1939. A recent overview is Catherine Gousseff, 'Les déplacements forcés des populations aux frontières occidentales, 1914–1950', in S Audoin-Rouzeau, A Becker, C Ingrao, H Rousso, eds., *La violence de guerre 1914–1945*, Paris, Éditions complexe, 2002, pp. 175–91.

Chapter 2: Latvian Refugees and the Latvian Nation State during and after World War One

1. Miroslav Hroch, *Social Preconditions of National Revival in Europe: A Comparative Analysis of the Social Composition of Patriotic Groups among the Smaller European Nations*, Cambridge University Press, Cambridge, 1985. See also EJ Hobsbawm, *Nations and Nationalism since 1789*, Cambridge University Press, Cambridge, 1990, p. 12.
2. A Švābe, *Latvijas vēsture, 1800–1914* [*History of Latvia, 1800–1914*], Stockholm, 1962; A Šilde, *Pirmā Republika* [*The First Republic*], Rīga, 1993; U Ģērmanis, 'Latvijas neatkarības idejas attīstība' ['The development of the idea of Latvia's independence'], *Jaunā Gaita* [*New Peace*], Orangeville, Canada, Ceļinieks, vol. 11, no. 58, 1966, p. 62; E Blanks, *Latvju tautas ceļš uz neatkarīgu valsti* [*Latvia's path to an independent state*], Västerås, 1970; F Cielēns, *Laikmetu maiņā: Atmiņas un atziņas* [*Change of Times: Memoirs and Opinions*], vol. 1, Lidingö, Memento, 1961.
3. D Hening, 'Nacionālā kustība un nacionālas valsts tapšana Latvijā' ['The national movement and formation of a nation-state in Latvia'], *Latvijas Vēstures Institūta Žurnāls* [*Journal of the Institute of History of Latvia*], 1995, no. 1, pp. 64–79.
4. Ibid., pp. 71–2.
5. Ģērmanis, 'Latvijas neatkarības idejas attīstība', *Jaunā Gaita*, vol. 12, no. 62, 1967, pp. 33–4.
6. See Peter Gatrell, *A Whole Empire Walking: Refugees in Russia during World War One*, Indiana University Press, Bloomington, 1999.
7. See K Bachmanis, *Latvju tauta bēgļu gaitās* [*Latvian People's Refugeedom*], Rīga, 1925; K Bachmanis, *Latvieši Ukrainā 1917–1919 gados* [*Latvians in the Ukraine, 1917–1919*], Rīga, 1926; J Dūks, *Latviešu tauta lielo maldu un iznīcības ceļos* [*The Latvian People on a Wrong and Destructive Path, 1915–1940*], Grand Haven, 1974; S. Paegle, *Kā Latvijas valsts tapa* [*How Latvia's State Came into Being*], Rīga, 1923.
8. Ģērmanis, 'Latvijas neatkarības idejas attīstība', *Jauna Gaita*, vol. 12, no. 58, 1966, pp. 36–7; Ā Šilde, *Latvijas vēsture* [*History of Latvia, 1914–1940*], Stockholm, 1976, p. 248; J Līgotnis, *Latvijas valsts dibināšana* [*The Establishment of the Latvian State*], Rīga, 1925, pp. 495–504. In 1925 Latvia had 1,845,800 inhabitants, some 72 per cent of the prewar population.
9. Valters was one of the 38 politicians who proclaimed an independent Latvian state on 18 November 1918; he served as Minister of the Interior in the first Latvian government. See Sarma Boge, 'Latvijas valstiskuma ideja un citi nacionālā valstiskuma aspekti latviešu socialdemokrātu savienības laikrakstā 'Proletāriets' (1903–1904 gads)' ['The idea of loyalty to Latvia and other aspects of the national question in the newspaper of the Latvian Social Democratic Association 'Proletariets', 1903–1904'], *Latvijas Vēstures Institūta Žurnāls*, 1996, no. 3, pp. 73–89.
10. Švābe, *Latvijas vēsture, 1800–1914*, pp. 610–13; L Dribins, *Nacionālais jautājums Latvijā, 1850–1940* [*The National Question in Latvia, 1850–1940*], Rīga, 1997, pp. 73–122.

11. Arnis, 'Jānis Akuraters mūsu nacionālpolitiskajā dzīvē' ['Jānis Akuraters in our national-political life'], in J Akuraters, *Kopoti raksti* [*Collected Works*], Rīga, J Roze, 1923, vol. 4, pp. 1–100; K Skalbe, *Mazās piezīmes, 1917–1920* [*Small Notes, 1917–1920*], Rīga, 1999.
12. P Zālīte, *Latviešu tautas dvēsele ar iepriekšēju dvēseles jēdziena un tautu dvēseles apskatu* [*The Soul of the Latvian People, with a Preliminary Analysis of the Notions 'Soul' and 'People's Soul'*], Rīga, 1932, pp. 41–2; Līgotnis, *Latvijas valsts dibināšana*, pp. 20–2.
13. *Dzimtenes Atbalss*, 18 February 1917; U Ģērmanis, 'Latvijas neatkarības idejas attīstība', *Jauna Gaita*, vol. 11, no. 59, 1966, p. 12.
14. E Blanks, '700 un 200 gadi', *Dzimtenes Atbalss*, 42, 1917, p. 1; see also L Laicens, *Latvijas valsts* [*The Latvian State*], n.p., Maskavas grupa, 1917, p. 16; J Lapiņš, *Latvija mijkrēslī: piezīmes par Latvijas valsti* [*Latvia in the Twilight: Notes on the Latvian State*], Rīga, n.p., 1917, p. 27.
15. Gatrell, *A Whole Empire Walking*, pp. 157–60, 179–87.
16. A Bērziņš, *Kārlis Zariņš dzīvē un darbā* [*Kārlis Zariņš, his Life and Work*], London, Rūja, 1959, p. 140; *Latviešu bēgļu apgādāšanas centrālkomiteja* [*The Latvian Central Welfare Committee*], Rīga, V. Olava fonda sabiedrība izdevums, 1931, p. 47.
17. Šilde, *Pirmā Republika*, p. 77.
18. *Latvija*, 10 January 1914, p. 1.
19. *Līdums*, no. 8, 1917, p. 1.
20. See V Olavs, 'Latviešu literatūras kavēkļi' ['Hindrances of Latvian literature'], in V Olavs, *Kopoti raksti* [*Collected Works*], Rīga, 1924, p. 158.
21. Bērziņš, *Kārlis Zariņš*, p. 146.
22. Bachmanis, *Latvju tauta bēgļu gaitās*, pp. 309–10.
23. Bērziņš, *Kārlis Zariņš*, p. 151.
24. *Ziņas par Latviju* [*News about Latvia*]. Six issues were published during 1918.
25. Bachmanis, *Latvieši Ukrainā*, pp. 240–2.
26. V Salnājs, 'Sibīrijas latviešu nacionālā kustība' ['The Latvian national movement in Siberia'], in *Latvijas Republika desmit pastāvēšanas gados* [*The Republic of Latvia during its First Decade*], Rīga, 1928, pp. 39–40.
27. Cielēns, *Laikmetu maiņā*, pp. 463–6; Šilde, *Latvijas vēsture, 1914–1940*, pp. 244–5.
28. Bachmanis, *Latvju tauta bēgļu gaitās*, pp. 76–212.
29. *Līdums*, 170, 1915, p. 3; ibid., 175, 1915, p. 2; ibid., 202, 1915, p. 3.
30. Ibid., 202, 1915, p. 3.
31. *Pie Bābeles upēm: Raksti par latvju tautas bēgļu laikiem* [*By the Rivers of Babylon: Writings on Latvian People's Refugeedom*], Rīga, Valters un Rapa, 1929, p. 123.
32. *Latviešu Bēgļu Apgādāšanas Centrālkomitejas Ziņojums* [*Latvian Central Welfare Committee's Information Bulletin*], no. 51, 1916; Gatrell, *A Whole Empire Walking*, pp. 94–5.
33. Bērziņš, *Kārlis Zariņš*, pp. 157–62.
34. A Ķeniņš, '1917 gada Fonds' ['The fund of 1917'], *Dzimtenes Atbalss*, no. 7, 1917, p. 1.
35. For the Tatiana Committee see Gatrell, *A Whole Empire Walking*, pp. 40–2.

36. V Šalda, 'Latviešu kultūras birojs Maskavā, 1915–1917' ['The Latvian Culture Bureau in Moscow, 1915–1917'], *Latvijas Zinatņu Akadēmijas Vēstis. A daļa* [*Proceedings of the Latvian Academy of Sciences. Section A*], vol. 53, 1999, p. 27.
37. AD Smith, *National Identity*, London, Penguin, 1991, pp. 8–15.
42. K Zariņš, *Par Latvijas tapšanu* [*On Latvia's Emergence*], Melbourne, K Zariņa fonds, 1962, pp. 15–16.
43. *Pie Bābeles upēm*, p. 12.
44. Bērziņš, *K Zariņš*, p. 163. The Baltic German Committee closed its office in Petrograd in August 1918. The Moscow office followed suit two months later.
45. Ā Klīve, *Brīvā Latvija* [*Free Latvia*], Brooklyn, Grāmatu Draugs, 1969, p. 333.
46. T Bartele and V Šalda, 'Latviešu repatriācija no Padomju Krievijas, 1918–1921', ['The repatriation of Latvians from Soviet Russia, 1918–1921'], *Latvijas Vēsture*, 1998, no. 1, pp. 70–4.
47. Ibid., no. 2, pp. 28–30.
48. K Siliņš, *Mana dzīve: manu dienu atmiņas* [*My Life: Memories of the Days*], Veiverly, Latvju Grāmata, 1965, pp. 64–5.
49. *Latvju Enciklopēdija*, volume 1, 1951, p. 233.
50. *Latvijas Bēgļu Reevakuācijas Biedrības darbības pārskats, 1920–1922* ['Survey of the Work of the Latvian Refugees' Re-evacuation Society, 1920–1922'], Riga, 1922, p. 4.
51. *Valdības Vēstnesis* [*Government Herald*], 1920, no. 134, pp. 1–3.
52. *Latvijas Bēgļu Reevakuācijas Biedrības*, pp. 4–12.
53. *Latvijas Sargs* [*Guard of Latvia*], 1920, no. 150, p. 2; no. 205, p. 3. Provisional passports were issued for a period of 10 days and had to be exchanged for a permanent passport upon arrival at one's permanent residence.
54. *Krievijas Cīņa* [*Russia's Fight*], 1920, 16 October, p. 1.
55. *Valdības Vēstnesis*, 1920, no. 153, p. 2.
56. *Laukstrādnieks*, 1920, no. 20, p. 2.
57. Ā Klīve, *Latvijas neatkarības gadi* [*Years of Latvia's Independence*], Brooklyn, Grāmatu draugs, 1976, pp. 126–7.
58. A Stranga, *Latvijas-Padomju Krievijas miera līgums 1920 gada 11. augustā* [*The Latvian–Soviet Russian Peace Treaty of 11 August 1920*], Rīga, Fonds Latvijas Vēsture, 2000, pp. 79–81.
59. Bartele and Šalda, 'Latviešu repatriācija', *Latvijas Vēsture*, 1998, no. 4, pp. 24–5.
60. Stranga, *Latvijas–Padomju Krievijas miera līgums*, pp. 82–3.
61. A Aizsilnieks, *Latvijas saimniecības vēsture 1919–1945* [*History of the Latvian Economy, 1919–1945*], Stockholm, Daugava, 1968, pp. 194–228.
62. Ibid., pp. 233–51. However, the economic motives behind the reform, which divided estates into small farms that could support only one family, are not entirely clear. Several years elapsed before these farms were able to produce a surplus.
63. A Beika, 'Latvijas pavalstniecības optēsanas problēma Sibīrijā 20.gs. 20 gadu sākumā' ['The problem of Latvian citizenship optation in Siberia at the beginning of the 1920s'], *Latvijas Arhīvi*, 1994, no. 2, p. 29.
64. Aizsilnieks, *Latvijas Saimniecības vēsture*, p. 231.

65. E Ķiploks, *Profesors Voldemārs Maldonis: Dzīve, darbs, liktenis* [*Profesor Voldemārs Maldonis: His Life, Work and Times*], Rīga, LELBA apgāds, 1995, pp. 49, 59–64.
66. P Dāle, *vēsturisks pārskats par Latvijas Augstskolas nodibināšanu un viņas darbību pirmā (1919/1920) macības gadā* [*Historical Survey of the Establishment of the Higher School of Latvia and its Work in the First (1919/1920) Academic Year*], Rīga, Latvijas Augstskolas izdevums, 1921, p. 58.
67. *Dzimtenes Vēstnesis* [*The Herald of the Fatherland*], 1917, nos. 108, 109 and 118.
68. V Bērziņs, *Latviešu strēlnieki – drāma un traģēdija* [*The Latvian Riflemen – Drama and Tragedy*], Rīga, Latvijas vēstures institūts, 1995, p. 240.
69. D Handelman, 'The organization of ethnicity', *Ethnic Groups*, 1977, pp. 187–200.

Chapter 3: In Search of National Support: Belarusian Refugees in World War One and the People's Republic of Belarus

1. In this chapter we use the name 'Vilno' (the contemporary Russian form) instead of the Lithuanian 'Vilnius' or Polish 'Wilno'.
2. The difficulties of establishing the size of the refugee population are discussed by VS Utgof, 'Reevakuatsiia belorusskikh bezhentsev pervoi mirovoi voiny, nachal'nyi etap, struktury, formy, organizatsiia', in MM Krom, ed., *Istochnik, istorik, istoriia*, St Petersburg, European University, 2002, pp. 396–416, esp. p. 397.
3. See the summary by Ia. Miranovich, in *Bezhanstva 1915 goda*, Belastok, SPHU Podlaska, pp. 5–12. The broader context is provided by IP Shcherov, *Migratsionnaia politika v Rossii, 1914–1922*, Smolensk, n.p., 2000.
4. Vejas G Liulevicius, *War Land on the Eastern Front: Culture, National Identity and German Occupation in World War One*, Cambridge, Cambridge University Press, 2000, p. 62.
5. This is one of the themes of ES Kancher (Kanczer), *Belorusskii vopros: sbornik statei*, Petrograd, izdatel'stvo Belorusskogo otdela Kommissariata po delam natsional'nostei, 1919.
6. See Antoni Czubinski, *Walka o granice wschodnie Polski v latach 1918–1921* (*The Struggle for Poland's Eastern Borders in the Years 1918–1921*), Opole, Instytut Slaski w Opolu, 1993.
7. The standard text in English, which has still not been superseded, is Nicholas P Vakar, *Belorussia: The Making of a Nation*, Cambridge, Mass., Harvard University Press, 1956. Polish administration of western Belarus and its impact on the Belarusian population have generated a large literature. A recent summary is Werner Benecke, 'Kresy: die weissrussischen Territorien in der Polnischen Republik 1921–1939', in Dietrich Beyrau and R Lindner, eds., *Handbuch der Geschichte Weissrusslands*, Göttingen, Vandenhoeck und Ruprecht, 2001. See also Werner Benecke, *Die Ostgebiete der Zweiten Polnischen Republik: Staatsmacht und Öffentliche Meinung in einer Minderheitsregion 1918–1939*, Köln, Vandenhoeck und Ruprecht, 1999, and VS Utgof, 'Nekotorye aspekty kolonizatsionnoi politiki Pol'skoi respubliki na Poles'e, 1921–1939', in *Formula Rossii: tsentr i periferia*. Sankt-Peterburg, Nestor, 2000, pp. 94–9.

8. Among recent surveys particular mention should be made of AM Babkov, 'Bezhency v Belorussii v gody pervoj mirovoj vojny 1915–1916' (Refugees in Belarus in the World War One), *Gistarychnaia navuka i gistarychnaia adukatsyia u respublitse Belarus (Historical Science and Historical Education in the Republic of Belarus)*, kniga 1, *Gistoruja Belarusi (History of Belarus)*, Minsk, 1994, pp. 131–8; and VP Karnjaljuk, 'Prablema gistoruka-demagrafichnaj kharaktarystyki bezhantsay z belaruskih zjamel', 1914–1918' (The problem of historical-demographic characteristics of refugees from Belarusian lands, 1914–1918), *Vesnik Grodnenskogo Gosudarstvennogo Universiteta, Seryja* 1, no. 2, 2000, pp. 20–6. Shorter surveys include A Mikalaevich, 'Berzency' (Refugees), *Belaruskaj minuvshchyna (Belarusian Past)*, 1994, no. 3, pp. 60–1.
9. In Russian, *Belorusskoe obshchestvo po okazaniiu pomoshchi postradavshim ot voiny.*
10. Vakar, *Belorussia*, pp. 87–92 discusses the significance of *Nasha Niva*. For brief English-language accounts of their careers, see Jan Zaprudnik, *Historical Dictionary of Belarus*, Scarecrow Press, Lanham Md., 1998.
11. Rossiiskii Gosudarstvennyi Voenno-Istoricheskii Arkhiv (hereafter RGVIA), f. 13273, op. 1, d. 113, l. 1.
12. Ibid., l. 1 ob.
13. See the reports of the BSAVW inspections of Grodno province, of Vilno (authored by Lastowski), and of the western part of Vitebsk province. RGVIA, f. 13273, op. 1, d. 113, ll. 4, 5.
14. Ibid., ll. 20b.
15. Ibid., l. 2. On the Tatiana Committee see Peter Gatrell, *A Whole Empire Walking: Refugees in Russia during World War One*, Indiana University Press, Bloomington, 1999, pp. 40–2. One tsarist official commented that 'we failed to establish the reasons why the Tatiana committee provides greater financial support for some organisations than it does for others. However the very fact cannot be denied and the current state of affairs is hardly desirable in future'. A Miller, *Doklad po revizii uchrezhdenii i organizatsii, vedaiushchikh okazaniem pomoshchi bezhentsam v g. Moskve*, Moscow, 1917, p. 6.
16. RGVIA, f. 13273, op. 1, d. 113, l. 12.
17. Ibid., d. 12, l. 7–51.
18. Ibid., d. 2, l. 12.
19. Pseudonym of Anton Lewicki (1869–1922), one of the foremost Belarusian writers who helped establish modern Belarus literature.
20. Pseudonym of Vladislav Golub (1882–1937), actor and theatre director, one of the founders of the professional theatre in Belarus.
21. Fal'skii (1886–?) was a professional actor involved in the creation of the Belarusian theatre.
22. Pseudonym of Ludwiga Sawicka (1892–1991), writer who started her publishing career in 1911, in the newspaper *Nasha Niva*. Her works included a major dictionary of botanical terms in Lithuanian and other languages. After 1923 she moved to Polish-administered Vilno.

23. V Skalaban, 'Veto surovoe vremia', *Neman*, 1981, no. 12, p. 142. Further details on the activities of the BSAVW will be found in the Belarusian State Archive-Museum of Literature and Art (Belorusskii Gosudarstvennyi arkhiv-muzei literatury i iskusstva, hereafter BGAMLIM), f. 3, op. 1, d. 125, ll. 5–12.
24. M Szczaulinski, 'Bezhancy i belaruski natsyianal'ny rukh u gady pershai susvetnai vainy' ('Refugees and the Belarus nationalist movement in the years of the First World War'), *Belaruski Gistarychny Chasopis (Belarusian Historical Journal)*, 1999, no. 3, p. 24. See also Gatrell, *A Whole Empire Walking*, chapter 7.
25. RGVIA, f. 13273, op. 1, d. 84, ll. 11–34.
26. See the list of societies registered in Petrograd, in Tsentral'nyi Gosudarstvennyi Istoricheskii Arkhiv Sankt-Peterburga (hereafter TsGIA SPb), f. 1935, op. 1, d. 1, l. 1. The Petrograd Society was formally established on 12 January 1916. Its activities escaped the attention of Gatrell, *A Whole Empire Walking*, pp. 165–6. On the early career of Epimakh-Shipillo see Vakar, *Belorussia*, pp. 84–5. See also I Hlebcevicz, *Belorusskii nauchno-literaturnyi kruzhok studentov Sankt Peterburgskogo Universiteta*, Sankt-Peterburg, 1914.
27. 'Statute of the Belarusian Society in Petrograd for Assisting the Victims of War', in TsGIA SPb, f. 1935, op. 1, d. 1, l. 2.
28. Ibid., d. 3, ll. 42–3.
29. BGAMLIM, f. 3, op. 1, d. 126, ll. 118–9. On the German cultural programme in the *Land Ober Ost*, see Liulevicius, *War Land*, pp. 112–50, where it is described as 'native culture ... bracketed by German institutions which would define native identity and direct their development'. The key document was prepared for Ludendorff in May 1916. By 1918 the German authorities had approved the creation of 1,350 primary schools, the majority of which were Lithuanian. Around 90 were 'White Ruthenian', that is Belarusian.
30. V Skalaban, 'V eto surovoe vremia', p. 147; Maksim Adamavich Bahdanovich (Bogdanowicz), 'Proshenie Belorusskogo obshchestva po okazaniiu pomoshchi postradavshim ot voiny' in *Pouny zbor tvorau (Complete Works in Three Volumes)*, volume 3, Minsk, Navuka i tekhnika, 1995, pp. 195–8.
31. Ibid. Skalaban believes that the petition was written by Bogdanowicz himself.
32. RGVIA, f. 13273, op. 1, d. 185, ll. 54ob.-55. Details of these organizations will be found in Gatrell, *A Whole Empire Walking*, pp. 155–6, 165.
33. Z Veras, 'Uspamny pra zsyccie' ('Remembering my life'), manuscript in BGAMLIM, f. 3, op. 1, d. 3a, l. 41.
34. M Os'mak, 'Agliad pracy za pershy god Minskaga addzela Belaruskaga Tavarystva dlia pomaczy paciarpelym ad vainy' ('A review of the first year's work of the Minsk section of the Society for Assisting the Victims of War'), *Polymia [The Flame]*, 1981, no. 12, p. 191.
35. Z Zhylunovicz (1887–1937), Belarusian publicist and poet, who used the pseudonym Gartny. He became a member of the Academy of Sciences of Belarus in 1928.
36. Bud'ko was one of the founders of the Belarusian Christian Democratic Party. Some

time in 1916 he left Minsk, where he had belonged to the BSAVW, for Petrograd. He is mentioned briefly in Vakar, *Belorussia*, pp. 85, 246.

37. T Gartny, 'Uciakaczy' ('Refugees'), *Dziannica*, 1916, no. 1, p. 2. The verses were later reprinted in the newspaper of the Belarusian National Commissariat, likewise entitled *Dziannica*, 29 August 1918, pp. 2–3.

38. V Skalaban, 'Newiadomy artykul paeta' ('An unknown article by the poet'), *Polymia*, 1981, no. 12, p. 189; *Dziannica*, 27 November 1916. Skalaban demonstrates that the article was written by M Bogdanowicz and published under the pseudonym M Os'mak. In 1917 Bogdanowicz published an article in *Ukrainskaia zhizn'* on the activities of the Minsk BSRVW; this was an abridged translation of the article that Os'mak had published earlier in *Dziannica*.

39. Z Zhylunowicz, 'Luty-kastrycznik u belaruskim nacyianal'nym ruhu' ('February to October in the Belarusian national movement'), in A Stasheuskaha, ed., *Belarus: narysy historyi, ekonomiki, kul'turnaha i revoliutsyinaha rukhu*, (*Belarus: works in history, economics, culture and the revolutionary movement*), Minsk, BSSR Central Executive Committee, 1924, p. 184.

40. The Belarusian societies were omitted from a semi-official list of institutions responsible for refugee relief published in 1916. See *Spisok organizatsii, vedaiushchikh delo pomoshchi bezhentsam, na 1 maia 1916, vypusk 1*, Moscow, 1916.

41. Gatrell, *A Whole Empire Walking*, pp. 165–6.

42. V Grynewicz, 'Na rekah Vavilonu' ('By the waters of Babylon'), *Spadczyna*, 1997, no. 4, pp. 165–81.

43. TsGIA SPb, f. 1935, op. 1, d. 2, l. 15.

44. P Miadzelka, *Sciezkami zsyccia* (*Along the pathways of life*), Minsk, Mastackaja litaratura, 1974, p. 80.

45. F Kudrinskii, *Liudskie volny: berzency*, Petrograd, 1917, reprinted in *Neman*, 1997, no. 6, pp. 79–193.

46. Kancher, *Belorusskii vopros*, p. 113.

47. Z Zhilunovicz, 'Z'ezd belaruskih nacyjanalnyh arganizacyj 25 sakavika 1917 g.' '*The congress of Belarusian national organisations, 25 March 1917*', *Polymja*, 1925, no. 6, p. 202.

48. Vakar, *Belorussia*, pp. 96–7. Vakar is almost completely silent on refugee questions. On developments during 1917 see Gatrell, *A Whole Empire Walking*, pp. 173–87.

49. F Turuk, *Belorusskoe dvizhenie: ocherk istorii natsional'nogo i revoliutsionnogo dvizheniia belorussov*, Moscow, Gosudarstvennoe izdatel'stvo, 1921 (reprinted, Minsk, 1994); Vakar, *Belorussia*, pp. 96–7.

50. S Rudowicz, *Czas vybaru: Prablema samavyznaczennia Belarusi u 1917 g.* (*Moment of Decision: The Problem of Belarusian Self-Determination in 1917*), Minsk, Tehnalogia, 2001, p. 78. These names are also listed in Vakar, *Belorussia*, p. 246. Vakar gives Fal'skii's profession as an engineer, although this appears to be an error.

51. Ibid., p. 96.

52. RGVIA, f. 13275, op. 1, d. 113, l. 21.

53. *Vol'naia Belarus'*, 28 May 1917, p. 4; Vakar, *Belorussia*, pp. 96–7.

54. Natsional'ny Arkhiv Respubliki Belarus' (hereafter NARB) (National Archive of the Republic of Belarus'), f. 325, op. 1, d. 2, ll. 29–30.
55. NARB, f. 325, op. 1, d. 2, l. 29.
56. PM Kraskovskii, 'Kto byl' na Pervom Vsebelorusskom s"ezde?' ('Who attended the First All-Belarusian Congress?'), NARB, f. 325, op. 1, d. 6, l. 130b.
57. Ibid., l. 300b.
58. Ibid., l. 34.
59. *Belarusskaia Rada*, 8 December 1917, pp. 1–2; 14 December 1917, p. 1; 17 December 1917, p. 1.
60. The resolutions prepared by the refugee section of the First All-Belarusian Congress were printed in *Belorusskaia Rada*, 21 December 1917, p. 2.
61. See the resolution of the organizing commission of the Second All-Russian Congress of Refugees, TsGIA SPb, f. 5318, op. 2, d. 1, l. 4.
62. Vakar, *Belorussia*, p. 99.
63. Ibid., p. 103.
64. Article 2 of the agreement in February 1918 on the repatriation of civilian subjects entitled persons 'who have been removed during the war from their places of residence that were located on territory occupied by the adverse party' to return home. *Dokumenty vneshnei politiki SSSR*, volume 1, Moscow, 1957, pp. 47–51, 644.
65. The statutes of the Central Belarusian Refugee Committee are in BGAMLIM, f. 3, op. 1, d. 232, ll. 16–16ob.
66. Ibid., d. 233, l. 17.
67. *Czyrvony szliach (Red Road)*, 1918, nos. 7–8, pp. 20–1; NB Szczawlinski, 'Belorusskie organizatsii v 1917–1918 gg. v Odesse', *Vesnik Belaruski Dziarzhauny Universiteta*, series 3, gistoriya, 1996, no. 1, p. 25.
68. NARB, f. 325, op. 1, d. 8, l. 350b.
69. 'Raport Narodnogo sekretaria finansov V Zakharki', *Arkhivy Belaruskai Narodnai Respubliki*, Vilnius and New York, Belaruski instytut navuki i mastatstva, 1998, volume 1, part 1, p. 241.
70. Kancher, *Belorusskii vopros*, pp. 114–6. Kancher had spent the war years in Turkestan before moving to Petrograd. By 1918 he had become a Soviet official, employed by the Belarusian department of the 'Union of Communes of the Northern Region' (*Soiuz kommun Severnoi Oblasti*).
71. Quoted in *Bezhanstva 1915 goda*, pp. 33–4. See also *Dziannica*, 19 August 1918.
72. NARB, f. 4, op. 1, d. 55, l. 238, letter from Moscow city union of refugees to Belnatskom; Kancher, *Belorusskii vopros*, p. 116.
73. 'Z pratakola bezsancau-belarusu Grodzenskaj gubernii', in *Pamjac: gistoryka-dakumentalnaja hronika Bresckaga rajena [Memory: Historical-Documentary Chronicle of the Brest Region]*, Minsk, Belta, 1998, p. 91. This statement is dated 29 April 1918.
74. 'Rezoluciia obshchego sobraniia bezhentsev Belorussii g. Saratova 7 iiulia 1918 g.' (The resolution of the general meeting of refugees from Belorussia in Saratov, 7 July

1918), *Protokoly, postanovleniia i materialy Vserossiiskogo s"ezda bezhentsev iz Belorussii v Moskve, 15–21 iiulia 1918g.* Moscow, 1918, p. 74.

75. 'Deiatel'nost' Belorusskogo Natsional'nogo Kommissariata za fevral'-oktiabr' 1918g.', *Czyrvony szliach*, 1918, nos. 9–10, p. 38; D Zhilunovicz, 'Ot oktiabria 1917g.do fevralia 1918g.', *Polymia*, 1924, no. 1, pp. 163–73. See also VA Krutalevich, 'Organizatsiia i deiatel'nost' Belorusskogo Natsional'nogo Komissariata (1918–1919gg.)', *Istoriia SSSR*, 1963, no. 6, pp. 115–26. The first head of Belnatskom was AG Cherviakov; his deputy was VV Skorinko.
76. NARB, f. 4, op. 1, d. 38, l. 8. Memorandum to Belnatskom, 26 April 1918.
77. Ibid., d. 45, l. 1.
78. VV Skalaban, 'Izdatel'skaia deiatal'nost' Belorusskogo Natsional'nogo Kommissariata 1918–1920gg.', in M.P.Strizhonok ed., *Istoriia knigi, knizhnogo dela i bibliografii v Belorussii*, Minsk, Tsentral'naia nauchnaia biblioteka AN BSSR, 1986, pp. 26–49; Krutalevich, 'Organizatsiia', pp. 120–1. A total of 49 issues of *Dziannica* were published between 1 March 1918 and 24 April 1919.
79. Utgof, 'Re-evakuatsiia', p. 399.
80. *Czyrvony szliach*, 1918, nos. 5–6, pp. 3–5. According to Krutalevich, 'Organizatsiia', p. 121, this journal was to begin with strongly influenced by 'the nationalistic sentiments of elements of the Belarusian intelligentsia'.
81. NARB, f. 4, op. 1, d. 44, l. 40; Krutalevich, 'Organizatsiia', pp. 117, 119.
82. TsGIA SPb., f. 75, op. 1, d. 143, l. 57, 'Protokol soveshchaniia bezhenskogo otdela Tsentral'nogo kollegii po delam plennykh i bezhentsev s predstaviteliami Narkomnatsa', 13 December 1918.
83. NARB, f. 325, op. 1, d. 21; d. 32, ll. 1–4; 'Deiatel'nost' Belorusskogo Natsional'nogo Kommissariata', p. 38; Kancher, *Belorusskii vopros*, pp. 21–22.
84. 'Raport Narodnogo sekretaria finansov V Zakharki', pp. 140–2.
85. NARB, f. 325, op. 1, d. 16, l. 57.
86. Ibid., d. 8, ll. 107, 130ob.
87. Vakar, *Belorussia*, pp. 104–5. See also VA Krutalevich, 'Osvobozhdenie Belorussii ot okkupatsii posle annulirovanii Brest-litovskogo', *Istoriia SSSR*, 1968, no. 1, pp. 42–56.
88. 'Radiogramma MID Germanii Narodnomy Komissariatu Inostrannykh Del RSFSR ob usloviiakh vozvrashcheniia pol'skikh bezhentsev na rodinu' ('Radio message from the German Ministry of Foreign Affairs to the People's Commissariat of Foreign Affairs of RSFSR on conditions of repatriation of Polish refugees'), in N Khrenov and N Govserovskaia-Grabovskaia, eds., *Dokumenty i materialy po istorii sovetsko-pol'skikh otnoshenii*, volume 1, Moscow, Nauka, 1963, p. 346.
89. GARF, f. R-3333, op. 4, d. 45, l. 160b.; *Protokoly*, p. 87.
90. GARF, f. R-3333, op. 4, d. 45, l. 160b.
91. TsGA SPB, f. 5424, op. 1, d. 18, l. 332.
92. Ibid. f. 142, op. 1, d. 28, l. 119.
93. 'O deiatel'nosti politico-pravovykh podotdelov natsional'nykh otdelov Komissariata po delam natsional'nostei SKSO' (On the activities of the political and

legal sections of the departments of nationalities of the Commissariat on the nationalities of the Union of Communes of the Northern District), in TsGA SPb, f. 143, op. 4, d. 8, l. 25.
94. *Bezhanstva 1915 goda*. Belastok, 2000, p. 42.
95. TsGA SPb, f. 54, op. 1, d. 66a, l. 34.
96. See the chapters by Stadnik and Balkelis.
97. NARB, f. 325, op. 1, d. 8, l. 91.
98. *Bezhanstva 1915 goda*, p. 29.
99. *Protokoly*, p. 68. See also 'Iz obzora pechati belorusskogo stola informatsionnogo otdela Narodnogo Komissariata po delam natsional'nostei o Vserossiiskom s"ezde bezhentsev iz Belorussii', AI Azarov, ed., *Bor'ba za Sovetskuiu vlast' v Belorussii, 1918–1920: sbornik dokumentov i materialov*, volume 1, Minsk, Belarus', 1968, p. 162; Krutalevich, 'Organizatsiia', pp. 121–2.
100. *Protokoly*, p. 48.
101. Ibid., pp. 16–18, 63–4.
102. NARB, f. 4, op. 1, d. 67, l. 4.
103. Ibid., d. 128, l. 250b.; Utgof, 'Re-evakuatsiia', p. 407.
104. Grynewicz, 'Na rekah Vavilonu', p. 177.
105. GARF, f. R-3333, op. 4, d. 45, l. 25.
106. Quoted in Krutalevich, 'Organizatsiia', p. 121.
107. Utgof, 'Re-evakuatsiia', p. 406, citing NARB f. 4, op. 1, d. 14, l. 2, telegram from Belnatskom officials to the Petrograd office, 20 February 1918.
108. Kancher, *Belorusskii vopros*, p. 118. See also NARB, f. 4, op. 1, d. 14, l. 5.
109. Krutalevich, 'Organizatsiia', pp. 122–3.
110. NARB, f. 40, op. 1, d. 86, l. 2.
111. *Belaruski Gistaryczny Czasopis*, 1993, no. 1, p. 71. Determining the geographical borders of the Belarusian lands, Belnatskom had used the map of Academician Karskii, which marked the territorial distribution of ethnic Belarusian population, as the basis for defining the sphere of their activities. By contrast, the *Rada* of the BNR had defined its territory as consisting of Mogilev, Minsk, Grodno, Vilno, Vitebsk, Smolensk and Chernigov provinces.
112. NARB, f. 40, op. 1, d. 94, l. 33–330b.
113. Ibid., f. 325, op. 1, d. 25, l. 81.
114. Utgof, 'Re-evakuatsiia', p. 413.
115. IV Poluian, *Zapadnaia Belorussiia v period ekonomicheskogo krizisa 1929–1933gg.*, Minsk, Navuka i tekhnika, 1991, p. 4. Poluian suggests somewhat fancifully that 'most participated in active revolutionary struggle'.
116. TsGA SPB, f. 75, op. 2, d. 37, ll. 50–500b.
117. See the remarks of Arsen' Lis, 'Pasliasloue' ('Epilogue'), in A Cvikievicz, *Zapadnorusizm*, Minsk, 1994.
118. Brief English-language accounts of their careers will be found in Zaprudnik, *Historical Dictionary of Belarus*.
119. *Neman*, 1997, no. 6, editor's note.

120. Z Zhilunovicz, 'Baliuzhae pytanne'(A sore point), *Savetskaia Belarus'*, 3 April 1921.
121. This is a theme of Terry Martin, *The Affirmative Action Empire: Nations and Nationalism in the Soviet Union, 1923–1939*, Cornell University Press, Ithaca, 2001, quotation on p. 9.
122. A specialist study is B Chiari, "'Nationale Renaissance': Belorussifierung und Sowjetisierung: Erziehungs- und Bildungspolitik in Weissrussland 1922–1924", *Jahrbücher für Geschichte Osteuropas*, 42, 1994, 521–40.
123. See Martin, *The Affirmative Action Empire*, pp. 263–5.

Chapter 4: In Search of a Native Realm: The Return of World War One Refugees to Lithuania, 1918–24

1. Although the declaration of independence was issued on 16 February 1918, the German government refused to acknowledge it and remained in control of Lithuania. German forces stayed in the country until late 1918, while on November 7, 1918 the Lithuanian Council (Taryba) formed the first Lithuanian government under A Voldemaras.
2. The figure of 550,000 refers to all former residents who left what was now Lithuanian territory, not only ethnic Lithuanians. As Minister of the Interior from June 1920 until February 1922, Skipitis was responsible for the return of refugees to Lithuania. His memoirs are thus an important source for the historian of population displacement in postwar Lithuania. See, Rapolas Skipitis, *Nepriklausomą Lietuvą statant* [*Building an Independent Lithuania*], Chicago, Terra, 1961, p. 265.
3. Čepėnas, Pranas, *Naujųjų laikų Lietuvos istorija* [*History of Modern Lithuania*], Chicago, 1976, vol. 2, pp. 78–9.
4. Skipitis, *Nepriklausomą Lietuvą statant*, p. 259.
5. Juozas Švaistas – Balčiūnas, *Dangus debesyse: autoriaus išgyvenimai 1918–1919* [*The Sky in The Clouds: Memoirs 1918–1919*], London, 1967, p. 60.
6. Jurgis Jakelaitis, *Jeigu kas nors skaitys: atsiminimai* [*If Someone Will Read: Memoirs*], Kaunas, 1991, pp. 218–31.
7. This is my approximate estimate of the total.
8. *Lietuva* [*Lithuania*], 144, 13 July 1920.
9. For the text of the agreement see, 'Tremtinių grąžinimo sutartis tarp Lietuvos ir Rusijos' in *Vyriausybės žinios* [*Government News*], Kaunas, August 3, 1920, pp. 1–3.
10. Lithuanian Ministry of the Interior (hereafter LMI) Fond [Fondas] 377, subsection [Aplankas] 7, file [Byla] 4, p. 194. The deadline of late 1921 apparently did not apply to the Lithuanian refugees and optants in Siberia.
11. However, groups of refugees and individual refugees continued to make their way to Lithuania until as late as 1930. LMI 377, s. 5, f. 212, 213.
12. The term 'fixing', as applied to refugees, here implies any practice by state officials to monitor, control, select, screen, indoctrinate, isolate and quarantine refugees. Thus the term will be used to denote both a state's political and ideological strategies to control political or national loyalties of refugees, as well as its physical measures, such as disinfections and quarantine.

13. The Lithuanian historian Adolfas Šapoka also acknowledged that 'the committee conducted this great welfare work with a certain political idea', Adolfas Šapoka, *Lietuvos istorija* [*Lithuanian History*], Kaunas, 1936, p. 535.
14. Martynas Yčas, 'Rusijos lietuvių pastangos kovose už Lietuvos nepriklausomybę', in J Barkauskas, ed., *Pirmasis nepriklausomos Lietuvos dešimtmetis, 1918–1928* [*The First Decade of Independent Lithuania, 1918–1928*], Kaunas, 1990 (3rd edition), p. 25.
15. Ibid., p. 27.
16. Lithuanian Ministry of the Foreign Affaires (hereafter LMF) 83, s. 5, f. 45, p. 251.
17. Raštikis Stasys, *Lietuvos likimo keliais: iš mano užrašų* [*Along the Road of Lithuania's Fate: From My Notes*], Chicago, 1982, p. 108.
18. *Lietuvos žinios* [*Lithuanian News*], Kaunas, 136, 1922, pp. 140–1.
19. Veronika Janulaitytė-Alseikienė, 'Kūno pacientai ir dvasios draugai', [*Body Patients and Spiritual Friends*] *Šiaurės Atėnai*, Vilnius, 43, 2001, p. 9.
20. Ibid.
21. Švaistas, *Dangus debesyse*, p. 77.
22. Ibid., p. 78.
23. Jakelaitis, *Jeigu kas nors skaitys*, p. 218. There was a generational divide among the Lithuanian refugees in Voronezh: most of the students who attended the local Lithuanian gymnasium enrolled in the ranks of the Soviet militia, while adult refugees kept their distance from the Bolsheviks.
24. Skipitis, *Nepriklausoma Lietuva: atsiminimai* [*Independent Lithuania: memoirs*], Chicago, 1967, p. 55.
25. Raštikis, *Lietuvos likimo keliais*, p. 108.
26. Skipitis, *Nepriklausoma Lietuva*, p. 48.
27. Ibid., p. 57.
28. Janulaitytė-Alseikienė, 'Kūno pacientai ir dvasios draugai', p. 9.
29. Skipitis, *Nepriklausoma Lietuva*, p. 48.
30. LMI 377, s. 9, f. 2, p. 7.
31. Ibid., p. 95.
32. Skipitis, *Nepriklausomą Lietuvą statant*, p. 261.
33. Jakelaitis, *Jeigu kas nors skaitys*, p. 221.
34. Ibid., pp. 227–9.
35. Ibid, pp. 229–30. We do not know how many refugees joined the Lithuanian army after their return, but some, like Raštikis, found the idea attractive. The fact that all army volunteers were promised land served as an inducement to join the army.
36. A Lithuanian refugee hospital originally formed in Minsk continued its work in Vilno with a staff of 20. It expanded by taking care of those refugees who were returning through Vilno to Lithuania. With occasional grants from the authorities in Kovno it took care of 700 Lithuanian refugee orphans in 1918–19. Janulaitytė-Alseikienė, 'Kūno pacientai ir dvasios draugai', p. 9.
37. Mikų Dėdė, 'Lietuvos tremtiniai iš Ukrainos' ['Lithuanian Refugees from the Ukraine'], *Lietuvos žinios*, Kaunas, 1922, no. 136, pp. 140, 141.

Notes

38. 'Tremtinių gražinimo sutartis tarp Lietuvos ir Rusijos', *Vyriausybės žinios*, Kaunas, (42) 3 August 1920, pp. 1–3.
39. Ibid, p. 1.
40. The Refugee Division at the LMI was established in the first half of 1919 (See, LMI 377, s. 10). From October 1919, under a new ministry of E Draugelis, it was incorporated into the Department of Work and Social Protection at the LMI. Its main function was the return of war refugees to Lithuania.
41. Skipitis, *Nepriklausomą Lietuvą statant*, p. 263. The government officials in whose hands lay the fate of every deportee were Indreika and Josiukas, both members of the prewar patriotic Lithuanian intelligentsia, personally selected by Skipitis and described by him as 'serious people'. The fact that Indreika was indirectly involved with the military anti-government mutiny in Panemunė in February, and sentenced to death but later acquitted, did not deter the liberal-minded Skipitis from making his choice. At the time there was a great shortage of educated Lithuanian government officials and every loyal member of the intelligentsia was a potential recruit for the state. Later Indreika became an independent lawyer, while Josiukas represented the Farmers' Union in the Lithuanian parliament for three consecutive terms.
42. LMF 377, s. 5, f. 12, p. 153.
43. Ibid., 83, s. 5, f. 45, p. 44.
44. In a letter to the Minister of Foreign Affairs, Juozas Purickis, Skipitis expressed his concern over the inefficient work of the Lithuanian Mission to Ukraine and criticized his chairman, Prof. Mošinskas: 'The Lithuanian Mission to the Ukraine organised its work so poorly that we are forced to return 50 per cent of deportees from each train. At the same time they are crossing out from the lists of deportees true Lithuanians. ... Prof. Mošinskas pays little attention to such facts. The fact that his secretary is a person of Polish orientation serves as grounds for complaints from many people.' Ibid., p. 136.
45. Ibid., p. 176.
46. LMI 377, s. 5, f. 12, p. 160.
47. LMF 83, s. 5, f. 45, p. 97, 156.
48. Ibid., pp. 234–5.
49. Skipitis, *Nepriklausomą Lietuvą statant*, p. 229.
50. Ibid., p. 264.
51. LMI 377, s. 5, f. 34, p. 115.
52. See the letter of Foreign Minister, Jurgutis, to Minister of the Interior, Oleka, dated 20 August 1922, in ibid., f. 4, p. 189. Jurgutis complained that these refugees were thus able to enter Lithuania through Joniškis or Kaišiadorys, evading the quarantine facility at Obeliai.
53. LMI 377, s. 5, f. 12, p. 154.
54. Švaistas, *Dangus debesyse*, pp. 98–9.
55. Ibid., p. 98.
56. LMI 377, s. 7, f. 78, p. 104.

57. Ibid., s. 4, f. 12, p. 154.
58. Ibid., s. 5, f. 12, p. 144.
59. Letter dated 13 December 1921, in LMF 383, s. 5, f. 45, p. 3.
60. Čepėnas, Pranas, *Naujųjų laikų Lietuvos istorija*, Chicago, 1976, vol. 2, pp. 83–121.
61. LMF 83, s. 5, f. 45, p. 48.
62. LMI 377, s. 5, f. 12, p. 7.
63. Ibid., pp. 37–141.
64. Ibid., p. 142.
65. The Ministry of the Interior charged a fee of 200 marks per family for their transportation through Russia. See LMF 83, s. 5, f. 45, 44, letter dated 6 October, 1921.
66. LMI 377, s. 5, f. 12, p. 32.
67. Ibid.
68. LMF 83, s. 5, f. 45, p. 90.
69. Ibid., p. 76: 'Despite everything, the local troops allowed and still are allowing individual refugees coming from Vilno. This creates chaos and threatens the country with a danger of epidemics' (Skipitis to the Minister of Defence, J Šimkus, dated 1 June 1921).
70. Ibid., p. 72.
71. Ibid., p.52, telegram of Skipitis to the quarantine in Obeliai, 26 May, 1921.
72. Ibid., p. 59.
73. Ibid., p. 61.
74. Ibid., p. 67, letter of Purickis to the Cabinet of Ministers, 6 July 1921.
75. Ibid.
76. Ibid., p. 73, letter of Baltrušaitis to the Director of the Eastern Department, Lisauskas, 23 May 1921.
77. Skipitis, *Nepriklausomą Lietuvą statant*, p. 267.
78. Ibid.
79. *Darbininkas [The Worker]*, Kaunas, 19, 30 July 1921, p. 7.
80. *Tėvynės sargas [The Fatherland's Guardian]*, Kaunas, 20 February 1920, p. 78.
81. One of the ideological leaders of 'Vilkolakis', Antanas Sutkus, later wrote that 'in Obeliai there was supposed to be a state institution which had "to sift through" the returnees.' However, officials there conducted 'the lucrative sale of citizenship rights', withholding documents from Lithuanian refugees in favor of strangers who possessed sufficient financial means to bribe them. See Antanas Sutkus, *Vilkolakio teatras [Vilkolakis theatre]*, Vilnius, 1969, pp. 90–3. The picture on page 128 shows some of the actors from 'Quarantine of Sheep' dressed up in 'Jewish' style.
82. Skipitis, *Nepriklausomą Lietuvą statant*, p. 270.
83. *Tėvynės sargas*, Kaunas, 11, 30 January 1922, p. 50.
84. *Lietuvos žinios*, Kaunas, 25, 28 March 1922, p. 3.
85. For the full text of the resolution see LMI 377, s. 5, f. 12.
86. Sutkus, *Vilkolakio teatras*, p. 91.
87. Skipitis, *Nepriklausomą Lietuvą statant*, pp. 268–9.

88. See 'Kazimieras Oleka', in: *Lietuvių enciklopedija* [*Lithuanian Encyclopedia*], Boston, vol. 21, 1963.
89. LMF 83, s. 5, f. 45, p. 71.
90. *Lietuvos žinios*, Kaunas, 170, 28 September 1922. Official data suggest that among the total number of 69,728 refugees who returned in 1921, Jews formed 37.4 per cent of the total and Lithuanians 42.5 per cent. However, the number of Jews who never returned to Lithuania from the former Russian empire was 80,000, compared to 35,000 Lithuanians. Thus the supposition that most of the refugees in 1921–2 were Jews is incorrect.
91. LMI 377, s. 5, f. 12, p. 61.
92. Ibid., p. 6, letter from the Director of the Refugee Division, Kubilius, to Skipitis, 6 July 1921.
93. *Lietuvos žinios*, Kaunas, 52, 3 May 1922.
94. LMI 377, s. 5, f. 12, p. 146.
95. Ibid., p. 132.
96. Sutkus, *Vilkolakio teatras*, p. 92.
97. LMI 377, s. 5, f. 12. In his report to the minister Kubilius indicated: 'The director [of quarantine] explained that at one moment he forbade any entrance of the public into the quarantine. However, people then would meet and even trade along the fence. ... I agreed to give a permission to build a second fence.'
98. LMI 377, s. 5, f. 12, pp. 66–8.
99. Ibid., pp. 64–5.
100. Ibid., p. 158.
101. Ibid., p. 161.
102. In 1924 the Ministry of Jewish Affairs was closed. In 1926 an authoritarian right wing regime of A. Smetona came to power and in 1927 suspended the Lithuanian parliament.

Chapter 5: Population Displacement and Citizenship in Poland, 1918–24

1. Wojciech Roszkowski, *Historia Polski 1914–1991* [*History of Poland 1914–1991*], Wydawnictwo Naukowe PWN, Warsaw, 1992, p. 32.
2. Rogers Brubaker, *Nationalism Reframed: Nationhood and the National Question in the New Europe*, Cambridge University Press, Cambridge, 1997, pp. 85–6.
3. Voievodship (*województwo*) – an administrative unit in interwar Poland (in the case of the Kingdom of Poland, the voievodship replaced the Russian guberniya).
4. Brubaker, *Nationalism Reframed*, pp. 99–100. Also Ivan Berend, *Decades of Crisis. Central and Eastern Europe before World War II*, University of California Press, Berkeley, Los Angeles, London, 1998, p.157; Werner Benecke, *Die Ostgebiete der Zweiten Polnischen Republik. Staatsmacht und Öffentliche Ordnung in Einer Minderheitenregion 1918–1939*, Böhlau Verlag, Köln – Weimar – Wien, 1999, pp. 10–18, 25–6.
5. See, for example, Jeff Schatz, *The Generation: The Rise and Fall of the Jewish Communists of Poland*, University of California Press, Berkeley, 1991.

6. Haus-Hof und Staatsarchiv Wien (hereafter HHStA) Ministerium des Äußern 1848–1918 (hereafter MA) Politisches Archiv I (hereafter P.A. I) 899a, pp. 406–7; HHStA MA P.A.I 522, pp. 774–5. Also Arthur Hausner, *Die Polenpolitik der Mittelmächte und die österreichisch-ungarische Militärverwaltung in Polen während des Weltkrieges*, Hollinek, Vienna, 1935, p. 4.
7. *Izkor buch chelm*, ed. M Bakalczuk-Felin, Khelmer Landmenshaft, Johannesburg, 1954, p. 75; Konrad Zieliński, *Żydzi Lubelszczyzny 1914–1918* [*Jews in the Lublin Province, 1914–1918*], Wydawnictwo LTN, Lublin, 1999, pp. 82–3.
8. For the development of Polish attitudes to the Jews from 1914, see YIVO Institute for Jewish Research in New York (hereafter YIVO), Wolf Lucien and Mowschowitch David, Papers 1865–1957 (hereafter WM), 59, ff. 4880, 4890; YIVO WM, 112, ff. 14136–8; YIVO WM, 129, f. 15969; Zieliński, *Żydzi Lubelszczyzny*, pp. 78–81, 83–7.
9. Jerzy Tomaszewski, 'Wokół obywatelstwa Żydów polskich, 1918–1939' ('Around the citizenship for the Polish Jews, 1918–1939'), in *Narody. Jak powstawały i jak wybijały się na niepodległość?* [*The Nations. How they arose and how they won their independence?*], Państwowe Wydawnictwo Naukowe, Warsaw, 1989, p. 509. See also Archiwum Państwowe w Lublinie (hereafter APL) Urząd Wojewódzki Lubelski 1919–1939 (hereafter UWL) Wydział Społeczno-Polityczny (hereafter WSP) 1323, p. 61.
10. As early as February 1918 the Polish government under the auspices of Germans and Austrians prohibited some groups of refugees and immigrants from Russia from settling in certain regions of the country. For instance, Russians and Ukrainians could not settle in territories bordering with Lithuania (so-called Kaunas Lithuania) or in those parts of Ukraine subordinated to Germany. See circulars in Dierzavnyj Archiv Lvivskoj Oblasti w Lviv (hereafter DALO) f. 1, op. 52, d. 45, ll. 5–6.
11. Semen Petliura was an outstanding politician and organizer of the Ukrainian army, the High Hetman of the Ukrainian armed forces. See Waldemar Rezmer, 'Symon Petliura (22 V 1879 – 25 V 1926). Szkic biograficzny' [*Symon Petliura (22 May 1879 – 25 May 1926). A biographical study*], in Zbigniew Karpus, Waldemar Rezmer, Emilian Wiszka, eds, *Polska i Ukraina. Sojusz 1920 roku i jego następstwa* [*Poland and Ukraine. The Alliance of 1920 and its Consequences*], Wydawnictwo UMK, Toruń, 1997, p. 160.
12. Brubaker, *Nationalism Reframed*, p. 100.
13. These authorities were, among others, leaders of the Central Welfare Council (*Rada Główna Opiekuńcza*) in Warsaw, the Central Citizens' Committee (*Centralny Komitet Obywatelski*) in Lublin and the Central Citizens' Committee of the Kingdom of Poland in Russia (*Centralny Komitet Obywatelski Królestwa Polskiego w Rosji*) with its branches in Kiev, Moscow, Petrograd and Minsk. The most active persons were a Catholic priest, Wacław Bliziński, chairman of the Relief Commission for Reemigrants from Russia and Prussia (*Komisja Organizacyjna Pomocy dla Reemigrantów z Rosji i Prus*); Władysław Grabski, chairman of the abovementioned Central Citizens' Committee of the Kingdom of Poland in Russia; and Stanisław

Moskalewski, chairman of the Kiev branch of that Committee. See Ryszard Bender, *Katolicka myśl i działalność społeczna w Polsce w XIX i XX wieku* [*Catholic political thought and social activity in Poland in the 19th and 20th centuries*], Wydawnictwo Katolickiego Uniwersytetu Lubelskiego, Lublin, 1987, pp. 52–3; Jerzy Holzer, Jan Molenda, *Polska w pierwszej wojnie światowej* [*Poland during the First World War*], Wiedza Powszechna, Warsaw, 1963, pp. 322–5.

14. Peter Gatrell, *A Whole Empire Walking: Refugees in Russia during World War One*, Indiana University Press, Bloomington, 1999, pp. 17–24, 27, 155–6; Mariusz Korzeniowski, *Na wygnańczym szlaku... Działalność Centralnego Komitetu Obywatelskiego Królestwa Polskiego na Białorusi w latach 1915–1918* [*On the refugee route... The activity of the Central Citizens' Committee of the Kingdom of Poland in Belarussia in the years 1915–1918*], Wydawnictwo LTN, Lublin, 2001, pp. 106–11, 144–9.
15. Archiwum Akt Nowych w Warszawie (hereafter AAN) Tymczasowa Rada Stanu 1916–1918 (hereafter TRS) 15, pp. 187–8.
16. W Chocianowicz, 'Sejm Wileński w 1922 roku' ['The Vilno Parliament in 1922'], *Zeszyty Historyczne* [*Historical Notebooks*], 1963, z. 4, p. 40.
17. Janusz Faryś, *Piłsudski i Piłsudczycy. Z dziejów koncepcji polityczno-ustrojowej 1918– 1939* [*Piłsudski and his supporters. On the origins of the political system 1918–1939*], Uniwersytet Szczeciński, Szczecin, 1991, pp. 12–5; Włodzimierz Mich, *Obcy w polskim domu. Nacjonalistyczne koncepcje rozwiązania problemu mniejszości narodowych 1918–1939* [*An alien in the Polish Home. Nationalist conceptions of the solution of the national minorities problem 1918–1939*], Wydawnictwo UMCS, Lublin, 1994, pp. 12–3, 15–6; Helmut Pieper, *Die Minderheitenfrage und das Deutsche Reich 1919–1933/34*, Institut für Internation. Angelegenheiten d. Universität Hamburg, Hamburg, 1974, pp. 56–8; Roman Wapiński, 'The Endecja and the Jewish question', *Polin: Studies in Polish Jewry*, vol. 12, 1999, pp. 271–2.
18. The *Endeks* rejected the calls for ethnic autonomy made by Ukrainians and Belarusians and postulated complete assimilation with Polish society. According to *Endeks*, Jews should be isolated from Polish society, and the German minority should be deprived of its position in politics and economy. See Andrzej Chojnowski, *Koncepcje polityki narodowościowej rządów polskich w latach 1921– 1939* [*Conceptions of ethnic-national policy of the Polish governments in the years 1921–1939*], Ossolineum, Wrocław, 1979, pp. 19–21.
19. See, for example, Marian Eckert, *Historia polityczna Polski lat 1918–1939* [*Political history of Poland, 1918–1939*], Wydawnictwa Szkolne i Pedagogiczne, Warsaw, 1988, pp. 69–91; Zbigniew Landau, Jerzy Tomaszewski, *Zarys historii gospodarczej Polski 1918–1939* [*History of the Polish Economy 1918–1939. An outline*], Książka i Wiedza, Warsaw, 1999, pp. 327–34; Tomasz Nałęcz, *Rządy Sejmu 1921–1926* (*Rule of the Sejm 1921–1926*), Krajowa Agencja Wydawnicza, Warsaw, 1991, pp. 74–5, 78–81.
20. Henryk Chałupczak and Tomasz Browarek, *Mniejszości narodowe w Polsce 1918– 1995* [*National minorities in Poland 1918–1995*], Wydawnictwo UMCS, Lublin, 1998, p. 48.

21. Tomaszewski, *Wokół obywatelstwa Żydów polskich*, p. 507.
22. Chałupczak and Browarek, *Mniejszości narodowe w Polsce*, pp. 48–9.
23. To a lesser extent the same can be said about the residents of Galicia, formerly part of the Austro-Hungarian Empire. Generally speaking, this referred to Eastern Galicia, which was inhabited mainly by Ukrainian-speaking people.
24. In practice, to prove Polish origin when this was not obvious was quite simple – people usually had documents, could request testimonials from relatives, former neighbours or acquaintances, or sometimes they knew Polish language. Of course, there were doubtless occasions when non-Poles were able to convince officials of their 'Polish origin'. This would rarely have been the case for Ukrainian or Russian farmers or orthodox Jews.
25. Tomaszewski, *Wokół obywatelstwa Żydów polskich*, pp. 508–9.
26. Brubaker, *Nationalism Reframed*, p. 85.
27. Ibid., p. 86.
28. Chałupczak and Browarek, *Mniejszości narodowe w Polsce*, p. 48.
29. Ibid., pp. 48–9; Henryk Chałupczak, *II Rzeczpospolita a mniejszość polska w Niemczech* [*The Second Republic and Polish minority in Germany*], Instytut Zachodni, Poznań, 1992, pp. 186–7.
30. Stanisław Alexandrowicz, 'Sytuacja ludności polskiej za "ryską granicą" 1921–1939' ['Situation of the Polish population behind the "Riga border" in the years 1921–1939'], in *Traktat ryski 1921 roku po 75 latach* [*The Treaty of Riga of 1921 after 75 years*], Wydawnictwo UMK, Toruń, 1998, pp. 214–5.
31. Ibid.
32. 'Dziennik Ustaw' 1920, no. 71. Also APL UWL Wydział Organizacyjny (hereafter WO) 368 no page number (hereafter n.p.), 'Sądownictwo doraźne, 1922' ('The Temporary [i.e. military – KZ] Judicature, 1922'); UWL WSP WO 369 n.p., 'Sądownictwo doraźne, 1923' ('The Temporary Judicature, 1923'). See also Jarosław Hrycak, *Historia Ukrainy 1772–1999. Narodziny nowoczesnego narodu* [*History of Ukraine 1772–1999. The birth of the modern nation*], Instytut Europy Środkowo-Wschodniej, Lublin, 2000, pp. 188–93; Jan Kęsik, 'Pomiędzy współpracą a irredentą. Ukraińska mniejszość narodowa w II Rzeczypospolitej' ['Between cooperation and rebellion. The Ukrainian minority in the Second Republic'] in *Tematy polsko-ukraińskie. Historia, Literatura, Edukacja* [*Polish–Ukrainian themes. History, literature, education*], ed. R Traba, Wspólnota Kulturowa Borussia, Olsztyn, 2001, pp. 90–1; Zachar Szybieka, *Historia Białorusi 1795–2000* [*History of Belarusia, 1795–2000*], Instytut Europy Środkowo-Wschodniej, Lublin, 2002, pp. 283–6.
33. Different sources (e.g. Polish committees in Russia, Polish relief committees in the Kingdom of Poland and Galicia, the Tatiana Committee etc.) give different estimates of the number of Polish soldiers, refugees, POWs, and inhabitants of former Polish territories living in Russia at this time, varying from 617,000 to 1,500,000. See Korzeniowski, *Na wygnańczym szlaku*, pp. 107–10. Also Gatrell, *A Whole Empire Walking*, p. 214. It should be noted that none of these estimates includes new immigrants to Poland (mainly Russian émigrés). Documents in the collection of the

Polish Bureau of Agitation and Propaganda of the All-Russian Communist Party [Bolsheviks'] (*Polskie Biuro Wszechrosyjskiej Partii Komunistycznej [bolszewików]*, 1917–1931) could be useful to explore this topic. See, for example, the Russian State Archive of Socio-Political History (*Rossisskii Gosudarstvennyi Arkhiv Sotsial'no-Politicheskoi Istorii*, the former Soviet central party archive, hereafter RGASPI) f. 63, op. 1, dd. 16, 157, 158, 159, 163, 164.

34. *Rocznik statystyki Rzeczypospolitej Polskiej 1923* [*Statistical Yearbook of the Polish Republic, 1923*], Główny Urząd Statystyczny, Warsaw, 1923 p. 28. At this time, re-emigration and emigration from Russia was much smaller: about 36,000 people arrived in Poland during the period 1923–4. See Edward Kołodziej, *Wychodźstwo zarobkowe z Polski 1918–1939. Studia nad polityką emigracyjną II Rzeczypospolitej* [*Work emigration from Poland 1918–1939. Studies on the emigration policy of the Second Republic*], Książka i Wiedza, Warsaw, 1982, pp. 56–7.

35. Jerzy Kumaniecki, 'Repatriacja Polaków z ZSRR, 1921–1924' ['Repatriation of Poles from the USSR, 1921–1924'] in *Z dziejów rozwoju państw socjalistycznych* [*Socialist States – History and Development*], vol. 2, 1984, no. 1–4, p. 228. See also Norman Davies, *White Eagle, Red Star: The Polish-Soviet War 1919–1920*, Macdonald & Co., London, 1972, p. 32; Eugene M Kulischer, *Europe on the Move: War and Population Changes, 1917–1947*, Columbia University Press, New York, 1948, pp. 130–1.

36. APL UWL Wydział Pracy i Opieki Społecznej (hereafter WPOS), 48, p. 10.

37. AAN, Przedstawicielstwo Rady Regencyjnej Królestwa Polskiego w Rosji Radzieckiej 1916, 1918–1919 (hereafter PRRR) 99, pp. 1–9, 'W sprawie Dekretu Rady Komisarzy Ludowych O wyjściu niektórych kategorii osób z obywatelstwa rosyjskiego' ['On the Decree of the Council of People's Commissars [Sovnarkom] on denationalisation of some groups of Russian citizens']. See also RGASPI f. 17, op. 63, d. 4, l. 12; f. 63, op. 1, d. 35, ll. 46–50; ibid., d. 321, l. 37.

38. APL UWL WO 552 nnp.

39. AAN Ambasada Rzeczypospolitej Polskiej w Londynie 1916, 1919–1945 (hereafter ARPL) 1358, pp. 7–8.

40. See Henry L Feingold, *A Time for Searching. Entering the Mainstream 1920–1945*, The Johns Hopkins University Press, Baltimore, London, 1992, pp. 1–34; Matthew F Jacobson, *Whiteness of a Different Color. European Immigrants and the Alchemy of Race*, Harvard University Press, Cambridge, London, 2001, pp. 78–99; Michael M Marrus, *The Unwanted: European Refugees in the Twentieth Century*, Oxford University Press, New York, 1985, pp. 59–65; Mark Wischnitzer, *To Dwell in Safety. The Story of Jewish Migration since 1800*, Jewish Publication Society of America, Philadelphia, 1948, pp. 151–4.

41. AAN ARPL 1358, p. 7.

42. Ibid., pp. 8–9, 13–15. See also Jerzy Tomaszewski, *Zarys dziejów Żydów w Polsce w latach 1918–1939* [*History of Jews in Poland in the Years 1918–1939. An Outline*], Wydawnictwo Uniwersytetu Warszawskiego, Warsaw, 1990, pp. 13–17.

43. APL UWL WSP 1323, p. 30.

44. Unfortunately, I have not found these reports and diplomatic notes in the Foreign Ministry archive. Some are mentioned in voievodship offices. See, for example, APL UWL WSP 1296, p. 213. See also Marrus, *The Unwanted*, p. 66; Zosa Szajkowski, 'Western Jewish aid and intercession for Polish Jewry, 1919–1939,' in *Studies in Polish Jewry 1919–1939. The Interplay of Social, Economic and Political Factors in the Struggle of a Minority for Its Existence*, ed. Joshua Fishman, YIVO Institute for Jewish Research, New York, 1974, pp. 150–75; Jerzy Tomaszewski, 'Czechoslovak diplomats on the national minorities in Poland, 1924–1939,' in *Acta Sueco-Polonica*, 1994, no. 2, pp. 54–9.
45. APL UWL WSP 1323, p. 30.
46. Ibid., WSP 1306, p. 155.
47. Ibid., WO 557, n.p.
48. There was no common deadline for the whole of Poland, but was settled individually for particular territories. WSP 1322, p. 12.
49. AAN ARPL 1352, pp. 1–6, 10, 17–8.
50. APL UWL, WSP 1323, pp. 26, 30, 33, 60–1. APL Komenda Wojewódzka Policji Państwowej w Lublinie, 1919–1939 (hereafter KWPP) 473, n.p; APL KWPP 474, p. 4.
51. APL UWL, WSP 1301, p. 219; ibid., WSP 1323, pp. 60–1.
52. Ibid, p. 213; AAN ARPL 430, p. 10.
53. AAN ARPL 1358, p. 5; DALO, f. 1, op. 52, d. 232, l. 15.
54. Most of the 156 Jews who presented certificates at the Polish border affirmed that they had the right to a Polish passport. According to the law, however, they had no such right because they had never lived in Poland. It is likely that they had either crossed the border illegally or had bribed the border guards. See APL UWL WSP 1323, p. 61; see also Kumaniecki, 'Repatriacja Polaków z ZSRR', p. 221.
55. AAN ARPL 1358, pp. 1–6, 67; APL UWL, WSP 1145, pp. 49–51. See also Kołodziej, *Wychodźstwo zarobkowe z Polski*, pp. 54–5.
56. YIVO WM, 121, p. 13.
57. Tomaszewski, *Wokół obywatelstwa Żydów polskich*, p. 509.
58. APL UWL, WSP 1323, p. 62.
59. AAN ARPL 430, p. 2; APL UWL WPOZ 48, pp. 26–7. This happened most often to farms situated in the eastern voivodships, which were abandoned by Ukrainians. See Stanisław Tomkowicz, *Wycieczka w Lubelskie [An Excursion to Lublin Province]*, Drukarnia 'Czasu', Kraków, 1916, p. 6.
60. AAN ARPL 430, pp. 8–9; AAN Towarzystwo Straży Kresowej 1918–1927 (hereafter TSK) 213, p. 43; APL UWL, WO 451, n.p., 'Protokoły zgłoszenia mienia opuszczonego' ['Registers of deserted property reports']. See also Krystyna Gomółka, *Między Polską a Rosją. Białoruś w koncepcjach polskich ugrupowań politycznych 1918–1922 [Between Poland and Russia. Belarusia in Conceptions of the Polish Political Parties, 1918–1922]*, Gryf, Warsaw, 1994, p. 164.
61. APL UWL, WO 552, n.p.

62. See, for example, APL UWL, WSP 1296, p. 8.
63. Ibid., WO 367, n.p.; WO 369, n.p.; WO 369, n.p.; *Dziennik Ustaw* [*Register of Laws*], 1920, no. 71, item 479.
64. There is a large volume of such material (mainly reports) sent by the Polish Bureau of the All-Russian Communist Party (bolshevik) to the Central Committee in Moscow. See e.g.: RGASPI, f. 17, op. 4, d. 95, l. 11; d. 100, ll. 1–5; op. 63, d. 4, ll. 2, 5, 12,15; f. 63, op. 1, d. 30, ll. 1–5; d. 35, ll. 40, 44, 50, 59, 64, 94; d. 36, ll. 29–31; d. 66, l. 8; d. 73, ll. 10, 15, 18, 20–1, 37, 63, 66; d. 322, ll. 15, 19, 26–7. See also Kumaniecki, 'Repatriacja Polaków z ZSRR', p. 226.
65. AAN TSK 324, pp. 8–11; APL UWL WSP 1145, p. 183. See also Richard Pipes, 'Jews and the Russian Revolution: a note', in *Polin: Studies in Polish Jewry*, vol. 9, 1996, p. 57; Janusz Szczepański, *Społeczeństwo polskie w walce z najazdem bolszewickim 1920 roku* [*Polish society in the fight against the Bolshevik invasion of 1920*], Naczelna Dyrekcja Archiwów Państwowych, Warsaw, Pułtusk, 2000, pp. 386–8.
66. Tomaszewski, *Zarys dziejów Żydów w Polsce*, pp. 32–4.
67. APL UWL, WSP 215, p. 42.
68. See, for example, Wacław Kostek-Biernacki, 'Wpływy rosyjskie na Polesiu – liczebność, rozmieszczenie i charakterystyka ogólna – referat wojewody poleskiego, 1933 r.' ['The Russian influence in Polesie: demography and a general study of the community, 1933'], in ibid., WSP 414, pp. 3–4, 6–7.
69. AAN Komitet Rosyjski w Polsce 1919–1939 (hereafter KRP) 9, np.; AAN TSK 68, pp. 2–3; APL UWL, WSP 414, n.p.
70. Wojciech Stanisławski, 'Emigracja i mniejszość rosyjska w II Rzeczypospolitej: Próba charakterystyki społeczności', ['The Russian emigration and Russian minority in the Second Republic: A first study of the community'), *Sprawy Narodowościowe – Seria nowa* [*Ethnic Issues – New Series*], 1996, vol. 5, no. 2 (9), pp. 36, 38–9. See also Alicja Bełcikowska, *Stronnictwa i związki polityczne w Polsce* [*Political parties and organizations in Poland*], Dom Książki Polskiej, Warsaw, 1925, pp. 633–4, 961–4.
71. APL UWL, WSP 1301, pp. 165, 219; ibid., WSP 1323, p. 30.
72. After the Uprising of 1863, the Russian government excluded Poles, Catholics and in many cases even Russians married to Polish women from employment in administration. As Theodore R Weeks wrote, 'Ironically, it was easier for Poles to make a career in the Russian interior, where such restrictions did not exist. This fact gave rise to large Polish communities in the Russian capital and elsewhere', in 'Defining us and them: Poles and Russians in the "Western Provinces", 1863–1914', *Slavic Review*, 1994, vol. 53, no. 1, pp. 33–4. See also Andrzej Chwalba, *Polacy w służbie Moskali* [*Poles in Moskal [i.e. Russian] service*], Wydawnitwo Naukowe PWN, Warsaw, Kraków, 1999, pp. 68–9, 86–7.
73. 'Nauczycielstwo narodowości rosyjskiej. Informacje i opinie, 1926' ['Russian teachers, information and opinions'], in APL UWL, WSP 434, pp. 10–63. See also Stanisławski, *Emigracja i mniejszość rosyjska*, p. 35.
74. APL UWL, WSP. 1352, p. 81

75. Ibid., WSP 1323, p. 69; APL KWPP 474, p. 3.
76. APL UWL, WSP 1323, p. 62.
77. See the examples in ibid., WSP 1305, p. 602.
78. Ibid., WSP 1323, p. 1.
79. Stanisławski, *Emigracja i mniejszość rosyjska*, pp. 29–31.
80. AAN KRP 9, pp. 62, 74–5, 112, 177, 290. See also RGASPI f. 63, op. 1, d. 197, l. 2; d. 198, l. 6. Also Benecke, *Die Ostgebiete der Zweiten Polnischen Republik*, pp. 45–6.
81. Szczepański, *Społeczeństwo polskie*, pp. 432–3.
82. Bułak-Bałachowicz, tsarist officer, organized one of the first anti-Bolshevik forces in the western provinces of the former Russian Empire. This formation, as a Polish ally, had taken a part in the Battle of Warsaw in August 1920. Peremykin, a Russian Major-General, was commander of the so-called Third Army. His detachment was the last allied formation created in Poland. See Zbigniew Karpus, 'Traktat Ryski a polscy sojusznicy z okresu wojny polsko-bolszewickiej 1920 roku' ['The Treaty of Riga and Poland's allies from the Polish-Bolshevik war of 1920'] in *Traktat ryski 1921 roku po 75 latach*, pp. 233–7.
83. Examples are to be found in Komitet Rosyjski w Polsce: AAN KRP 36, pp. 34, 66, 69, 150; AAN KRP 39, pp. 78, 206.
84. Karpus, *Traktat Ryski a polscy sojusznicy*, p. 240.
85. Szczepański, *Społeczeństwo polskie*, pp. 434–5.
86. For attempts to create Russian and Ukrainian military units to fight on the Polish side, consisting of both refugees and Soviet POWs, see the archives of the Russian Committee in Poland (*Komitet Rosyjski w Polsce*, 1919–1939). This collection is located in the Archive of Modern Documents (*Archiwum Akt Nowych*) in Warsaw. The collection was copied by the Soviets during the Communist era, and identical materials are thus to be found in Russian archives. The collection of the Central Military Archive (*Centralne Archiwum Wojskowe*) in Warsaw also sheds light on this topic.
87. Jerzy Tomaszewski, *Z dziejów Polesia 1921–1939. Zarys stosunków społeczno-ekonomicznych* (From the History of Polesie. An Outline of Social-economic Conditions)', Państwowe Wydawnictwo Naukowe, Warsaw, 1963, p. 24. For the results of the 1921 census for the whole of Poland, see *Pierwszy powszechny spis Rzeczypospolitej Polskiej z dn. 30 września 1921 roku* [*The First Census of the Polish Republic from 30 September 1921*], vols 22, 23, Główny Urząd Statystyczny, Warsaw, 1924. In Polesie, the 'local' language was a mixture of Belarusian and Russian with Polish and Lithuanian components. The authorities had problems with categorizing speakers of this language in terms of nationality, but usually regarded them as Belarusians.
88. According to the Second General Register and the language criterion (mother tongue) applied in 1931 as a mark of the national identity, the Russian population in the Second Republic represented 0.4 per cent (138,713 people) of the total population of Poland. The largest number lived in the eastern voievodships: Vilna (3.4 per cent), Białystok (2.1 per cent), Polesie (1.4 per cent) and Wohłynia (1.1 per cent). See:

Włodzimierz Mędrzecki, 'Liczebność i rozmieszczenie grup narodowościowych w II Rzeczypospolitej w świetle wyników II Spisu Powszechnego (1931 r.),' in *Dzieje Najnowsze* [*Modern History*], 1983, vol. 15, nos 1–2, pp. 233–7. John H Simpson offers some estimates of the proportion of native to immigrant Russians in Poland see *The Refugee Problem. Report of a Survey*, Oxford University Press, Oxford and New York, 1939, pp. 63–116, 269–81.

89. Stanisławski, *Emigracja i mniejszość rosyjska*, p. 27.
90. It is worth mentioning that some groups of inhabitants of Polesie defined themselves as *tutejsi*, literally 'people from here'. Ethnically they were closest to Belarusians. These people, who were usually poor and backward peasants, were unable to define their nationality or the mother tongue, at least in the categories recognized by the Polish authorities. Their language was a mixture of Belarusian and Ukrainian with an addition of Polish and Russian components. See for example: Janusz Obrębski, 'Dzisiejsi ludzie Polesia', in *Przegląd Socjologiczny* [*Sociological Review*], 1936, vol. 4, no. 3–4, pp. 416–17. We can see some similarities with Ruthenians in Galicia: as a contemporary observer wrote of the Ruthenians, 'they belong so much to the land of Galicia and the land to them, that, in ordinary parlance, they are often simply called "Galicians", a term which would never be applied without qualification to the Poles or Jews of that country'. See John Pollock, 'Thoughts on the Polish Question,' in *The New Europe*, 1916, vol. 1, no. 7, p. 243.
91. APL UWL, WSP 414, pp. 6–7.
92. Ibid., pp. 3–4.
93. Ibid.
94. Ibid, pp. 22–5, 34, 47; ibid., WSP 434, pp. 10–63. See also Stanislawski, *Emigracja i mniejszość rosyjska*, p. 52.
95. See, for example, *Sprawy Narodowościowe* (Ethnic Issues), 1928, vol. 2, no. 3; ibid., 1930, vol. 4, no. 1; ibid., 1932, vol. 6, nos 2–3. More information is to be found in the Russian Committee in Poland and Ministry of Interior Affairs (*Ministerstwo Spraw Wewnętrznych*) collections in the Archive of Modern Documents in Warsaw.
96. Brubaker, *Nationalism Reframed*, pp. 84–103.
97. APL UWL, WO 556, n.p.
98. AAN KRP 36, p. 69.
99. APL UWL, WO 556, n.p. A Conjoint agent wrote, 'Jews escape not so much because they cannot live under Bolshevik rule, but because they are afraid of being killed off sooner or later by bands and groups of peasants who are only awaiting their chance to make new pogroms upon the Jews', in YIVO WM, 121, p. 13.
100. Jerzy Tomaszewski, 'Niepodległa Rzeczpospolita' ['Independent Poland'], in *Najnowsze dzieje Żydów w Polsce* [*The Recent History of the Jews in Poland*], ed. J Tomaszewski, Warsaw, 1993, pp. 148–9.
101. In 1916, for the first time in the history of the Kingdom of Poland, its inhabitants were allowed to vote in elections for town councils. See Zieliński, *Żydzi Lubelszczyzny*, pp. 130–2, 148–51.
102. See, for example, Berend, *Decades of Crisis*, pp. 158–9.

Chapter 6: The Repatriation of Polish Citizens from Soviet Ukraine to Poland in 1921–22

1. Within the Secretariat-General the Central *Rada* created a Secretariat for Nationality Affairs which had a separate Polish Division. This became a Ministry following the official proclamation of the Ukrainian People's Republic in November 1917. The Ministry was responsible for the development of the national-cultural autonomy of the Polish minority in Ukraine. Unfortunately, the attempts by the Central *Rada* to develop Polish national-cultural autonomy in 1917 were in effect rejected as soon as the government was overthrown. The Soviet authorities subsequently resorted to these tactics by granting national minorities, including Poles, the right to form territorial administrative units where they constituted a majority. Set up in 1924, the national Soviets constituted basic administrative units of the Soviet regime until their final liquidation in 1939. However, no Polish Soviet was established in Donetsk province. For detail see *Polacy na Ukrainie: Zbiór dokumentów, lata 1917–1939* [*Poles in Ukraine: Collection of Documents, 1917–1939*], Part 1, Południowo-Wschodni Instytut Naukowy w Przemyślu, 1998, pp. 245–47; *Natsional'ni menshyny v Ukraini u 1920–1930 rr.* [*National minorities in Ukraine in the 1920s and 1930s*], Kyiv, Institute of International Relations and Political Science, 1996, pp. 5–8, 52–61.
2. These episodes involved different Ukrainian political authorities, namely the Central *Rada* of the Ukrainian People's Republic, the government of the Western Ukrainian People's Republic, the Directorate of the Ukrainian People's Republic, and finally, the Council of People's Commissars of the Soviet Ukraine. For details, see Henry Abramson, *A Prayer for the Government: Ukrainians and Jews in Revolutionary Times, 1917–1920*, Cambridge, Mass., Ukrainian Research Institute, chapter 5.
3. Norman Davies, *Europe: A History*, Oxford and New York, Oxford University Press, 1996, p. 935.
4. Norman Davies, *White Eagle, Red Star: The Polish–Soviet War 1919–20*, London, Macdonald, 1972, p. 32.
5. Successive Ukrainian governments attempted to deal with the nationalities problems and related issues of internees and refugees. On 1 February 1919 officials of the Western Ukrainian People's Republic (ZUNR) and representatives of the Polish POW Affairs Commission signed the Lwiw Agreement on prisoners of war. The defeat of the ZUNR left unclear the legal validity of this agreement. P. Pavlenko, *Ukrains'ki viis'kovopoloneni i internovani u taborakh Pol'schi, Chekhoslovachyny ta Rumunii: stavlennia vlady ta umovy perebuvannia, 1919–1924 rr.* [*Ukrainian Prisoners of War and Internees in Polish, Czechoslovak and Rumanian Camps: The Attitudes of the Authorities and Terms of Incarceration, 1919–1924*] Kyiv, Ukrainian Institute of History, 1999, pp. 46–63.
6. *Dokumenty vneshnei politiki SSSR* [Documents of Soviet Foreign Policy] volume 2, Moscow: Ministry of Foreign Affairs, Gospolitizdat, 1958, pp. 180–5; volume 3, 1959, pp. 249, 464–7; T Eremenko, 'Politichni ta dyplomatychni vidnosyny radians'koi

Ukrainy z Pol's'koju Respublikoju (1921–1923)', ['Political and diplomatic relations between Soviet Ukraine and the Polish Republic, 1921–1923'] *Ukrainian Historical Journal*, 1998, no. 4, pp. 61–2. See also Zielinski, this volume.

7. Copies of this top-secret document were posted to each *Gubkom* in order to coordinate their activity throughout the period of re-evacuation. GADO, f. 1, op. 1, d. 366, l. 194.
8. The Polish section of the *Dongubkom* was established on 23 June 1920. On 17 October 1920 it was reorganized as the Polish Bureau, which remained in existence until 6 November 1922. GADO, f. 1, op. 1, d. 19, ll. 51, 123; d. 1309, l. 43. Thereafter Polish representatives were assigned to the 'Nationalities section' of the local committee of the Communist Party. Administratively, these sections constituted a subunit of the Party's Department of Information and Propaganda (*Agitprop*). Their main task was to implement Party decisions concerning the Sovietization of the Polish population. The personnel of the Polish sections was recruited mainly from leftist Polish prisoners of war. However, most such sections had only a modest staff, insufficient to discharge their responsibilities. Ibid., d. 652, l. 57. See Binyamin Pinkus, 'The extra-territorial national minorities in the Soviet Union, 1917–1939: Jews, Germans and Poles' in *Studies in Contemporary Jewry. Jews and Other Ethnic Groups in a Multi-Ethnic World*, Institute of Contemporary Jewry, The Hebrew University of Jerusalem, volume 3, Oxford University Press, New York and Oxford, 1987, p. 78.
9. GADO, f. 1, op. 1, d. 834, l. 43. Before the revolution, public organizations such as the All-Russian Union of Zemstvos and the Union of Towns assisted the government in refugee relief. During 1917 and 1918 the hostility between the Bolshevik authorities and provincial *zemstvos* (such as in Khar'kov and Ekaterinoslav) made concerted action impossible. No provincial soviet was likely to recruit former zemstvo workers as members of its re-evacuation staff. See Grigorii Gerasimenko, *Zemskoe samoupravlenie v Rossii* [Zemstvo Self-government in Russia], Moscow, Nauka, 1990, p. 220. It should be noted that, in contrast to the Right-Bank provinces, there was little Polish settlement in Donetsk prior to 1914 and thus no established local Church presence. See *Polacy na Ukrainie*, pp. 88, 89, 117–9, 214–16.
10. GADO, f. 1, op. 1, d. 834, l. 43.
11. Ibid., l.44. See below for further discussion of the role of the *politrabotniki*.
12. GADO, f. 1, op. 1, d. 837, ll. 8, 30; d. 1309, l. 52; Wojciech Materski, *Pobocza dyplomacji: Wymiana wiezniow politycznych pomiedzy II Rzeczapospolita a Sowietami w okresie miedzywojennym* [*The Margins of Diplomacy: The Exchange of Political Prisoners between the Second Polish Republic and Soviet Russia in the Inter-War Period*] Warszawa, Instytut Studiow Politychnych PAN, 2002, pp. 97–8.
13. GADO, f. 1, op. 1, d. 837, l. 8; d. 834, l. 42.
14. Ibid., d. 19, l. 52.
15. Soviet representatives of this Commission operated from Warsaw while their Polish counterparts were based in Moscow.
16. Between September and November 1921 the Soviet authorities sent several

diplomatic notes and one memorandum dealing with 'the obstacles put by the Polish authorities in the way of the repatriation campaign'. Materski, *Pobocza dyplomacji*, p. 33.
17. GADO, f. 1, op. 1, d. 837, l. 8. See below.
18. Materski, *Pobocza dyplomacji*, p. 90.
19. Under the Repatriation Agreement, Russia and Ukraine were responsible for conveying to each place of exchange no fewer than 4,000 people. But by reducing the number of candidates for repatriation to Poland the Polish authorities made it difficult to stick to the agreed programme. NS Raiskii, *Pol'sko-Sovetskaia voina 1919– 1920 i sud'ba voennoplennykh, internirovannykh, zalozhnikov i bezhentsev* [The Polish–Soviet War of 1919–1920 and the Fate of Prisoners of War, Internees, Hostages and Refugees] Rossiiskaia Akademiia Nauk, Moscow, 1999, p. 33. For its part, the Polish side blamed the Soviets for deliberately overloading refugee contingents so as to facilitate the entry of Bolshevik agents. Materski, *Pobocza dyplomacji*, p. 95.
20. GADO, f. 1, op. 1, d. 370, l. 24.
21. The number of returnees to the Soviet Union between 1920 and 1938 has been put at 200,000. Pavel Polian, *Immigratsiia: kto i kogda v XX veke priezhal v Rossiiu* [Immigration: Who came to Russia and When during the Twentieth Century] forthcoming. See also YP Pisarevskaja, 'Dve Rosii v Manchzhurii: socialnaja adaptaciia i reemigraciia v 1920–1930' ['Two Russian lands in Manchuria: social adaptation and re-emigration, 1920s–1930s'] in *Nowy istorichekij vestnik*, no. 2, 2000, pp. 7, 10–13.
22. In August 1922 the All-Union Central Executive Committee of the Communist Party issued a decree on the administrative deportation of all persons deemed to be socially 'insecure'. Foreigners were particularly vulnerable. See the article 'Concerning Polish espionage in the USSR', *Kochegarka* [*Fireman's News*], 18 June 1924.
23. GADO, f. 1, op. 1, d. 837, l. 10; f. 1, op. 1, d. 834, ll. 106, 107. We should note here that the introduction of NEP may have magnified their anxieties, because the policy was associated with an increase in unemployment in the short and medium term. See Maurice Dobb, *Russian Economic Development since the Revolution*, second edition, Routledge, London, 1929, pp. 189–90.
24. Peter Gatrell, *A Whole Empire Walking: Refugees in the Russian Empire in World War One*, Indiana University Press, Bloomington, 1999, pp. 31–2, 47.
25. GADO, f. 2442, op. 1, d. 34, l. 54.
26. The last branch office in Russia (Khabarovsk) closed down in August 1925. Materski, *Pobocza dyplomacji*, p. 179. Five exchanges under the extradition agreement took place in the 1930s.
27. Materski, *Pobocza dyplomacji*, p. 263.
28. See, for example, a Party document recommending that the Polish Bureau facilitate the departure to Poland of one 'Comrade Petrovskii' who 'is willing to work there in the clandestine Communist Party'. GADO, f. 1, op. 1, d. 839, l. 67.
29. Ibid., d. 1309, l. 19.
30. Ibid., d. 834, l. 133; d. 837, l. 7.

31. See below for further discussion of the issue of professionals and their decision to migrate.
32. GADO, f. 1, op. 1, d. 370, ll. 56, 57.
33. According to the Gubevak the total number of Polish refugees in Donetsk guberniia in July 1921 stood at 20,000. See Ibid., d. 837, l. 8.
34. This is also true of Khar'kov *guberniia*. Here the All-Ukrainian Re-evacuation Committee registered 16,500 Poles willing to leave for Poland while the Polish section of the Khar'kov Gubkom counted 15,000 people, 'including 4,000 workers, 2,000 prisoners of war, and 9,000 other civilians'. See the Report of the Polish Section of the Khar'kov Gubkom for the period from September to May 1921, in ibid., d. 834, l. 133.
35. Donetsk *guberniia* was legally established in April 1920, and comprised two *uezds* of Khar'kov province, three from Ekaterinoslav, and part of the Don oblast; it also included the territories of Taganrog and Shakhtinsk, which six years later were annexed to the Russian Federation. In 1925, the term *guberniia* was abolished, and replaced by *okrug*. In 1930 this suffered the same fate, and a new administrative system with cities and districts was launched. The 'Stalin region', made up of Stalin, Mariupol, Artemovsk, Starobelsk and Lugansk was created in 1932. See Iu A Poliakov, *Sovetskaia strana posle okonchaniia grazhdanskoi voiny: territoriia i naselenie* [*The Soviet Land in the Aftermath of the Civil War: Territory and Population*] Moscow, Nauka, 1986, pp. 65–6.
36. GADO, f. 1, op. 1, d. 837, l. 13.
37. Op. cit., l. 8.
38. Op. cit., l. 14.
39. These stories were based on the situation in the Polish–Ukrainian borderlands in 1921 and 1922. According to the report of the Special Commission for Health Care established within the Polish Commissariat for Repatriation, the authorities had no means at their disposal to fight the epidemics among evacuees. Materski, *Pobocza dyplomacji*, pp. 97–9.
40. *Kochegarka*, 27 June 1924.
41. GADO, f. 2442, op. 1, d. 34, l. 24.
42. Ibid., l. 1.
43. For purposes of re-evacuation the Polish Committee for Return to the Homeland [*Komitet Powrotu do Kraju*], established in 1917, prioritized as follows: urban and rural managers of enterprises; zemstvo activists; skilled workers; merchants; and unskilled labourers and farmers. Archiwum Akt Nowych (Warsaw), f. 53, op. 2, d. 3, ll. 43–52.
44. GADO, f. 1, op. 1, d. 837, l. 11.
45. Under the Repatriation Agreement two categories of soldiers had been defined: former prisoners of war, to be treated as refugees (that is, those who resided on the Polish territory until 1 January 1914 but had been held captive during World War One); and second, prisoners of war (combatants of the Polish army or separate forces, units or detachments taken prisoner by the Red or Ukrainian armies on the

Russian–Ukrainian–Polish front or other fronts where they were disarmed and interned by the Russian or Ukrainian authorities). As a rule, each echelon was restricted to one particular category of evacuees. Thus, former prisoners of war might find themselves among refugees, but they were usually re-evacuated separately. Most of those re-evacuated from Donetsk province could be classified as refugees (those who resided on the Polish territory until 1 January 1914, but during World War One or the Russian–Ukrainian–Polish war abandoned their places of residence occupied or threatened by the hostile forces and those who were expelled [*vyslannye*] by order of military or civil authorities). Polish prisoners of war were largely concentrated in the nearby Khar'kov province: some 1,500–2,000 people were taken to specially created labour units (one regiment and one battalion) and worked at the local factories and railway station up to their re-evacuation. GADO, f. 2442, op. 1, d. 62, ll. 55–6; Raiskii, *Pol'sko-Sovietskaia voina*, p. 26. The figure of 2,000 was given in the report of the Polish section of the Khar'kov province Party Committee in May 1921. GADO, f. 1, op. 1, d. 834, l. 133.

46. Alan Ball, *And Now My Soul Is Hardened: Abandoned Children in Soviet Russia, 1918–1930*, Berkeley, University of California Press, 1994.
47. Between 8,000 and 20,000 children were reported as awaiting return to Poland. See Konrad Zielinski and Kateryna Stadnik, 'Abandoned children in Poland and Soviet Ukraine: making future citizens', in Nick Baron, ed., *Displacement, Delinquency and Child Welfare in Twentieth Century Eastern Europe*, forthcoming.
48. The file of correspondence between the Polish Bureau and the DonGubkom indicated the number of children and their distribution among the various 'echelons'. See GADO, f. 1, op. 1, d. 839, l. 48.
49. Ibid., d. 370, l. 271.
50. For more details, see Zielinski and Stadnik, 'Abandoned children'.
51. GADO, f. 2442, op. 1, d. 62, l. 85. This letter was probably sent first to the Provincial Re-evacuation Committee (*Gubevak*) in Iuzovka but never forwarded to the Central Committee.
52. Materski, *Pobocza dyplomacji*, p. 106.
53. GADO, f. 1, op. 1, d. 834, l. 9.
54. Ibid., d. 837, l. 20. No data are available for the other six *uezds* where there were no Party cells responsible for record keeping.
55. These lists did not give precise numbers of Polish-speaking people. For instance, although they reported that 1,556 people lived in Grishino as of November 1921, the instructor of the DonGubkom contradicted this claim when he visited Grishino and found only 15 Polish families. In other localities numbers were also often underestimated. GADO, f. 1, op. 1, d. 837, l. 20.
56. See the report, 'Przedląd krytyczny prasy zakordonnej' ['Critical review of the foreign press'], ibid., d. 838, ll. 87–9.
57. Ibid., d. 834, l. 107.
58. Report by Khar'kov Gubkom to the Polish Bureau of DonGubkom in the summer of 1921. Ibid., ll. 133, 134, 77, 78.

59. Ibid., d. 652, l. 57.
60. A troika member called Schliumi reported on 20 March that in Chuguev, 270 Polish prisoners of war were fed with eight pounds of flour, seven pounds of oil, eight pounds of beetroot and five pounds of salt. Thus one ration was reckoned to include up to 0.03 pounds of flour, oil and beetroot and about 0.02 pounds of salt. GADO, f. 1, op. 1, d. 834, l. 107. Unfortunately, it has proved difficult to locate any data on the rations available to refugees. Apparently, pressures on foodstuffs varied over time (even within a calendar year, as food supply largely depended on the seasons) and localities (as proximity to transportation links or food-producing areas might ease the pressure). But throughout 1920 and 1921 the authorities in the Donbass tried to find funds to fight the widespread food shortage.
61. GADO, f. 1, op. 1, d. 837, ll. 30, 31.
62. The first line of the famous Polish song composed in 1797 by Jozef Wybicki to a folk-tune. This song was a hymn of Dąbrowski's Polish legions in the Napoleonic Army and became the national anthem of the independent Polish state under Piłsudski.
63. GADO, f. 1, op. 1, d. 1308, l. 23.
64. Ibid., d. 834, l. 77.
65. Ibid., d. 839, l. 67.
66. Ibid., d. 834, l. 72.
67. No reports on re-evacuation appeared following the reorganization of the Polish Bureau in November 1922, although the mass repatriation campaign continued until June 1924. The decision to restructure the *Guberniia* Polish Bureau may be taken as an indication that the repatriation of Poles from Donetsk province had been largely completed.
68. GADO, f. 1, op. 1, d. 1308, l. 21.
69. Some 15–25 per cent were Poles, 65 per cent Ukrainians and Belarusians, and 10 per cent other nationalities. Eremenko, 'Politichni ta dyplomatychni vidnosyny', pp. 63–4.
70. Ibid., p. 64.
71. GADO, f. 1, op. 1, d. 865, l. 37.
72. *Kochegarka*, 14 June 1924. However, a *Gubkom* report on nationality policy in the Donbass in 1925, based on the *guberniia* Census, failed to give any figure for the Polish population in the region. GADO, f. 1, op. 1, d. 2366, ll. 1–23.
73. There is a curious note in the newspaper *Kochegarka* dated 27 June 1924: 'Each Turkish citizen is eligible for free travel. All other foreigners willing to repatriate are eligible for free travel to the border, if they comprise a group of no less than 25 people.'
74. Ibid.

Chapter 7: 'Sybiraki': Siberian and Manchurian Returnees in Independent Poland

1. Robin Cohen, *Global Diasporas: An Introduction*, London, UCL Press, 1997, p. 7.
2. A Walaszek, ed., *Polska diaspora* [*The Polish diaspora*], Krakow, Wydawnictwo Literackie, 2001, pp. 9–10, 23–6.

3. The term 'Polish diaspora' was first used in Poland in 1971 and has gained widespread currency since this time. It coexists with the term 'Polonia', which is the traditional name for Polish communities living outside Poland. See Walaszek, *Polska diaspora*, p. 8. In the period 1914–24, the term 'wychodźca' ('exile') was generally used to describe Poles living in the Russian interior.
4. Indigenous residents of the Eastern marches of Poland had of course been swallowed up by the Russian empire during the successive Partitions of Poland.
5. See, for example, Nick Baron and Peter Gatrell, 'Population displacement, state-building and social identity in the lands of the former Russian empire, 1917–1923', *Kritika: Explorations in Russian and Eurasian History*, 4, 2003, pp. 51–100; John Urry, *Sociology Beyond Societies: Mobilities for the Twenty-First Century*, London, Routledge, 2000.
6. This affinity with Siberia's landscape was a central theme of returnee literature in the 1920s, for discussion of which see below. For a general introduction to the history of Siberia, see Alan Wood and RA French, eds., *The Development of Siberia: People and Resources*, Basingstoke, Macmillan, 1989.
7. A Kuczyński, ed., *Syberia: Czterysta lat polskiej diaspory* [*Siberia. Four Hundred Years of Polish Diaspora*], Wrocław, Atlas, 1998, p. 10.
8. M Wrzosek, *Polski czyn zbrojny podczas pierwszej wojny światowej 1914–1918* [*Polish Military Actions during the World War, 1914–1918*], Warsaw, Wiedza Powszechna, 1990; Peter Gatrell, *A Whole Empire Walking: Refugees in Russia during World War One*, Bloomington, Indiana University Press, 1999; Alon Rachamimov, *POWs and the Great War: Captivity on the Eastern Front*, Oxford, Berg, 2002.
9. Kuczyński, *Syberia*, p. 106.
10. A Patek, 'Z dziejów Wojska Polskiego na Syberii i dalekim Wschodzie' ['From the History of the Polish Army in Siberia and Far East'], *Zeszyty Naukowe Uniwersytetu Jagiellońskiego, Prace Historyczne* [*Scientific Annals of the Jagiellonian University: History Series*], 112, 1994, p. 62. Based on research in Polish and foreign archives, this is one of the few scholarly treatments of this subject. See also Z Łukawski, *Ludność polska w Rosji 1863–1914* [*The Polish Population in Russia, 1863–1914*], Wrocław, Ossolineum, 1974, p. 94.
11. A Winiarz, 'Polska diaspora w Mandżurii' ['The Polish diaspora in Manchuria'], in Walaszek, *Polska diaspora*, p. 388. See also K Grochowski, *Polacy na Dalekim Wschodzie* [*Poles in the Far East*], Harbin, Harbin Daily News, 1928, and David Wolff, *To the Harbin Station: The Liberal Alternative in Russian Manchuria, 1898–1914*, Stanford, Stanford University Press, 1999.
12. Grochowski, *Polacy na Dalekim Wschodzie*, p. 74.
13. J Neja, 'Charakterystyka środowiska V Dywizji Strzelców Syberyjskich' ['Description of the Milieu of the Fifth Siberian Rifleman's Division'], in A Kuczy'nski, ed., *Syberia w kulturze i historii narodu polskiego* [*Siberia in the culture and history of the Polish people*], Wrocław, Wydawnictwo Silesia, 1998, p. 277.
14. Patek, 'Z dziejów Wojska Polskiego', p. 64. The agreement was signed in Omsk on 23 July 1918.

15. S Biegański, 'Repatriacja jeńców 5 Dywizji Syberyjskiej' ['The Repatriation of Prisoners of War of the Fifth Siberian Division'], in *Polacy na Syberii: Szkic historyczny* [*Poles in Siberia: An Historical Survey*], Warsaw, n.p., 1928, p. 74. Neja writes that Polish soldiers often married 'local' women, but does not indicate whether they were marrying local Poles, Russians or even Siberian natives. See J Neja, 'Charakterystyka środowiska', p. 283.
16. Patek, 'Z dziejów Wojska Polskiego', p. 69. See also Zofia Lech, *Syberia Polską pachnąca* [*The Scent of Poland in Siberia*], Warsaw, Verbinum, 2003, pp. 239–52. For a bibliography of works devoted to the history of the Fifth Division see *Sybirak*, 1 (9), 1936, pp. 14–18.
17. W Sholze-Srokowski, 'Po katastrofie: Podróż dookoła świata. Ucieczki' ['After the Catastrophe: Journey around the World. Departures'], in *Polacy na Syberii*, p. 67.
18. Ibid., p. 68.
19. Biegański, 'Repatriacja jeńców', pp. 69, 70, 71.
20. Ibid. On the origins of *Tsentroplenbezh* see Gatrell, *A Whole Empire Walking*, pp. 188–90. For more details on procedures for repatriating Polish refugees from Soviet territory, see the chapter by Kate Stadnik in this volume.
21. S Biegański, 'Repatriacja jeńców', p. 72.
22. M Cabanowski, *Tajemnice Mandżurii: Polacy w Harbinie* [*Secrets of Manchuria: Poles in Harbin*], Warsaw, Muzeum Niepodległości, 1993, p. 42.
23. S Lubodziecki, 'Polacy na Syberii i Dalekim Wschodzie w latach 1917–1920: Wspomnienia' ['Poles in Siberia and the Far East, 1917–20: Reminiscences'], *Sybirak*, 3/4, 1934, p. 5.
24. Lubodziecki, 'Polacy na Syberii ...', *Sybirak*, 2, 1936, pp. 52–3.
25. Cabanowski, *Tajemnice Mandżurii*, pp. 46–7, Lubodziecki, 'Polacy na Syberii ...', *Sybirak*, 2, 1938, pp. 47–51.
26. Lech, *Syberia Polską pachnąca*, p. 297.
27. W Theis, *Syberyjskie dzieci* [*Siberian Children*], Warsaw, Wydawnictwo Uniwersytetu Warszawskiego, 1992.
28. Lech, *Syberia Polską pachnąca*; Lubodziecki, 'Polacy na Syberii ...', *Sybirak*, 4, 1935; 2, 3, 1936; J Kumaniecki, *Po Traktacie Ryskim* [*After the Riga Treaty*], Warsaw, Książka i Wiedza, 1971, p. 252.
29. *Sybirak*, 4, 1935, p. 78.
30. Ibid., 1, 1935, p. 52.
31. Ibid., p. 65.
32. Ibid.
33. W Bączkowski, 'Istota problemu tradycji sybirackiej' ['Essence of the Problem of Sybirak Traditions'], *Sybirak*, 3–4, 1934, pp. 1–4.
34. Ibid., 1, 1935, p. 64. By 1938 the number of clubs had grown to twelve.
35. The Board of Control was an internal commission that audited the Association's accounts and checked that its activities corresponded to its constitution. The Court of Arbitration dealt with any conflicts that arose among the membership.
36. For Sieroszewski's career, see K Czachowski, *Wacław Sieroszewski: Życie i twórczość*

[*Wacław Sieroszewski: Life and Works*], 2nd ed., Łódź, Poligrafika, 1947; H Małgowska, *Sieroszewski i Syberia* [*Sieroszewski and Siberia*], Toruń, Wydawnictwo Uniwersytetu Toruńskiego, 1973. Sieroszewski wrote many novels and several scientific works, including one of the earliest ethnographic accounts of the Yakuts, *Dwanaście lat w kraju Jakutów* (*Twelve Years in the Land of Yakuts*), Russian edition 1896, Polish edition 1900. His numerous novels, such as *Zamorski diabeł (Foreign Devil)*, 1903, and *Miłość samuraja* (*Love of the Samurai*), 1926 were often situated in Siberia and the Far East.

37. The film, entitled *Bohaterowie Sybiru* ('Heroes of Siberia') was made in 1936, and depicted the final battle of the Fifth Division. Despite the appearance of several famous Polish film stars, the film flopped.
38. See Jerzy Holzer, *Mozaika Polityczna Drugiej Rzeczypospolitej* [*Political Mosaic of the Second Republic*], Warsaw, Książka i Wiedza, 1978, pp. 314, 347.
39. *Encyklopedia historii Drugiej Rzeczypospolitej* [*Historical Encyclopedia of the Second Republic*], Warsaw, Bellona, 1999, p. 92.
40. Some members of the Association had been exiled for having been active members of the Polish Socialist Party, to which Piłsudski had belonged.
41. *Sybirak*, 2, 1934, p. 17.
42. The most comprehensive collection is the series of essays edited by a deportee, Stanisław Lubodziecki, and published at intervals throughout the 1930s. See Lubodziecki 'Polacy na Syberii ...', *Sybirak*, 1–4, 1934; 1–4, 1935; 2–3, 1936; 1, 1937; 2–4, 1938; 1–3 1939.
43. Bączkowski, 'Istota problemu', p. 3.
44. Feliks Gross, 'Syberia, zesłanie, nauka' ['Siberia, exile, learning'], *Droga* [*The Way*], 9, 1934. Replies to this article were published in *Sybirak*, 2, 1934.
45. Polish achievements in 'discovering and civilizing' Siberia are a major theme of Michał Janik, *Dzieje Polaków na Syberii* [*Activities of Poles in Siberia*], Kraków, Krakowska Spółka Wydawnicza, 1928. Most subsequent publications rely heavily upon this book. See also note 36 above.
46. Mieczyslaw Bohdan Lepecki, *Syberia bez przekleństw*, Warsaw, Towarzystwo Wydawnicze Rój, 1934.
47. Bączkowski, 'Istota problemu'.
48. A Zabęski, 'Syberia z przekleństwem czy bez?' ['Siberia with curses or without?'], *Sybirak* 1, 1935, p. 29. Zabęski was an editor and frequent contributor to *Sybirak*.
49. M Sabatowicz, 'O nasz stosunek do Sybiru' ['On our attitudes to Siberia'], Ibid., 6, 1935, p. 15.
50. K Wyka, 'Literatura podróżnicza' ['Travel Literature'], *Rocznik Literacki* [*Literary Yearbook*], 3, 1934, p. 225.
51. E Kajdański, *Fort Grochowski*, Olszyn, Wydawnictwo Pojezierze, 1988, p. 189.
52. Lech, *Syberia Polską pachnąca*, p. 302.
53. Maria Kuncewicz, *Cudzoziemka*, Warsaw, Spółdzielnia Wydawnicza 'Wiedza', 1936.
54. Igor Neverly, *Wzgórza Błękitnego Snu*, Warsaw, Wydawnictwo Czytelnik, 1988.
55. Stefan Żeromski, *Przedwiośnie*, Warsaw, Wydawnictwo J Mortkowicza, 1925.

Chapter 8: Refugees in the Urals Region, 1917–1925

1. Peter Gatrell, *A Whole Empire Walking: Refugees in Russia during World War One*, Bloomington, Indiana University Press, 1999; AN Kurtsev, 'Bezhentsy pervoi mirovoi voiny v Rossii (1914–17)', *Voprosy istorii*, 1999, 8, pp. 98–113; TM Bartele and VA Shalda, 'Latyshskie bezhentsy v Rossii v gody Grazhdanskoi voiny', *Otechestvennaia istoriia*, 2000, 1, pp. 18–31.
2. In particular, I have made use of the following collections: GASO fond r-511, the Ekaterinburg Department of the Regional Administration (*Ekaterinburgskii otdel upravleniia guberniei*, abbreviated as *Gubotuprav*), which includes the materials of the Regional Committee for Prisoners of War and Refugees (*Gubplenbezh*); fond r-1646, the Ekaterinburg Regional Administration for Evacuation (*Ekaterinburgskoe gubernskoe upravlenie po evakuatsii naseleniia*, hereafter *Gubevak*); and fond r-1159, the Kamyshlovskaia Uezd Commission for Prisoners of War and Refugees (*Kamyshlovskaia uezdnaia komissiia o plennykh i bezhentsakh*). The statistical reports of the railway authorities of Ekaterinburg and Cheliabinsk are also very interesting, because a careful registration of migrant groups was attempted at major junction stations (although railway officials were not able to inspect all groups, because the stopping time of trains was very brief). These sources have been supplemented with documents from fond r-3333 (*Tsentroplenbezh*) of the State Archive of the Russian Federation (GARF).
3. GASO, fond r-239, opis' 1, delo 45, list 164, 165 (hereafter archival references will be abbreviated as f., op., d., l.); ibid., d. 460, ll. 1, 1 ob.
4. Ibid., f. r-1646, op. 1, d. 1, l. 5; f. r-511, op. 1, d. 363, l. 6; f. r-239, op. 1, d. 45, ll. 96, 95 ob.
5. This chapter considers only materials for the period after 1917.
6. GARF, f. 3333, op. 2, d. 236, ll. 21ob, 22.
7. Ibid., l. 8 ob.
8. GASO, f. r-511, op. 1, d. 363, l. 5.
9. Ibid., f. r-239, op. 1, d. 32, l. 1.
10. Ibid., l. 2.
11. Kurtsev, 'Bezhentsy', pp. 104, 108.
12. GARF, f. r-3333 op. 3, d. 218, l. 14.
13. GASO, f. r-1159, op. 1, d. 54, ll. 6, 60b.
14. For example, certificates or receipts for rent paid or for property insurance purchased in the previous place of residence for an extended period of time, a state savings book indicating the holder's address, etc.
15. One pud is equal to 16.38 kg.
16. GASO, f. r-511, op. 1, d. 351, l. 23.
17. Ibid., d. 363, l. 1.
18. GARF, f. 3333, op. 2, d. 236, ll. 93, 93ob.
19. GASO, f. r-1159, op. 1, d. 54, l. 19.
20. Ibid., ll. 30, 30ob.
21. GARF, f. 3333, op. 3, d. 218, l. 41.

22. GASO, f. r-511, op. 1, d. 363, l. 250b.
23. Ibid., d. 261, ll. 109, 109ob.
24. Ibid., d. 351, l. 2.
25. Ibid., d. 352, l. 43.
26. Ibid., l. 42.
27. Ibid.
28. Ibid., f. r-88, op. 21, d. 12, l. 15.
29. Ibid., f. r-511, op. 1, d. 363, ll. 27–30, 30–3.
30. Ibid., f. r-1646, op. 1, d. 15, l. 9.
31. Ibid., f. r-511, op. 2, d. 199, ll. 50–75.
32. Ibid., d. 363, l. 250b.
33. Ibid., f. r-1646, op. 1, d. 15, l. 68.
34. For a detailed analysis of the famine in the Urals, see DV Karakulov, *Golod 1921–1922 godov na Urale*, Abstract of dissertation submitted for the degree of Candidate of History, Ekaterinburg, 2000.
35. GARF, f. 3333, op. 2, d. 236, ll. 93, 93ob, 94.
36. Ibid., l. 94.
37. GASO, f. r-512, op. 1, d. 1, l. 61.
38. Ibid., f. r-7, op. 1, d. 220, ll. 56, 56ob.
39. Ibid., f. r-511, op. 1, d. 452, l. 440ob.
40. Ibid., d. 362, l. 46.
41. Ibid.
42. Ibid., f. r-512, op. 1, d. 1, l. 58ob, 59.
43. Ibid.
44. *Sovetskaia derevnia glazami VChK-OGPU-NKVD: 1918–1939. Dokumenty i materialy*, Volume 1, 1918–2, Moscow, Rosspen, 2000, pp. 646, 649, 598.
45. GASO, f. r-512, op. 1, d. 1, l. 61.
46. *Sovetskaia derevnia glazami VChK-OGPU-NKVD*, p. 464.
47. GASO, f. r-88, op. 21, d. 3, l. 11.
48. Ibid., f. r-512, op. 1, d. 1, l. 52ob.
49. Ibid., f. r-239, op. 1, d. 33, ll. 28, 29, 30.
50. Ibid., ll. 25, 26, 27ob.
51. Ibid., d. 45, ll. 98, 99, 100, 100ob.
52. Ibid., d. 212, l. 19.
53. Ibid., f. r-245, op. 1, d. 230, l. 38.
54. *Vsesoiznaia perepis' naseleniia 1926 goda. Ural'skaia oblast'*, section 3, 'Otdel'nyi ottisk tablichnoi chasti', Moscow, TsSU, 1930, p. 116.
55. GASO, f. r-1646, op. 1, d. 3, ll. 131, 131ob.
56. Ibid., f. r-511, op. 1, d. 379, l. 1.
57. Ibid., f. r-1646, op. 1, d. 2, l. 14.
58. Ibid., f. r-1159, op. 1, d. 1, l. 8.
59. Ibid., f. r-1646, op. 1, d. 44, l. 36.
60. Ibid., d. 46, l. 33.

Chapter 9: Armenia: the 'Nationalisation', Internationalisation and Representation of the Refugee Crisis

1. Backed up in principle, in the case of 'minority' populations, by the League of Nations.
2. Hannah Arendt, *The Origins of Totalitarianism*, second edition, New York, Meridian Books, 1958, p. 267.
3. There is a huge literature on the 'Eastern Question'. The first major text in English was JAR Marriott, *The Eastern Question: An Historical Study in European Diplomacy*, Oxford, Clarendon Press, 1917. An authoritative overview is MS Anderson, *The Eastern Question, 1774–1923*, London, Macmillan, 1966. See also Manoug Somakian, *Empires in Conflict: Armenia and the Great Powers, 1895–1920*, London, IB Tauris, 1995; Bernard Lewis, *The Emergence of Modern Turkey*, second edition, London, Oxford University Press, 1968.
4. From a Turkish point of view, the treaty softened the impact of the Treaty of San Stefano, which provided for a continued Russian occupation of Ottoman territory until such reforms had been implemented.
5. William Thomas Stead, *The Haunting Horrors in Armenia*, London, Series 'Political Papers for the People', 1896, and Edwin M Bliss, *Turkey and the Armenian Atrocities*, London, T Fisher Unwin, 1896. An important contribution by the future Prime Minister of France was Georges Clemenceau, ed., *Les Massacres d'Arménie: Témoignages des Victimes*, Paris, Mercure de France, 1896.
6. James Bryce had formed the Anglo-Armenian Society in 1893. The Friends of Armenia originated in 1897, with Lady Frederick Cavendish as its President. See the general survey by ADz Kirakosian, *Velikobritaniia i armianskii vopros*, Erevan, Aiastan, 1990. This Armenophile imagination is the subject of the PhD dissertation by Jo Laycock, currently in preparation at the University of Manchester.
7. John Craig Havemeyer, *The Relation of the United States to Armenia*, reprinted from the *New York Times*, Yonkers, New York, 1896; Robert Mirak, *Between Two Lands: Armenians in America, 1890–World War 1*, Cambridge, Mass., Harvard University Press, 1983; Thomas Bryson, 'The Armenia-America Society: A factor in American-Turkish relations, 1919–1924', *Records of the American Catholic Historical Society of Philadelphia*, 82, 1971, pp. 83–105.
8. See Susan Layton, *Russian Literature and Empire: Conquest of the Caucasus from Pushkin to Tolstoy*, Cambridge, Cambridge University Press, 1994; Ronald Grigor Suny, *Looking Toward Ararat: Armenia in Modern History*, Bloomington, Indiana University Press, 1993, p. 46. The population estimate is from Anne Elizabeth Redgate, *The Armenians*, Oxford, Blackwell, 1998, p. 271. The Dashnaktsutian (the Armenian Revolutionary Federation) had been formed in 1890. They directed attacks on Ottoman officials and property, in pursuit of their demand for greater autonomy. The Hnchaks sought complete independence from Turkey.
9. A key figure here was the renowned international lawyer André Mandelstam (1869–1949). Mandelstam spent 15 years as a diplomat in Constantinople until the

outbreak of the world war. See KJ Partsch, 'Die Armenierfrage und das Völkerrecht in der Zeit des ersten Weltkrieges: zum Wirken von André Mandelstam', in M Dabag and K Platt, eds., *Genozid und Moderne, Band 1: Strukturen kollektiver Gewalt im 20. Jahrhundert*, Opladen, Leske und Budrich, 1998, 338–46 (thanks to Peter Holquist for this reference); Lubor Jilek, 'Violences de masse et droits de l'homme: André Mandelstam entre Constantinople et Bruxelles', *Cahiers de la Faculté des Lettres de Genève*, 2000, pp. 64–71; and Dzovinar Kévonian, 'Les politiques et avènement du 'droit humain': la pensée juridique d'Andre Mandelstam (1869–1949), *Revue d'Histoire de la Shoah*, 177–8, January–August 2003, pp. 245–73. Mandelstam's key works include *Le sort de l'empire ottoman*, Lausanne and Paris, Librairie Payot, 1917, and *Das armenische Problem im Lichte des Völker- und Menschenrechts*, Berlin, G Stilke, 1931.

10. Somakian, *Empires in Conflict*, pp. 82–3; D Kirakosian, *Zapadnaia Armeniia v gody pervoi mirovoi voiny*, Erevan, izdatel'stvo Erevanskogo universiteta, 1971, pp. 420–26.

11. Mandelstam, *Le sort de l'empire ottoman*; Vahakn N Dadrian, *The History of the Armenian Genocide: Ethnic Conflict from the Balkans to Anatolia to the Caucasus*, Providence, Berghahn, 1995, pp. 221–2; Robert Melson, *Revolution and Genocide: On the Origins of the Armenian Genocide and the Holocaust*, Chicago, Chicago University Press, 1992; Donald Bloxham, 'Three imperialisms and Turkish nationalism: international stresses, imperial disintegration and the Armenian genocide', *Patterns of Prejudice*, 36, 2002, pp. 37–58.

12. Stanley E Kerr, *The Lions of Marash: Personal Experiences with American Near East Relief, 1919–1922*, Albany, State University of New York, 1973, pp. 28–32; *Izvestiia Vserossiiskogo Souiza Gorodov*, 29–30, 1916, p. 215; RGIA f. 1322, op. 1, d. 16, l. 38, report of the governor of Erevan to MVD, 21 January 1916.

13. Christopher J Walker, *Armenia: The Survival of a Nation*, London, Croom Helm, 1980, pp. 193, 203; Aviel Roshwald, *Ethnic Nationalism and the Fall of Empires: Central Europe, Russia, and the Middle East, 1914–1923*, London, Routledge, 2001, p. 110.

14. On the vexed question of German knowledge of the genocide see Vahakn Dadrian, 'The Armenian question and the wartime fate of the Armenians as documented by the officials of the Ottoman empire's World War 1 allies: Germany and Austria-Hungary', *International Journal of Middle East Studies*, 34, 2002, pp. 59–85. The context of German intervention is provided by Ulrich Trumpener, *Germany and the Ottoman Empire, 1914–1918*, Princeton, Princeton University Press, 1968, and Wolfdieter Bihl, *Die Kaukasus-Politik der Mittelmächte: Teil I: Ihre Basis in der Orient-Politik und ihre Aktionen 1914–1917*, Vienna, Hermann Böhlaus Nachf., 1975.

15. Arnold Toynbee and James Bryce, *The Treatment of Armenians in the Ottoman Empire*, London, HM Stationery Office, 1916; A Nassibian, *Britain and the Armenian Question 1915–1923*, London, Croom Helm 1984; Arthur Beylerian, *Les grandes puissances, l'empire Ottoman et les Arméniens dans les archives françaises, 1914–1918*, 3 volumes, Paris, Publications de la Sorbonne, 1983; BS Papazian, *The Tragedy of Armenia*, Boston, Pilgrim Press, 1918.

16. *Mshak*, 53, 12 March 1915, p. 3; *Ashkhatank*, 58, 1917, p. 4; Emily Robinson, *Armenia and the Armenians*, London, n.p., 1916; Aurora Mardiganian, *Ravished Armenia: The Story of Aurora Mardiganian*, New York, Kingfield Press, 1918.
17. Editorial, *Armiane i voina*, 1, March 1916, p. 1; Peter Gatrell, *A Whole Empire Walking: Refugees in Russia during World War One*, Bloomington, Indiana University Press, pp. 150–4, 185–6.
18. On the power politics see the essays in Marian Kent, ed., *The Great Powers and the End of the Ottoman Empire*, second edition, London, Cass, 1996.
19. Richard G Hovannisian, *Armenia on the Road to Independence*, Berkeley, University of California Press, 1967, p. 100; Somakian, *Empires in Conflict*, chapter 5.
20. On the Transcaucasian Federation see Richard Pipes, *The Formation of the Soviet Union*, revised edition, Cambridge, Mass., Harvard University Press, 1964, pp. 193–5.
21. Richard Hovannisian, *The Republic of Armenia: Volume 2, From Versailles to London, 1919–1920*, Berkeley, University of California Press, 1982, pp. 6, 10, 300–1.
22. Madeleine de Bryas, *Les peuples en marche: les migrations politiques et économiques en Europe depuis la guerre mondiale*, Paris, A Pedone, 1926, p. 31.
23. Richard G Hovannisian, *The Republic of Armenia: Volume 1, The First Year, 1918–1919*, Berkeley, University of California Press, 1971, pp. 44, 49.
24. Kerr, *Lions of Marash*, pp. 36, 41–51.
25. Hovannisian, *The Republic of Armenia*, volume 1, chapter 9.
26. Ibid., pp. 450–4.
27. Ibid., pp. 126–30.
28. Hovannisian, *The Republic of Armenia*, volume 2, chapters 2 and 3; idem, *The Republic of Armenia: Volume 3, From London to Sèvres, February–August 1920*, Berkeley, University of California Press, 1996, p. 113; Somakian, *Empires in Conflict*, pp. 210–14. The French withdrew from Cilicia in October 1921.
29. Hovannisian, *The Republic of Armenia*, volume 3, p. 19 for this usage.
30. Hovannisian, *The Republic of Armenia*, volume 1, p. 450.
31. Quotation in ibid., pp. 461–8, our emphasis.
32. Ibid., pp. 144–50, 448–9; Hovannisian, *The Republic of Armenia*, volume 2, pp. 280, 286–315; Hovannisian, *The Republic of Armenia*, volume 3, pp. 254–89.
33. Ibid., volume 2, pp. 43, 299–300.
34. Report by Oliver Wardrop to the British Foreign Office, 19 October 1919, in India Office Library, L/PS/11/158/6847. For other reports on the displaced population see James G Harbord, 'The American military mission to Armenia', *International Conciliation*, 151, June 1920, pp. 275–312; Hovannisian, *The Republic of Armenia*, volume 2, pp. 284–6; Mary Matossian, *The Impact of Soviet Policies in Armenia*, Leiden, EJ Brill, 1962, p. 30.
35. EA Yarrow, quoted in Hovannisian, *The Republic of Armenia*, volume 2, p. 6.
36. Harbord, 'American military mission', p. 287; Hovannisian, *The Republic of Armenia*, volume 2, p. 296.
37. Ibid., volume 3, pp. 3–19, 57–60.

38. Hovannisian, *Republic*, volume 2, pp. 29–30, 303; ibid., volume 3, pp. 278–9, 309.
39. Ibid., volume 4, pp. 265, 267, 340.
40. Anderson, *The Eastern Question*, pp. 362–3; Somakian, *Empires in Conflict*, pp. 214–42.
41. Suny, *Looking Toward Ararat*, p. 139.
42. Sevtap Demirci, 'The Lausanne conference: the evolution of Turkish and British diplomatic strategies, 1922–1923', unpublished PhD dissertation, London School of Economics and Political Science, 1998. See also Lucy Mair, *The Protection of Minorities*, London, Christophers, 1928, p. 218. The signatories to the treaty were Britain, France, Turkey, Italy, Japan, Greece, Romania and Serbia.
43. This point is made by See Dzovinar Kévonian-Dyrek, 'Les tribulations de la diplomatie humanitaire: la Société des Nations et les réfugiés arméniens', in Hans-Lukas Kieser, ed., *Die armenische Frage und die Schweiz*, Zurich, Chronos, 1999, pp. 279–310.
44. Hovannisian, *The Republic of Armenia*, volume 4, p. 145. Some of the difficulties they encountered in the repatriation process are described in the League of Nations, report of Fifth Committee to Sixth Assembly, 25 September 1925, Appendix 2, India Office Library, L/E/7/1315/3774.
45. SV Kharmandarian, *Armianskaia SSR v pervyi god novoi ekonomicheskoi politiki, 1921–1922*, Erevan, AN ASSR, 1955, pp. 26, 114; AO Marukhian, *Vosstanovlenie narodnogo khoziaistva Armianskoi SSR: materialy i dokumenty za 1921–1928gg.*, Erevan, AN ASSR, 1958.
46. Suny, *Looking Toward Ararat*, p. 147; Kharmandarian, *Armianskaia SSR*, pp. 144–51; Matossian, *The Impact of Soviet Policies*, pp. 35–58. Repatriation was halted in April 1922, and resumed in 1923. According to Kharmandarian, this enabled the government to improve conditions for prospective returnees.
47. Matossian *The Impact of Soviet Policies*, pp. 48–9.
48. Report by Dr. Nansen to League of Nations. *Official Journal, Special Supplement no. 38, Sixth Assembly, Fifth Committee* (28 July 1925), 983–6. India Office Library, L/E/7/1315/3774.
49. The Armenian Red Cross was popularly known as 'Miss Robinson's Fund', after its honorary secretary, Emily Robinson, daughter of the editor of the *Daily Mail*.
50. See *The Plight of Armenian and Assyrian Christians: Report of a public meeting organised by the Lord Mayor's Fund, held at Central Hall, Westminster, on December 4, 1918*, London, Spottiswoode, Ballantyne and Co., 1918.
51. Minute book of the British–Armenia Committee, 13 October 1915–21 February 1921. British-Armenia Committee papers, Rhodes House Library, Oxford, Ms G506. The Committee was formed in 1912, with Noel Buxton, Liberal MP for North Norfolk, as its first chairman.
52. In November 1918 the British-Armenia Committee sent a deputation to the Foreign Office to press for Allied troops to protect Armenian civilians, to help in the repatriation of Armenians who had fled from or been thrown out by the Turks, and to

return women and children who had been kidnapped by the Turks and Kurds. British-Armenia Committee minutes, 7 November 1918, Rhodes House Library, Oxford.
53. Christopher J Walker, *Visions of Ararat*, London, IB Tauris, 1979, p. 129.
54. Joseph Burtt, *Report on Armenian Refugees in the Near East*, London, Society of Friends, 1925; idem, *The People of Ararat*, London, privately printed by Leonard & Virginia Woolf, 1926; Richendra Scott, *Quakers in Russia*, London, Michael Joseph, 1964, pp. 204, 210; Skran, *Refugees in Interwar Europe*, pp. 177–82.
55. Robinson, *The Truth About Armenia*, p. 3.
56. Robinson, *Armenia and the Armenians*, p. 7.
57. Rouben Paul Adalian, 'La reconnaissance du génocide des Arméniens aux États-Unis', *Revue d'Histoire de la Shoah*, 177–178, 2003, pp. 425–35. See also Jay Winter, ed., *America and the Armenian Genocide*, Cambridge, Cambridge University Press, 2003, which appeared after this chapter was completed.
58. James L Barton, *The Story of Near East Relief, 1915–1930: An Interpretation*, New York, Macmillan, 1930; Frank A Ross et al., *The Near East and American Philanthropy: A Survey*, New York, Columbia University Press, 1929; Clarence D Ussher and Grace Knapp, *An American Physician in Turkey; A Narrative of Adventures in Peace and in War*, Boston and New York, Houghton Mifflin Co., 1917; Mabel Evelyn Elliott, *Beginning Again at Ararat*, New York, Fleming Revell, 1924 (Elliott was Medical Director of Near East Relief). See also Esther Pohl Lovejoy, *Certain Samaritans*, New York, Macmillan, 1927, pp. 73–130; Kerr, *The Lions of Marash*, passim; Oliver Baldwin, *Six Prisons and Two Revolutions: Adventures in Trans-Caucasia and Anatolia, 1920–1921*, London, Hodder and Stoughton, 1925, pp. 86–7. A Soviet-era treatment is AE Ioffe, 'Deiatel'nost' amerikanskogo 'Komiteta pomoshchi Blizhnemu vostoku' v Zakavkaz'e, 1921–1930gg.', *Istoriia SSSR*, 1963 no. 3, pp. 18–36. Between 1915 and 1918 the American Committee for Armenian and Syrian Relief published numerous short accounts of the situation in Armenia. Nor should we overlook the activities of German missionaries and volunteer relief workers.
59. Ioffe, 'Deiatel'nost'', pp. 29, 31.
60. Northcote, letter to his sister, 5 July 1919. Northcote Papers, British Library. Add. Ms. 57559.
61. Northcote was the son of a former British Chancellor of the Exchequer and Foreign Minister. During World War One he was stationed in Mesopotamia, where he rose to the rank of Lieutenant. Baqubah lies 33 miles north of Baghdad and about 400 miles due south of Erevan. The term 'concentration camp' appears in the 'Memoranda on the Armenian and Assyrian refugees at present in camp at Ba'quba', Baghdad, Government Press, 1919.
62. Northcote Papers, British Library. Add. Ms. 57559–61.
63. Harold Buxton, 'Enquiry into famine conditions, December 1921 to January 1922'. Report from the Lord Mayor's Fund to the High commissioner for Relief in Russia. Northcote Papers, British Library Add. MS. 57559. Buxton was the director of the Lord Mayor's Fund relief operation in Armenia and honorary secretary of the

British Armenia Committee. His books and pamphlets on the region included *Transcaucasia*, London, Faith Press, 1926.
64. 'Armenian Refugees in Mesopotamia'. Statement from the Colonial Office, 24 September 1921. Northcote Papers, British Library Add. MS. 57559.
65. 'Memorandum concerning the proposed dispersal of refugees in Mesopotamia, 19 July 1921'. Northcote Papers, British Library Add. MS. 57559.
66. *The Times*, 30 September 1921; 6 October 1921.
67. Emily Robinson had written before the war that 'When they leave their country, their ability no less than their loyalty soon wins them positions of trust and importance and makes them most valuable colonists.' Robinson, *The Truth About Armenia*, London, n.p., 1913, p. 18.
68. Northcote, Letter from the Armenian Refugees, Lord Mayor's Fund, 15 October 1921. Northcote Papers, British Library, Add. 57559.
69. Miss Karen Jeppe, report dated 9 August 1924, India Office Library, L/E/7/1230/1585.
70. Northcote Papers, British Library, Add. 57559. The information about Northcote's time with the refugees in Erevan is of a different nature. There are fewer letters to his family but more factual information about the work carried out by the various relief agencies operating in Armenia at this time.
71. S Tchirkina, January 1921, from a note filed in the India Office Library, L/P&S/11/194/P1134.
72. Mr G Carle, report of 1925, filed in the India Office Library, L/E/7/1315/3774. The image of a disreputable mercantile population emerges also in the report of James Harbord, who concluded that Armenians were admired rather than liked, since they 'incur the penalty which attaches among backward races to the banker, the middleman, and the creditor.' Predictably, Harbord drew an analogy with Jews in Poland and Russia. Harbord, 'The American military mission', p. 296.
73. India Office Library, L/E/7/1315/3774, comments made by Pio Lo Savio.
74. Quoted in Skran, *Refugees in Interwar Europe*, p. 179.
75. István Mocsy, *The Effects of World War 1. The Uprooted: Hungarian Refugees and Their Impact on Hungary's Domestic Politics, 1918–1921*, New York, Columbia University Press, 1983, p. 5.
76. Such as the *Comité central des réfugiés arméniens* in Paris, under the chairmanship of Léon Pachalian. See Kévonian-Dyrek, 'Les tribulations de la diplomatie humanitaire'.
77. Skran, *Refugees in Interwar Europe*, pp. 148–55. Arendt, *The Origins of Totalitarianism*, pp. 283–6, discusses the failure of, respectively, repatriation and naturalization as 'remedies' for statelessness. See also the important new study by Dzovinar Kévonian, *Réfugiés et diplomatie humanitaire: les acteurs européens et la scène proche-orientale pendant l'entre-deux-guerres*, Paris, Publications de la Sorbonne, forthcoming, which we have been unable to take into account here.
78. FP Walters, *A History of the League of Nations*, Oxford, Oxford University Press, 1952, volume one, pp. 187–9. See also Simpson, *The Refugee Problem*, pp. 198–203.
79. Skran, *Refugees in Interwar Europe*, pp. 173–4, 180.

80. India Office Library, L/E/7/1315/3774, mission of Colonel J Procter, as reported to Fifth Committee to the Sixth Assembly of the League of Nations, 25 September 1925.
81. The Treaty of Sèvres refused to recognize all conversions to Islam that had taken place since 1 November 1914. It further required Turkey to 'afford all the assistance in its power ... in the search for and deliverance of all persons, of whatever race or religion, who have disappeared, been carried off, interned or placed in captivity' since that date. Hovannisian, *The Republic of Armenia*, volume 3, p. 92.
82. Prime Minister Ohandjanian, reported in ibid., p. 255.
83. See the speech given by the Minister of Education on the first anniversary of Armenian independence (29 May 1918), extracts in Hovannisian, *The Republic of Armenia*, volume 1, p. 460, and the speech given by the Speaker to the Khorhurd (Parliament) on 1 August 1919, in ibid., p. 476.
84. Melville Chater, 'The land of stalking death', *National Geographic Magazine*, 36, November 1919, pp. 403, 417–18.
85. Kerr, *The Lions of Marash*, p. 42.
86. James Bryce, *Transcaucasia and Ararat: Notes of a Vacation Tour in the Autumn of 1876*, London, Macmillan and Co., 1877, p. 406; Arnold Toynbee, *Armenian Atrocities: The Murder of a Nation*, London, Hodder & Stoughton, 1915, pp. 19–20.
87. Northcote, 'Memorandum concerning the proposed dispersal of refugees in Mesopotamia'.
88. Gatrell, *A Whole Empire Walking*, p. 123.
89. Edmund Harvey MP, 14 July 1924, as reported in India Office Library, L/E/7/1315/3774.
90. Mademoiselle Vacareso, 'Statement with regard to the deportation of women and children in Turkey and the neighbouring countries'. Northcote Papers, British Library. Add. 57559.
91. Hebe Spaull, 'Mothering children for the League of Nations: Froken Jeppe', in idem, *Women Peacemakers*, London, Harrap, 1924, pp. 49–62.
92. Miss ED Cushman, report to Secretary General of League of Nations, 16 July 1921, India Office Library, L/E/7/1230/1585. Cushman, an American citizen, was a member of a commission of enquiry into deported women and children. See also Kévonian-Dyrek, 'Les tribulations de la diplomatie humanitaire', pp. 280–1.
93. Elliott, *Beginning Again at Ararat*; Lovejoy, *Certain Samaritans*; Robinson, *Armenia and the Armenians*.
94. Vacareso, 'Statement'.
95. India Office Library, L/E/7/1230/1585, Report of Miss Karen Jeppe on behalf of the 'Commission for the protection of women and children in the Near East', dated 28 July 1927. Emphasis added. See also Kévonian-Dyrek, 'Les tribulations de la diplomatie humanitaire', pp. 284–88.
96. Report by Fifth Committee on Deportations to League of Nations, 22 September 1921, India Office Library, L/E/7/1230/1585.
97. See note 95.

98. India Office Library, L/PS/11/159/P7105.
99. Hovannisian, *The Republic of Armenia*, volume 2, p. 6, quoting EA Yarrow, 'Winter conditions in the Caucasus', *Journal of International Relations*, 11, July 1920, p. 111.
100. Matossian, *The Impact of Soviet Policies*, pp. 49, 61, 77.
101. DS Northcote, 'Armenia' (manuscript), 1926. Northcote Papers, British Library, Add. 57560.
102. Guildhall Library, London, MS16509, speech by EA Brayley Hodgetts.
103. Harbord, 'American military mission', p. 284. Harbord placed great emphasis upon the potential for 'ordinary' Armenians and Turks to coexist peacefully. In his opinion, the baleful events in 1915 were the product of organized government and military provocation.
104. Northcote, 'Armenia', passim.
105. Vacareso, 'Statement'.
106. Kharmandarian, *Armianskaia SSR*, pp. 115–23.
107. Lieutenant HL Charge prefaced his report on the refugee camp at Baqubah by stating 'I have had to write from knowledge derived from intercourse with the Refugees themselves, much of which on close examination having proved to be quite unreliable.' 'Memoranda on the Armenian and Assyrian refugees', Baghdad, Government Press, 1919.

Conclusions: On Living in a 'New Country'

1. Professor A Mal'kov, quoted in Donald Raleigh, *Experiencing Russia's Civil War: Politics, Society, and Revolutionary Culture in Saratov, 1917–1922*, Princeton, Princeton University Press, 2002, p. 187.
2. As quoted in the proceedings of the *European Health Conference, held at Warsaw from March 20th to 28th 1922*, Geneva, League of Nations, 1922, p. 3. Note the deliberate use of the term 'zone', rather than 'sanitary cordon'.
3. Decree issued 1 June 1921, reprinted in *Pogranichnye voiska SSSR 1918–1928: sbornik dokumentov i materialov*, Moscow, Nauka, 1973, pp. 172–3.
4. See also Utgof, this volume, as well as Peter Gatrell, *A Whole Empire Walking: Refugees in Russia during World War One*, Bloomington, Indiana University Press, 1999, pp. 174–5.
5. Peter Holquist, '"Information is the alpha and omega of our work": Bolshevik surveillance in its pan-European context', *Journal of Modern History*, 69, 1997, pp. 415–50; David Hoffmann, 'European modernity and Soviet socialism', in David L Hoffmann and Yanni Kotsonis, eds, *Russian Modernity: Politics, Knowledge, Practices*, Basingstoke, Macmillan, 2000, pp. 245–60.
6. General Max Jonge, as quoted in Alon Rachamimov, *POWs and the Great War: Captivity on the Eastern Front*, Oxford, Berg Publishers, 2002, pp. 193–4.
7. ES Kancher, 'Sud'by bezhentsev', in idem, *Belorusskii vopros: sbornik statei*, Petrograd, 1919, p. 116.

Index

agriculture in Latvia 49
Akurates, Jānis 38
American Jewish Joint Distribution Committee (JDC) 9, 25, 28
American Polish Typhus Relief Expedition 25, 29
American Red Cross, in Poland 28
American Society of Friends 14
Anglo-American Jewish Committee 109
anti-Semitism, in Poland 100, 111, 117
Arab populations 196, 198
Arendt, Hannah 179, 210
armed conflict 18, 19
Armenia 4, 8, 11, 13–15, 19, 20, 179–208
    British involvement in 180–93, 195–9
    children 194, 195, 197, 198
    Christian tradition in 191, 192, 194
    refugee crisis in 5, 8, 26, 179–200
    and Turkey 17, 18
    Soviet Armenia 186
    women in 195-200
'Armenian question', in western Europe 180, 184
Association of Siberian deportees 146–50, 206
Azerbaijan 4, 19

Bahdanovich, Maksim 56–7
Balkelis, Tomas 7, 74–97
Baltic German Committee 27, 45–6
bandits, in Urals 173
Baron, Nick 1–9, 201–8
Barrow, Florence, Quaker relief worker 30–1
Belarus 4, 5, 7, 17, 18, 19, 53–73
    education and culture in 56–9, 68
    independence 71
    farming in 24
    national consciousness 53, 58, 73
    newspapers in 58
    partition of 69
    Polish occupation of 22
    refugees in 15, 23, 30, 53–73
Belarusian National Commissariat *see* Belnatskom
Belarusian People's Republic (1918) 53–73
Belarusian Society for Assisting the Victims of War 54–6, 71
Belarusian Soviet Socialist Republic (1919) 54, 69
Belnatskom 59, 64, 65, 67–9, 72, 73
Berlin, Russian exiles in 27
Bolsheviks 16–18, 21, 24, 27, 30, 34, 46, 122–6, 132–4
    repression by 48, 106, 107
    terror in Latvia 51
    see also October revolution
borders, establishment of 24, 88, 96, 102
    see also Treaties, Peace
Brest-Litovsk Peace Treaty, *see under* Treaties, Peace
British involvement with Armenia 180–93, 195–9
British Society of Friends, *see* Society of Friends
British troops in Caucasus 17
bubonic plague 145
Buxton, Harold 188–90

cannibalism, reports of 171
Catholic Church 125, 135, 140
Caucasus 10, 17, 18, 20, 33, 47

Central Committee for Prisoners of War and Refugees (Tsentroplenbezh) 24, 65, 143, 158–9
Cheliabinsk base station, Urals 21, 159
children 64, 129–30, 172, 194–5, 197–8
cholera 88, 93, 128, 145, 202
Christian tradition in Armenia 191, 192, 194
citizenship in Poland 98–118
Citizenship Regulations, Poland 110
Civil War, Russian 8, 16–23, 157
Civil War refugees in Urals 166
class enemies 123, 124
coal-mining, Ukraine, 128
Commissariat for Polish Affairs, Moscow 24
Commissariat of Latvian National Affairs 46
Communist Party members, Russia 121, 125, 131
Conrad, Joseph 18
conscription 11, 12
Constantinople, Russian exiles in 27
Cossack troops, removal 21
counter-revolution 187
Crimea, refugees 26, 47
criminal activity 125, 187
culture 3
  Belarus 58
  and education in Latvia 45
  history 202–3
  of Lithuania 76
Czechoslovakia 18, 21, 27

deportation of refugees from Poland 107, 109
discrimination 7, 122, 204
  by Polish government 105
  towards immigrants 107–9
diseases see also bubonic plague, cholera, influenza, malaria, typhus
  contagious and infectious 46, 93–6, 121, 164, 202, 205
  epidemic threat 203
  screening for 34
  see also quarantine
documentation, 164–5
Donbass region, Ukraine 128, 129, 136

economic
  crisis in Poland 117
  deprivation 202
  expansion in Siberia 147
  problems in Lithuania 86
education and culture, Belarus 56–9, 68
education, for refugees 64
  see also schools
Ekaterinburg
  base station, Urals 159
  refugees in 165–8, 170–1, 175
Elliott, Mabel 30, 33, 206
Erevan 13, 20
Estonia 3, 15, 26–7
ethnicity 91–3, 208
  of Belarusians 70
  in Poland 98–101, 103, 105–6
  of refugees 96
Europe 2, 3, 4, 7, 20
  and 'Armenian question' 180, 184
European peace settlement, Versailles 18
evacuation, of refugees 69, 163
exiles, Russian political 73, 77, 150

famine 22, 176–7, 183, 202, see also starvation
'famine refugees' 156–8, 169–74
Far East 8, 27
February Revolution (1917) 35
Finland, independence 16, 17
Finnish independence 16, 17
Finnish Parliament (Diet) 15
First World War, see under World War One
food parcels 83
French troops in Caucasus 17
France, intervention in Caucasus 17
frontier wars 95
funds, refugees have sufficient 110, 113, 117

Galicia 11, 12, 19, 22, 24
Gatrell, Peter 1–9, 10–34, 179–208
'genocide'
  by Turks 26
  in World War One 180–3
geographical distribution of refugees 160–1
Georgia 4, 19
  war relief committee 77
German
  authorities 77
  in Latvia 43, 51
  citizens in Poland 104

settlers in Russia 13
military occupation 17, 33, 41
   of Belarus 53, 54, 56, 62–3, 65–6, 72
   of Poland 15, 99, 100
   settlers in Russia 13
   of Vilno 55
Germany 16, 18, 19, 21
Goba, Alfreds, Latvian refugee 25, 32, 218
Goldmanis, Janis, Latvian politician 14, 38, 41, 48
Greece 11, 27
Grodno province 23, 54, 55
gypsies 12

Harbin, Manchuria 27, 140, 141, 144–7, 152
health screening 34
'homeland' 1, 77, 78, 138, 201, 207, 208
Hoover, Herbert, US President 27–8, 29
humanitarian
   crises 88, 89
   intervention 6, 8, 13, 14, 29, 30, 206
      in Armenia 188–93, 195–9, 200

ideology, Latvian 38
immigration 1, 6, 202
   policies 91, 92, 95
   quotas 118
   from Russia 105
   statistics, Lithuania 83–4
independence 35, 36, 37
   Belarusian state 71
   Latvian state 50
   Lithuanian state 78, 79
infectious diseases 205
influenza 202
intelligentsia 139
   Jewish 92
   need for, in Lithuania 79
Inter-Governmental Conference on the Refugee Question 28
internationalization 193–4
international opinion 180–3
Iraq, resettlement of refugees in 196
Islam 183, 194, 197 199, 200

Jeppe, Karen 197, 198
Jewish

farmers 26
immigrants to Poland 108–9
intelligentsia 92
minorities in national states 25
national committee 14
population 12
refugees 32–4, 89, 91–3, 123, 204
Jewish Society 57
Jews 7, 13, 24
   assimilation of 104
   Polish 128

Kancher, Evgenii 63, 66, 71
Kapraska, Łucja 7–8, 138–55
Karelian peasants 27
Kerenskii government, Latvia 39
Kiev, Ukraine 21
kinship ties 123, 125
Kornilov, Gennadii 8, 156–78

land reform 49, 207
landscape and migration 208
languages 45, 64, 81, 203
   native, in Polesie 114–15
Latvia 2, 3, 5, 7, 9, 14–16, 18, 20, 26, 35–52
   Commissariat of Latvian National Affairs 46
   independence, 50
   legal system 50
   literature 50
   national consciousness in 36, 45, 50–1, 52
   national independence movement 40–3
   religion 44
   ideology 38
   Soviet Republic of 46
   state-building in 38
   unemployment in 49
Latvian Refugees and Colonies Department 47
Latvian nation state 7, 35–52
Laycock, Jo 8, 179–200
League of Nations 27, 28, 180, 193–4, 206, 210
legal system in Latvia 50
literature, Latvian 50
Lithuania 3, 7, 9, 14, 20, 55, 74–97
   economic problems in 86
   independence 16, 78, 79
   nationalism in 75

national minorities in 84
German occupation of 17
and Poland 19
population movements in 5
refugees in 11, 15, 74–97
troops 10
Lithuanian Society 57
Lublin voievodship, Poland 99
Luckiewicz, Anton 71
Lutheran Church 43, 49

malaria 183
male recruits for armies 88–9
Manchurian 138
  railway company 140
  returnees in Poland 138–55
migrants
migration 1, 128–9, 156, 157–74 see also
    population displacement
  forced 6, 157, 158
  in Poland 98–101
  in the Urals 174
Moscow Latvian Society 44, 45

national consciousness 7
  in Belarus 53, 58, 73
  in Latvia 36, 45, 50–1, 52
  in Polesie 115–16
national independence 15, 16, 17
  movements 35, 36, 37
    Latvian 40–3
nationalism 2, 5, 205, 210
nationalities in Lithuania 84
nationality politics in Poland 98–101
Near East Relief 30, 206
newspapers in Belarus 58
Northcote, Dudley Stafford 189–92, 195–6

October revolution 11, 16–23, 59–62, 201
  aftermath, in Belarus 63
Olavs, Pastor Vilis 40, 41
Onishchuk, Jascha, murder of 30
orphanages 47, 56, 58, 60
orthographic reform 50
Ottoman empire 11, 179, 180-1, 184, 193
  Armenians in 13
  empire 179, 180, 181, 184, 193

Turkish troops 11
see also Turkey

patriotism 77
peace treaties 16, 23, 73
People's Republic of Belarus (1918) 54
Perm base station, Urals 159
Pēterburgas Avīzes newspaper 40
Petliura, Semen, Ukrainian leader 22
Petrograd Welfare Society 44
Piłsudski, Józef 19, 26, 148, 149
PKN see Polish National Committee
PKR see Polish Rescue Committee
PKW see Polish War Committee
Poland 9, 19, 20, 27, 69, 98–118
  armed forces 10, 34, 141–2
  citizenship regulations 110
  economic crisis in 117
  German occupation of 17
  nationality politics in 98–101
  population movements 5, 8, 139
  refugee problem 24, 28, 30, 65–6
  rivalry with Soviet Russia and Lithuania 88
  and Russia, war 22
  self-rule 15
  spy mania in 111–12
  and Ukraine 19
Poles 13, 128–9
  in the Far East 139–42
  in Siberia 139–42
  in Ukraine 126
Polesie voievodship 115
  national consciousness in 115–16
Polish
  citizenship 110, 112–13, 116
  diaspora 139, 146, 149
  government and migrants 106
  language speakers 131
  military units in Siberia 141
  territories 8, 24
  troops 10, 34, 141–2
Polish National Committee (PKN) 144, 145
Polish Rescue Committee (PKR) 145
Polish-Russian Treaty, Riga (1921) see under
    Treaties, Peace
Polish Society for Assisting the Victims of
    War 57

Polish-Soviet War (1920) 10, 22, 33, 111, 119
Polish-Soviet Repatriation Treaty (1921) 42–3, 120, 130
Polish Typhus Relief Expedition 28
Polish-Ukrainian war 119
Polish War Committee (PKW) 141, 144, 145
political
    agitation by Communist Party 132–4
    population displacement 10–34, 174–7, 201–2, 208 *see also* migration
        Armenia 183–8
        Belarus 53, 62–7
        and Jewish refugees 91
        Lithuania 74
        Poland 98–118, 136
        Soviet Union 127
        in the Urals 156
        wartime 61
possessions prohibited in travel 162
poverty 130, 133, 145, 158, 164
Prague, Russian exiles in 27
Priedite, Aija 7, 35–52
prisoners of war 143, 205
    Russian 113–14
    Serb 11–18
proletarians 34, 136
property and baggage 162, 164
Provincial Repatriation Committees 120–1

Quaker relief workers, 23, 28
    see also Society of Friends
quarantine 46, 47, 85–6, 88, 93, 94, 95
    see also diseases

rail transport 144, 160, 163–4, 168–70
Red Army 10, 20, 21, 30
Red Cross 25
re-evacuation campaigns 135, 136
refugees
    Baltic States 28
    of Belarus 53–73
    camps in Armenia 190–2
    'character' of 28, 110–14
    families 31, 32
    funds 110, 113, 117
    Latvian 42, 47
    Lithuanian 11, 87–91

'moral degeneration' 28, 110
organizations 60, 61, 62, 81
property 82
registration procedures 7, 162, 165, 174, 204
resettlement 193–4
screening 84–6
welfare 130–6
Refugees and Colonies Department, Latvia 47
registration, of refugees 7, 162, 165, 174, 204
relief organizations 25, 27–9, 56, 58, 59, 64, 109, 195
religion of Latvians 44
repatriation 46, 62, 67–9, 75–87, 93, 125, 143–6
    Armenia to Anatolia 186
    Belarusian refugees from Russia 65
    Lithuania 76, 80–3, 87
    mass 93
    obstacles to 48
    of Polish citizens 119–37, 142–4, 203
    of Russians 193
Repatriation Treaty, Polish-Soviet 142–3
revolution, *see* October revolution
revolution 16–23, 59–62
Riga, German army occupation of 41
Romanian refugees 18, 28
Russia 7, 10, 14, 19, 20 *see also* Soviet Russia
    Latvians, permission to leave 48
    Lithuanian refugees in 75
    famine in 8
    emigration from 26
    population movements in 5
    revolution and civil war 16–23
Russian
    émigrés in Poland 111–12
    empire 3, 10, 11, 12, 15, 17, 20
    famine in 8
    immigrants to Poland 108–9
    nationalist exiles 27
    partition of Belarus 69
    prisoners of war 113–14
    refugees 5, 8, 47
    revolution 10, 15
    revolution, *see* October revolution
    territory 43–5
    troops 12
Russian Army 12, 140
Russian borderlands (1914–24) 10–34

Russian Civil War 8, 21, 157
Russian Commissariat of Nationalities 46
Russian Red Cross 144
Russian Social Federal Soviet Republic 8
Russians 24, 99
  in Polesie 114–16
russification campaign 11
Ruthenians
  in Poland 117
  Russian 23

Save the Children Fund 28
schools 45, 49–50, 56
  see also education
Second All-Russia Refugee Congress (1917) 61
secret police 120, 125, 204
secret-service agents 125
self-awareness, national 36
self-realization, individual 29, 30, 31, 32, 33
Serb prisoners of war 11, 18
Siberia 8, 13, 138
  economic expansion in 147
  exile tradition 149
  Latvian colonies 44–5
  natural beauty in 151, 152, 153
  Polish nostalgia for 153
  returnees to Poland 138–55
  Polish returnees from 138–55
  see also Association of Siberian deportees
Sieroszewski, Wacław 148, 150
socialist revolutions 124
social upheaval 34, 202
Society of Friends 14, 28
soldiers returning 202
soup kitchens 56
Soviet
  citizenship 144
  obstructive tactics 143
Soviet Armenia, *see* Armenia, Soviet
Soviet Central Administration for Prisoners of War and Refugees 24
Soviet Central Collegium on the Affairs of Refuges and Prisoners of War 65
Soviet Central Committee for Prisoners of War and Refugees 143
Soviet-German relations 65

Soviet Latvian Republic, *see* Armenia, Soviet Republic of
Soviet-Polish Agreement on Repatriation, *see* Polish-Soviet Repatriation Treaty
Soviet-Polish war, *see* Polish-Soviet War
Soviet Russia 2, 3, 4, 5, 18, 34 *see also under* Russia
Soviet Russian Commissariat for Polish Affairs, Moscow 24
Soviet Ukraine, see Ukraine, Soviet
spy mania in Poland 111–12
Stadnik, Kateryna 25, 119–37
starvation 130, 158, 169, 185 *see also* famine
state building 10–34, 74, 117, 204
  Latvian 38
Strong, Anna Louise 32
Sybirak (*The Siberian Exile*) 138, 139, 148, 149–54

Tatiana Committee 14, 44, 45, 55, 218, 223
Transcaucasian Federation 19
Transcaucasus 13, 179
transport 80, 81, 82, 83, 85, 87, 121–2, 145
Treaties, Peace
  Brest-Litovsk (March 1918) 17, 23, 45, 54, 62, 63, 67–8, 75, 76, 101
  Kars (March 1921) 20
  Lausanne (July 1923) 20, 186–7
  Riga (March 1921) 22, 54, 100, 104, 119, 145, 146, 215
  Sèvres (August 1920) 20
  Versailles (June 1919) 18
  Warsaw 119
Tsentroplenbezh *see* Central Committee for Prisoners of War and Refugees
Turkey 11, 13, 17, 19, 184, 196
  Allies kept in check by 18
  and the Armenian 'genocide' 8
  occupation of Armenia 26, 186–7
  territorial demands 20
Turkish
  'genocide' 8
  harems 197
  invasions 196
  occupation of Armenia
  rule 13, 182
  troops 17

typhus 23, 25, 28, 93, 121, 128, 169, 183, 202, 203
  epidemic 28, 169

Ukraine 2, 4, 17-18, 119–37
  conflicts 18
  immigration to Poland 108
  independence 16, 17
  and partition of Belarus 69
  population movements in 5
  refugees in 47
  settlements 26
  Soviet Socialist Republic of 125
Ukrainian Peoples' Republic 119
Ukrainian Rada 16
Ukrainian Relief Committee 77
Ukrainian Soviet Socialist Republic 125
Ukrainians 7, 13, 24, 99
  in Poland 101, 108, 117
  troops 10
unemployment in Latvia 49
Urals region (1917–25) 8, 156–78
  Civil War refugees 166
  'famine refugees' in 156–8, 169–74
  planned resettlement in 158
USSR *see under* Russia *and* Soviet
Utgof, Valentina 53–73

vaccination 46
Vilnius province 54, 55
Vilno (Vilnius) 19
Vitebsk province 54, 55
Vladivostok 21

Voronko, Jazep, Belarusian nationalist 67

war 10–34
  in Belarus 54–6
  refugees, Lithuania 76, 78
Warsaw 27, 28
wartime displacement of populations 13
welfare 25
  of refugees 130–6
White Army 10, 21
White Ruthenians 23, 216
  see also Belarusians
Wilson, Woodrow, US President 20
women 207
  in Armenia 195–200
workers, skilled 126
World War One 9–16, 22, 40, 53, 74, 138, 180–3, 201
  and Latvia 37–40, 41, 45–50
  and migration 179
  population displacement 33, 35, 179
  refugees and forced migrants 157, 167
  and Belarus 72

Yčas, Martynas, Chair of Lithuanian War Relief Committee 14
Young Men's Christian Association, US 28
Yugoslavia 27

Zālītis, P, Latvian politician, 38, 41, 49
Zielinski, Konrad 7, 25, 98–118

www.ingramcontent.com/pod-product-compliance
Lightning Source LLC
Chambersburg PA
CBHW052104230426
43671CB00011B/1928